D1589278

ANYBODY'S NIGHTMARE

by Angela & Tim Devlin

Introduction
by Frances Gibb
legal correspondent, *The Times*

Copyright Tim Devlin Enterprises (TDE). All rights reserved.
No part of this book may be reproduced,
stored in any retrieval system or transmitted in any form
or by any means without the prior permission of TDE.

Published 1998 by Taverner Publications
Taverner House, East Harling, Norfolk NR16 2QR

Distributed by TDE
Ramsons, Maidstone Road, Staplehurst, Kent TN12 0RD
Tel. 01580 893176

Printed by Postprint
Taverner House, East Harling, Norfolk NR16 2QR

ISBN 1 901470 04 0

To the Friends of Sheila Bowler and
the Trial and Error Team
with grateful thanks

And to the Bowler family
in admiration for their courage in reliving the nightmare
to help us write this book

Dans notre societé tout homme qui ne pleure pas
à l'enterrement de sa mère risque d'être condamnée à mort.

In our society, every man who does not weep
at his mother's funeral risks being condemned to death.

Albert Camus, *L'Etranger,*
Paris 1955

CONTENTS

INTRODUCTION
by Frances Gibb, legal correspondent, *The Times*

I have come across few cases in 15 years as legal correspondent of *The Times* as bizarre as the case of Sheila Bowler, the Sussex piano teacher convicted of murdering her husband's Aunt Flo. It had all the ingredients of an Agatha Christie mystery. If Sheila Bowler had not pushed the frail and seemingly immobile old lady into the river, then who had?

But when Tim Devlin first told me of the case, he insisted there was no murder, merely a tragic accident. The elderly woman could – despite the odds against it – have walked to her death down a lonely country lane and fallen into the river in the dark. The theory seemed implausible. Equally implausible, maintained Tim and his wife Angela, was that Sheila Bowler, pillar of the small Sussex community of Rye for many years, would have committed murder.

He outlined his theory in detail on September 20 1994 in the law pages of *The Times*. It was explored further that night on television by Channel Four in its *Trial and Error* programme. It was the first public suggestion that Mrs Bowler, dubbed the Black Widow by the tabloids after her conviction in July 1993, might after all be innocent. Her first appeal in the wake of the article and television programme failed. But Michael Howard, then Home Secretary, referred the case back to the Court of Appeal and in July 1997 the Lord Chief Justice, Lord Bingham of Cornhill, quashed her conviction and ordered a re-trial. After four and a half years in prison, Mrs Bowler was released on bail.

I became intrigued by the case. The Devlins would not champion such a cause lightly. Their conviction in Mrs Bowler's innocence prompted me to drive to Rye and with them walk along the remote winding lane down to the River Brede where Aunt Flo met her death. Seeing the 500 metres she would have had to wander in the dark from the car (abandoned by Mrs Bowler as she sought help for a flat tyre) I found it impossible to believe that a frail, semi-demented woman of 89 years, said by everyone to be unable to walk more than a few steps unaided, could have managed the journey.

Then there was Mrs Bowler herself. I felt certain that after interviewing her I would have a firm feel as to her innocence or otherwise. At her home she was busy preparing for her forthcoming trial in just a few days' time. She had been back there since being released on bail a few months before. Despite the exceptional circumstances – the mantelpiece bore rows of good luck cards – it was easy to glimpse what her life must have been four years earlier. Tidy, ordered and utterly respectable.

She, too, seemed remarkably composed, despite confessing to nerves about the trial the next week. One could see why the police officers, visiting her after the discovery of Aunt Flo's body, might have been suspicious, thought her behaviour odd for someone whose relative had just disappeared. She had carried on as normal, making biscuits. She was not an easy interviewee, hard to pin down and much of the time preoccupied with hunting for her new kitten in the garden or making telephone calls on the finer details of her re-trial. She talked without anger or bitterness – even with humour – of her time in prison. Her emotions were under control. It was by no means impossible to see how the Prosecution, at her first trial, could have depicted her as 'cold, calculating and callous.'

The Devlins readily admitted that Sheila Bowler's own personality had helped bring about her conviction. So why had they embarked on the campaign to free her? They had known Sheila Bowler for some 15 years before the death of Aunt Flo, but more as acquaintances than friends. Their daughters were at the same primary school in Rye. Four factors however convinced them of her innocence: first, she doted on her daughter Jane and was passionate about her musical career. If she had planned to murder Aunt Flo, she would never have done so in the middle – as it then was – of Jane's music degree finals. Second, she was an intelligent woman: the 'murder plot,' if such it was, was doomed to fail because Mrs Bowler herself was aware that everyone believed the old woman incapable of walking any distance. So the finger of suspicion would immediately fall on her. Third, she was a compulsive talker with an abrasive personality – she easily offended people and would have infuriated the police. But fourth, beneath her brusque front, she had a heart of gold – many local people testified to her good deeds. Above all, as the Devlins describe in the book, she had cared lovingly for Flo and her sister Lil for many years and was extremely fond of her.

The first trial had formulated the case in this way: if Mrs Bowler did not kill her aunt, then who did? The idea that there might have been an accident was never postulated. As part of their campaign, the Devlins undertook lengthy research to show Aunt Flo was not the querulous, fragile old lady content to sit in a chair in the old people's home where she lived. She was by nature an explorer, a traveller. She took off in her 60s, flew to New York, hailed a cab and demanded to be taken to the notorious Bowery district to look around. In her 70s she set off for Canada, where she knew no one, and spent two months back-packing across the country, staying in youth hostels and returning as a steerage passenger in a Russian ship. In her 80s she joined the Bowlers on a family holiday in Germany and insisted on taking a trip in a ski-lift.

More significant, perhaps, was the evidence brought forward that elderly people thought unable to walk more than a few steps can, and do, in situations of stress, accomplish the unexpected. Professor Archie Young, a leading geriatrician, argues it is entirely possible that Aunt Flo could have walked to her death. His evidence was not heard at Mrs Bowler's first appeal against conviction but was significant in the second appeal.

By the time of the re-trial, in January this year, the arguments were essentially polarised: Anthony Glass, QC, a formidable advocate, argued convincingly for the Crown that Mrs Jackson could not have walked the distance to the river. Jeremy Roberts, QC, for the Defence, argued equally persuasively that Mrs Bowler – and he called several witnesses as to her character – could not, would not, have committed the murder. It was a stark choice between two improbable scenarios.

The Crown's case, on the face of it, was forceful: Mr Glass cited a list of factors which seemed to suggest guilt. But, as Mr Roberts eloquently put it, they were all circumstantial. Indeed this was a case, he said, of circumstantial evidence par excellence. In other words, there was no 'direct evidence' to link Mrs Bowler with the crime, nothing, he argued, to show she was in any way involved. No one had seen her at the alleged scene of the crime, nor was there any scientific or forensic evidence to connect her with it.

Above all, in his quiet but compelling opening address to the jury, he insisted that it was not necessary to be sure as to what happened that night to Florence Jackson. The circumstances of her death were likely to remain a mystery to which 'none of us,' he said, 'is likely ever to know the answer.'

The court – judge, jury, lawyers, press and supporters – watched as Mrs Bowler entered the witness box to give evidence. Everyone was mindful that, a widow now aged 68 years, she had served four and a half years and was only too well aware of the consequences of failure at this last attempt to assert her innocence. The remainder of the 12-year sentence could yet have to be served – and if she was sent back, she told me, she would undoubtedly die in prison.

This book recounts how a tragic series of misunderstandings, too–ready assumptions and prejudices led to Sheila Bowler's conviction for murder. It describes the harrowing ordeal for the piano teacher of her time in police cells awaiting interrogation, and of her first weeks in Holloway prison. Angela Devlin's own extensive research into prison life gave her an added insight into what Sheila Bowler experienced. *Anybody's Nightmare* also draws on Mrs Bowler's personal prison diaries and prison reports to complete the picture of what she endured – not least the moving letter she wrote to her son and daughter, as she waited pessimistically for the result of her first appeal, telling them to get on with their lives.

On a human level, this book is a sad and moving story. But it also prompts questions about the legal system in which Sheila Bowler believed so profoundly. She never worried, over all the months leading up to her first trial, because – as she put it – she had faith in British justice. When Lord Justice Rose recently quashed the conviction of a man hanged for murder 40 years ago, he reflected on the dangers of the death penalty in a system where human error is bound to be involved. No such system can be infallible. *Anybody's Nightmare* is a salutary reminder of the need therefore for vigilance – and the need, above all, to leave room for doubt.

Frances Gibb
April 1998

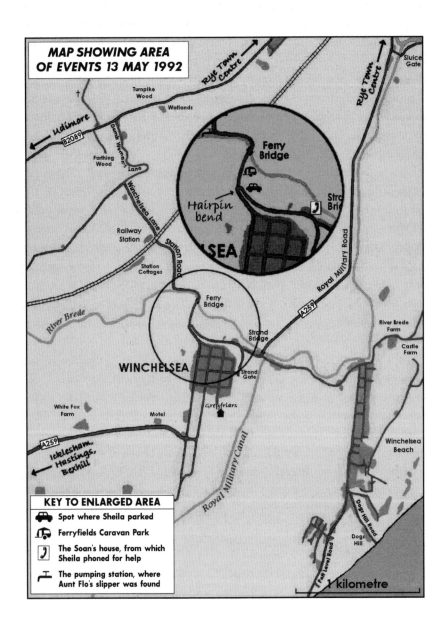

MAP SHOWING AREA OF EVENTS 13 MAY 1992

KEY TO ENLARGED AREA

Spot where Sheila parked

Ferryfields Caravan Park

The Soan's house, from which Sheila phoned for help

The pumping station, where Aunt Flo's slipper was found

1 kilometre

CHAPTER ONE

LOOKING AFTER AUNTIE

It was a nightmare that could have happened to anyone.

One night in May 1992 Mrs Sheila Bowler, a widowed piano teacher in her sixties, was driving home to the picturesque town of Rye in Sussex. At some point between 9.30 and 10pm she had reached Winchelsea, another quaint medieval hill-top town just a few miles from Rye, when she noticed something seriously wrong with the steering on her elderly Audi car. She drove carefully down Ferry Hill, one of the steepest gradients in the south of England, and parked just round the hairpin bend at the bottom. She got out. Sure enough, the front nearside tyre looked as if it had a puncture. She dared not drive any further.

In the front passenger seat sat Mrs Florence Jackson, the 89 year old aunt of Sheila's late husband Bob. Sheila had collected her earlier that evening from a local old folks' home to spend a couple of days with her in Rye. Sheila checked the boot: she had left the spare tyre in her garage at home. Now she explained to the old lady she must go and telephone for help and would be back in a few minutes. Clutching her shoulder bag and a torch she set off along the busy A259.

At the bottom of Ferry Hill the road is bordered by heavy undergrowth and overhanging trees. The first houses you see are set far back off the road in the fields, and Sheila did not fancy walking down one of the long dark driveways. She quickened her pace and hurried on round the bend. But it was still a good five minutes before she came to a row of cottages with their front gardens bordering the pavement. The first few were either in darkness or had only the bedroom lights on. But at Number Four Tanyard Cottages, there were lights blazing all over the house. Sheila went up the path and rang the doorbell.

She recognized the householder, a local barber, and they chatted for some minutes before she managed to interrupt and explain her problem. The breakdown service took some time to answer her phonecall and it was about twenty past ten before she managed to get through. The rescue truck would be there within the hour. The barber and his wife offered to walk her back to her car and keep her company till it arrived. By the time they reached the hairpin bend, Sheila must have been away for about half an hour. When they were a few feet from the Audi, Sheila realised that Aunt Flo's white hair was no longer visible through the windscreen. In fact there was no sign of her at all.

Next morning the body of Mrs Florence Jackson was found floating face down in the River Brede, about 500 yards from the car. Fourteen months later Sheila Bowler sat in a cell in Holloway Prison, sentenced to life imprisonment for murder. Her life as a respectable piano teacher was shattered, her daughter Jane's promising musical career lay in ruins.

Jane Bowler was 22 at the time of Aunt Flo's disappearance. On the evening of Wednesday 13 May, while Sheila was driving down Ferry Hill, Winchelsea, she was studying in her West London studio flat for her final music degree examinations. A gifted cellist, she hoped soon to embark on a career as an orchestral musician. She had done the first two exams about a week earlier and the next was on May 26.

Jane always kept in close contact with her mother, who still lived in the Rye house where Jane was brought up. Sheila, a cellist herself as well as a pianist, proudly supported her daughter's musical ambitions. They would speak on the telephone every few days. That evening Jane had a particular reason to call: Sheila was planning to stay the Friday night with her daughter on the way to spend the weekend with friends in Bishop's Stortford and Jane wanted to finalise arrangements.

But it was Jane's brother Simon, 25, who answered her phonecall at about 8 o'clock.

'Mum's still out,' he said. 'She's gone to fetch Aunt Flo from the old folks' home. She's bringing her to stay for a couple of days.'

When Jane rang again at 11pm Sheila was still not back.

'It's Aunt Flo,' said Simon, 'She's gone missing – she's lost!'

The nightmare had begun.

Aunt Flo – Mrs Florence Jackson – was Jane's great aunt, and she was very fond of the old lady. There are photographs in the family album of Aunt Flo, a widow, and her unmarried younger sister Aunt Lil – Miss Lilian Gillham – unwrapping presents at Christmases spent at 25 Fair Meadow, the Bowlers' comfortable modern detached house on the hill just outside Rye.

Sheila was brought up in Essex and was always musical. She played the violin, piano and cello at school, went on to study music at Trinity College and became a music teacher. At the age of 32 she married Robert Bowler, a divorced man with three teenaged children aged 13, 15 and 19. Bob had custody of the children. Bob and Sheila set up home in Ilford. Four years later their son Simon was born, followed after three years by Jane. They moved to Rye in August 1970. Sheila wanted to live in one of the cobbled streets in the town centre, but Bob preferred a large modern house on the outskirts. They bought 25 Fair Meadow and by 1978 they had paid off the mortgage.

In 1971 Bob's aunts Flo and Lil, then in their sixties, decided they would also move to the historic Sussex town from their home near Ilford, because their nephew Bob and his second wife Sheila were so good to them, and the childless aunts were so fond of the children. They loved to go with the Bowlers on family holidays, and particularly enjoyed a special trip to Germany to see the Oberammergau Passion Play.

Lilian, Florence and Bob Bowler's mother Rose were three of the six children born in the early 1900s to William and Emma Gillham, a rather remarkable family who lived in Cubitt Town on the Isle of Dogs in London's East End. There was also a pair of twin boys, who died in infancy. Their home, 115 Alpha Road, was just a few streets away from the Thames, and Flo and Lil would have been familiar with the sights and sounds of the great river. William was a lighterman – his job was to help load and unload the lighters, the flat-bottomed boats that ferried goods to and from the great ships anchored in the East India Docks.

The Gillham children did quite well for themselves. Though John was killed in the Great War at Passchendaele, another brother, Harry, became a London headmaster and in his spare time made magnificent marquetry furniture. A sister, Annie, ran her own ironmongers' shop. Though born just four years apart, and in their later years inseparable, Lil and Flo were not particularly close in their youth. Flo, the elder of the two, born on 10 August 1902, was always much more adventurous than Lil. Perhaps the sight of the ocean-going freighters in the London docks fostered a longing to see foreign countries, for Flo always loved travelling. In her twenties – remarkably for a woman of her class and times – she set off alone to live in

Australia, where she stayed for ten years, extensively exploring both Australia and New Zealand.

She returned to England and got married rather late in life to Albert Edward Blenkinsop Jackson, a clerk in the Ministry of Works. They settled in South Shields, but in 1943, when Albert was just 48, he died of stomach cancer, leaving Flo a widow at 41. She returned to London and resumed her independent life, getting herself a job in Whitehall, at the Foreign Office.

Meanwhile Lil's life followed a far more traditional pattern: she became the companion to an elderly lady, keeping herself busy with intricate embroidery. But when the old lady died, Flo used her Whitehall contacts to find Lil a job at the Home Office. At this point the sisters grew close, commuting daily together to central London from the flat they shared in Greenwich. They used to rise at crack of dawn and be in town by eight, where they would take breakfast together before work.

Flo remained fiercely independent and impulsive throughout her long life. She continued to travel widely: Christopher Gillham, one of her great-nephews, recalls meeting her in her sixties. 'Florrie was talkative and expansive, while Lily was quiet, dull and even rather disapproving.' Flo had told him about a recent trip to New York, when she persuaded a reluctant taxi driver to take her to the notorious Bowery district, and got out and walked around, oblivious of any danger.

At the age of 70, perhaps recalling the cargo ships of her riverside childhood, she suddenly decided to travel alone by freight ship to Canada, where she knew not a single soul. She spent two months there, crossing from one side of the country to the other by train. On her return the Bowlers watched her alight from a Russian steamer when they went to collect her at Tilbury Dock. In Canada Flo slept in youth hostels. She was used to this kind of basic accommodation: whenever she travelled from Rye to London she would stay overnight at a youth hostel in Tottenham Court Road, and continued to do so until she was well over 70. At 80 during the German holiday Flo insisted on taking a ride on a ski-lift – an event proudly documented by Bob in a jerky home movie using the family's cine camera (bought by Sheila with saved-up Green Shield stamps).

Aunt Flo had retired from her job at the Foreign Office before the move to Rye, but Aunt Lil carried on commuting to London to her Home Office job, continuing well past retirement age. When they first came to live in the town, they bought a small house at 25 North Salts, a select 'seventies development of neo-Georgian houses at the bottom of Rye Hill, where they used regularly to babysit Jane and Simon. The Bowler family went to tea with the great aunts every other Sunday.

'We always had exactly the same food,' remembers Jane. 'It was invariably cold meat and salad and the aunts used to cut it up small for me and Simon. The trouble was, they went on doing it well into our teenage years!'

Lil and Flo delighted in shopping trips by train to Hastings and Eastbourne, often taking Jane and Simon to Debenhams for fish and chips, or to the amusements arcade on the pier where they gave them pennies for the slot machines. Later, as Jane's musical talents emerged, they enthusiastically supported her. They especially enjoyed a local concert when Jane played in a quartet. Flo and Lil insisted on paying for a strong cello case so Jane could transport the instrument safely home after her lessons. Sheila thought the cost – £300 – was far more than the old ladies could afford and paid the money back into their building society account.

The sisters lived happily at the North Salts house for fourteen years.

As they grew older Flo and Lil, now also retired, became familiar Rye characters in a town famous for elderly eccentrics. Every Sunday Flo would attend morning service at St Mary's, the beautiful Rye parish church which stands high above Romney Marsh, a landmark for homecoming sailors. She always sat in the same pew behind her nephew Bob in his church warden's chair, and one morning a week she sold books and curios to tourists at the church bookstall. Meanwhile Lil stayed at home busying herself about the house. Flo had never liked housework, but she would sit for hours and knit toys for Sheila to sell at the NSPCC Christmas Fair.

Flo and Lil were universally known with affection as The Aunts. Just as they used to breakfast together in London, now each weekday they would stroll into town for a 'second breakfast' – and sometimes lunch too – at Simon the Pieman, a quaint tea room next to St Mary's. But at Christmas, when the restaurant offered special concessions for pensioners, Lil and Flo stayed at home: they would rather pay the full price for their lunch than reveal their age and accept 'charity.'

Both ladies remained remarkably active: one of their great pleasures was their regular 'constitutional' walk, and well into their seventies they would set out along the Military Road outside their house and walk the six miles across the Marsh to Appledore. Sometimes they would catch a bus back but often they would walk the return journey as well. People of that generation were used to walking, and even their 'short' walks were enough to daunt someone half their age. A favourite stroll took them past Rye railway station and out along the road towards Udimore for about a mile. They would then turn left past Carpenters, the home of one of Rye's famous residents, the comedian Spike Milligan, and along a winding narrow road with the Hardyesque name Dumb Woman's Lane. They would potter on past Winchelsea Station and then alongside the River Brede till the lane emerged on to the busy A259. They would hurry on along this major trunk road back towards Rye till it was time to cross the Marsh and inspect the ruins of Camber Castle, one of the fortresses built by Henry VIII.

But these hearty walks ended for Aunt Lil when she came home one day feeling dizzy, possibly because of a slight stroke, fell down the stairs and broke her leg. Sheila and Bob ordered Meals on Wheels but the aunts furiously cancelled them. Finally it was decided that the house was too large and they would be safer without stairs to manage. In 1985 they moved to a ground floor flat, 59 Ferry Road, closer to the town centre.

Aunt Lil, always much more houseproud than her sister, had been in the habit of doing all the cleaning. After her fall she was less capable, and, says Jane, 'that sort of thing never interested Aunt Flo. She never cared what the house looked like, nor how she looked herself.' Instead Flo would sit reading library books – historical novels and the travel books that reminded her of her globetrotting days. Her eyesight and hearing were good and she never needed spectacles or a hearing aid. But in February 1986 she was admitted to Rye cottage hospital with a suspected slight stroke. She made good progress and was discharged after nine days.

As the sisters grew older and even more eccentric, Sheila's task became more arduous, and it was only her dutiful care of the old ladies that enabled them to continue living independently in Ferry Road. She tried everything to make sure they ate properly, returning at lunchtime to prepare a hot meal (Meals on Wheels were again ordered and again angrily cancelled). She finally had to resort to nutritious fillings for sandwiches. Meanwhile the aunts were busily sabotaging her efforts, with Aunt Flo trotting to the shops for the biscuits and sweets she and Lil loved, or persuading Mary Edwards, their cleaning lady, to make the purchases for them. After the move to the flat Lil was diagnosed as being diabetic and was forbidden sugar. But Aunt Flo insisted on buying sugar or borrowing a cup or two from neighbours for Lil's secret supply.

At this period in her life, Sheila was kept quite busy for a woman nearing retirement age. She worked hard for local charities, especially the NSPCC, and helped Bob by carrying out door-to-door collections for the British Legion Poppy Fund. For years Rye has put on an annual arts festival, and Sheila was the person to ask if you wanted someone to provide refreshments for a visiting brass band or group of actors. She was entirely reliable and thought nothing of entertaining twenty young people to a delicious tea in her comfortable living room.

Her teaching workload was quite heavy too. As a peripatetic music teacher she had to drive considerable distances between the three private schools in Kent and Sussex where she taught all day on Mondays and Tuesdays, as well as Wednesday afternoons. But she always found time to lend a hand to local people in trouble, and many of them were later to come forward, offering to testify how she had helped them or their relatives at times of sickness and distress, always ready with a bunch of flowers, a home-made cake, a hospital visit or a friendly chat.

Even her closest friends, however, admitted that tact was not Sheila's strong point. Her manner could be abrupt, she had a sharp tongue which she sometimes used without thinking, and she did not suffer fools gladly. A former Rye primary school teacher has been a close friend for twenty years and her comment is typical of many: 'Sheila is a very outspoken person who does not mince her words, sometimes falling foul of people in defence of her family and those in her care. Before I taught her son I already knew of her as an "awkward parent" from other staff.'

Sheila was also a great talker: Rye friends and acquaintances spoke fondly of her good deeds, but admitted crossing the street to avoid her if they were in a hurry. As Mrs Biddy Cole, the aunts' next-door neighbour, said, 'Sheila had verbal diarrhoea. Talking to her was like being battered by a battering ram!'

But everyone who knew Sheila Bowler well agreed that she was reliable and dutiful, especially in her care of her husband's elderly aunts. Carol Brigham has been a friend for about thirteen years and the two ladies would meet early most mornings for coffee in Rye before starting their working day: 'We would discuss the day ahead, then Sheila would go off "to do the aunts," taking them ham sandwiches because they often forgot to eat. She would have to clean them up and never once in all those years did I hear her complain about doing it.'

'Mum used to get up about 6am and go along to the flat every morning before work,' remembers Jane. 'As the aunts got older they would sometimes be in quite a mess when she got there and she'd have to clean them up. Mum went on like this for about seven years, apart from the odd week or two when the aunts went into an old people's home for respite care.' Mrs Cole, who with her husband runs a pottery business further along Ferry Road, was a daily witness to Sheila's unflagging care. The back of the aunts' flat extended into their garden in an L shape, and Biddy could see them there from her own bedroom window:

'The ladies were elderly and slightly dotty – growing more so over the years. In time the aunts wandered. Flo would suddenly turn up in our kitchen without warning. I'd be doing the washing up and I'd turn round and find her there. Whenever I had cause to be up during the night they were nearly always up and dressed and having cups of tea in their kitchen. I have seen them setting out for a walk at two or three o'clock in the morning. I don't think time meant a great deal to them.

'As they grew older and more fragile Sheila visited them daily and quite often two or three times a day. They were *devoted* to her – they used to wait for her to come and she would take them out for trips in her car. I never heard her shouting at them. She was a brusque woman but she was very nice indeed to the aunts, even though towards the end there were some very nasty messes for her to clean up. She struck our family as a very caring carer who really was extremely fond of the old ladies.'

Dr Peter Lewis, whose wife Rosemary is head of Bricklehurst Manor, one of the prep schools where Sheila gave piano lessons, recalls that 'on a number of occasions Sheila revealed that she had been up early, around five o'clock, so that she could visit her husband's aunts to deal with their bedding, cleaning and tidying their flat. Sheila always sounded most caring toward them and their needs.'

In May 1989 Lil spent several weeks in Rye Hospital. She was said to be 'muddled, with memory short term only, diabetic, sight poor.' Back at home Flo sat sleeping in her chair waiting for her sister's return. By this time Social Services were becoming concerned about the aunts and there were discussions with the Bowlers about the possibility of the sisters moving into residential care. But the old ladies were firmly set against such a move.

That same year Magdala House, a new day care centre for the elderly, opened in Rye, funded by East Sussex Social Services. It happened to be conveniently situated in Ferry Road, immediately opposite the aunts' flat, and they were referred there on 7 June and were soon attending three times a week. Social Services workers would come and help them across the road – they provided the ladies with a zimmer frame and walking sticks which they kept hanging at the ready on the back of their chairs – and the day-care workers even held a key to number 59.

At Magdala House Flo and Lil could have a cup of tea, a meal and the company of other elderly people. But Mrs Polly, Magdala House's senior care worker, found Sheila difficult to deal with. Sometimes the aunts had to be given a bath because of their incontinence: when Sheila came to see them in the flat after work she would find a bag of soiled clothes left by Magdala House staff for her to deal with. She was irritated to find Flo and Lil dressed in somebody else's old clothes. Later in a statement to the police Mrs Polly was to say that Sheila 'did not understand the needs of the elderly.' Once again – and this was Sheila's tragedy – her sharp tongue gave the lie to her genuine care for the aunts over so many years.

Meanwhile the aunts were becoming more and more vulnerable. One day that same year Sheila arrived at the flat to find Aunt Flo looking upset: 'I did a silly thing, Sheila,' she confessed. A week earlier a confidence trickster posing as a roofer had come knocking at the door. He told the sisters that a tile was missing and offered to mend it for them. But he would need £700 in cash – in advance. He persuaded Aunt Flo, who had no idea of the cost of roof repairs, to walk into town to her bank while he followed behind in his van. He parked at the back of the building, then walked into the bank and waited while she took the money out and gave it to him. Then he immediately drove off.

Sheila told the police but it was too late – the swindler had had seven days to make his getaway. It was not the first time he had struck in Rye, a fertile hunting-ground because of all the elderly people living there; a few months earlier warnings had been printed in the local newspaper and shown on local TV. Bob was furious: when he first heard the media warnings he had thought of his aunts and had taken the trouble to write to the bank warning them to look out for any major payments. About a month later, Sheila and Bob were stunned to find the same thing had happened again. This time Flo had been persuaded by the bogus roofer to write a cheque for £1100: he said the roof was now in need of major repairs. Bob protested even more furiously to the bank, and eventually the sisters received £500 in compensation.

These two incidents are significant because they show that Bob and Sheila had no direct control over the aunts' finances. The old ladies still wrote their own cheques to repay the Bowlers for household jobs they arranged. The garden had to be dealt with and a recurring problem was the removal of a bees' nest underneath some wooden steps at the back of the Ferry Road flat leading to the apartment above.

While Lil was content to potter around the flat, Flo, always energetic and restless as she had been all her life, would often wait at her front gate for Sheila to arrive, sometimes wandering up Ferry Road to meet her. In October 1989 Dr Jeelani, the local GP who was the family doctor for both the aunts and the Bowlers, requested that Flo be admitted to St Helen's Hospital, Hastings, because of tiredness, unreliable eating habits and impaired balance.

She stayed there from 10 October to 1 November, and hospital notes describe her wandering round the wards feeling lost and asking to go home, though she was 'mobilizing very well' and there had been no falls during her stay. On 19 October a hospital note reads: 'She remains wandering at times and loses her whereabouts on the ward. She is adamant she does not want to be resettled (in a residential home) and wants to go back home.'

When she was brought back to Ferry Road she was disorientated and at first failed to recognize Lil. The next month she had to be treated at the Rye cottage hospital again, this time for a burn to her leg. Sheila recalls that the aunts insisted on switching off the electric storage heaters and using instead an electric fire, often sitting too close to it, so it had to be taken away.

On 10 February 1990 Dr Jeelani made a report to the DHSS so that Flo could receive a mobility allowance. He said she had signs of brain failure and multiple falls at home and her mobility was restricted, though she could dress and undress and make drinks for herself. But he was later to admit in the Court of Appeal that he had exaggerated her infirmity, as is quite common when kindly doctors seek help for the elderly. Because in January 1991, nearly a year later, Flo was still certainly not immobile. She spent a couple of days in hospital for tests that detected a small internal polyp. Hospital notes confirm that she could 'mobilize well, shuffles purposefully and appears steady on her feet without any aids.'

Throughout 1991 Social Services officials began to grow more and more concerned about the old ladies continuing to live on their own in the Ferry Road flat. On April 12 social workers rang Bob to tell him that everyone dealing with Flo and Lil was worried. Their notes made at the time record a phonecall to Bob registering their concern: 'Told him the ladies are no longer able to make decisions for themselves and he must take responsibility. Everyone voiced their concerns and felt the ladies should be in care. Mr Bowler said he agreed but his aunts wish to stay at home and he has to go along with this.' The notes also recorded that Greyfriars, a local authority residential care home in Winchelsea, about three miles from Rye, would have two vacancies that September, and would be happy to take both sisters. But the following day Bob rang Social Services saying he could not agree to his aunts going permanently into a care home against their wishes. On 15 April Flo was once more in hospital, this time in Hastings, when a simple fracture to the left wrist was diagnosed and plastered. The plaster was removed exactly a month later and the fracture had left no ill effects.

That summer Bob Bowler finally agreed to short-term respite care to give his wife a break, and the aunts stayed at Greyfriars from 15 July to 17

August. Sheila telephoned regularly to see how they were, and on August 10, Flo's 89th birthday, she took her chocolates. She also managed a break with Bob in Cornwall, followed by a short holiday in Vienna for the Mozart bicentennial celebrations. An extra attraction of the trip was to see Jane playing her cello there with the East Sussex youth orchestra. When they returned, Flo and Lil left Greyfriars and went back to Ferry Road.

One day in the autumn of 1991 Sheila turned up to find that Flo was not at home. She discovered her outside Rye railway station, a walk of about half a mile. She was, she said, off to go shopping in Hastings. In the past this had been one of her regular jaunts. But this time she had no money and no idea what to do next.

On October 23 Bob and Sheila attended a case conference at the Social Services 'patch office' in Rye. Again, social workers insisted the old ladies needed twenty-four hour care. Again, the notes record Bob as stating emphatically that his aunts said they did not want to go into Greyfriars, even though again the general feeling was that the old ladies should be in permanent residential care. But he agreed on another trial week, and Flo and Lil returned to the Home from 25 October until November 1st. Because this stay, like the summer session, was regarded as temporary respite care, they were charged at only a minimal basic rate.

These case conferences were at times rather fraught occasions. At one, Sheila, in combative mood, complained that many of the old ladies' own clothes had been lost by Magdala House because of the staff's continuing refusal to issue them with incontinence pads. They frequently soaked themselves, and Sheila said she was constantly having to replace lost and ruined garments. Mrs Polly complained that she sometimes found Mrs Jackson and Miss Gillham had gone without breakfast. 'This was quite untrue,' says Sheila. 'Often by the time I arrived in the morning Aunt Flo had already made the toast, and if not I prepared breakfast for them.' Yet now Mrs Polly seemed to be accusing Sheila of neglecting the old ladies. On this occasion Bob Bowler, known in Rye as the mildest of men, lost his temper. 'Don't you dare speak to my wife like that!' he shouted.

In early November 1991 Aunt Lil had a heart attack. The home help found her and she was rushed to St Helen's Hospital in Hastings where, on 11 November, in her eighty-sixth year, she died. Aunt Flo went on living in the flat but she was lonely without Aunt Lil, who had shared her home for the past fifty years. The sisters had had a love-hate relationship, often quarrelling furiously over trivia: 'Aunt Lil would look out of the window of the flat at the roadside bench opposite,' says Jane, 'and she would insist there was a man in a green jacket sitting on it. "Nonsense!" Aunt Flo would shout, "That's a green litter bin!" Then Aunt Lil would look outside when a Force Six gale was blowing and say, much to Aunt Flo's annoyance, "There's not a leaf moving on the trees!"'

Nevertheless the sisters were inseparable: they chattered to each other constantly and after the great hurricane of 1987, which alarmed them greatly, they shared the same single bed. They refused to use the bathroom at night but would keep a bucket next to the bed. There were many accidents and inevitably once again it was Sheila who, uncomplaining, cleared them up. Now with her sister gone, Aunt Flo sunk into a deep depression.

On 19 November, a week after Lil's death, Social Services rang Bob and asked him to go to Ferry Road and pack a suitcase for Mrs Jackson as she was 'very distressed and did not want to stay at home.' Would he take her straight to Greyfriars? Bob said his wife would visit the old lady, and the following day he telephoned to say Flo was perfectly all right. The social workers were told firmly to leave well alone. According to Sheila, 'It seemed Aunt Flo said one thing to them and another to Bob and me. Bob felt he just couldn't force Aunt Flo against her will to move, as she became more and more obstinate when Greyfriars was mentioned, just as she did when anyone mentioned her going to hospital.' Anyone used to dealing with elderly relatives will recognize this familiar pattern.

On November 21, two days after Bob's conversation with Social Services, and ten days after Aunt Lil's death, Sheila arrived at the flat in the morning rather later than usual. 'I called out and Aunt Flo didn't answer, and to my horror she was lying in a pool of blood near her chair. There was blood on her hair and on her face. She was conscious and the first thing she said was, "I don't want the doctor." I phoned an ambulance immediately and they came about ten minutes later.'

It was never established whether the blood was a cause or a result of the fall. The old lady was taken to the Royal East Sussex Hospital in Hastings but Sheila could not accompany her in the ambulance – she had to stay behind for a short time to clear up the mess and lock up the flat. Just before Sheila left, Mrs Polly came rushing across from Magdala House to see if there was anything she could do. Sheila explained that everything was under control and drove off after the ambulance, managing to catch it up on the Hastings Road. When she had seen the old lady comfortably settled, and the hospital told her there was nothing more she could do, she went about her usual shopping errands then went on to work.

In hospital Flo seemed to recover – certainly enough to shuffle around the ward. She was transferred to St Helen's Hospital where less than two weeks earlier Aunt Lil had died. She continued to make good progress and according to the hospital notes of 22/23 November, she could move around independently using a zimmer frame. The notes say she 'can be wandersome' and 'is mobilizing short distances round bed area.' By 28 November she had 'got up to the commode unaided.' On her discharge on December 6 it was noted that she could walk with a zimmer, though she was still slightly confused. So Aunt Flo left the hospital and was taken straight to Greyfriars.

Bob and Sheila were by now quite familiar with the residential home. But nevertheless they were hurt and angry that Flo's transfer from the hospital was arranged with Greyfriars officials without their knowledge, especially as the very day before Flo's discharge, a member of St Helen's staff had told them she needed more time in hospital. They only discovered Flo had been moved when they turned up at St Helens to visit her: 'We both felt Greyfriars had manoeuvred her into their care without Bob or I knowing. We did know there had been some liaison between the hospital and Greyfriars but we thought the move should have been discussed with us first.'

It was an inauspicious start to the period of long-term care planned at Greyfriars by Social Services. The short holiday breaks had gone quite well, but the more the Bowlers saw of the place, the less impressed they became with the standard of care provided: 'I used to sit with Aunt Flo sometimes at the evening meal to persuade her to eat as she did not want to, but no-one else bothered,' says Sheila.

On December 8 Sheila went into Greyfriars, bringing extra clothes for

Aunt Flo, and on the 18th she and Jane went again together. On Christmas Day the whole family visited the old lady.

Never the most tactful woman, Sheila was soon making herself very unpopular with the Matron, Mrs Joan Dobson, and her staff. She felt that the care Aunt Flo was getting was quite inadequate.

'Mum was always complaining because she just wasn't happy with the way Aunt Flo was being treated,' says Jane. 'Mum's got extremely high standards, she didn't think the staff were doing their job properly and she made that obvious. Mum doesn't beat about the bush and the staff certainly didn't like her very much.'

On 9 January a Greyfriars care assistant called Deborah Freeman took Flo to St Helen's Hospital in Hastings by car. She was given a colonoscopy to examine the large bowel but no abnormalities were detected. Up until mid-January Bob and Sheila visited the old lady frequently. As in many old people's homes, visitors could come and go more or less as they pleased as long as it was not too late at night. At first no record was kept of visits, though by February 1992 a visitors' book had been set up in the entrance hall, and visitors were asked to sign. Whenever Jane was home from London she accompanied her mother and admits they often forgot to sign: 'One of us was always popping in and out and we didn't always sign the book. It hardly seemed worth it – sometimes we'd only be there a few minutes because Aunt Flo might be sleeping.' At other times there was, frankly, nothing to talk about. Aunt Flo's chatter had been silenced since her sister died and conversation soon flagged.

According to Jane, the old lady, independent as ever, was not at all happy at Greyfriars and longed to be back in her own flat in Ferry Road: 'Aunt Flo never liked being in the Home even when Aunt Lil was there to keep her company, and she certainly didn't want to be there without Aunt Lil. Every time I went to see her, she always used to ask me when she could come home. She seemed to be very low and depressed.'

Bob and Sheila were becoming increasingly worried. The social workers seemed to be putting ever more pressure on the family to have Flo registered as a permanent resident at Greyfriars. The question of the payment of the Home fees also needed to be settled. Aunt Flo's financial position had been assessed, with her property and pension being taken into consideration. As a result – like any elderly person with assets of more than £8,000 – she had to pay the maximum contribution of £242.62p per week for her keep at Greyfriars. Her pensions (her state pension and a small pension from her job as a civil servant) were diverted to be paid to the Home but they did not meet the full fees and a backlog soon began to mount up. Social Services were of the opinion that the Ferry Road flat should now be sold to meet the bills.

As the weeks went by and the Greyfriars debt steadily increased, tensions rose between Social Services and the Bowlers. The family was in a quandary. Various options were discussed. One was to redecorate the flat and rent it out to lodgers. The rent would pay the Greyfriars bills and Aunt Flo's flat would still be there for her if she were ever able to return. Jane, now back in London, was kept in touch by phone: 'Aunt Flo kept complaining to Mum that she didn't like being in the Home: all she did was sit in a room all day and a lot of the other old people were much worse off than her. Aunt Flo more or less had all her marbles and some of the other poor souls weren't right in the head. But I think she did accept that she wasn't well and she was just coming round to the idea that she might have to stay there. I thought she should stay, because I knew what an effort it was for Mum to keep her going in the flat, and I said so. It was all very well for Dad – he didn't have to do all the work. But still, Dad was very much against making Aunt Flo sell her flat. He was adamant that no action should be taken without her consent. Then Dad died and nothing was ever resolved.'

Bob Bowler was a relatively fit and healthy man for his 73 years. He had joined the Post Office at the age of 14 as a delivery boy and had spent his whole career there, apart from the war years when he took part in the Normandy landings as a gunner. He distinguished himself in active service, reaching the rank of Captain by the age of 27 when the war ended. He returned to the GPO and joined the Investigations Department and by the time he retired in 1978 he had reached the responsible position of Assistant Controller, commuting daily from London after the family moved to Rye. The journey was long and tiring, with a change of trains at Ashford, but Bob felt it was worth carrying on for the excellent pension he stood to earn. He had kept himself very busy for the past thirteen years, working for the British Legion on their annual Poppy Appeal, helped by Sheila, and fulfilling his duties as a church warden.

In mid-January Bob began complaining of pains in his stomach. He was violently sick several times, and on Sunday 19 January he was admitted to the Royal East Sussex Hospital in Hastings (now replaced by a more modern hospital, the Conquest). Extensive tests over the next few days showed he would need routine surgery to remove a small benign growth in the lower bowel. The operation was performed on Thursday 23 January and Bob began to recover, but then seemed to deteriorate again. Jane went to visit her father on Sunday the 26th and thought he looked very weak. By the following Tuesday he had begun to haemorrhage and Sheila was becoming terribly worried. She was told he was to go back to the operating theatre to check there was no major problem.

She had just arrived back home from the hospital – either on the Tuesday or the Wednesday, she cannot now recall – when there was a ring at the doorbell. The woman on the doorstep said she was Heather Phillips, the visiting officer from the council. She wanted to speak to her about Mrs Jackson's Greyfriars fees. She produced a property form for Sheila to sign. There had, she said, been problems in the past when elderly people had died, and the beneficiaries of their wills had refused to pay the bills for their care in council homes.

'But of course,' she said, glancing around the spacious, elegantly furnished hall, 'I'm sure we wouldn't have problems like that in your case.'

Sheila refused to sign anything. She explained that Mrs Jackson was her husband's aunt, not hers. He would have to make any such decision, he was in hospital recovering from surgery, and at the moment was too ill to be troubled.

'I'm not sure of the exact wording of the form,' says Jane, 'but I think if Mum signed it, Aunt Flo's flat would have had to be sold to pay the Greyfriars fees. But as I said before, Aunt Flo had always said, right from the beginning, that she never wanted the flat sold. She wanted it there, even if she couldn't go back to it, and Dad always used to say, "We can't force Aunt Flo to stay in an old people's home. We certainly shouldn't sell her flat while she's still alive."'

On Wednesday January 29, Mrs Jackson was taken by Greyfriars staff to the outpatients clinic where the surgeon discharged her, describing her as

'Well – symptom-free – on examination fit for her age.'

The next day, Thursday January 30, Sheila spent all day with her husband, not returning home until 6.30pm. She did mention the property form to him but did not trouble him too much, as he seemed so weak: 'But he did say I was to sign nothing without Aunt Flo's consent.'

Tragically, these turned out to be almost Bob's last words. Something seems to have gone horribly wrong in the aftermath to what should have been a routine operation. At 9pm that evening Sheila telephoned the hospital, to be told he was very poorly, but there was no point in her returning. At 11pm she called again and was told he was 'comfortable.' It was a very foggy night. Sheila hated driving in the fog, and – worried she might have to return to the hospital later – she contacted a local taxi firm and asked for a cab to be on standby. She went to bed partly dressed in readiness.

At 2am in the early hours of Friday January 31 the hospital called: Bob had been rushed into intensive care – could Sheila get there immediately? The taxi dashed over the Marsh through the fog to get her and Simon to the hospital but it was too late: by the time they arrived Bob was dead.

'We were all devastated – it was such a shock,' recalls Jane, 'but at the time I never saw Mum cry. I know how upset she felt but she kept her feelings to herself for the sake of me and Simon.' Sheila's lifelong friend Audrey Mummery explains: 'Sheila is very resilient and does not show her emotions to the outside world. Her father was a respected solicitor and member of our local Methodist church, and he expected high standards. He taught his two daughters that in adversity you faced up to the difficulties – you did not burden others.' That Sunday evening Sheila went with Simon and Jane to the Candlemas Service at St Mary's and her friends remarked on their courage. But afterwards Jane remembers her mother breaking down in tears in her bedroom as she sat with her two children and grieved over the shockingly sudden loss of her husband of almost thirty years.

But soon Sheila's emotions were firmly back under control. Her father had taught her to keep a stiff upper lip and that is exactly what she did. Bob died on a Friday and on the Monday she was back teaching at Marlborough House, the Kent prep school where she had several pupils.

'That was just Mum's way of coping,' says Jane. Audrey Mummery agrees: 'Everyone copes differently with grief. Sheila's way was to keep herself busy, immersing herself in music. Her children, particularly Jane, were grieving badly, so she hid her own grief from them.'

The funeral was held the following Friday – a quiet family affair. A more public memorial service was planned for later in the year.

On Thursday 6 January – less than a week after her husband's death – Sheila received a letter from Sarah Silberston, an assessment officer at the County Council's financial department in Lewes. She offered her condolences and apologized for troubling Mrs Bowler at this time. But she explained that because Mrs Jackson would not be returning to her home in Ferry Road, the old lady would now have to consider selling the flat to pay the Greyfriars fees, due to rise by a further £10 a week at the beginning of April. By now the arrears had reached almost £3,000.

But Bob's unexpected death meant that any decision about Aunt Flo had to be put on hold. Social Services and their property form were forgotten as Sheila tried to deal with other more pressing practical considerations. She was having meetings with hospital staff about possible negligence claims following her husband's death. She also wrote to Sir David Lumsden, Director of the Royal Academy, expressing her concern that the bereavement would affect Jane's performance in her degree finals. Sir David wrote a personal letter in reply, assuring her that Jane's tutor had been made aware of the situation and would make allowances. Bob Bowler had been a Freemason and on February 28 John Smith and Dan Neville, two members of the Rye masonic lodge, called on Sheila to ask her if she needed any financial help. Sheila declined – she was comfortably off, she said, with a reasonable income from her teaching and her pensions and no mortgage to pay. But if they cared to give Jane a little help in her musical career, she would be very grateful.

When things settled down a little, the family's thoughts returned to Aunt Flo. Sheila knew how passionately Bob had upheld his aunt's determination to keep her flat: indeed he had defended that right on the very last day of his life. So while she characteristically pulled herself together and went back to her teaching and charity work, the flat remained unsold and the old lady remained at Greyfriars.

Although Aunt Flo was depressed, she seemed to be doing quite well physically, according to notes made by staff. The Matron, Mrs Dobson, wrote that she 'got around very well ' and was 'reasonably fit for a person approaching her 90th year,' though she was confused and could not wash herself. ('She was never a great one for washing herself anyway!' recalls Jane).

On 26 February Sheila attended her first case conference about Bob's aunt without the benefit of his support. By this time she was seriously considering whether she could manage to have Aunt Flo living at home with her. It was now nearly a month since Bob's death and Sheila had several times confided to Jane that she hated returning home to an empty house: she would often delay that moment by dropping in after work at a friend's home for coffee. She would also telephone Audrey Mummery and ask to come and spend a few days when she felt lonely. She thought about ending her piano teaching at Battle Abbey, the school on the site of the Battle of Hastings, and re-scheduling lessons at the other two schools so they fitted into just one day's teaching a week. She had discussed Aunt Flo's unhappiness with Audrey and described this new plan. Now she told Social Services about it.

There was another reason for her new idea: after Bob's death she had had a phonecall from a distant nephew living in Norfolk. He had heard about Aunt Lil's death and wondered how Aunt Flo was. He asked whether he and his wife could help in caring for her, perhaps having her to stay.

Mrs Dobson attended the 26 February meeting and according to Sheila she was very much against the idea: 'Mrs Dobson said they had no intention of letting Aunt Flo home as she doubted I was capable of seeing to her needs.' But Social Services disagreed. Despite past differences they supported Sheila's plan. They noted the possible input of the nephew – an encouraging new factor – and liked the idea of some form of 'rotating care.' They even offered to provide care themselves to look after Aunt Flo on the one day each week when Sheila would be teaching.

But yet again, no final decision was reached. Taking on someone of Aunt Flo's age was a big responsibility and Sheila was still trying to recover from Bob's sudden death. She also knew Jane would be unlikely to approve: she thought her mother already worked too hard. So a further meeting was fixed for 26 March, when the nephew and his wife could come and meet them. (In the event the meeting had to be cancelled because the nephew rang to say his wife was ill. The arrangement he had suggested seems to have fallen by the wayside, for he never made any further contact).

On 4 March, Sheila was asked to take Flo to the hospital outpatients' department for further tests. Once again, the same surgeon described Flo as 'on examination, fit for her age.' But as she had complained of a pain in her side, she stayed in hospital for five days. On 7 March a suspected urinary tract infection was diagnosed. When Sheila went back for the test results, the surgeon told her privately he thought 'there was something there' but that no action should be taken: Flo would be too old to cope with an operation. 'I don't think it will be long,' he commented – a remark which Sheila took to refer to the old lady's life expectancy. She assumed he had diagnosed something as serious as stomach cancer. (Flo had had radical mastectomy of her left breast in the past, though this was many years earlier). At this point Sheila did not mention her assumption to Jane for fear of upsetting her while she was studying for her degree finals. Flo returned to Greyfriars on 10 March. Hospital notes for that day recorded that she could wash herself and 'walk with one nurse to the toilet.'

While Flo was safe in hospital, Sheila had been able to throw herself into preparations for Bob's memorial service, being organized by the Reverend Paddy Buxton at St Mary's, Rye, where Bob had been churchwarden for so many years. On the day, Friday 20 March, more than 450 people came to pay their respects to this quiet, much-loved man. Old soldiers from his regiment stood next to former work colleagues from the Post Office. Members of the Rye British Legion rubbed shoulders with Freemasons from the Rye masonic lodge – Bob had been an active member of both organisations. Elizabeth, one of Bob's three children by his first marriage, read out Maya Angelou's moving poem *When great souls die*. Canon David Maundrell gave the address, and the music was stirring: Bach's *Toccata and Fugue,* the Pachelbel *Canon,* Albinoni's *Adagio* and the *Pie Jesu* from Fauré's *Requiem.*

After the service was over Sheila's thoughts again turned to Aunt Flo. The rest in hospital and the change of scene may have done her good, because her health seemed to have improved physically – she was even able to go on a coach trip with other residents on 20 March, the day of the Memorial Service, in a special coach provided by Magdala House. But two days later she was covered with a rash, and her keyworker Lynda Hanson took her by car to Rye to see Dr Jeelani. On March 25 the rash had worsened, and Dr Jeelani's wife, also a GP, was called to Greyfriars where she treated her for a chest infection. On 8 April she went for a further check to the Royal East Sussex Hospital outpatients' department where her notes read, 'Everything is fine now, no further appointments.' But on 13 April, Greyfriars notes record that she 'fell during the night getting out to commode. No injury.'

In case Flo became too infirm mentally to deal with her own affairs, Sheila, now responsible for her since Bob had died, sought advice from her own solicitor, John Sperring, who suggested a limited power of attorney. In fact the appointment with Sperring was not made primarily to discuss Aunt Flo's affairs. Sheila had never bothered to make a will herself, and Bob's death had made her aware she should do so. At this point she did not even have her own solicitor, but had met John Sperring through her acquaintance with his mother. She was given a form to sign and took it into Greyfriars, where a Rye friend, Edna Adamiw, acted as a witness. But in fact the power of attorney was never needed: to the end of her life Aunt Flo continued to sign all her own cheques. Sheila had no access to Flo's bank or building society accounts, and nobody ever knew what happened to the considerable profit the sisters must have made when they sold the house in North Salts and downsized to the Ferry Road flat. There may have been other incidents like the bogus roofer, because when Aunt Flo died her only asset was her small flat.

Sheila, Jane and Simon were spending the week before Easter – the first without Bob – with Sheila's elder sister Mary and her husband Albert at their home in Royston in Hertfordshire. They returned to Rye on Easter Sunday, and that afternoon, Greyfriars rang to tell them that on Maundy Thursday, 16 April, Aunt Flo had had an accident. 'They were very apologetic,' remembers Sheila, 'and obviously felt guilty about the incident.' It seemed that as Flo was walking on her own from the dining room to the big lounge after supper, possibly trying to use her zimmer frame though nobody was there to see her, she slipped and fell, while attempting to negotiate a ramp or some steps. Three days earlier she had fallen in the night while getting out of bed trying to reach the commode. But this second fall was more serious. Flo had fractured her right wrist and sustained a black eye. She was taken by ambulance to the Royal East Sussex Hospital at 7.10pm, had a long wait in casualty, and was not brought back to Greyfriars until 2am. Greyfriars notes record: 'Fracture had been reduced, plaster, must wear a sling and do finger exercises.'

Sheila and Jane went to Greyfriars on Easter Monday, 20 April, the day after their return from Royston, to take Aunt Flo back to the hospital for her plaster to be checked, and to bring her a belated Easter egg. They found her even more subdued than usual, and were shocked by the heavy bruising on the right side of her face. Her arm was in a sling as well as a plaster, though it was not long before she insisted on dispensing with the sling, which irritated her.

The fracture clinic notes record that she was 'to have arm out of sling on Wednesday. To attend fracture clinic May 25th.' By 30 April, Greyfriars staff noted in their records, Flo 'has a very poor appetite at the moment, but appears to have very little pain from her fractured wrist.'

Throughout this period relations continued to worsen between Sheila and the Greyfriars staff. She complained to Jane that they opened letters sent to Aunt Flo by the local health authority to fix check-up appointments, and failed to let her know the contents. This meant that some of Aunt Flo's appointments – at the Royal East Sussex, at the Rye cottage hospital, and with Dr Jeelani, were made without her knowledge. She felt very strongly that she was being sidelined.

Meanwhile the Greyfriars fees were still mounting up. Despite the Social Services assessment Aunt Flo had no savings of her own readily available to meet the backlog, which by the end of March had reached £3589.70.

As the months went on Sheila knew she would soon have to make a decision: to pay off the arrears Aunt Flo's flat would have to be sold. Again she was presented with the same property form to sign.

She made another appointment with her new solicitor John Sperring to ask his advice. Now that Bob was no longer around she needed professional help to know how best to proceed. It was quite clear that something really must be done about Mrs Jackson's future. Should she stay

Anybody's Nightmare

on and become a permanent resident in the Home where she was plainly unhappy? Should she perhaps be moved to a different residential home, and if so, would she have the financial means to pay for it? She took the property form to show Sperring. He told her it was not a legally binding document and she could ignore it. The local authority had no power to force the sale of an elderly person's property, though they could inform the land registry when the property was eventually sold, and would have first claim on any profits to repay fee arrears – provided that £8,000 capital remained in the estate.

Perhaps now Sheila should make a serious attempt – as she had discussed with her friends and with Social Services – to look after Aunt Flo at 25 Fair Meadow.

CHAPTER TWO

AUNT FLO GOES MISSING

At the beginning of May Sheila finally decided on a course of action. It was now three months since Bob's death and she felt more positive than of late. She would bring Aunt Flo back to Fair Meadow for a couple of days as a kind of trial run, to see how things went. If the visit was successful she would follow it with a more extended visit on August 10 – the old lady's 90th birthday – when she planned a small family celebration. With these ideas in mind she telephoned Greyfriars and fixed a date – Wednesday 6 May – to collect Aunt Flo. Greyfriars notes for May 4 record: 'Mrs Bowler has decided to take Flo home for a few days to see if they can cope. Will come for her on Wednesday pm.'

When Wednesday came Sheila realised this day was a foolish choice: she had extra lessons to teach that evening and after that it would be too late – and she would be too exhausted – to fetch Aunt Flo. At 6pm she telephoned Greyfriars and spoke to the matron, Mrs Dobson. A new appointment was fixed for the same day the following week – Wednesday 13 May. Sheila said that she would be coming along about 8 o'clock in the evening after work to collect Aunt Flo.

At ten minutes past three on the afternoon of May 13 she rang Greyfriars to confirm the arrangement. Joyce Law, one of the care workers, took the call and Sheila asked her particularly not to give Aunt Flo her bowel medication that day. The previous week Greyfriars staff had made this suggestion in case of incontinence on the way home, and now Sheila reminded Joyce Law of the arrangement. The staff were themselves concerned about Flo's incontinence: the Home's daily diary contains a note made on 4 May, after Sheila had first telephoned: 'We must ensure that Mrs Bowler keeps a record of when Flo goes to the toilet as we could end up with a problem after her stay at home.' Now the Greyfriars notes recorded: 'Flo is going to stay with Mrs Bowler until Friday.'

Immediately after making the call Sheila set out from Fair Meadow for Battle Abbey, the girls' school where she was teaching that afternoon. Before she left she chose a walking-stick for Aunt Flo from a collection belonging to Bob and Simon in the hall cupboard and put it between the two front seats beside the gear stick. On the front passenger seat she put a plastic refuse sack with a folded towel on top in case Aunt Flo had one of her increasingly common accidents. The family car was a 1979 Audi 80 saloon in immaculate condition. Though it had done so many miles that a new engine had had to be installed, Bob and Sheila had taken good care of the vehicle and its metallic green bodywork shone as brightly as the day they drove it out of the showroom in St Leonards thirteen years earlier.

Sheila took her usual route to the school – the Udimore Road out of Rye which coincidentally passes Aunt Flo's Ferry Road flat, now standing forlorn and empty. As she drove along Sheila glanced at her watch. Would there be time for her to make a detour to Hastings, about twelve miles from Rye and three miles from Battle? She needed to collect some sheet music for her piano pupils from B & T Keyboards, a Hastings music shop, and she also had in the car a pair of Simon's shoes, neatly packed in a plastic bag. They had been badly repaired by a Hastings cobbler and Sheila – ever the perfectionist and perpetually returning goods to exasperated shopkeepers – was keen to return them and demand satisfaction. Also on the back seat of the car were two new bath mats, still in their shop bags, that she intended to change: she was certainly a customer hard to please.

About a mile and half out of Rye, Sheila was approaching a small side road on the left when she made a decision. She would take a short cut through to the A259, the major trunk road leading straight to Hastings. It was only 3.20 and her first lesson was at 4.15. She indicated left and turned into Dumb Woman's Lane.

As it happened, the route she chose exactly retraced one of the aunts' favourite 'constitutional' walks. Dumb Woman's Lane is the narrow winding road they used to take on their way to see Camber Castle. It turns into Winchelsea Lane, then leads past Winchelsea Halt railway station (where its name changes to Station Road) and then, meandering on beside the River Brede on the right, it passes a brick-built pumping station set well back off the road, and a little further on there is a caravan park called Ferryfields on the left – the kind with permanently fixed mobile homes for holidaymakers to rent, rather than visiting tourist vans. Then Station Road joins the main road, the A259. Before you reach the caravan park the road crosses the Brede at Ferry Bridge, and as she approached this bridge, Sheila felt there was something odd about the Audi's steering. The car seemed to be veering to the left and bumping slightly. She stopped, got out and inspected the tyres.

Two weeks earlier, on April 30, Sheila had noticed a similar problem. She was on her way home from Hastings on a scenic route via the clifftop hamlet of Fairlight, with its spectacular sea views. With her was an elderly Rye friend, Mrs Helen Goodwin, whom Sheila knew because she had been a neighbour of the aunts at North Salts. In one of her characteristic good deeds, Sheila had taken Mrs Goodwin to Debenhams in Hastings to buy her a hat for a wedding. They had lunch in the store's restaurant and now stopped to look at the view of the sea. When Sheila started up the car again and drove slowly off down the steep hill, she told her companion she thought there was something wrong with the steering and she would have to take it into the garage. 'It absolutely sticks in my mind,' recalled the old lady later, 'because I thought, Oh dear, what if we crash and I don't get to the wedding to wear my lovely new hat!'

Sheila admits she was slightly neurotic about the Audi's tyres. 'I was always worrying Bob about the tyre pressures, though I actually used to leave him to pump them up.' But then the problem seemed to disappear. If there was a fault with the tyres, it only occurred intermittently.

As when Mrs Goodwin was in the car two weeks before, Sheila's fears now once again seemed groundless – the tyres looked fine. So Sheila drove on towards Hastings. But this delay, and a traffic jam tailing back along the road between the villages of Guestling and Ore, further along the route, made her worry about being late for her pupils. It was a warm afternoon – the temperature was around 20 degrees Celsius – and she didn't want to get hot and flustered. So she changed her mind about the shopping, took a right turn at the next major junction, drove along the road known locally as The Ridge, and arrived at Battle Abbey School at about 4.10, just in time for her first lesson.

The girls' piano lessons varied in length: some lasted half an hour, some just fifteen minutes. The last child, a ten year old Colombian boarder, finished her lesson at about 7.05 and hurried off to Boarders' Assembly which started on the hour. Sheila gathered up her music, and then went to the telephone in the staffroom to phone Simon and let him know she was collecting Aunt Flo that evening and intended to bring her to stay for a couple of days. He would otherwise have been expecting his mother home at 7.45.

Simon no longer lived at 25 Fair Meadow. He had lodgings in Maidstone, where he worked as a Customs and Excise officer, returning to Rye only at weekends. But this week he had come home on Tuesday evening because he had a day off on the Wednesday. He had to attend a course in Brighton the following weekend and wanted to collect some belongings. He was working in the garden when the phone rang. It was a little while before he came in to take the call. He had taken off his wristwatch to do the gardening and had to squint at a wall clock instead. Simon's vision is impaired enough for him to carry an official 'partially disabled' card.

After a short conversation with her son, Sheila spent a few minutes in the staff toilet then left the building. All the day staff had gone home, and she saw none of the boarding staff before she left. Perhaps they were all in Assembly.

As usual after these evening lessons Sheila had to struggle to open the large wooden double gates leading out of the majestic Abbey. One gate had to be secured by a hook in the wall, the other by a bolt shot down into the gravel drive. If they were not properly fixed they could swing back and damage the car, and this had happened more than once to staff cars. After she had driven through, Sheila then had to get out and close the gates behind her. So it was at least 7.20 before she set off back to Winchelsea.

When she passed Hillcrest School in Ore, the village she had avoided earlier because of the traffic jam, she saw a telephone box beside the road and stopped to ring Simon again. This time she wanted to tell him that she might be back later than she had first said. It was such a lovely evening that she thought Aunt Flo might enjoy a country drive, and Sheila had a package she needed to pick up in Cooden, a village near Bexhill-on-Sea, a few miles beyond Hastings.

By this time Sheila estimates it was between 7.40 and 7.45. When Simon answered this second call he was in his bedroom getting ready to go out. He had still not put his wristwatch back on. He said he would be staying in till 10pm, then planned to go off to a local pub for a drink. Sheila said she hoped to be back before that.

When Sheila finally arrived at Greyfriars it was about 8pm, near enough the time arranged earlier. She rang the bell as the door was locked in the evenings and someone let her in. Then Barbara Jones, one of the care workers, appeared. Coincidentally, Mrs Jones knew Flo and Lil from her days as a waitress at Simon the Pieman where the sisters used to take breakfast. There was also a connection with Sheila: Mrs Jones's husband Ted would do odd garden jobs for the Bowlers. Just before the 1987 hurricane he had, at Bob's request, felled a large tree in their garden.

Barbara Jones went off to fetch Flo from the television room where she was waiting. She helped Aunt Flo up the same four wide steps with the adjacent ramp where the old lady had fallen a month earlier.

Erica Britton, one of Barbara's colleagues, went upstairs to Flo's room to collect the old lady's black suitcase with its tartan lining. Mrs Britton had packed it herself that afternoon, with just a few underclothes and washing things. She also collected her three-quarter-length camel-hair coat. Flo's room was on the first floor at the back of the rambling building, some distance along the corridor from the lift and stairway. The old lady was wearing a button-through dress with a black and white floral pattern and a bright blue cardigan. She wore slippers on her feet: she had large bunions and found slippers more comfortable than shoes. When she returned, Mrs Britton helped Aunt Flo into her coat and did up the buttons.

Sheila waited while Mrs Britton went off to collect Flo's medication – diazide, paracetamol, lactose and fybogel. She mentioned to another carer, Carol Pierce, that she was planning to drive to Bexhill with Aunt Flo that evening. Mrs Britton came back with the medication, explained how it should be administered, and gave Sheila a note on East Sussex County Council headed paper with more detailed instructions. Then Mrs Jones and Sheila helped Aunt Flo into the car, parked about five feet from the front door. The old lady complained that she would never be able to walk that far – she was in the habit of making that kind of remark – but with Sheila chivvying her along in her usual brisk manner, she finally reached the passenger seat. Sheila helped her into the car, lifting her legs over the door sill, and she settled back into the seat. Sheila went back to the hall to collect the suitcase.

There was some discussion whether or not Sheila would need to take a zimmer frame with her. Barbara Jones was in favour of taking it, but Erica Britton said the uneven pressure on Flo's injured arm could cause damage. Sheila knew she had a walking stick ready for Aunt Flo to use if necessary – so the zimmer was left behind. Sheila told the care-workers she would bring Flo back on Friday afternoon as agreed. She got in the car, fastened Aunt Flo's seatbelt and her own, and drove off. The carers waved goodbye.

All this took time and it was some minutes before the Audi was rumbling over the gravel drive and out through the streets of Winchelsea on to the A259 towards Hastings, proceeding at a stately pace. Aunt Flo disliked being driven fast and would readily complain, so Sheila kept at a steady 30 to 40 miles an hour.

As they drove along, Sheila told Aunt Flo of the plan to drive to Bexhill and the old lady nodded and commented on the lovely evening. She was used to travelling about in the big comfortable Audi – before she entered Greyfriars Sheila would regularly take her and Lil on trips and to the hairdressers – and now she settled comfortably down in her seat. She did not talk much: she just enjoyed looking out at the trees and late spring flowers in the evening sunshine. She had already had her evening meal and it was a treat to be out and about instead of sitting in the gloomy Greyfriars lounge with the other residents staring at the television screen. Flo particularly resented being put to bed far too early for her liking – indeed on one occasion she had obviously resisted, because Sheila had found her sitting up late in front of the TV long after the other Greyfriars residents were fast asleep in bed. In Ferry Road she would often stay up to all hours, as her neighbour Biddy Cole had witnessed. She liked watching snooker on television, to the fury of Aunt Lil who had loathed the game. She would watch late into the night, making comments about her favourite players: Alex 'Hurricane' Higgins was one of her heroes.

As the car left Icklesham, a few miles from Winchelsea, Sheila noticed that Aunt Flo was rubbing her left side. She had seen her do this on other occasions recently and thought of the Hastings surgeon's prognosis in early March when he had told her privately he 'thought there was something there' and said 'I don't think it will be long.'

She pulled into a layby. The old lady had slipped a little down the seat – possibly because of the slippery plastic bag under the towel. Sheila undid the seatbelt, moved the seat-back to a more upright position, hoisted Aunt Flo up in her seat, adjusted the seatbelt to fit, and gave her a mint and a tissue. She said the pain had now gone, so Sheila set off, with Aunt Flo, now comfortable again, admiring the scenery once more. At one point the walking stick slipped down between the front seats and Sheila pulled it up again, saying she had brought it in case Aunt Flo needed to use it at some point.

Sheila explained to Flo that she wanted to collect a special health food protein product from her friend Mrs Day in Cooden and this seemed a good opportunity. It was a tin of nutritional drink mix and had been ordered a few days earlier in a telephone call from Mrs Helen Goodwin, the lady whom Sheila took to buy the wedding hat a fortnight before. Sheila had met Jenny Day about three years earlier at Ahmet's, the Bexhill hairdressers they both attended. The two women got talking about the importance of taking regular vitamin supplements, and Mrs Day told Sheila that she and her husband were the agents for Shacklee Health Supplements, an American range of natural products ranging from vitamins to shampoos – though the original stockists had now been replaced by Nature Sunshine Products. Sheila and Bob had then themselves become distributors, selling the products to acquaintances and friends. Mrs Goodwin had remarked how tired she became after her heart attack, and Sheila recommended the protein.

Sheila glanced at her car clock as they approached the outskirts of Bexhill: it was about 8.45 – not too late to disturb Mrs Day. She turned into King Offa Way and arrived at the house five or ten minutes later, parking in the wide driveway at the front. She switched on some music on the car radio for Aunt Flo and went and rang the doorbell.

Tom Day came to the door. He had just turned on the television, but when he realised it was an episode of *Lovejoy*, a programme he did not like, he reached for a TV listings paper to find out what else was showing. At this moment the doorbell rang and he switched off the set.

He had not seen Sheila since Bob's death: he commiserated and Sheila told him her concern about possible medical negligence. Unfortunately Jenny was out, Tom said, and he could not give Sheila the protein product because he and his wife had not been there that morning when it arrived. It was at the Parcel Force depot waiting to be collected. Normally the delivery man left it in the shed – in the past Sheila had collected it from there herself – but for some reason on this occasion he did not.

Sheila said it didn't matter: the following day she might be in the area again – she never worked on Thursdays and this could be another pleasant trip for Aunt Flo. Tom suggested she might prefer to pick up the protein from Elan, a ladies' dress shop in Bexhill town centre, where Jenny would be setting up a new display next day. She was very creative and made a little money from window dressing in local shops.

Tom invited Sheila in but she declined because Aunt Flo was sitting waiting in the car. The Audi's engine had been left running and indeed in the front passenger seat he could see the head and shoulders of a white-haired lady. He did not go and speak to Aunt Flo – he had never met her though he had heard Bob and Sheila referring to her. The conversation ended and Sheila called out to Aunt Flo, 'It's not there – they haven't got it!' – a reference to the protein. Though she was standing just a few feet away from the car she had to raise her voice to be heard above the music playing on the car radio.

She said her goodbyes and drove into Bexhill town centre via St Leonards Road and the sea front to check that she knew where the Elan shop was. It would be easier to find it now than the following day when traffic in the town centre would be much busier. Then she and Aunt Flo set off for home.

It was getting dark as they drove along the A259 towards Winchelsea. Sunset that mid-May day was at about 8.40, with darkness falling about half an hour later. Along the stretch of road known locally as the Icklesham Straight – where on the outward journey Aunt Flo had complained of her stomach pain – Sheila noticed that the Audi was handling badly again, a return of the trouble that had worried her earlier, first with Helen Goodwin, then at Ferry Bridge that very afternoon. She was now sure there must be something wrong with the steering.

As they approached Ferry Hill, the steep hill leading down from the hilltop town, she slowed down, and by the time they were half way down the hill – one of the steepest gradients in the south of England – and approaching the hairpin bend at the bottom, the car was veering so badly, pulling to one side and shuddering, that there was nothing for it but to stop as soon as it was safe to do so. In the half light she looked ahead: the only traffic was a group of two or three motorcyclists parked in a layby near the bottom of the hill.

Sheila drove carefully round the hairpin bend and pulled up near the kerb on the main road. The motorcyclists seemed to have disappeared. She was just a few yards past the junction with Station Road – the short cut she had taken earlier that afternoon when she planned to go to Hastings to buy the sheet music. She glanced back up the hill: she was rather too near the bend but it couldn't be helped. To drive any further would be dangerous and would also risk ruining the inner tube.

Aunt Flo asked why they had stopped and Sheila explained that she would have a look in a moment, but she was worried about the tyres. She switched on the hazard warning lights and sat in the car for a few minutes, wondering what to do. She was still worried about the motorcyclists – was it safe to get out of the car? Just as she was wondering if she had really imagined them in the poor light (by now it must have been about a quarter to ten and the moon was not yet fully up) a second group of bikers came roaring down the hill, slowed down and stopped in the layby on the bend behind her – a small inlet she knew led to the sewage works. Glancing over her shoulder she watched them suspiciously, saying nothing to Aunt Flo for fear of frightening her. Two more bikers came down the hill and joined the group, then, after a minute or two, they all revved up their machines and roared off towards Rye.

Sheila breathed a sigh of relief. She got out of the car, bent down and looked at the wheels. Sure enough, the front nearside tyre was deflated. She checked in the boot: as she'd feared, she was not carrying the spare wheel. She had taken it out a few days earlier to make room for boxes of jumble for a local sale and had forgotten to put it back. It was sitting in the garage back at home in Fair Meadow. The spare, she said later, was 'in and out of the boot like a yo-yo: I was always moving it to make room for Jane's cello, or some other clobber.'

She got back into the car and spoke to Aunt Flo: 'I don't like the feel of the tyres – the car's not steering properly. I think I've got a puncture. I'll have to go and get help.' Then she opened the glove compartment and found the details of the Britannia Recovery Service, to which she subscribed.

She fiddled with the car radio, hoping to find some music to keep Flo entertained – the old lady liked the kind of loud, cheerful music she had been listening to outside the Days' house. But no music could be found. Aunt Flo said she 'didn't want any talking' on the radio: she would be quite all right without anything. Sheila said she was just going up the road for help. She picked up a torch from under Aunt Flo's seat, tucked her shoulder bag under her arm and set off, half running along the A259 towards Rye to find a telephone and call the recovery service.

At the bottom of Ferry Hill there is a long uninhabited stretch of the A259 which is bordered by trees and undergrowth. Then there are some large houses quite far back off the road. Most of them are at the end of long, dark drives. Sheila hurried on round the bend until at last she reached some cottages on the main road. Some were in darkness, and she did not feel she could disturb people whose bedroom lights were already switched off. But at Number Four Tanyard Cottages there were lights on everywhere so she walked up the front path without hesitation and rang the bell.

She realised immediately that by chance she knew the man who came to the door. He was John Soan, who used to work as a barber near the Landgate, the historic arched entrance to the town of Rye, then moved to another shop in the Rope Walk arcade. Indeed Simon used to have his hair cut there. She was surprised to see him because last time they met she was knocking on the door of his former house in Playden, a few miles from Rye, during one of her regular collections for the NSPCC. Mr Soan only vaguely remembered her at first but then recalled she was the wife of the Mr Bowler he knew from the Rye British Legion Club to which both men belonged. Both inveterate talkers, he and Sheila spent a few minutes chatting on the doorstep before Sheila had a chance to explain why she needed to use Mr Soan's telephone and he invited her in.

Soan offered to change the wheel for her but she explained that she had no spare tyre. He had heard about Bob's death and commiserated when Sheila explained the tragic circumstances. He launched into a lengthy description of his own health problems – he suffered from diabetes. Sheila said she knew about the illness – her stepdaughter Rosemary was a sufferer. Changing the subject and trying to hurry Mr Soan up, Sheila asked how he liked living at Tanyard Cottages. He did not like his new home at all, he said, and wanted to move yet again, because of unpleasantness from the neighbours. Sheila listened sympathetically but again tried to hurry him along. 'I'd better make that call now,' she said. 'I'm a bit worried about my aunt, waiting in the car.' Mrs Soan offered Sheila a glass of orange squash as she waited for her call to be answered.

Britannia Rescue is a much smaller operation than the AA and RAC and subscribers may have to wait a while before their calls are answered. At the first attempt the phone was engaged, then nobody answered for some time. It was 10.21 before Sheila finally got through to a woman operator – the call was logged at the service's office in Huddersfield. She explained that she had a puncture, told the operator where the car was and – 'to chivvy them up to be a bit quicker' as she said later – she told them she was with her elderly aunt. The operator asked if the old lady would be able to climb into a transporter and Sheila said she thought she could, with help. Britannia said they would prioritize the job and get to her as quickly as possible, though they might take an hour to arrive.

John and Catherine Soan offered to escort Sheila back to the car: they were concerned that two elderly ladies might have to wait alone for up to an hour for the breakdown truck to arrive. All three set off along the narrow pavement, Sheila leading the way and the Soans following behind.

The Audi was clearly visible, its hazard lights still flashing, as they rounded the bend in the road. A huge articulated lorry lumbered down the hill and John Soan thought it might hit the stranded car, parked so near the turn. As they drew nearer, Sheila noticed that the passenger door, which she remembered closing tightly shut, was now just caught on the latch. When they were about a car's length away, it was clear that the Audi was empty. Aunt Flo's distinctive tuft of white hair was no longer visible through the windscreen. In fact there was no sign of her at all.

'I don't think she's there!' Sheila was amazed. 'Where could she have got to?'

Mr Soan thought he could see the old lady, 'but he was obviously looking at the headrest,' said Sheila later. When they reached the car she peered inside. It appeared that nothing had moved except an old towel, which Sheila kept folded beneath the pedals to stop her shoes scuffing.

Now it was draped over the gear stick as if someone had pulled it towards the passenger side.

'She must have got out and walked off,' said Mr Soan.

Sheila was incredulous: 'She can't have gone far,' she replied, 'She can't walk without a walking frame!'

Anxiously she told Mr Soan about the bikers, 'rough-looking types,' who had been there earlier.

All three began to search, Sheila's torch beam scouring the darkness. Mrs Soan was the first to set off down Station Road, the short cut Sheila had taken earlier that day. Mr Soan followed her, like his wife calling out Mrs Jackson's name. Sheila joined them though she was sure Aunt Flo could not have got this far, and all three peered into the ditches on either side of Station Road. There was no response. They all came back to the car and Mr Soan then walked back towards his own house – could the old lady have tried to follow Sheila? Still no sign.

Sheila and the Soans now walked back together along Station Road, this time as far as the caravan park entrance. 'She *can't* have gone this far!' said Sheila, 'She just wouldn't be able to make it!'

They agreed that Sheila should stay and go on searching while the Soans went back home to phone the police. Sheila called out Aunt Flo's name but there was no response.

While John Soan went indoors, his wife rushed on past her own house to the home of Major Cameron-Clarke and his wife Peta, a local magistrate. They lived in the Old Malt House, the last house before the Bridge Inn, and were just going to bed. Donald Cameron-Clarke answered Mrs Soan's insistent ringing and within a few minutes the couple had dressed and gone out to join the search.

First they walked up to the Strand Bridge, away from the Station Road junction, then they drove their brown Mini along past the stranded Audi and parked it in the sewage works layby beyond, where earlier Sheila had seen the bikers stop.

Sheila knew Mrs Cameron-Clarke very slightly. They had met at a Conservative coffee morning, and more recently in Budgens, a Rye supermarket, just before Christmas when Aunt Flo was first admitted to Greyfriars, and Sheila had mentioned her worries about the old lady.

Now Sheila explained that Aunt Flo had gone missing but that she couldn't walk far. Mrs Cameron-Clarke took charge of the search, shouting 'Mrs Jackson!' in an authoritative tone befitting her magistrate's rank.

All then returned to the car, and Sheila, Mrs Soan and Mrs Cameron-Clarke went off again to the caravan park. By this time Mr Soan was back from ringing the police and remained by the Audi while the women went on hunting among the mobile homes and calling out Mrs Jackson's name. Perhaps she had headed towards the lights of the caravans, though at night the caravan park seems a hostile place with each mobile home moored in its own pool of light and threatening dark areas in between. The holiday season had yet to start properly with the Bank Holiday at the end of May, and few of the mobile homes were yet occupied.

At 10.50 a breakdown truck arrived, driven by a Mr Steven Coulmanhole, the owner of the Elva recovery service in St Leonards-on-Sea, who acted as one of the local agents for Britannia Rescue. He parked in front of the Audi and was greeted by Mr Soan who explained that an old lady had gone missing. Mr Coulmanhole walked past the Audi, noting that the nearside front tyre was deflated. He and Mr Soan joined Sheila and Mrs Soan at the caravan park, searched again, then returned to the car. A red car came along Station Road and on to the A259 and Mr Soan stopped the driver and asked if he had seen anyone. He said he had not. Mr Coulmanhole went off with Major Cameron-Clarke to search the allotments behind the houses.

At 11pm two police officers, PC Anthony Millington and PC Stephen Doswell, arrived in response to Mr Soan's call, received while they were in the Fairlight area of Hastings in their patrol car. Sheila described what Aunt Flo looked like and explained about the flat tyre and how she had been away for ages, looking for a phone and trying to get through to the breakdown service. She thought it must be at least half an hour. She added that despite her initial scepticism that Mrs Jackson could have got out and walked off, the old lady was much more mobile than people thought, and the car door was nice and wide and would have been easy to get out of.

The police looked in the glove compartment in case anyone had left a note, and it was at this point that Sheila noticed that the walking stick she had brought for Aunt Flo was missing. She asked the police to phone her son in case he was worried about her being late: they tried several times but Simon had already gone out: he was by this time at the bar of the Globe Inn at the bottom of Rye Hill, a short walk from Fair Meadow.

PC Doswell stayed at the scene and PC Millington drove off in the patrol car to Greyfriars where he spoke to the few staff on duty. They said they had no knowledge of Mrs Jackson's whereabouts: they told him they could not believe the old lady was capable of getting out of the car by herself and walking off. PC Millington cruised around the town for a further search then returned to the Station Road junction, where he radioed for a dog search unit to attend the scene.

Sheila wondered for a fleeting moment whether Simon could have come out looking for them and walked back with Aunt Flo. But she soon dismissed the idea. It would have taken far too long for him to walk there, and Simon cannot drive – his poor eyesight has always prevented his owning a car. In any case he was with friends at the Globe by this time, unaware that anything was amiss.

Three more officers, WPS Janet Clark, PC Barry Webster, and PC Watson, were despatched to Fair Meadow to see if Mrs Jackson was there. When they arrived, PS Yardy, an officer on duty at Rye Police Station, rang PC Webster from Rye to tell him Simon had at last been contacted. He had spent about an hour at the Globe pub, had only just returned home and knew no more than the police did. He suggested they check at 59 Ferry Road in case Flo had somehow found her way back to her old home. But the flat was empty. The police checked at a few other nearby properties, then returned to Greyfriars to question the night staff once again.

By now it was about an hour and a half since Sheila had left Aunt Flo alone in the car. Soon after PC Millington arrived back at the scene, the dog search team arrived from Hastings and began to scour the immediate area, looking in the ditches close to the Audi, then gradually moving further afield, but there was no sign of the old lady. She seemed to have disappeared completely. Sheila was asked to open up the car boot: 'I suppose you have to do these things in case I'm hiding something in the car!' she remarked. The police saw that there was indeed no spare wheel. Sheila's briefcase and Mrs Jackson's suitcase were still there.

At 12.20am the police radioed for help from the East Sussex police helicopter, codenamed HOTEL 900, which is equipped with heat-seeking equipment and is often used in search and rescue operations. At this point the police officers told Sheila she might as well go home with the breakdown truck. There was nothing more she could do and they would continue the search with the dog team and let her know when they had any news.

The Audi was loaded on to the trailer and Sheila got into the front passenger seat. On the way home she asked, 'If the police find Aunt Flo, will they let me know?' 'Yes, I should think so,' said Mr Coulmanhole.

It was between 12.30 and 12.40am by the time they pulled into the drive in front of the garage at number 25. Simon waited anxiously as the Audi was unloaded: he told his mother he thought there had been an accident. When Sheila said it was a puncture, Simon reminded her he had seen the spare wheel where she had left it in the garage. He then had to help Mr Coulmanhole push-start his truck: he had left his beacon flashing light running for so long while he joined the search that the truck's battery had gone flat. Sheila took her briefcase out of the boot as she always did after work, leaving Aunt Flo's suitcase where it was.

Mr Coulmanhole drove off and about 1am a police car arrived. PC Doswell and PC Millington brought in a 'MISPER' – a missing persons form – and asked Sheila to help them complete it. The officers complained that the helicopter was late but finally they heard it overhead. According to the pilot's log it had left Eastbourne at 1.35am. Then the police left Sheila and Simon alone at 25 Fair Meadow.

Jane phoned and Sheila explained what was happening. Then she had a bath and got ready for bed. Through the open window she could still hear the distant whirring of helicopter blades. Peering through the curtains she saw the lights of the helicopter as it circled near Winchelsea Hill. She climbed into bed and fell into a fitful sleep, half expecting the police to ring at any minute and tell her Aunt Flo had been found wandering around.

Meanwhile back at Station Road the search was continuing as the police observer travelling with the helicopter pilot radioed down to the police on the ground to ask the purpose of the search.

The helicopter flew around but found nothing, and called off the search till morning. According to the pilot's log it arrived back at base at

Shoreham Airport at 2.25am. The dog unit carried on hunting until dawn was beginning to break about 4am. There was illumination from the moonlight – May 13 was just three days short of a full moon and it was a clear night. Then they too gave up the search.

PCs Doswell and Millington got back into their car and made another search round the streets of Winchelsea. Finally they drove the whole length of Station Road, finding nothing. At 6.15am they handed over to Inspector Hodgson and returned to Rye police station. PC Doswell had forgotten to ask Sheila for authority to put out a call for information in the local media, so he immediately telephoned her from the station. Sheila was already awake, having slept hardly at all. Rather dubiously she agreed. At 7am Doswell and Millington went off duty.

At 8am the helicopter returned and began circling overhead again. Mrs Cameron-Clarke was up early too. At 8.45 she drove her Mini to the pumping station, did a three-point turn and came back. She saw nothing.

At 9.45am Police Sergeant John Tickner, the official observer in the police helicopter, and Ian Morrison, the paramedic accompanying him, spotted the body of Mrs Florence Jackson floating face down in the River Brede about 20 yards downstream from the pumping station close to the opposite bank – a distance of about 500 yards from the car.

Could the old lady have grown tired of waiting for her niece and walked off? Her short-term memory was poor and maybe it seemed to her that Sheila had been away for hours rather than minutes. In the past she had got out of hospital beds at night to reach the commode, and on other occasions had been found wandering round the wards looking lost. Perhaps, desperate for the toilet, or terrified of being left alone, she had summoned up unexpected strength and set out on her own, meeting a tragic end in the waters of the River Brede where once she and Aunt Lil liked to walk.

But the police had other ideas. Although they had asked Sheila to help them complete a missing persons form, there are significant pointers which suggest that for the police officers, this was no ordinary missing person search.

Why did the police telephone Tom Day and wake him soon after 2am asking if he could confirm that Mrs Bowler and her aunt had called on him the previous evening? He said later, 'I found it very strange to ring me up at that time of night for information that could not help them find somebody who was missing.'

At 2.25am on his return to base, the helicopter pilot wrote up his flight log. Nearly eight hours before Mrs Jackson's body was found, he recorded: 'Informed by Inspector that woman very rich. That the nursing home where she lived didn't trust the niece and the car's flat tyre had been a ploy. CID are making enquiries!'

What had happened in the three hour period since the police first arrived at Station Road to transform a commonplace search for an elderly missing person into a sinister murder investigation?

CHAPTER THREE

PRIME SUSPECT

While Sheila tossed and turned in her bedroom in Rye, Mrs Joan Dobson, the Matron of Greyfriars, was also lying awake. By the time PC Millington arrived at the Home soon after 11pm that evening, Mrs Dobson had gone off duty, as had her deputy Mrs Valerie Nye. So it was perfectly natural, as soon as the police had left, for the night duty staff to put a call through to senior officers, and Mrs Dobson was told the news: one of her residents, Mrs Florence Jackson, was missing.

It must be the constant concern of staff at homes for the elderly that a resident will go wandering off and come to some harm. Every day, carers have to tread the fine line between keeping their charges safe and keeping them over-restricted and confined, because if a tragic accident should occur, it is the staff who will bear the responsibility. To anyone caring for vulnerable people in an official capacity – whether it be children, the mentally disordered or the elderly – the issues of accountability and responsibility are absolutely crucial, and at the time of her disappearance, Mrs Jackson was not officially Greyfriars' responsibility.

This may partly explain why, at 2.05am, as recorded in the police duty logs, Mrs Dobson picked up the telephone and dialled the number of the Sussex Police operations room. The duty sergeant answered the call. Afterwards he wrote in the log: 'I have spoken to Mrs Joan Dobson, the officer in charge of the home. She expressed great concern about the circumstances of the disappearance, and was scathing of Mrs Bowler. Although she didn't openly accuse Mrs Bowler of doing harm to her auntie, she left me in no doubt that she thought it a distinct possibility.'

It would be simplistic in the extreme to suggest that the police were naive enough to take Mrs Dobson's phonecall at face value and immediately set about treating the case as murder. The call is obviously important, but it should not be seen in isolation.

Before they ever received Joan Dobson's call, the police officers investigating Florence Jackson's mysterious disappearance already had two reasons for treating the circumstances as suspicious. The first was Sheila's own behaviour. Far from conducting herself in the distraught manner considered appropriate for a lady in such a situation, Sheila carried on in the unemotional, matter-of-fact way in which she dealt with any crisis, including her husband's sudden death. Helena Kennedy, in her book *Eve was Framed**, catalogues the way women are stereotyped by the criminal justice system, giving numerous examples of how women presenting before the police and courts with 'feminine' characteristics (those who weep, look fragile and vulnerable, or come across as 'good wives and mothers') are treated more leniently than their stronger, more feisty sisters. The police response to Sheila is a typical example: her brusque, impatient, no-nonsense manner must have seemed to them an odd and churlish response – considering that everyone was trying to help her find an elderly relative. And the police were not alone: eye-witnesses like Mr Soan, Mr Coulmanhole and Mrs Cameron-Clarke were all later to remark on how oddly Sheila behaved. A psychologist would doubtless relate her response to this stress to her recent bereavement. But no psychologist was there to see her. She later told friends that she was in fact extremely worried but forced herself to remain calm, convincing herself that the police would find Mrs Jackson.

But that was not how it looked to PC Millington. In his official statement the following day he said that 'at this stage' (after his return from his first visit to check with Greyfriars staff) Mrs Bowler 'appeared totally unconcerned about what had happened to Mrs Jackson.' He added that at 1am when he and PC Doswell had gone to Fair Meadow to take details for the MISPER form, 'I again noted the apparent total lack of concern for Mrs Jackson's wellbeing by both mother and son.'

PC Doswell corroborated his colleague's opinion. His statement made on the same day as PC Millington's contains some identical expressions [our italics], suggesting the officers had discussed Mrs Bowler's reaction: 'At this stage I was surprised to see the apparent *lack of concern* for Mrs Jackson's safety from Mrs Bowler especially as she herself had said, "I would be surprised if she could get out of the car by herself".' Like PC Millington he also comments on the visit to 25 Fair Meadow: 'Again I was a little taken by *lack of concern* from *both Mrs Bowler and her son* Simon.'

*Vintage, 1993

He added: 'Just before we left Mrs Bowler said, " I think I shall get some sleep as I'm up at five"'.

The second reason for suspicion is likely to have been the response that police received from Greyfriars night staff. There is a very brief official record of what they told officers during the two visits they made to the Home that evening – the first by PC Millington soon after he and PC Doswell arrived on the scene at 11pm, the second by officers Webster, Clark and Watson after they had established that Mrs Jackson was neither at Fair Meadow nor at Ferry Road, and returned to Greyfriars for a further check.

The duty staff made the following note in the daily diary – presumably it must have been written up early on the morning of Thursday May 14: 'Flo left with niece Mrs Bowler at 8pm to stay a few days. Police came round to Greyfriars at 11.05pm to say that Flo had been reported missing by her niece. Apparently the niece's car had broken down. She left Flo in the car while she went for help. When she arrived back at the car Flo had disappeared. There were police dogs and helicopters out searching for her. The police want to know who was in the car and how much help Flo needed to get in and out of the car. They were told by us that it was unlikely that Flo could walk away. Mrs Dobson was informed at 11.50... Phoned back at 2am. She had spoken to the police herself.'

The note gives only a brief account of the interchanges between the police and the duty staff, but knowing the poor relationship between Sheila and the Greyfriars workers, and knowing what Mrs Dobson was to say to the duty sergeant, their comments about her are hardly likely to have been complimentary.

A local Age Concern worker, Mrs Barbara Wild, who knew Joan Dobson and the rest of the Greyfriars staff, as well as Sheila herself, was aware that, 'Sheila's relationship with them was abysmal. She is meticulous and can be peremptory. The Greyfriars staff would resent her commanding attitude. No doubt this was immediately apparent to police.'

Although we have no way of knowing exactly what Mrs Dobson and her staff told police on the night of 13 May, the statements they made over the next few days are available, and it seems most unlikely that they would have changed their views in such a short period of time.

Take Mrs Dobson: her statement was made on 14 May, just a few hours after she first spoke to the police. Presumably she was responding to police questioning about Mrs Jackson's physical and mental capabilities when she said that Mrs Jackson was 'mentally frail and physically dependent.' She added that since Mrs Jackson's fall 'her mobility and confidence decreased markedly.' In any case she 'did not like the dark' and 'the likelihood of Mrs Jackson being able to walk 500 to 600 yards in the dark without support is very unlikely.' She had never seen Mrs Jackson use a walking stick and, she added, 'I doubt whether she would know how to use it' – though Social Services, with whom Mrs Dobson was constantly in touch, had in fact presented Aunt Flo with both a zimmer and two walking sticks at the Ferry Road flat.

All these responses were perfectly in keeping with police speculation about the possibility of Mrs Jackson wandering away from the car. But Mrs Dobson's statement – like her 2am telephone call – also contains a number of apparently gratuitous pieces of information which cannot have been prompted by the police who at this early stage would have no knowledge of Mrs Jackson's recent history.

Mrs Dobson said that 'Rye Social Services had been recommending care (residential care in Greyfriars) for some time,' though 'Mr and Mrs Bowler had declined this.' She mentioned the Greyfriars fees of '£252.56 pence per week' and said that Mrs Bowler had visited Mrs Jackson just six times during the time (about five months) she was at Greyfriars – which, she added pointedly, 'includes the collection by car on the evening of the 13th May 1992.' (These were the only visits recorded in the visitors' book, which the Bowler family rarely bothered to sign. In fact the book was later revealed to have been started up only in February, when Mrs Jackson had already been in residence for two of the five months she spent at Greyfriars). For no particular reason Mrs Dobson also volunteered that an earlier trip – which proved abortive – had been planned for the previous week and, most significantly, she said that though she had not been on duty when Mrs Bowler had collected Mrs Jackson, she 'saw the car drive off at approximately three minutes past eight. The car left at a faster rate than I would have expected.'

The precise time is interesting. Mrs Dobson was later to say she glanced at her office clock as the Audi left the drive. Of the eight care workers interviewed, only four were on duty at the time Sheila arrived. Two of them more or less corroborated Dobson's timings: Barbara Jones said Mrs Bowler arrived at 7.50, Erica Britton put it at 8pm. But the police chose the much earlier time of arrival estimated by Carol Pierce – between 7pm and 7.30 – to use in their briefing notes to detectives who later investigated the case.

It also seems reasonable to assume that the information given by the other Greyfriars workers that night would match what they said in subsequent statements. The night shift at the Home, according to one of the carers, Deborah Freeman, began at 8.30pm, so the staff who handed Aunt Flo over to Sheila at 8pm would just have been ending their period of duty, and would have left by the time the police called at 11pm. But all eight Greyfriars staff (Nye, Hanson, McGlanaghy, Pierce, Freeman, Jones, Britton, Law) who made statements to the police over the next few days were unanimous in their view that since her fall Mrs Jackson could only walk with the aid of a carer, so it seems likely that whoever was on night duty would have said the same. Like Mrs Dobson, some of the eight volunteered further information which would have confirmed the adverse opinion the police had already formed of Sheila Bowler.

Lynda Hanson, who had been Flo's key worker, said she had made notes at the meeting arranged by Social Services on 26 February to discuss Mrs Jackson's future. She commented in her statement: 'My personal view of Mrs Bowler at this meeting was that she was delaying the decision whether to allow Flo to have full-time personal care at Greyfriars.' Valerie Nye, Mrs Dobson's deputy, mentioned the cancelled arrangement the previous week and added that 'Mrs Jackson's only visitor was her niece-in-law Mrs Bowler whose visits were infrequent and short.'

Carol Pierce's statement contained a similar sentence: 'The only visitor that Florence used to have was a Mrs Bowler who used to visit infrequently for short periods of time. She was a niece.'

Joyce Law described packing Mrs Jackson's suitcase for the 6 May visit which 'Mrs Bowler cancelled at short notice.' A week later, at 3.10 on 13 May, she had taken a call from Mrs Bowler. She had confirmed she would be arriving to collect Mrs Jackson between 7.30 and 8pm and requested that she should not be given her bowel medication. When Law protested that the old lady needed it 'because she gets very constipated... Mrs Bowler just laughed and the conversation was ended.'

Erica Britton described the cancellation on 6 May at length: 'After supper that day Florence was all ready to go, her bags had been packed and she was in the lounge.' Mrs Britton also explained how, one week later, on the evening of May 13, she had advised against Barbara Jones's suggestion that Mrs Bowler should take the zimmer.

However, Barbara Jones's statement gives a quite different version: 'I asked Mrs Bowler whether she required Flo's zimmer and Mrs Bowler said she wouldn't need the zimmer' – a comment open to sinister interpretation.

Britton added that she recalled 'hearing Mrs Bowler say out loud, "Oh come on!" and she sounded impatient, this comment was made when Florence was near the car.'

There is a third reason for police suspicion: Sheila's appearance. She is a tall, thin, angular woman – only a few inches off six feet tall – with steely grey hair and strong features that soften when she smiles, but which can look harsh, even forbidding, when she is under stress. That night she was wearing a black reversible anorak with the black fur on the outside, a longish black skirt and a white blouse. Her appearance – that of a rather strict school-marm or slightly haughty daughter of the manse – would raise no eyebrows in church or at a charity function. But it might seem more sinister on a dark night when an old lady had gone missing and her carers had painted such an unflattering portrait of her niece.

In the circumstances then, it is perhaps unsurprising that the police had murder on their minds at such an early stage, before a body had even been found. It is indeed true that the vast majority of murder victims are killed by someone they know, often a family member. It is also true that the most likely suspect is bound to be the person who was with the victim at or near the time of death. But as Anthony Hooper QC (now a High Court Judge) was later to say, discussing this case in a television interview, such a conclusion should only be drawn if there are no alternative explanations for death – if, for example, the victim and the prime suspect are locked in a room together and when the room is unlocked, one is alive and one is dead.

In other miscarriage of justice cases, commentators have remarked upon police 'tunnel vision': once they have an idea firmly fixed in their minds, it is said, police officers have a frightening tendency to pursue it to the end, excluding all other possibilities. Was this just such an example?

By 6am on the morning of Thursday 14 May Sheila, always an early riser, was dressed and eating her breakfast. Simon left for work to catch an early train – the 6.20 or the 7am – to Maidstone via Ashford. Sheila was up and ready to answer PC Doswell's early morning call seeking her authority to ask for help on the radio. By 8am she was out on the drive trying to pump up the Audi's tyre with Bob's footpump, which had a pressure gauge attached to it. Fair Meadow is a good walk from the town centre and Sheila hated to be without transport because it meant carrying heavy shopping bags home up the long hill. She had no lessons to teach that day but she might be called upon to fetch Aunt Flo and take her to hospital – who could tell?

Sheila shuddered. She was now beginning to feel seriously worried. Where could Aunt Flo be after all this time? Of course it had occurred to her during the restless small hours that the old lady might after all have managed to wander off and come to some harm. But Sheila had never been one to anticipate trouble before it happened, or to panic in a crisis. As usual she pulled herself together and threw herself into something practical, shutting out any fears from her mind. After all, Aunt Flo would probably be brought back safe and well, and there would be shopping to do, visits to make – perhaps another trip to Bexhill to see Jenny Day and pick up the protein supplement for Helen Goodwin. The car had to be sorted out first. She would pump up the tyres and then drive the car to her usual garage at Rye Harbour. She got the tyre out of the garage and with some difficulty lifted it into the boot.

Car maintenance was something Sheila had always left to Bob, and now she was not having much success. She managed to pump up three of the tyres to 26 pounds per square inch, but could not get the front nearside tyre anywhere near that pressure. Leaving the footpump attached to the tyre valve, she went inside again and rang Roger Capps, known to everyone as Lofty. He was a mechanic at the Rye Harbour garage: 'Shall I go on trying to pump up the tyre and try and bring the car over to you?' she asked, 'Or will you come and collect it?'

'Don't you worry about that,' said Lofty. 'I think it's best if I come along to you.' Sheila went outside again and was about to detach the pump when a police car drew up and two officers got out. By this time it was about twenty minutes to nine.

The officers introduced themselves as Inspector Hodgson and PC Brian Reese. Sheila asked if Aunt Flo had been found. No, they said, she had not. PC Reese looked at the pressure gauge still attached to the front nearside tyre: it read 17 pounds per square inch. He kicked the tyre. 'It doesn't look very flat to me,' he said. Sheila said that wasn't surprising as she had just been trying to pump it up. She told the Inspector she had had a puncture and now her mechanic was on the way to collect the car. 'Oh no he's not, we're taking it with us,' said one of the officers.

Sheila assumed this was to test the car for fingerprints. Obviously they would want to eliminate her own, and maybe they feared Aunt Flo had been abducted – she had always had her suspicions about those rough-looking bikers.

Reese got into the Audi and appeared to be about to drive off, but Sheila asked him to pump up the tyre fully before they drove to the police station – she was afraid, as she had been the previous evening, that the inner tube would be damaged. PC Reese used the footpump to inflate the tyre up to 20 pounds per square inch.

Sheila wanted to know when she would be likely to get the car back. She could do without it until after the weekend – she was travelling by train to stay with friends in Bishop's Stortford the following day – but would need it first thing on Monday morning to get to work. The officers told her to ring Detective Superintendent Brian Foster at Rye Police Station over the weekend.

In the statement he made two weeks later, PC Reese explained that he had pumped up the tyre as Sheila asked. He said he was attempting to reach 24 to 26 psi but 20 was the highest he could manage. He detached the pump but – again according to his subsequent statement – he could not recall whether he replaced the dust cap. Then he got into the Audi and drove slowly off to Rye, followed by Inspector Hodgson in the police car. They drove down Rye Hill, turned right down the narrow twisting Dead Man's Lane (Rye specializes in picturesque street names) and along to the police station in Cinque Ports Street. He experienced no problems in the car's handling, though he had to negotiate several sharp bends and occasionally reached the town speed limit of 30 mph. The distance from Fair Meadow to the police station was eight-tenths of a mile.

At the station the Audi was handed over the following day to PC Derrick Watson of the police traffic division, who carried out a series of tests on the vehicle, concentrating on the tyres and steering. He did not begin the tests until 5.30 that evening. He checked the tyre pressure on the police gauge. It now registered 15 psi, a hefty five pounds lower than when it stood outside 25 Fair Meadow, reinflated by PC Reese. This was a loss of 25 per cent in a journey of just eight-tenths of a mile. All the other tyres remained at the recommended pressure of 24-25 psi. PC Watson recorded that he found the tyre in poor condition.

Left at home without the car, Sheila rang Lofty to say he need not bother to come along. Then she busied herself round the kitchen. At around 9.30 she set about baking a batch of cinnamon biscuits. It was her habit to keep the biscuit barrel full in case visitors dropped by. She had just put the first tray of biscuits in the oven when the doorbell rang. It was about 10am. On the doorstep stood a young female police officer and an older male officer.

'I have to tell you,' said the male officer, 'that the body of Mrs Florence Jackson was found in the River Brede at 9.45 this morning.'

The woman offered to put the kettle on and make some tea. 'This is WPC Sarah Ellis,' said the policeman. 'I'm going off now so I'll just leave her with you.'

'On guard?' asked Sheila Bowler.

The two officers exchanged glances. People who know Sheila would understand that this was an awkward joke to hide her embarrassment at any emotion she might be feeling, and irritation that these strangers were there to witness it. She had made a similar joke the evening before when asked to open her car boot for the police. But to already suspicious police officers it must have seemed strange indeed.

'No, not at all. She's very good at this sort of thing – making tea and so on,' said the male officer. 'Actually, this is the first time I've ever done anything like this,' confided the young policewoman as her colleague left the house.

There is no record of any statement from WPC Ellis, so we can only surmise what she felt as she sat with Sheila in the kitchen, drinking tea and waiting for the biscuits to cook.

When the biscuits were ready, the policewoman ate one, then suggested they sit outside in the garden. The mid-May sunshine was warm and she took off her uniform jacket and sat in her shirt sleeves. 'I felt a little bit uneasy,' Sheila was to say later, 'because I couldn't understand what the police lady was doing there. I couldn't understand how she could help because I'm a fairly independent person and I like to get on with things. If I grieve I like to grieve alone. I don't like to grieve on anyone's shoulder. I remember telling her that I felt that I just had to keep busy because that's the way I react. In fact it was *me* making *her* cups of tea throughout the morning.'

After a few minutes Sheila got up again and went inside to put the next batch of biscuits in the oven and to pour an extra mug of tea: Robin Piggott, a local painter and decorator, had arrived and begun work, painting the outside of the house. The Bowlers cared for their property as carefully as they cared for their car. They had finished paying the mortgage on the large red-brick detached house twelve years earlier, so there was money to spend on maintenance. Sheila gave Robin the tea and went back into the garden. WPC Ellis stood up and removed her black epaulettes: 'We don't want to upset the neighbours,' she said.

By 12.30 Sheila and WPC Ellis had got through several more cups of tea and most of the biscuits when another police car drew up and a second, older woman got out. She was smartly dressed in a lemon-coloured suit. She introduced herself as Detective Sergeant Booth.

Linda Booth was to say in her statement, which was not written out formally until 21 August, more than three months later, that her role in attending 25 Fair Meadow was 'to offer support to Mrs Bowler and also to obtain antecedent history and detailed information from her as to the circumstances leading up to the disappearance of her aunt Mrs Jackson.' Indeed she seems to have presented herself to Sheila as a kind of bereavement counsellor.

Throughout this visit and in subsequent visits up to the time of Sheila's arrest on 25 May, WDS Booth made what she later referred to as 'scribble notes' which in August she wrote up as formal officer's reports and submitted to the incident room at Hastings police station. At no time during this first two-hour interview, nor during the eleven day period of intermittent questioning between 14 and 25 May, was Sheila Bowler given a formal caution, nor was a solicitor present – although we know from the police logs that she was the prime suspect almost eight hours before a body was ever discovered.

So Sheila was alone, with no legal advisor to check the consistency of her statements, or to point out any errors she might make under questioning in these stressful circumstances. Nor did it ever occur to Sheila to contact her solicitor John Sperring. At this point she still had no idea she was under serious suspicion of causing the death of Aunt Flo.

Like her colleagues Millington and Doswell the previous evening, Linda Booth expressed surprise that Sheila Bowler, when introduced to her by WPC Ellis, 'showed no signs of distress,' and 'appeared very sprightly and jovial, having just learned that she had been informed of the death of Mrs Florence Jackson.'

Throughout the rest of her 'scribble notes,' Booth made a number of similarly subjective judgements. As Sheila, prompted by the policewoman, ran through her recent family history and relationship with Aunt Flo, Booth concluded that she was 'clearly obsessed by the injustice of her husband's death,' but 'was quick to state that after her husband's death she continued with her life even to the surprise of her immediate family.' Booth then went on to question Sheila closely about her movements the previous evening. 'During the course of my conversation with Mrs Bowler that afternoon,' commented Booth, 'she kept jumping up to tend to the workmen and various other excuses and albeit answered my questions appeared reluctant to do so.'

Sheila was presented in Booth's report as suspiciously changing her story: at first, said Booth, she claimed that Florence Jackson had stayed with her regularly, but then stated that the last occasion 'was some three years ago.' At first, said Booth, Sheila claimed she had removed the spare tyre to accommodate her daughter's viola case (Jane is in fact a cellist, and Sheila would never have used the word 'viola': it is a small mistake in itself, but it casts doubt on the accuracy of Linda Booth's memory, perhaps inevitable in a statement written up three months after the events). 'However, she has subsequently told me it was in fact for some large boxes of jumble.'

At about 2.45, the interview was adjourned and Linda Booth asked Sheila for the shoes she had been wearing the previous evening. Sheila went to the utility room and produced a pair of black patent shoes with a slightly wedged heel, which she said had been muddy, but she had 'rubbed them up' ready to wear the following day – another remark which aroused further suspicion.

She asked the policewoman where Aunt Flo's body had been found and Booth told her it was about half a mile away from the car. Sheila, according to Booth, 'appeared surprised and said that in no way could her Aunty have made that distance on her own.'

As WDS Booth left, armed with the black patent shoes, she told Sheila that she would have to go with a police officer to identify Aunt Flo's body.

'Do I have to?' asked Sheila. 'Couldn't someone from Greyfriars go?' No, said Booth, Sheila must do it herself. WPC Ellis arrived to take over from WDS Booth.

At about 5pm a male officer, PC Joyce, arrived to take Sheila to the Royal East Sussex Hospital in Hastings where Florence Jackson's body had been taken. There in the mortuary an attendant pulled back a sheet and Sheila nodded that yes, this was indeed her aunt-in-law. She noticed that there was a graze on her forehead. 'It was the first dead body I had ever seen. I had not wanted to see Bob. Seeing Aunt Flo in the mortuary was not a pleasant experience. I identified the body very quickly.'

PC Joyce drove Sheila back to Rye and soon after they arrived at Fair Meadow, at about 6.30pm, WDS Booth returned with Sergeant Levett and another male officer.

The officers said they had come to take official statements from Sheila and Simon, who had by this time returned from work. 'How long are you going to take?' asked Sheila, 'My son and I are going out to eat this evening.' Booth said it might take about an hour and a half – they needed to ask her more questions. 'Surely it can wait till the morning,' said Sheila crossly. In the words of Booth's 'scribble notes': 'she expressed that she was extremely tired and felt that she'd really been inconvenienced enough by the police over this matter. She stated that albeit she may be interested in finding out the cause of her Aunt's death she had other priorities such as her daughter to consider at present.'

Plainly WDS Booth had never come across anyone quite like Sheila Bowler before. Her incredulity shines through her 'scribble notes.' Later during the official interrogation, Booth was to tell Sheila that in the course of her work as a police officer she had the painful duty of meeting many recently bereaved people. Never, she said, had she met anyone who showed so little emotion as Sheila. Never had she seen anyone set about baking a batch of biscuits the minute after hearing of the death of a loved one: 'During the course of the conversation that evening with Mrs Bowler,' Booth wrote in the 'scribble notes,' 'she was evasive and had a number of phone conversations with her daughter. She stated her daughter Jane was very upset by the whole incident and was surprised at her mother's resilience at which point Mrs Bowler explained that life must go on and that she managed in the same manner after the death of her husband and was back at work within two days.'

Anyone who has studied the psychology of bereavement is aware that it is not at all uncommon for the bereaved, especially those brought up like Sheila in a culture that demanded fortitude and self-denial, to react in the way she did. Her friends, many of them raised in the same culture, where public displays of emotion are interpreted as signs of weakness, found it perfectly normal. Her octogenarian friend Helen Goodwin subsequently praised Sheila for it in a sworn statement to her solicitors: 'I can say that in the time that I have known her she has never been emotional. She didn't cry in my presence following her husband's death and at the Memorial Service for Bob she *behaved fabulously'* (our italics). Mrs Goodwin was later to tell the investigative journalist David Jessel proudly in a television interview: 'Sheila wouldn't burst into tears in front of the police – not Sheila. Nor would I have done.'

Another interviewee on the same programme, a man of about the same age, an upright military type sporting a smart cravat, bridled at the very suggestion: 'She cannot cry, she cannot show her emotions,' he said. You felt he admired her for what many regard as a peculiarly English quality. After all, many commentators remarked on the fortitude of Princes William and Harry at their mother's funeral. Some admired it, some felt it would have been more natural for them to weep. But nobody suggested they were not grieving.

There was an added dimension to Sheila's particular bereavement: it must have gradually been dawning on her as Booth's questions continued throughout the day that she was being treated with real suspicion. She, who for the past seven years had dutifully tended two old ladies who were not even her blood relations! She, who was only carrying out her late husband's wishes not to sell Aunt Flo's home! How dare the police behave in this way! But Linda Booth knew nothing of the past seven years. Her only information about Sheila's relationship with Mrs Jackson came from the Greyfriars staff, who had reason to resent their client's interfering niece.

Now Sheila's manner, prickly and haughty, was bound to enrage the investigating police officers. Far from being intimidated and deferential as most people would have been in the circumstances, Sheila made it clear that this was her house, she was mistress of it, and they were unwelcome intruders getting in the way of her daily routine. She got up as Booth was in the middle of taking her statement and, according to the policewoman, 'went to the kitchen to prepare some food for the cat and remarked that it was frozen.'

'I'd never have made such an idiotic remark!' snapped Sheila waspishly when she was later shown Booth's statement. 'Of course it was frozen – I was getting it out of the freezer, wasn't I!'. Booth suggested she defrost it in her microwave 'to which she told me she had not got one and then remarked that she had absolutely no food in the house and would have to be going to the pub at the top of the hill to eat that evening.' Booth then scribbled a note that, trivial as it may seem, became an important plank in the Prosecution case: 'This struck me as being strange in view of the fact that she was due to have her Aunt to stay that evening one would have expected her to have food in readiness.'

Another small domestic point was also to assume enormous importance at the trial. Booth notes, 'When asked what sleeping arrangements she had made at 25 Fair Meadow to accommodate Mrs Jackson, she states she was going to sleep her on the bed-settee on the ground floor.'

In fact, these apparently *ad hoc* arrangements were entirely appropriate: Sheila knew Aunt Flo would already have had her supper at Greyfriars and

– like most elderly people – would want no more than a cup of tea so late in the evening. Of course Sheila had a freezer full of food, but after a long and stressful day she had no intention of setting about cooking a meal for herself and Simon at this time of night. As Jane says, 'When Mum says there's no food in the house, she means there isn't a three course meal ready on the table!' Besides, she had had enough of impertinent questions from police officers when she had done nothing wrong at all.

As for the bed for Aunt Flo: there was a bed already made up in Jane's bedroom. If the old lady could manage the stairs, she could sleep there. Otherwise, Sheila planned to bring downstairs an old-fashioned Relyon folding mattress usually kept in Simon's room. A lightweight and easily portable contraption which she could get down the stairs without any problem, it was designed to unfold into a single bed and she would make it up in the living room. It was all eminently sensible.

Booth's 'scribble notes' twice mention Sheila's financial situation: 'She also remarked that she was finding it extremely difficult making ends meet on a widow's pension and that she had started to write down everything she spent.' Sheila denies ever saying any of this, but as no solicitor was present to back her up, the police officer's version was accepted as the correct one.

Booth continues: 'When discussing the financial affairs of Florence Jackson, she stated that there would be some transfer of funds from/to [the confusion seems significant] Florence's account to her own. She said that albeit she held Power of Attorney, she still got Florence to sign any cheques as required. She also mentioned having some money from Aunt Lil's which was for the payment of her funeral, yet she had not got around to paying it.' (When she later saw the statement, Sheila explained that this was money released by the bank from Aunt Lil's account to pay for her funeral – a perfectly proper and common arrangement.) Booth's questions about money are significant in view of the incorrect police assumption, recorded in the police helicopter log, that the aunt was 'very rich.'

While Linda Booth was interviewing Sheila in the dining-room that evening, her male colleagues were in the lounge taking a statement from Simon about his movements the previous day. His account differed from his mother's on one significant point. He remembered the second call from

Sheila at about 9.15pm, not at 7.40 when his mother said she phoned from the kiosk in the village of Ore. Maybe the interviewing officers did not know at the time the true extent of Simon's visual impairment. Officially registered 'partially disabled,' he can read and tell the time only if he is able to peer very closely at a newspaper or wristwatch. He had taken his wristwatch off to do the gardening, and would have had to rely instead on a wall-clock which he would have found much harder to see accurately.

Simon said he told his mother he intended to go out at 10 for about an hour. He duly left at 9.55 and was at the Globe pub till 11.05, returning home by 11.15. Though he did not mention it in his statement, he later recalled that at the pub he changed a cheque for a small sum of money – about £20 – with the landlord Mick Haffenden. This was a fortuitous act which gave him a cast-iron alibi if the police suspected him as an accessory to the murder of his great aunt.

Asked about the tyre, Simon said it was not all that bad and he felt his mother could have got further. As for Aunt Flo's mobility, he said, like his mother, that she 'couldn't walk any distance without assistance. She used a zimmer frame or walking stick. I don't believe she could get out of a car without the assistance of another person opening the door and helping her out.' He later added, 'To my knowledge my aunt has never gone wandering or tried to escape in the past.' The policemen, like WDS Booth, were also very concerned about the absence of any bed made ready for Aunt Flo. Simon said, 'I'm not sure whether a bed had been made up for my Aunt but there are usually beds made up.'

Meanwhile in the dining-room Sheila, never a patient woman, was becoming more and more irritated. The whole session seemed such a ridiculous waste of time. The police had been with her on and off all day and she was hungry and tired. At Booth's request she handed over the black anorak and skirt she had been wearing the previous evening, along with the key to Aunt Flo's flat in Ferry Road. She also went and found two photographs of the old lady for the police to publish in the local press to help them, they said, get further information.

Then, says Booth in her 'scribble notes,' Sheila remembered something else: 'It is interesting to note that during the evening she suddenly recalled that she had in fact travelled down Winchelsea Lane towards the railway station earlier in the afternoon of the 13th May. This is something she had not mentioned previously and she had appeared quite vague as to when she would have last been down there.'

Booth added, 'Again it is interesting to note that she could relate the name of Ferry Bridge Cottage, however, she maintained she does not know the area well.' In fact Sheila knew the name of the cottage because Bob had once told her it had been the birthplace of an elderly Rye gentleman they both knew.

Now fingerprints – said by the police to be 'elimination prints' – were taken from both Sheila and Simon. Then Sheila, crosser than ever, told the officers that the Top O' the Hill pub stopped serving food at nine and pointedly asked them if these interviews could end at 8.45. When 8.45 came she asked them for a lift down to the pub on the corner of Fair Meadow, where that road joins Rye Hill.

Her blunt attempt to get rid of these intrusive strangers was the last straw for Linda Booth : 'Soon after this she virtually ushered myself and some fellow officers who were taking a statement from her son out of the house saying she needed to go and get a meal and could assist us no further that evening. I had impressed upon her the importance of her assistance in view of the fact that she was our main source of information.'

Nevertheless the policewoman – probably flabbergasted at her suspect's coolness – drove her to the pub, and the male officers followed, dropping Simon off to join his mother.

CHAPTER FOUR

OPERATION DACE

Simon and Sheila Bowler sat down to eat their pub meal together, apparently unaware that they were now at the centre of a full-scale murder investigation. The murder enquiry, appropriately codenamed Operation Dace – presumably by a keen police fisherman (the dace is a small freshwater fish of the carp family) – had been launched in earnest that morning when Mrs Florence Jackson's body was found floating face down in the murky waters of the River Brede. It later became apparent that it had really begun nearly eight hours before the body was actually spotted. But the intensity of police activity on 14 May reveals their determination to prove that Sheila Bowler had indeed killed Florence Jackson.

Police Sergeant John Tickner, described in police logs as 'Observer One' in the police helicopter, says in his own statement that at 9.45am he spotted Mrs Jackson's body in the river, landed in the adjoining field and pulled it on to the river bank: 'She had apparently been in the water for some considerable time and I established that there were no signs of life.' He says that Ian Morrison, the paramedic accompanying him, confirmed this opinion, though no statement was taken from him until over a year later. They covered the body with a blanket and waited on the scene until Detective Inspector Newnham arrived.

At 10.32 the police surgeon Dr Jeelani, who was still of course Mrs Jackson's own GP in Rye, and indeed officially Sheila's doctor as well, examined the old lady's body and signed her death certificate. The Bexhill police immediately set up an incident control vehicle for Operation Dace in Station Road, Winchelsea, and just after midday PC Marshall was on duty there when a Mrs Spriggs, a London holiday-maker staying at Ferryfields Caravan Park, turned up with a silver spanner she had found on Station Road near a grass verge. PC Marshall dutifully marked the spot with waterproof chalk, but Mrs Spriggs's public-spirited act does not seem to have borne fruit. Nothing more was ever heard of the spanner.

Police divers were called out to search the river for other clues.

Jonathan Ashe, a senior photographer for the police, arrived at 11.45am with a civilian scenes of crime investigator called Victor Booth and at

12.02 Ashe started taking photographs and making a video of the body of Florence Jackson, still lying on the western bank of the River Brede. She was still wearing her buff-coloured coat and her sky blue cardigan. The buttons of both were undone. In her left hand she was still clutching the paper tissue Sheila had given her when they stopped near the layby at Icklesham. She had no slippers on her feet. Mr Ashe photographed her right slipper lying on the opposite bank above a concrete culvert near the pumping station (the left slipper was nowhere to be seen) and a number of tyremarks on the hardstanding area nearby. Mrs Jackson's body was then put into a body bag and taken to the Royal East Sussex Hospital mortuary.

At 1.20 Ashe and Booth went off to Rye police station and photographed the Audi, both inside and out, and Victor Booth made a list of the items it contained. He removed the front passenger seatbelt clip and a grey torch from the same front seat.

Ashe had one further duty that day. At 7pm that evening, after Sheila had identified the body at the hospital mortuary, he went along there and photographed every stage of the post-mortem as instructed by Dr Heath, the Home Office pathologist conducting the examination. In attendance were five police officers: Detective Superintendent Foster, the officer in charge of Operation Dace; Detective Inspector Cook, Detective Inspector Newnham, Scenes of Crime Officer Detective Sergeant Taylor, and Scene Investigator PC Mullan. Three other officials also attended: the Coroner's Officer, Scene Investigator Victor Booth, and a senior mortuary anatomical technician called Mr Howard. Such a large police presence at the mortuary strongly suggests that less than ten hours after her body was discovered, Mrs Jackson's death was now officially regarded as the result of foul play.

All day long a large number of police officers detailed to work on the case had been going round taking statements from key witnesses. They visited the Soans, Major and Mrs Cameron-Clarke, Mr Coulmanhole, Greyfriars Matron Joan Dobson and some of her staff, and Tom Day.

John Soan said he and his wife had had visitors who left at 9.30. They were watching TV when Sheila rang the door bell – he estimated it was between 10 and 10.15. He described their conversation and the delay while Sheila waited for the recovery service to answer the telephone. He had commiserated with her about the death of her husband. 'She said, " Yes he bled to death, it should never have happened." 'Up until this point,' added Mr Soan, 'she had been very calm but on talking about her husband she became up-tight.'

He thought she was in the house for fifteen minutes at most, 'though I do recall her saying that it had taken twenty minutes to half an hour to find us which was the only house to have the lights on downstairs.' He said he and his wife had then walked back to the car with Sheila, and when they were about 50 yards from it, they saw a big articulated lorry turn the bend: 'I thought it was going to hit the car.' As they drew nearer and were about 30 yards from the Audi, 'Mrs Bowler turned to me and said, "She's not in the car." I couldn't see this but it might have been that Mrs Bowler had picked this up in the headlight of the articulated lorry.'

Soan went on to describe Sheila's insistence that the old lady couldn't have walked off alone, and her mention of three rough-looking motorcyclists she had seen earlier. He told how he had stopped a red car coming out of Station Road but the driver had seen nothing. (The red car was never seen again and its driver never identified). He and his wife went home to telephone the police and then returned to help with the search. In his concern for the old lady he failed to notice whether the Audi had a puncture. Finally he added, 'Mrs Bowler was, and remained, very calm upon finding the Aunt missing from the car.' Mrs Soan's statement confirmed what her husband had said, adding that all the doors and windows of the Audi were closed. Unlike him, however, she had noticed that the 'tyre on the front nearside wheel was totally flat.' She added that she had rushed off to fetch the Cameron-Clarkes and then had returned to join the search. Detective Constable Poplett, interviewing Catherine Soan, must particularly have asked her about Mrs Bowler's shoes, because she recorded that 'they appeared clean and smart in keeping with her general appearance.' Unless prompted it seems most unlikely that she would have volunteered this information in a general description.

Mrs Cameron-Clarke's statement explained her own role in the search for Mrs Jackson. The official typed statement refers to Sheila throughout as 'Shirley Bowler,' though this mistake may well have been a transcription error. She said she knew 'Shirley' as an acquaintance and recounted the conversation in Budgens supermarket when Mrs Bowler 'talked about her Aunty being a bit of a worry as she was getting old and confused.' She added, 'I got the impression that she was fond of the Aunty and saw quite a bit of her.' She emphasized that 'Shirley' said several times during the previous evening that searching down Station Road was 'ridiculous as the old woman wouldn't have been able to walk that far.' 'Shirley' had also mentioned the bikers. On the morning of 14 May, about an hour before Mrs Jackson's body was found, Mrs Cameron-Clarke said she had herself driven along Station Road and had to do a three point turn near the pumping station to come back. She said she noticed that the gate leading onto the piece of concrete hardstanding next to the brick building was open and thought it strange as the gate was always shut.

Her husband confirmed his wife's account of the search, adding that he had spent some time helping Mr Soan look for Mrs Soan when she walked off alone. He and Mrs Cameron-Clarke had, he said, returned home about 1am.

Mr Coulmanhole, the Britannia Rescue truck-driver, said he arrived at about 10.50 and was immediately asked by Mr Soan to help search for an old lady who had gone missing. He glanced at the Audi as they passed and could see that the nearside front tyre was flat, though unlike Mrs Soan he thought it 'did not look completely flat.' He met Mrs Bowler and asked her how long she had been away from the car: 'She said, "I must have gone before 10pm." I think she said that she had been gone for half an hour.'

Mr Coulmanhole's statement goes on to describe his meeting with the Cameron-Clarkes, his search with the Major around some allotments, and a conversation with a police handler about dogs. After another twenty minutes he helped one of the officers search the car. In the front passenger footwell he found what he described as 'a tyre leaver [sic] sized 2 inches by a foot.' The police then asked him to take Mrs Bowler home. He drove the Audi on to his truck, confirming his earlier view that 'the front tyre was not completely deflated.' By the time he had got Mrs Bowler into the front passenger seat it was about 12.15am.

Mr Coulmanhole's account of his conversation with Sheila on the homeward journey is particularly significant, because it gave the police further evidence about her odd behaviour: 'I then drove towards Rye and

said to Mrs Bowler, "This is very strange." She said, "Yes." Every time that
I tried to talk about the old lady Mrs Bowler changed the subject.'

When they reached the Top o' the Hill pub, says Mr Coulmanhole, 'I
said, "Wherever they find your aunt they'll give you a ring." She said, "Will
they ring any time?" I said, "Yes." She said, "I go to bed late and get up at
half past four since my husband died. The last thing I want is the police
phoning me at 2 o'clock and I'll get no sleep." I recall her saying, "I hope
they find her in the morning and then at least I'll get my sleep!'

According to Sheila, she never said anything of the sort. She has always
maintained that she simply asked Mr Coulmanhole whether the police
would ring to let her know when they found Aunt Flo and he replied, 'Yes,
I should think so.' If she is correct, it is difficult to explain how the
recovery driver would have known anything about Bob's death unless the
police told him – but by May 14 when this statement was made, they
would hardly be aware of Sheila's personal sleeping habits themselves. It is
possible that Mr Soan discussed the matter with Mr Coulmanhole or the
Cameron-Clarkes as they searched together for Mrs Jackson.

But it may be that Sheila, edgy and tired (Mr Soan described her as
'up-tight' when talking about her husband's death) became excessively
garrulous and made some clumsy joke like the others described earlier. She
may have spoken about not wanting to be disturbed in an attempt to
convince herself and anyone listening that she was not really at all worried
about Mrs Jackson. To admit she *was* worried would be tantamount to
admitting a dereliction of duty in leaving the old woman unattended – and
everyone who knows her says Sheila is above all a dutiful woman. Now
she reacted by battening down the hatches on her own emotions and fears
and giving a convincing – though false – impression of calm. It was the
same reaction later to be interpreted by WDS Booth as a callous lack of
concern.

Whatever was said in the conversation between them, Mr Coulmanhole's
impression of Sheila on the night Aunt Flo went missing was the same as
Mr Soan's. He ends his statement, 'My impression of Mrs Bowler was that
she did not appear to be very concerned or worried about the old lady's
disappearance.'

For the final statement taken on May 14, Police Sergeant Levett drove
over to Cooden, near Bexhill-on-Sea, to interview Tom Day about the visit

the previous evening from Mrs Bowler and her aunt. Mr Day had already been woken in the early hours of that morning to confirm that the two women had been with him but now Sergeant Levett needed further details.

Day said he was certain the ladies arrived after 8pm because he had switched on the television and turned it off because the programme *Lovejoy* (which began at 8) was showing. He explained the arrangement whereby Sheila would collect protein supplements supplied by his wife's parents, though that evening the parcel she needed had not been delivered in time. He thought Sheila left the engine running and said the car was parked facing the house, so he could see the elderly lady in the front seat. Usually, he said, Sheila would come in and chat but this time she explained she would not stay, as her aunt was waiting in the car. He told her the location of the Elan shop where she could meet his wife the following day. Sheila went back to the car, opened the door and said in a loud voice, 'They haven't got it,' then drove off. Finally he added that 'it was light and very bright at the time Mrs Bowler called, in fact the sun was shining on the car as it was setting.' The police were later to confirm that on 13 May 1992 sunset was at 8.38pm and 'the hours of darkness' began at 9.08pm.

But a later police briefing note, dated 22 May, records a Detective Inspector Bunce as reporting that 'Mr Day cannot give a more certain timing of Mrs Bowler's visit than between 8pm and 9pm.'

Armed with the information from this first batch of witnesses, Detective Sergeant Booth returned to Fair Meadow next morning, Friday 15 May. With her was a male detective. He had a distinctive white streak running through his black hair from front to back. This was Detective Sergeant David Renno: the Bowler family were later to nickname him 'Badger.'

When the detectives arrived just after 11, they told Sheila they wanted to take the rest of the statement they had begun the following day. 'But first,' said David Renno, 'We're going out for a little drive.' In his own statement, written that same day, he says, 'we covered a route from Rye to the A259 at Winchelsea, at Mrs Blower's direction' (the statement refers to Sheila throughout as 'Mrs Blower'). 'I made notes of our route and also of tracing a telephone kiosk Mrs Blower used on 13.5.92.'

Travelling in Linda Booth's red BMW they took the route Sheila had taken the previous evening. Sheila was in the front passenger seat giving directions, Booth was driving and Renno sat in the back, taking notes.

They took the route Sheila had taken two days earlier: up Udimore Road, left down Dumb Woman's Lane, along Station Road and up the hill by-passing Winchelsea Town. The officers particularly wanted to know where Sheila had stopped on the Icklesham Straight when she had hitched Aunt Flo up in her seat, and which telephone kiosk she had used to call Simon. Sheila was puzzled: 'I couldn't understand why they wanted me to do this because it's the only telephone along there and it's obvious which one it is.' Later she said she thought she was being watched for her reactions: 'And I must have made them cross on the way back because I knew Renno was making notes and I made comments to him, like, "Have you got that?"' Still inwardly fuming at being dragged about by the police in this undignified manner, she told Booth and Renno that the posters their colleagues had placed near the Station Road site, seeking information from the public, were far too few and too small for people to see.

When the car returned Sheila to Fair Meadow the officers began to ask further questions. Sheila was even more irritated: she might miss her train to Bishop's Stortford. 'WDS Booth said to me that I was going to have my journey to London curtailed a bit, and I said, "Oh no I'm not!". I said Jane would be expecting me and there was nowhere I could contact her. I'd arranged to meet her in the café on the first floor of the Charing Cross Hotel at 2.30, so we could have a talk on my way to Bishop's Stortford. I said I really must not miss the 12.45 from Rye. I said, "My daughter's upset enough as it is, I don't want to be late"'. The officers said they would drive her to the railway station in good time. They asked for Aunt Flo's cheque book, which Sheila handed over, and for Sheila's own account number. After a few more questions, 'I told them I was teaching on Monday and Tuesday the following week but I could see them on the Wednesday if I rearranged my lessons. They arranged to come back at 2 o'clock on that day.'

It is hardly surprising that Booth and Renno dropped Sheila unceremoniously outside the police station, leaving her to walk the hundred yards or so along Cinque Ports Street to the railway station.

While Renno and Booth were interviewing Sheila Bowler, Detective Constable Poplett was taking a statement from Mr Denis Giddings, owner of the Ferryfields caravan park on Station Road. Mr Giddings described how on the evening of 13 May he had made four journeys along Station

Road. He had gone from his home past the pumping station at 6.30 to take his son Stuart to a karate class at Northiam village hall. On the way there he noticed a woman walking along the road just before Ferry Bridge. When he came back half an hour later she was still there, now much nearer to the pumping station. When Mr Giddings set out again at about 9.55 to collect his son, he noticed a family saloon car parked across the entrance to the pumping station with its reversing lights on. It was a greyish-coloured hatchback with not much of a boot (the Audi is metallic green and has a very pronounced boot) and was facing towards Winchelsea Station, away from the A259 junction. When he returned at 10.30 the car was gone.

Although the woman could not have been either Aunt Flo or Sheila Bowler (at that time Flo was at Greyfriars and Sheila at Battle Abbey) Mr Giddings was obviously someone who noticed things, and he would have noticed Aunt Flo during his second set of journeys if she had been wandering along the road. The car he saw did not match the Audi's description and it was facing the wrong way, but its presence was enough to firm up the suspicion that it *might* have been Sheila's car.

That evening, Aunt Flo's left slipper was found by a Mr Philip Stan who had learned that an old lady had died and offered to take police divers up the Brede in his friend's boat as they searched for her walking stick and slipper. Mr Stan's wife, with him in the boat, noticed at about 5pm that the slipper had lodged among reeds a few inches from the bank. He fished it out with a boat-hook. An hour later Mr Stan took Scene Investigator Victor Booth along the river to show him the spot.

On Saturday 16 May the police took a statement from a young motorist called Christopher Beckett, who said that on the evening of 13 May he had left his home in Udimore and taken the same local short cut down Dumb Woman's Lane and Station Road that Sheila had taken that afternoon when she planned to get to the Hastings shops. He spent ten to fifteen minutes at the Robin Hood pub in Icklesham, then drove back along the A259 to the Bridge Inn at Winchelsea, arriving there at 10pm. A few minutes before he got there he passed the Audi: 'I looked to see if anyone was in the car. I could not see anybody.' He said he saw a lady walking along the road about 50 yards from the car. But he described the lady as 'being aged 45 to 50 years old.. with black wavy shoulder-length hair...

She did not appear to be carrying anything.' Sheila was 62, grey-haired and was carrying a shoulder bag.

Sheila spent that weekend with the Cutmores, her friends in Bishop's Stortford. She tried to enjoy herself but was growing increasingly worried about the way the police had behaved towards her. She spoke on the telephone to Audrey Mummery, who had just returned from a fortnight's holiday and knew nothing about the incident on May 13. Audrey said later, 'She related everything that had happened on the fateful night, and that she was convinced the police thought she was responsible. I told her not to be stupid: it was obvious that Aunt Flo had got out of her car and walked somewhere. I told her that as long as she told the truth she had nothing to worry about. I was sure the police would have had experience of the wanderings of elderly people.'

From Hertfordshire on the Saturday afternoon Sheila telephoned Detective Superintendent Brian Foster at Rye police station to make sure her car would be returned to her before the end of the weekend. Though she was unaware of it, she was speaking to the officer directing the murder investigation in which she was the prime suspect. But when she arrived home that evening Foster had been as good as his word: the Audi was standing on the drive. 'I don't think WDS Booth was very pleased about that,' recalled Sheila years later, 'because she was the one who had to drive the car up to my house. She gave the keys to my neighbour Maria who told me she literally threw the keys at her and said that I seemed to be taking my aunt's death extremely well. Maria told her that was just the sort of person I was.'

On Monday 18 May, Detective Sergeant Renno took a statement from an 18 year-old engineer called Lee Apps. Apps told Renno that that morning at about 11.30 he had been driving along Pelsham Lane between Broad Oak and Peasmarsh, two villages a few miles from Rye, when he had seen a wooden walking stick lying in the road. He stopped, picked it up and handed it in to Hastings police station. At 3.20pm the same day he took Renno to the spot and showed him where the stick was found. The stick was photographed by WDS Booth with her polaroid camera.

That Monday, and the following day, Tuesday 19 May, Sheila went off to work as usual. She had cancelled her Wednesday lessons at Battle Abbey

School ready for her next appointment with the police. On the Tuesday afternoon she went to see David Teall, the headmaster of Battle Abbey. He had already heard of Mrs Jackson's tragic death, but now there was something else she had to tell him: 'I think you'd better know,' she said, 'that I feel I'm under suspicion of murder: the police seem to believe I killed Bob's Aunt Flo.' Mr Teall must have dismissed the idea as absurd, because he told Sheila to continue her work at the school as usual. The head teachers of Bricklehurst Manor and Marlborough House, the two prep schools where Sheila gave lessons, reacted in the same way.

One of Sheila's colleagues at Battle Abbey was Monica Steward, who had taught at the school for the past twenty years. At about 5 o'clock that Tuesday afternoon, 19 May, she was coming down the stairs near the school office. There was a staff meeting and she was on a duty patrol of the school when she bumped into Sheila who must have been between piano lessons: on Tuesdays she taught at the school from 4.15 to 7pm.

Sheila told Monica the news about Aunt Flo's death, briefly explaining the circumstances. She mentioned that Flo was incontinent and that her health had deteriorated since she went into Greyfriars. She told Monica she hadn't been sure whether or not the old lady needed a zimmer frame. This conversation, recounted nearly three weeks later in Monica Steward's statement to the police, reveals that Sheila was now becoming fully aware of the reality of her situation. Disbelief was giving way to a growing acceptance that there really was something to worry about.

Sheila told Monica she felt she had been treated like a criminal. The police, she said, had taken away her car for two days and they still had one of the wheels and the clothes Sheila was wearing the night Mrs Jackson disappeared. They had taken her bank books too and were bound to find out that the old lady had paid her money, but, Sheila explained, this was only used to settle Mrs Jackson's own bills. Sheila also mentioned her concern that police would find her tyre tracks on the lane near the river 'as she had been there several times before.' She said she had wondered whether her aunt had been raped. Finally she said she doubted the police's statement that the body had been found half a mile from the car. Perhaps, said Sheila, the distance was just a quarter of a mile and the body had been carried by the current – she wondered whether the currents had been checked.

The conversation lasted about fifteen minutes and Steward later told the police, 'I formed the impression from the way Sheila was talking to me that she was virtually thinking out loud and that she needed someone to speak to.' Those who know Sheila well are familiar with her tendency to think aloud, skipping from topic to topic with no apparent logic. In normal circumstances, for instance in a gossipy telephone conversation, it can be quite endearing for its very lack of artifice. In a murder suspect, it could be interpreted as deeply incriminating.

The question about rape is significant and may seem remarkable considering Mrs Jackson's advanced age, but Sheila had seen the bikers and, as she said later, 'these days you read such awful stories in the papers. After she was found dead this was just something that occurred to me.'

In fact it seems to have occurred to her even earlier: she may have hinted at it in the very first telephone conversation she had with Jane when she returned to Fair Meadow late on the night of May 13, long before Aunt Flo's body was found. Jane cannot remember any specific mention of sexual assault: 'But that night,' she says, 'I had the most terrible nightmares, of Aunt Flo in a ditch and the bikers doing awful things to her.' Sheila's immediate assumption of sexual attack is perhaps unsurprising for a woman of her age, class and upbringing. Four years in prison have made her far less judgemental, but in 1992 Sheila Bowler was the kind of woman who automatically tended to suspect people like bikers, or indeed anyone scruffily dressed, of all manner of ulterior motives. Her fears must have seemed justified when it later emerged that Aunt Flo's clothing had been disturbed. The pathologist's report noted that when she was found in the water, all the buttons of her jacket, cardigan and dress were found to be undone, and the back suspenders holding up her stockings were also unfastened. (This mystery was never to be explained, though one theory later suggested was that hypothermia could be the cause. It has been remarked that in cases of hypothermia, just before death, the sufferer may feel unnaturally hot and may try to remove all clothing. Could Aunt Flo have struggled long enough in the cold waters of the Brede to undo all her buttons? The suspenders are more easily explained. Many elderly ladies who wear girdles commonly leave the back suspenders undone because the hard fasteners dig painfully into their fragile skin.

Maybe Mrs McGlanaghy, the care-worker who had dressed Aunt Flo that morning, was aware of this and left them undone.)

The conversation between Sheila and Monica Steward ended and they went their separate ways, Monica on her rounds of the school and Sheila to her pupils. When the lessons were over she decided to drive to Bexhill and collect the protein supplement from the Days. Events had got in the way, but as she said when Bob died, life has to go on – and Helen Goodwin needed that protein.

Sheila's sudden decision to set off for Bexhill may seem odd, just like her sudden decision to rush off to Hastings on the way to work at Battle a week earlier. But everyone who knows Sheila Bowler well will tell you she is an impulsive woman. Just as in conversation she skips from topic to topic and back again, just as every friend will tell you she will pick up the phone and call you three times in five minutes with sudden afterthoughts, so she will suddenly go rushing off all over the country, often in half-formed gestures of kindness and generosity.

In the depths of her being, Sheila is a woman of impetuous, artistic and passionate temperament whom class and upbringing have forced to suppress all her most natural inclinations. She also has the misfortune to look like a starchy English matron instead of the slightly *distrait* musician she really is. Even her choice of clothes betrays this confusion as she alternates traditional tweeds with brilliant colours and flamboyant styles. It is this unresolved identity that makes her so hard to read on first acquaintance. There must be thousands of repressed middle-class Englishwomen like Sheila Bowler all over the country. Few of them are unlucky enough to end up on a charge of murder.

When Sheila arrived at the Days' house in Cooden, Jenny invited her in. 'The police know all about you and your proteins,' she laughed. 'They came and asked us all about you.' Her friends' jokes lightened Sheila's mood as she drove back to Rye, taking the same route as she had that fateful night less than one week earlier. But as she drove again along the Icklesham Straight, an awful thought suddenly struck her. She had given the policewoman the wrong shoes! The black patent shoes she had handed to WDS Booth on the afternoon of May 14 were not the ones she had been wearing the previous evening.

As she explained later, 'I often kept several pairs of shoes in the car and on that evening I had a spare pair on the floor under the driver's seat. They were the black patent ones I gave to the police. One had a slight split at the side and I thought they weren't good enough to wear, but were fine for driving. The shoes I was actually wearing that night were black leather ones with little red and green bits of decoration on the front. When I came back late that night in the breakdown truck, I carried the black patent shoes into the house along with my briefcase, took off the red and black shoes, gave them both a bit of a polish as I always do, and put the two pairs in the utility room.

'Then, days later as I drove along thinking things over, I said to myself, 'Oh my goodness – those weren't the shoes I was actually wearing! I was wearing the black ones with the little red bows on!' I remembered that because that evening as I helped Aunt Flo into the car she commented on them. She said, "You've got those pretty shoes on again." They were favourites of hers.'

Now Sheila was in a real quandary. Had she discovered the mistake earlier, she would have had no hesitation in telephoning the police and explaining. But we know from her conversation with Monica Steward that by now she felt threatened enough by the way the police were treating her to wonder what interpretation they might put on a mistake like this. They would be coming along the following day: should she hand over the right shoes? She needed more advice. Who better to ask than Mrs Cameron-Clarke? She had been most helpful during the search for Aunt Flo and she was a magistrate so would know the correct procedure.

By this time she had almost reached the foot of Ferry Hill, not far from the Cameron-Clarkes' house. So at about 9pm that evening, Sheila paid a visit to the Major and the magistrate, saying she had come to thank them for helping in the search for Aunt Flo.

The Cameron-Clarkes must have been a little taken aback by this unannounced visit, ostensibly just a courtesy call. People tend to retire early in the country and we know that Mrs Cameron-Clarke was undressed and ready for bed when Mrs Soan summoned her out to search for Aunt Flo six days earlier. It must have occurred to the couple that Sheila could have thanked them just as well in a telephone call. Nevertheless they invited her in and poured her a glass of sherry. Mrs Cameron-Clarke had spent the day at the Chelsea Flower Show and complained that her feet hurt, and that everything had been very expensive. In the statement she gave to the police three days later, Mrs Cameron-Clarke said that Sheila stayed about three-quarters of an hour and told her more about the events occurring after Mrs Jackson's body was found.

As in her conversation with Monica Steward, Sheila was again impetuously 'thinking out loud' without beginning to consider the implications of what she was saying. According to Mrs Cameron-Clarke's statement, Sheila said she could not understand why a policewoman had stayed with her that day, and left taking the clothes she had been wearing the previous night. Then, said Mrs Cameron-Clarke, Sheila explained that she had given the police the wrong shoes. She told Mrs Cameron-Clarke she knew the shoes were wrong 'because the pair she was wearing during the evening of 13 May had red bits on them and her late Aunt Flo liked them.'

Sheila had then asked for the magistrate's advice, which was unequivocal: 'I told her, "You must tell the police immediately and give them the right shoes"'.

Mrs Cameron-Clarke said Sheila mentioned a number of other matters which concerned her. She was worried that the police had taken away the 'short piece of steel piping' she kept in the car, and seemed evasive when Major Cameron-Clarke asked her why she kept it there. She had, she said, taken three recent trips down Station Road and was worried the police would find her tyre marks there. Mrs Cameron-Clarke told Sheila she herself had driven along that road in the morning before the body was found, so her tyre marks would be there too.

According to Mrs Cameron-Clarke, Sheila then told them that 'when she visited her friends at Cooden she parked in a different place to where she normally parked and it was lucky that the people could see Auntie very clearly.' She also mentioned other things that were worrying her: would her daughter's exam results be jeopardized if the police went and questioned her? Would the police have been shocked that the Ferry Road flat was untidy? Should she have kept account of the cheques signed by Aunt Flo and used to pay outstanding bills? Should the police have been given access to Aunt Flo's bank accounts? Finally Sheila asked Mrs Cameron-Clarke a question which the magistrate found extraordinary. It was the question she had asked Monica Steward a few hours earlier, the question that kept playing on her mind: 'Would it be all right if I asked the police if she had been raped?'

'Privately,' Mrs Cameron-Clarke was to tell the police, 'I was very surprised on hearing that remark from Mrs Bowler.' She added: 'Throughout our conversation Mrs Bowler did not display any sadness nor feeling of loss, bereavement or any compassion for Auntie Flo.'

Analysing Mrs Cameron-Clarke's statement, we see Sheila, garrulous, impetuous and ingenuous as ever, pouring out all her worries to the woman who had helped her the previous week, a respected magistrate. The daughter of a solicitor, Sheila had a great respect for the law and its practitioners. Here was one she thought she could trust with her private – and entirely understandable – fears. The conversation is very similar to the one she had had four hours earlier with Monica Steward.

Sheila, more illogical than ever in her anxiety, flitted from one topic to another. This was interpreted by Mrs Cameron-Clarke in her police statement as suspicious behaviour: 'It appeared that whenever my husband or myself made a pointed question Mrs Bowler went on to the defensive and made some sort of unintelligible reply.'

It is of course possible that Sheila was indeed on the defensive. Well-known by friends and acquaintances to be honest to a fault – indeed to the point of tactlessness – she was well aware that she had not given Mrs Cameron-Clarke an entirely honest reason for visiting her that evening. She was there not primarily to thank her for her part in the search, but to seek her advice as an officer of the law.

Secondly, she felt aggrieved and bitterly embarrassed that the police were treating her, a pillar of the community, like a common criminal, although she had done nothing wrong. This may perhaps have led her to try to ally herself with the respectable local magistrate who had after all shown support by helping in the search.

Thirdly, she must have felt a sense of guilt – not because she had murdered Aunt Flo but because she had left her alone in the car. This would explain much of the behaviour that seemed so odd to everyone. But in fact it is no odder than the behaviour of a loving parent who loses a toddler in a crowded supermarket, only to smack it furiously when it is found. Meticulous and dutiful, she had for once failed in her duty and Aunt Flo was dead as a result.

A different kind of person might have broken down and wept: Sheila's reaction was to go angrily on the defensive. After all, for the last fifteen years she had done her duty by Bob's two aunts – who were not even her blood relations. It was so unfair if she was now to be blamed for the first slip she had ever made. And this was no ordinary blame – incredibly, she was actually being suspected of *murdering* the old lady.

David Jessel, presenter of Channel Four's *Trial and Error* programme, was later to call the Sheila Bowler case a classic Agatha Christie mystery. Indeed it has all the elements of a game of *Cluedo*. Here we find a traditional English Major expressing his suspicions about a possible murder weapon – the metal bar found in Sheila's car. Sheila herself, no doubt brought up like the Major on a diet of murder-mystery thrillers, was equally worried about the artefact, though Mr Coulmanhole (who presumably as a recovery driver and engineer knew something about cars) identified it as nothing more sinister than a tyre lever. Sheila will now describe with some embarrassment how Bob put it there one day, 'in case I needed it to defend myself.' They had joked about it at the time: now it looked like becoming an instrument that would aid not Sheila's own defence but rather her prosecutors' case.

Whatever Major and Mrs Cameron-Clarke privately believed, they must have concealed their feelings very successfully because Sheila left feeling satisfied. She now knew the right thing to do. The following day she would hand in the red and black shoes when the police came to take her statement.

But when she got home, just to make doubly sure, she telephoned Audrey Mummery in Sevenoaks and asked her advice. Audrey told her to go to the police immediately: they would be sympathetic to such an understandable mistake. For women like these two friends, strictly raised in the Methodist faith, honesty must surely be the best policy.

On the morning of Wednesday 20 May Sheila received a letter from Heringtons, Aunt Flo's solicitors, containing a copy of the old lady's will. Everything had been left to her sister Lilian, and after Lil's death to her nephew Robert Bowler and his wife Sheila, or if they predeceased her, to Robert and Sheila's children. Jim Simpson, one of the partners at Heringtons' Rye branch, whom Sheila knew well, said in his letter that the police were asking for a copy of the will and he needed her consent before giving it to them. Sheila telephoned to agree, though she felt they were 'being a bit nosy.' The police had treated her with suspicion, so it was natural she should feel antagonistic. 'Why should we give it to them?' she asked. 'They can force us to hand it over if we don't,' said Jim.

Almost as an afterthought, Sheila told Jim that the police were coming along again at 2 o'clock that afternoon to finish taking a statement from her. Indeed they had been with her a great deal, off and on, since Aunt Flo's death. Simpson was horrified: 'Have you got anyone with you?' he asked. 'No,' said Sheila, 'Why should I? I haven't done anything.' 'I think you should have somebody there with you when the police come today,' said Simpson. 'I'll send Russell Parkes from our St Leonard's office. He's very good.'

As it happened, Russell Parkes, one of the younger members of Heringtons' staff, was spending that morning in Rye magistrates' court. By extraordinary coincidence he had just overheard a conversation between some police officers. They were not directly involved in the search for Mrs Jackson, but knew all about it. He told Sheila the gist of their conversation: 'That body we found in the river last week,' said one, 'We know the niece did it – all we've got to do now is get the proof.' So when Jim Simpson entered the courtroom, tapped Parkes on the shoulder and asked him to go up to number 25 Fair Meadow, he had more than an inkling of what it was all about.

When Parkes arrived he had another copy of Aunt Flo's will with him. He wanted to talk to Sheila before the police arrived, he said. 'We'll give them the will to read, that'll keep them happy.'

When DS Renno and WDS Booth drove up soon after Parkes, that is exactly what happened: they sat outside in their car and read through Mrs Jackson's will.

Alone with Sheila, Parkes came straight to the point. 'There's a rumour going round,' he said, 'that you have murdered your Aunt Flo.' Though Sheila had realised by this point that she was under suspicion, Parkes's bald statement was the first time she had heard anyone actually voice the amazing accusation. She sat down. 'I can't believe this!' she said.

Parkes stayed with Sheila while Linda Booth and David Renno took a full official statement. The process began with Booth reading aloud to Sheila and her new solicitor the first eight pages, which had been written down the previous day. This first section recounted her movements up to the point when she was waiting in the stranded car wondering what to do, having realised she had a flat tyre. The rest of the statement, which finally amounted to nineteen pages in all, was completed, and Sheila was asked to read it through, make any necessary alterations and endorse them with her signature, and finally sign the whole document.

Booth noted in her own later statement that as Sheila made a number of changes: 'Mr Parkes remarked, "It's your own fault for keep [sic] changing your mind."' Sheila disputes this version. She maintains it was DS Renno, not Russell Parkes, who made this remark: 'Russell Parkes would never have said a thing like that,' she says. The disparity is important: by attributing the remark to Parkes, Booth seems to be suggesting that even Sheila's own solicitor is turning against her.

Booth's statement contains some other significant additions. As advised by Monica Steward and Peta Cameron-Clarke, Sheila now asked the question that had been troubling her for days. Booth writes: 'Prior to the commencement of the statement, Mrs Bowler asked me if her Aunt Flo had been raped. I told her that to my knowledge there was no evidence to suggest this. She commented that her aunt must have been so frightened and this was the first occasion that she had expressed her concern for her aunt in my presence.'

Booth also noted that 'a number of discrepancies became apparent.' Sheila, meticulous as ever, now remembered that it was 8.45pm when she approached Cooden – though she had before been unable to be specific about times as Booth had requested. She also remembered going to Bexhill sea-front on the way back to check the location of the dress shop. Even more suspiciously, in police eyes, Sheila had, wrote Booth, 'changed her attitude and opinion as to her Aunt Flo's mobility.' Though at first Sheila 'had been adamant that she could not have got to the area (where) she was found on her own,' now she could not 'give an opinion as to whether she could have walked unaided or not'

Booth was also suspicious when Sheila asked her if the police had taken a silver torch from the glove compartment of the Audi: 'Mrs Bowler had not made mention of this silver torch when I asked her for an inventory of the car on 14/5/92.'

Finally Booth showed Sheila two items for her comment. The first was the polaroid photograph she had taken of the walking stick found by Lee Apps in Pelsham Lane. Sheila said it was not the one missing from the Audi.

The second was the metal bar that had worried Major Cameron-Clarke. When Booth showed it to Sheila, she confirmed that it was the one she always kept under the front passenger seat. Her late husband, she said, put it there for her own protection.

As the officers were about to leave, Sheila jumped up. She went to the utility room and produced the black and red shoes so admired by Aunt Flo. These were the shoes she had actually been wearing on the night of the 13th, she told Booth. The black patent shoes she had given the police earlier were the wrong ones. Although Sheila's explanation for the mistake was perfectly reasonable, Booth's suspicions were aroused still further: here was yet another 'discrepancy.' In her own statement she wrote that Mrs Bowler 'realised she had given us the wrong shoes which she was supposed to have been wearing on 13/5/92. Yet she was not at all hesitant when she handed me the first pair of shoes and, in fact, commented that she "rubbed them off" in preparation for the next day.'

Anyone who knows Sheila Bowler well could have explained to the police that the 'discrepancies' which they found so suspicious were in fact nothing more than symptoms of her meticulous, almost obsessive, attention to detail. Though she might have forgotten things during the course of her (uncautioned) first interviews, at a time when – despite appearances – she might well have been in a state of shock, she was now anxious that everything should be exactly correct. Why else would she have replaced the 'wrong' shoes? She was after all a solicitor's daughter.

Treated like a criminal by the police, she now began to feel like one. Indeed it is frightening to trace how even the most innocent action can be regarded as sinister once someone falls under suspicion.

Despite the police conversation he had overheard in court that very morning, Russell Parkes seemed unconcerned at anything he had witnessed later that day at 25 Fair Meadow. Perhaps he was simply trying to reassure his new client. As the two officers left, Sheila recalls him telling her, 'Of course they could arrest you. But I don't think they will, because they were too nice to you.'

After the police and Parkes had left, Sheila looked at her watch. The procedures had taken less time than she had expected and she would still be able to drive to Battle Abbey for the piano lessons she had provisionally cancelled.

In the staff-room at about 4.20 she met Monica Steward again and sat down for another chat. The police interview had worried her deeply: in her statement, Monica said Sheila was now 'clearly upset and concerned about the effect the whole affair was having on her daughter.' She mentioned to Monica the 'metal bar that she had kept in her car on her late husband's instructions in case she were ever in need of having to protect herself.' Appearing as it does in the Cameron-Clarke and Steward statements, Sheila's concern with the *Cluedo*-style 'weapon' must have seemed obsessive, and probably aroused police suspicion still further, but she was simply voicing her fears aloud to a colleague she felt she could trust. As Monica said, 'She also appeared concerned that there were items and circumstances that on the face of it may appear incriminating but that there was a rational explanation.'

Unfortunately for Sheila the teacher, as meticulously honest as Sheila herself, added in her statement: 'Sheila was concerned about the reputation she said the police had for rigging evidence.' It would be another 17 days before the East Sussex police were to hear Steward's account of Sheila's blunt scepticism about their integrity. If they had heard it earlier, they would not perhaps have seemed quite as 'nice' as Russell Parkes had concluded.

At 3pm that afternoon, while Sheila was driving to work at Battle Abbey, a Mr George Eldridge, aged 76, was giving a statement to a PC Turnbull. He explained that on the morning of Monday 18 May he was helping his wife into the family car. By coincidence they were setting out to drive to Greyfriars residential home in Winchelsea. Mr Eldridge said he put his stick on the roof of the car, forgot all about it and drove off. When they arrived at Greyfriars he remembered the stick. Now PC Levett showed him the stick handed in by Lee Apps two days earlier. Mr Eldridge identified it as his own and PC Turnbull handed it back to him.

In fact during the week between finding Mrs Jackson's body and returning to complete Sheila's statement on Wednesday 20 May, the police had been extremely busy. They had made discreet enquiries at Battle Abbey School, interviewing the last pupil taught by Sheila at Battle Abbey before she collected Mrs Jackson. Headmaster David Teall initially objected, but had to admit later that the interview was sensitively handled. The police officers asked the ten year old girl whether Sheila had finished the lesson early. The child thought long and hard, then shook her head.

During this same period the police also took statements from Dr Jeelani; five more of the Greyfriars care staff; Mr Abnett, the River Brede sluice-gate keeper, and Sarah Silberston, the Social Services assessment officer who had written to Sheila about the Greyfriars fees.

Police also took statements from thirteen motorists who had come forward because they were in the area on the night of the 13th. By the end of police investigations, a total of 28 motorists were to come forward in response to police requests, though it transpired that many of them could not assist police enquiries.

The police were particularly interested in the evidence of a Mrs Judith Pearson, who was pretty sure she had driven past the Audi at 9.50 on her way back from a restaurant meal. She did not notice anybody in the car, but, like Christopher Beckett, she noticed a lady hurrying along the road away from the Audi. But she put the time at ten minutes earlier than Mr Beckett, and her description is much more accurate than his: the woman had 'dark to grey colour' hair and was carrying a shoulder bag.

Dr Jeelani's statement gives a brief account of Florence Jackson's medical history, mentioning that when she was seen by Mr Yeo, a Hastings Hospital specialist, about two months earlier, he had said she was 'reasonably fit for her age.' It seems likely Dr Jeelani was asked by the police if he thought the old lady could walk the distance between the car and the spot where her body was found. He said, 'My observations from memory is that whilst visiting her at home, in Ferry Road, she could walk between her living room and kitchen by holding onto furniture or doors.' He said he could not comment on the state of her feet, but that she did have problems with incontinence' – suggesting that the police at this point may have been considering the need to urinate as a possible motive for getting out of the car.

Mr Abnett, the sluice-gate keeper, explained the mechanism of the sluice gates. The River Brede flows into the sea at Brede Sluice, Rye Harbour. At the Sluice there is a pair of gates with the function of controlling the flow of water in the River Brede. In the reclaimed flatlands of Romney Marsh, the sea will flow back up the river when the tide comes in, and if it were not controlled by gates the water would flood valuable grazing meadows. So the sluice gates are closed each time the tide comes in. They are opened again about four hours later when the tide goes out. When the gates are closed the level of the River Brede rises until the water overflows the top of the sluice gates. Mr Abnett said that two inches of water flow over the sluice gates, even when they are closed. So a walking stick could have floated over the gates and out to sea.

On the night of 13 May the gates were closed between 7.30pm and 11.30 pm and the level of the river at Ferry Bridge rose by about 9cm – 3 inches. During this period Mr Abnett estimated that the water in the River Brede would have been about two metres deep at the point where Mrs Jackson's body was found. At 11.30 the gates were opened again and stayed open till 8am on the morning of 14 May. While they were open the river level fell by about 6 cm – about 2 inches.

A police briefing note of 18 May has an Inspector Harmer reporting that the water flow had been checked and 'there would have been a reasonable flow.' Mr Abnett said the flow of the river would have been slow, though he could not give any accurate measurement. At 11.30pm when the gates were opened the flow would have been somewhat faster, slowing down again at 8am next morning when the gates were again closed.

But the pumping station near Ferry Bridge also has its own special effect on that particular stretch of the Brede. It is designed to pump water from one of the many Marsh drainage ditches into the river. The pump switches on and off automatically and a great surge of water comes rushing out from the large-bore pipe under the concrete parapet where Aunt Flo's right slipper was found. So although the Brede's flow was slow that night, the sudden outflow from the drainage tunnel would be violent enough to carry any object – a body, a walking stick or a slipper – quite swiftly downstream towards the sea.

Significantly, in view of Mrs Cameron-Clarke's surprise about the five-bar farm gate at the pumping station being open, Mr Abnett said that on the contrary, it had been pushed open in that position for at least the last ten months, and grass had grown up all round it.

The police interview with Sarah Silbertston, the Social Services assessment officer is illuminating. This statement, taken the very next day after Mrs Jackson's body was found, suggests the police decided early on that money was the motive for murder. By consulting her files at County Hall, Lewes, Silberston was able to tell police that as a householder, Mrs Jackson had been assessed as having to pay the maximum contribution to the Greyfriars fees, and that on 29 January that year Mrs Bowler had been asked to complete a property form regarding the Ferry Road flat. Not only had Mrs Bowler failed to sign the form, said Silberston, but she had cancelled all subsequent meetings with assessment officers, saying her solicitor had advised her not to sign the form. She ends her statement with the figure £3,589.70p – the sum owing by 29 March for the Greyfriars fees. More than six weeks had passed since the figure was reckoned, so the debt by the time of Aunt Flo's death would have grown to over £5000.

By this time the police must have felt they had a hard-hearted murderer with a motive. All that now remained was to work out the logistics of how Sheila Bowler managed to put her aunt-in-law in the River Brede at some point in the hour-long period between about nine o'clock when she left Tom Day's house and about ten o'clock when she turned up at the Soans – though the starting and finishing times of this period could not be exactly pinpointed.

It is clear that by the time the police came along to take Sheila's formal statement on 20 May, one week after Mrs Jackson went missing, they were sure she had devised a cunning plan which went as follows: furious at the rapid haemorrhage into Greyfriars fees of the money she expected to inherit from Aunt Flo, she decided to murder her before it could all drain away. Accordingly, on Wednesday 6 May she tried a 'dry run' of the plan, only cancelling the arrangement with Greyfriars at the last minute, either because she had cold feet, or something went wrong with the plot.

One week to the day later, at some time in the afternoon, she drove along beside the River Brede, stopped to check the best place to throw her aunt in, then callously carried on to Battle Abbey where she taught her lessons as usual. She then collected Aunt Flo, and instead of driving straight home, she used up the remaining hours of daylight – and tried to create an alibi – by taking the old lady on a lengthy detour in the opposite direction to Bexhill, on the pretext of collecting a protein supplement from Mr Day. She had then driven straight back to Winchelsea (rather than via Bexhill sea-front and the town centre as she later pretended), gone along Station Road to the edge of the river next to the pumping station, (a strange choice, incidentally, as there are better-concealed wooded areas further along the river), put Aunt Flo into the river, turned the car round and driven back on to the A259.

There she had parked just round the hairpin bend and let air out of the front nearside tyre to make it look as if the car had a puncture. She had then gone to the Soans' house on the pretence of seeking help.

It is perhaps worth mentioning at this point that two witnesses willingly came forward soon after Mrs Jackson's death and provided evidence that might have supported an alternative theory about the old lady's disappearance.

David Brown, a farmer in his mid-fifties, telephoned the police on the day Mrs Jackson's body was found in the river. He said he wanted to tell them that between 10.35 and 10.45 on the night of 13 May, he was driving along the A259 from Rye to Hastings and was just crossing Strand Bridge, near the Cameron-Clarkes' house, when a car going in the opposite direction – towards Mr Brown and away from the stranded Audi – hurtled dangerously across his path as its driver took a right turn and sped off down the road towards Winchelsea Beach. Mr Brown particularly noticed that the light-coloured car had one odd nearside door, in a burgundy colour. He drove on and noticed the stranded Audi and the breakdown truck nearby. Mr Brown's statement is dated 18 May, but later in court he was to maintain that the police did not come to take it until two weeks later.

The other witness was a woman called Bernadette Fiddimore. The officer who answered her call was PC Millington, whom she knew personally. She lived at Guestling, one of the villages on the A259 between Winchelsea and Hastings. She saw the posters seeking information and contacted the police. She said that she and her neighbour Bob Finch were in their adjoining gardens on the evening of May 13 putting up a fence when they counted no fewer than 72 motorcyclists on their way towards Hastings. She imagined some of them would certainly have returned along the A259 past the spot where Mrs Jackson had gone missing and might be able to help the police with their enquiries.

But no formal statement was ever taken from her by the police. Indeed in May 1992 the police seemed to dismiss the existence of any motorcyclists in the area that night, and to suggest they were a figment of Sheila's imagination, or part of her plot to blame an unknown abductor for the death of Aunt Flo. But five years later, when the case of Sheila Bowler had come to re-trial after going through two appeals, it emerged that the police had indeed investigated the bikers, and discovered that there were in fact two meetings of vintage motorcycle clubs that night, one at the Royal Oak pub in Pett, between Hastings and Winchelsea, the other at the Ash pub in Ashburnham, the other side of Hastings. Only at this point did Sheila's Defence team hear about Bernadette Fiddimore and her approach to the police. There is no record of the police questioning the bikers.

The police investigation was not of course confined to taking statements from witnesses. The Operation Dace team were also carrying out their own forensic experiments. While Sheila was being questioned on 20 May, the police scene photographer Jonathan Ashe had been summoned back to Winchelsea, where he was making another videotape, this time of Scene Investigator Victor Booth walking from the A259 along Station Road to the pumping station.

Mr Booth was also required to take tyre impressions and soil samples from the pumping station area, and floor sweepings and tyre scrapings from the Audi. But nothing appears to have been done with these soil samples. Five years later Booth would reveal that police decided not to send the soil samples from the car and the river bank off to a laboratory for scientific analysis and comparison 'because the soil was the same at the pumping station as it was all round the area for ten miles and indeed outside Mrs Bowler's house.'

The Crown were finally forced to admit, according to their own documents, that 'none of the casts matched the Audi's tyres and the police concluded that there was no scientific evidence to connect Sheila Bowler with the offence or with the pumping station.' Although Mrs Bowler's clothes and shoes were seized by the police, there is no record of any tests being carried out to see if anything on them connected her with the river bank. Either the police failed to test them for fibres, plant traces, seeds and so on, or they tested them and found nothing.

Mr Ashe, the police photographer, was to return to the scene for a third time, on May 26. This time the police asked him to take pictures of the soles of a new pair of slippers purchased by Victor Booth from Marks & Spencers in Eastbourne. Then he videoed a civilian called Deborah Bassett, doing the same walk as Mr Booth, but wearing the new slippers. He then re-photographed the soles of the new slippers to show the degree of wear after such a walk. In fact the experiment proved inconclusive, but the reconstruction shows that though Greyfriars staff and Mrs Bowler herself thought it unlikely that Aunt Flo could have walked to her death, the police were at least prepared to consider the walking theory, if only in seeking to disprove it.

The police also carried out another experiment to try and find out what could have happened to the walking stick that Sheila said she had left between the front seats of the Audi. Could it have fallen in the water and been swept out to sea? A police officer was instructed to find out and embarked on an experimental game of Poohsticks. His statement reads as follows: 'At 3pm I went to the scene on the River Brede and conducted an experiment with one of the walking sticks I had obtained from the Greyfriars Home. For a period of six minutes I placed the stick into the water. The stick floated. However it travelled a distance of about five metres before becoming lodged in the river bank.' No account appears to have been taken of the possible effect of the rushing outflow of water from the pumping station drainage pipe, nor the two-inches of water that Mr Abnett said always escaped out to sea over the top of the sluice-gates.

On Thursday 21 May, Sergeant Levett interviewed two professionals who had had direct contact with Florence Jackson. The first was Susan Clifton – the chiropody assistant who attended Greyfriars residents –

presumably in an attempt to establish the state of Mrs Jackson's feet and the effect of any foot problems on her mobility. Although Clifton needed to consult her treatment cards to recall that she had treated Florence Jackson, there is one significant paragraph in her statement, which throws doubt on the theory that Flo was almost crippled: 'If a resident's feet are in a really bad state,' recalls Clifton in the statement she made to Sergeant Levett, 'they are seen by the chiropodist Miss France. Mrs Jackson was assessed by Miss France and it was determined that I should tend to her.'

The second interview was more useful to the police's case against Sheila Bowler. Sergeant Levett went to take a statement from Mrs Ivy Polly, the Senior Care Officer at Magdala House, the day care centre opposite the Ferry Road Flat attended by the aunts three times a week. She confirmed that her staff would go across the road and collect the sisters. Mrs Jackson, she said, walked with the aid of a zimmer frame and, like her sister, was 'very frail.' She said she had never seen Mrs Jackson walk completely unaided, even within the centre. Although she conceded that the old ladies' flat was clean, she added that 'it lacked the personal attention that is required in running a home' and that her impression of 'the niece Mrs Bowler,' whom she had to contact if money was needed to buy such items as slippers, was that she 'didn't understand the needs of the elderly.'

Three other statements were made to the police that day. Two were from roadworkers employed on Wednesday 13 May to clear the sides of Station Road. But their work there was complete by 10am and they had nothing helpful to report.

The third statement was from Eric Gillham, Aunt Flo's nephew. He was the son of her elder brother Harry, to whom she had been so close in her youth. Indeed, Eric could be said to have greater expectations from Flo's will than Sheila, as, like Bob Bowler, he was her blood nephew. Eric had last seen Sheila at Bob's memorial service in St Mary's, Rye. But he was fond of his cousin-by-marriage and well aware of her kindness to his aunts and indeed to his own mother, Ivy, Flo's sister-in-law. He said he had been surprised to hear from news reports after Aunt Flo's death that she was not very mobile – he had remembered her as 'able to move around unaided.' He ended his statement: 'As far as I am concerned Sheila has always taken an interest in Florence as to her well-being.'

The following day, Friday 22 May, Detective Constable Shaun Kenyon took a trip all the way from Sussex to Huddersfield. He was collecting two cassette tapes recording two conversations with Linda Brierley, the Britannia Rescue operator who took Sheila's call at 10.21 on Wednesday 13 May. The first was between Brierley and Sheila: Brierley said Mrs Bowler informed her that she had an elderly lady passenger with her, so the job had been marked as a priority. The second cassette recorded the conversation between Brierley and Mr Coulmanhole, the recovery truck driver, asking for extra time to help search for a missing old lady.

The weekend of the late May Bank Holiday, Jane came down to Rye from London for a break from her studies – though her exams were not yet over. Sheila had been to a concert at the Barbican on the Friday evening, and Jane travelled back to Rye with her that night. On Saturday afternoon Sheila drove to Bexhill for a five o'clock hairdresser's appointment at Ahmet's, the salon where she had first met Jenny Day. On the way back she noticed a motorcyclist in a layby on the approach to Winchelsea. He was facing towards Hastings but as the Audi passed, he turned around and followed the car through the town. At the bottom of Ferry Hill he turned left along Station Road and Sheila drove on home to Rye.

Because of her suspicions about the motorcyclists on the night of May 13, Sheila made several attempts over that weekend to contact the police and tell them about the biker, but never managed to get a call through to the police station.

On the Sunday morning – 24 May – she made a telephone call to Mrs Cameron-Clarke. She had advised her about the mix-up over the shoes. Now perhaps, as a magistrate, said Sheila, she could give her some further advice. She had discovered that police officers had been along to question Aunt Ivy, Eric Gillham's mother – presumably at the same time as they had taken a statement from Eric, who with his wife lived in the same house as Ivy. The old lady was 95, and Sheila wanted to know whether the police had any right to do this. Mrs Cameron-Clarke asked whether Sheila had a solicitor and when Sheila told her Russell Parkes of Heringtons was acting for her, advised her to consult him. Then, according to Mrs Cameron-Clarke, Sheila raised another subject that was worrying her – the matter of the earlier journey down Station Road.

As soon as the phone conversation ended, Peta Cameron-Clarke picked up the receiver again and rang the police station. That afternoon at 2pm WDS Booth got back to her, and in the section of her statement headed 'Extract Report R7E (page 18 of Booth's statement), she gives her own account of their conversation: 'Mrs Cameron-Clarke explained that Mrs Bowler had phoned, she believes, on the pretext of seeking her opinion as to whether the police had the right to question her aunt. She went on to tell Mrs Cameron-Clarke that the police had been to see her Aunt Ivy, who was 95 years old and said, "Can they do this?" Mrs Cameron-Clarke enquired as to whether Mrs Bowler had a solicitor and she explained that she had seen Russell Parkes. Mrs Cameron-Clarke suggested that Mrs Bowler should address these questions to her solicitor who would obviously be in a position to advise her.'

Booth's statement continues as follows: 'Mrs Bowler then went on to say that while she was talking to Russell Parkes, he had told her not to mention the fact that she had been down Station Road prior to Aunt Flo's death. Mrs Cameron-Clarke felt this was the true reason behind Mrs Bowler's phonecall to her – in view of the fact that Mrs Bowler had already told Mrs Cameron-Clarke on the night of 13/5/92 that she had been down there before. She felt she was trying to drop the hint for Mrs Cameron-Clarke not to mention it.'

It is strange indeed that WDS Booth should pay so much attention to Cameron-Clarke's allegation that Sheila was trying to persuade her to suppress information. Booth knew quite well that Sheila had mentioned her earlier trip down Station Road very early on in her interviews with police. Indeed Booth herself records Sheila mentioning it on the evening of 14 May, the day Mrs Jackson's body was found. If Sheila had already told the police, what on earth was the point of trying to prevent the magistrate from doing so, a full ten days later? And why would Russell Parkes tell Sheila to suppress something the police already knew? It is much more likely that the solicitor advised her not to make a meal of it: he knew that there would be many tyre marks along the road and that to draw police attention to her fears about her own tracks would only arouse their suspicions still further.

Sheila had already told Monica Steward she suspected the police of being capable of evidence-rigging. What if they found the Audi's tyre marks and used them against her?

Sheila's concern at this point, ten days after Aunt Flo's death, was understandable. Although she was unaware of the full extent of police activity as they sought to find evidence to support a charge of murder, it was plain that their enquiries amounted to far more than simple 'elimination.' So although as a solicitor's daughter she would always abide by the instructions of her legal advisors, she was by this time worried enough to be dubious about Russell Parkes's calming assurances. She rang her own solicitor, John Sperring. 'Surely all this stuff is circumstantial,' she said. 'The police can't convict me on that.'

'I'm afraid they can,' said John Sperring.

On the morning of Tuesday, 26 May, Detective Superintendent Brian Foster issued a briefing statement to the officers involved in Operation Dace:

'A recap of the available evidence was carried out and we still do not have evidence to suggest that Mrs Jackson was in Mrs Bowler's car after the alleged puncture. In fact we have statements which lead us to believe she was not in the car. In view of the implausable [sic] accounts given by Mrs Butler [sic] together with these statements which tend to conflict with her account and her changing of the original stories to DS Booth, we must suspect Mrs Bowler of involvement in Mrs Jackson's death. As such, Mrs Bowler will be arrested on suspicion of murder today.'

CHAPTER FIVE

SHALL I BRING MY SHOPPING LIST?

At about 8.45 on the morning of Tuesday, 26 May, the telephone rang in the hallway of 25 Fair Meadow and Sheila hurried to answer it. Though it was half term week and there were no piano lessons to teach, Sheila was up as usual at crack of dawn.

The caller was Detective Sergeant Linda Booth. She wanted to drop by at 9.30, she said, to discuss something and to return the metal bar Sheila had kept in the car to protect herself. Sheila said she was planning to go out shopping but would wait until after Booth arrived.

'I've been trying to get hold of one of you over the whole weekend,' complained Sheila tartly. 'What were you all doing – sunning yourselves on the beach?'

She went on to describe the motorcyclist who had followed her on Saturday. 'I'll see you shortly,' she told the policewoman as the call ended.

At 9.40 a police car drew up outside number 25. But Linda Booth was not in it. Instead two policemen, Detective Constable Poplett and Detective Constable Rowley, got out of the car. DC Poplett takes up the story, as recounted in his official statement written that day, here reproduced exactly as it appears in the bundle of documents prepared for the trial:

'At 9.40am on Tuesday 26th May 1992 I was on duty with DC Rowley when we went to 25 Fair Meadow Rye Sussex.

A lady answered the door and I identified myself to her and then asked "Mrs Shirley [sic] Bowler" she replied "Yes" I said "I am arresting you on suspicion of murdering Florence Jackson." Bowler said "What do you mean" I then said to her "Let me finish please, your not obliged to say anything unless you wish to do so but what you say may be given in evidence do you understand" she replied "I don't believe this but why."

I said to Bowler "I am afraid we can't discuss the case with you but we'll take you to the Police Station where you'll be able to talk to WDS Booth, when everything that needs to be done has been done you will be brought home."

Bowler asked "Well what will be done." I said "Well they will obviously interview you so if you have a diary you might find it useful to refer to for times and dates and what have you"

She replied "Times and dates."

I said "Yes have you got a diary."

She replied "No I've got a calendar."

I said "Well you might find that useful."

Bowler then said "Can I telephone my decorator he's coming here this morning" Bowler then telephoned someone about her decorator Robin Piggott who arrived while she was on the telephone. She then went and spoke to the decorator, on her return she said "What questions can they want to ask me"

I replied "I can't discuss the case with you"

Bowler then said "Well I better not say anything else until my solicitor arrives he's at a trial this morning and won't be available until this afternoon so what will they do just wait."

DC Rowley said "Well we can get you another solicitor"

Bowler said "Well that's no good he won't know me, he won't know about the case."

Bowler then got herself ready and then said "How long will I be."

I replied "I don't know."

She said "Shall I bring my shopping list."

I said "Its up to you."

Bowler then said "Oh my kitchen calender [sic] you want me to bring that."

I said "You might find it useful."

She said "It's all such a shock especially when I'm innocent, how long will I be."

I replied "I don't know."

At 9.58 we left Bowlers address and conveyed her to Hastings Police Station on the way Bowler said as we went round Strand quay roundabout Rye "Oh we're going to Hastings not Rye."

DC Rowley said "Thats right."

As we travelled round the hairpin bend on the A259 at Winchelsea we drove past a Police witness appeal board, as we went round the bend Bowler said "You still can't read that sign."

DC Rowley said "No its in the wrong place."

She replied "Thats right, people coming round can't read it they're having to look where they're going."

There was no further conversation until we reached Hastings memorial where there was a brief discussion about pedal cyclist's wearing helmets.

At 10.30 am we arrived at Hastings Police Station where I handed Bowler over to the custody sergeant PS Sparks.'

At the police station Sheila was asked to read through the above record of the last 50 minutes that DC Poplett had just written in his pocket book. History does not relate whether she corrected his spelling and punctuation but she must have been sorely tempted. Her reactions throughout this period are reminiscent of her behaviour on the night of May 13. She said later that she was so shocked at the 'arresting speech' that she had to sit down on the telephone stool in her front hall. Her amazement is patent in her next remarks, and especially in her repetition of the officer's phrase 'times and dates,' as if she is momentarily stunned. But since childhood she had been taught to pull herself together at times of adversity and this is exactly what we see her doing here, taking refuge in the immediate practicalities of the situation just as she did after the news of Aunt Flo's death – though she has learned enough from her earlier experiences with the police to demand her own solicitor.

We see her sorting out the decorator and even asking DC Poplett if she can bring her shopping list – presumably thinking she is being taken to Rye police station for formalities which will be over soon enough for her to do her usual shopping errands. She is momentarily disorientated on the journey in the police car, when she realises they are bypassing the familiar Rye police station and heading instead for Hastings. But by the time they reach Winchelsea she has recovered her self-control and is back to her usual bossy manner, ticking off the police for placing the appeal posters in the wrong place and remarking on the need for pedal cyclists to wear helmets.

Nevertheless Sheila cannot have been prepared for what happened at the police station. It was one thing dealing with police officers in her own spacious and comfortable home, quite another being locked in a police station cell. Over a year later she wrote from Holloway prison, describing what she could remember, though on paper she expresses no more emotion than she does if she is describing the experience verbally: 'I was taken into a small room and all "vicious" items were taken from my handbag (scissors, nailfile, homeopathic tablets). Then I was locked in a cell. I asked for my solicitor and was told I could have the duty solicitor if mine was not available. The cell was very dirty, with just a box-like bed with a grubby thick plastic-covered mattress and toilet in the corner.'

Within the hour Russell Parkes had arrived with his assistant Emma Kerr. For the first time cracks began to appear in the shell Sheila had built round herself and for the first time since this nightmare began she broke down: 'I think I was in a daze and just didn't know what was going to happen next so when Russell arrived I burst into tears.'

Russell Parkes told Sheila that it was best for her to elect to make no comment at all to any questions the police put to her. Otherwise, he warned, 'they'll tie you up in knots and we'll never get you out of here.' He told her that seventy-five per cent of his clients chose to say 'No comment' to police questioning. Sheila, ever the dutiful solicitor's daughter, took his advice.

The first interrogation lasted just three minutes and like all the subsequent interviews was carried out by DS Renno and WDS Booth in the presence of Russell Parkes and Emma Kerr. Like all the interrogations it was tape-recorded. The transcripts of the tapes – the extracts printed here are reproduced just as they appear in the official police version – make fascinating but chilling reading.

At the outset, after giving her full name and date of birth, Sheila, as instructed by Russell Parkes, declares: 'I have nothing to say at this interview' and adds rather falteringly, 'And I do not wish to say anything unless in the presence of my, at any interview in, except in the presence of my solicitor.'

DS Renno asks her to run through her actions on 13 May and WDS Booth prompts her, asking if she would like to explain anything, for instance about her aunt. The emphasis from the outset is about financial arrangements: whether Sheila had power of attorney, whether she has ever signed or used any of the aunt's cheques. To every question Sheila replies, 'No comment.' After three minutes of this, Booth remarks, 'So you're making no comment because you're guilty of this offence?' and Renno warns that 'other officers are out at this moment seeing various members of your family.'

Although she dutifully continued to answer 'No comment' as instructed, Sheila later told friends she was in fact terribly worried about the effect the news of her arrest would have on Simon and Jane, especially as Russell had not at this point managed to contact them.

It is not surprising Simon was out of reach: he was himself being interviewed at work at the Customs and Excise Office in Maidstone by Police Sergeant Levett, the officer who had taken the first statement from him on the day Aunt Flo's body was found. It seems likely that Simon was still under suspicion, at least as an accessory to murder, because he was questioned about driving, though in fact he cannot drive at all. He had an alibi from 10.05 until 11.05 when he was at the Globe pub: if he was part of the plot the police thought Sheila had hatched, he would have had to leave the spot where Mrs Jackson entered the river and move very quickly indeed to be at the pub by 10.05 – the distance would be impossible to cover on foot in such a short space of time, and Sheila would not have had time to drive him there and then return to stage her breakdown. If she had done so as part of an evil plot, she would have risked being seen by plenty of witnesses: as it was, 28 motorists noticed the Audi parked on the A259.

Simon said he did not own a car and had never driven one. He was also asked once again about the walking sticks owned by the family, and the existence of the silver torch which Sheila thought was missing from the Audi's glove compartment. He said he had never seen such a torch. Finally he was asked whether his mother was the sole beneficiary of his father's will. Yes, he replied, she was. That evening he was interviewed again, this time at his lodgings in Maidstone.

While Sheila was undergoing her first interrogation that Tuesday morning, Jane was in central London, sitting at a desk at the Royal Academy of Music struggling with the third examination in her degree finals. It was a three-hour paper on music analysis, beginning at 10 o'clock. Jane knew she had not prepared for it properly because of her anxiety about the situation at home, and now she could not concentrate at all. In retrospect she thinks she might have had some strange premonition that something disastrous would happen that day: 'I kept fidgeting and in the end I thought I must be disturbing everyone else. So I got up and walked out. I left at 11.30am, half way through the exam. I went straight back to the flat, went to bed and fell asleep.'

While Jane was sleeping in her London flat, at Hastings police station lunch was being served to Sheila: 'It was handed to me through a hatch in the door. It was meat, potatoes, cabbage and carrots on a plastic plate with plastic utensils. I managed some of it but I couldn't eat whatever the pudding was – it was covered in custard. After a while Russell returned and said they would question me again later.' All afternoon Sheila sat alone in the police station cell and waited.

Jane was woken at 6pm by a ring on the doorbell. Still half asleep, she went downstairs. Her studio flat in South London was at the top of a family home but that evening she was alone. On the doorstep stood a long-haired woman and a man. Jane had no idea who these smartly dressed strangers were. They identified themselves as plainclothes police officers from Bexhill CID. The man said he was Police Sergeant Levett. In fact – though Jane did not know it – this was the officer who had interviewed Simon earlier. Jane cannot remember the woman officer's name.

Standing there on the doorstep, Levett broke the news: 'Your mother was arrested this morning on suspicion of murdering your Aunt Flo,' he said. 'We'd like to come in and ask you a few questions.'

Jane remembers shaking from head to foot as the officers followed her upstairs. The policewoman asked if she could put the kettle on. Jane nodded, stunned.

Jane asked how long all this would take – she had an exam next day and needed to study. 'It won't take very long,' said Sergeant Levett.

When the tea was ready the questions began. The officers wanted to know when Jane was last in Rye and then about the phonecalls she had made to her mother on the night of 13 May. They asked what Sheila had told Jane about her movements when she finally managed to speak to her that evening. According to her statement Jane replied simply that her mother 'had a puncture, parked the car then went off to get help leaving Aunt Flo in the car. Then when she returned she found Aunt Flo missing, the car door open and the walking stick missing.'

The officers asked when she had last seen Aunt Flo: Jane said it was at Easter when she took her an Easter egg. She described Aunt Flo's mobility as very limited, and that getting out of a chair was 'a major performance.' She said she was not aware at that time that Aunt Flo had stomach cancer: 'but I have since been informed by my mother that the Doctor at the Royal East Sussex Hospital had said that Aunt Flo had stomach cancer and only had a short period to live. I have only found out from my mother since Aunt Flo's death that the Doctor had stated she had a limited period to live.'

She remembered there being walking sticks in the hall cupboard at home. She recalled her mother 'mentioning the possibility of Aunt Flo staying with her for a few days... some while ago' and added that during the first of her four phonecalls on the night of 13 May, Simon told her that 'my mother was collecting Aunt Flo and bringing her back to the house for a few days.' Everything she said corroborated what Sheila had told the police at earlier interviews.

The interview lasted three hours, though the statement written down by PS Levett and signed by Jane amounts to just six pages. As they reached the end of each page, Jane was asked to check it through and sign it.

'I made them alter some things. They kept wanting to know how close I was to Aunt Flo. I explained that we used to be close but now she was a very old lady and relationships change.'

When the officers left at 9 o'clock they gave Jane the number of Hastings police station and said she could telephone her mother there in the morning.

Jane was still trembling: 'After they left I walked back upstairs shaking my head and saying, 'I can't believe it, I can't believe it' – the very words her mother had used when DC Poplett arrested her earlier that day.

While the police were interviewing Jane that evening, her mother was being taken from her cell in Hastings police station for her second interview. Russell Parkes had returned and the questioning began at 7.21 and this time lasted 27 minutes. It is worth examining the transcript in some detail because it reveals the way the police were constructing their case against Sheila. It also reveals the effect both on the interrogators and their interrogatee of Parkes's advice to keep silent.

Years later, Sheila was shown the transcripts of the taped interviews and was able to give the answers she would have given to the police had she been allowed. It is difficult to assess the wisdom of Parkes's advice that

Sheila should make no comment. Sheila's explanations might have cleared up many police misconceptions, but her manner – still furious so long after the events – might have alienated her interrogators still further.

David Renno again begins the interrogation. Immediately he suggests that there were plenty of witnesses who saw Sheila walking away from the car, and that one of them in particular was also willing to testify that at that time she was sure the car was empty.

When Sheila again makes no comment, Renno remarks, 'You say no comment so we'll assume that person's telling the truth?'

'No comment,' replies Sheila, raising her eyes to the heavens, no doubt in frustration at not being permitted to give these ridiculous questions a sharp riposte. This seems to infuriate Renno still further and he resorts to heavy sarcasm:

'Sorry, am I boring you? You're looking to the ceiling. I didn't know whether you was being bored.'

The interrogation proceeds, with Renno implying that Sheila invented the walking stick and refused to take the zimmer because she knew the old lady would not need it. That long before the Soans could see the car was empty, Sheila, the same distance away, was the first to say, 'Oh, she's not in the car' – because she knew very well that Aunt Flo was already in the river. That a motorist called Mr Beckett also drove past and also testified that the car was empty. That all the nursing home staff said Aunt Flo could not walk – and that even Sheila herself said the same thing on the first day of the enquiry. Renno becomes more aggressive and hectoring: Sheila's story about getting help is, he says, 'just a lot of nonsense.'

At this point WDS Booth intervenes, repeating Renno's assertion that there are many witnesses who saw Sheila walking away from an empty car, and that the old lady could not possibly have walked to her death alone. Booth then refers to the 'discrepancies' quoted in her own statement, notably the conversation with Mrs Cameron-Clarke when Sheila's earlier journey down Station Road was mentioned. Booth refers to Sheila's phonecall to the magistrate as a 'fishing expedition' (was this metaphor a subconscious allusion to the codename 'Operation Dace'?). Sheila was, says Booth, 'trying to find out certain things.' How can it be, asks Booth, that Sheila alleges she does not know the area, 'yet off the top of your head you were able to quote the name of the little cottage on the bend, Ferryfield Cottage.'

At this Booth notices that Sheila's 'No comment' takes on a different tone: 'Now you sounded cross. Were you, are you cross that I'm making these accusations?'

Sheila would like to have explained that yes, she was cross. The idea of the 'fishing expedition' was ridiculous as the police already knew all about her earlier journey down Station Road. She had told them about it herself on 14 May. She knew the cottage's name because Bob happened to have pointed it out to her as they drove past one day as the birthplace of Ted Hickmott, who assisted Bob in his churchwarden duties at St Mary's. Coincidentally he had also been an employee of Russell Parkes's own firm, Heringtons. But Russell had told her to keep silent. So to all Booth's challenging gibes that follow – her comments on Sheila's apparent lack of concern about Aunt Flo's death, her refusal to protest her innocence, the 'discrepancy' of the chrome torch – Sheila continues to repeat, 'No comment.'

Booth now produces an album of post-mortem photographs, presumably in the hope of shocking Sheila into a confession. She shows Sheila a picture of Aunt Flo's hand clutching a tissue.

'She's got her right arm plastered, she's got a tissue in her left hand. If you're trying to get us to believe that she's carrying the tissue in her left hand, she's also carrying a walking stick and a chrome torch...'

'No comment.'

Renno and Booth now alternate their questioning in classic interrogatory style, piling up the 'evidence' against Sheila in the hope that she will 'break' and confess to murdering Aunt Flo. They tell her that this very day 'tests are being carried out with identical slippers just to see what markings would be made if she did shuffle over there.' 'I am quite happy,' says Renno, 'they're going to be far more marked than poor Flo's were because she didn't shuffle round there, did she?'

'No comment.'

'Presumably,' says Renno, 'you want us to find the person concerned then presumably you would do all your best to help us and answer just some of the questions.'

'No comment.'

'So it tends to suggest,' goes on Renno, 'that we're not looking for anybody else... What we're saying to you is that Aunt Flo certainly wasn't in that car when you parked on the hairpin bend. Because there's no way she was mysteriously whizzed out of that car and out in the river half a mile away.'

Why, asks Renno, did Sheila not decide to do something about her tyre problem till she had Flo 'in the middle of nowhere in the dark.' He comments, according to the tape transcript: 'Total nonsense innit. Total nonsense!'

The questions move to the tyre damage then to Aunt Flo's injuries. 'You knew she'd have got a graze to her face, didn't you? Because you'd actually spoken to Mrs Cameron-Clarke about it.'

Of course I knew, fumed Sheila. I saw her face in the mortuary. But 'No comment' was all she said.

At this point Russell Parkes interrupts, stopping Renno in full flow, his voice introducing a moment of bathos in the tape transcript:

'I know this is an inappropriate time but I'm going to burst it's so hot. I wonder whether we could just have a breather.'

'Yeah, I can understand that, it is unbearably hot,' says Booth.

'Yeah, it is fairly, fairly warm in here,' mutters Renno.

'Mrs Bowler?' asks Renno, suddenly polite again, 'Do you wish to add anything?'

'No comment.'

And the second interrogation is over.

After a twelve minute break during which Russell takes the opportunity to warn Sheila that she is to be held overnight, the questioning begins again. This final session of the day lasts 23 minutes. Sheila continues to reply 'No comment' to every question.

Renno begins by returning to the allegation that the car was empty when Sheila left it. Why, he asks, if Aunt Flo was left sitting in the car, did nobody else see her? He dismisses two alternative explanations: that the old lady walked to her death; or that she was seized by an unknown abductor.

'The only other way she went is that she was taken to the river and dumped in the drink. And I think you were party to that.'

'No comment.'

The visit to Tom and Jenny Day was, says Renno, a 'charade': the only reason Sheila raised her voice to Aunt Flo was 'to try and impress upon Mr Day that your Aunt was in the car.'

'No comment.'

Renno then queries the timings recalled by Sheila, and Booth reminds her of the second suspicious pair of shoes and the journey in the police car when they passed Station Road. Melodramatically Booth demands,

'Did that send a shiver down your neck Sheila?'

'No comment.'

Renno reminds Sheila of Russell Parkes's words when he witnessed Sheila's statement (Sheila has always maintained they were in fact Renno's words, but on this occasion Parkes is present and does not contradict Renno).

'I think Mr Parkes who's here made some comment about you shouldn't keep changing your mind. Well you shouldn't change your mind so many times. Or words to that effect.'

'No comment.'

Booth reminds Sheila that she had no microwave and no food in the house prepared for Aunt Flo. Simon, she says, disagrees with Sheila's timings for the phone calls.

'No comment.' (sighs)

'Is Simon wrong?'

'Is he telling lies?'

Booth appeals to Sheila's sense of duty:

'If we go along with your story she was in the car, I would have thought a woman such as you should be concerned about leaving her in the car in that position. It's getting dusk, the light's not good, you talk about the big lorries coming round the bend and nearly hitting Mrs Cameron-Clarke's, you were worried about her car but not your own with poor old Flo sat in it unable to even get out or do anything... And why come and collect the woman at that time of night beats me anyway. At 8 o'clock, I mean most women of her age in the home, they're, they're ready for or getting ready for bed at half past seven in the evening. Here's you collecting her at 8 and taking her on a jolly round East Sussex to get back at home... would have been 10, quarter past the... It doesn't show a great deal of care or concern for an elderly relative does it?'.

'No comment.'

Finally the subject of Mrs Jackson's will is raised. Renno puts to Sheila that she was short of money, that she had power of attorney over Aunt Flo's accounts and that she was the sole beneficiary of both aunts' wills. Booth's final comment appeals to Sheila's personal feelings:

'You must feel yourself embarrassed even finding yourself in a police station [be]cause you've not been in this situation before that in itself must be uncomfortable but do you find the fact that we are sitting here accusing you of murder an uncomfortable situation?'

'No comment.'

Left alone for the night, locked in the police cell, Sheila felt nothing but a 'great feeling of disbelief that this was happening.' More than a year later, writing from Holloway prison, she recalled that 'by evening after Russell had left, the warder was a bit more kindly disposed towards me and let me go and have a shower or wash. I opted for the wash down as the shower was a bit public. Given toothpaste and towel. I was then given a cup of tea in a plastic cup and a cheese sandwich. The warder came back later with a blanket and a book for me to read – the *Readers' Digest.'*

In spite of the discomfort she managed to get some sleep but was awake at 6.45am when Jane phoned – only to be told that her mother was still asleep. When Jane tried again later she was told she could not speak to her.

At 7.30am Sheila was given a cooked breakfast of eggs, beans and a cup of tea and Russell Parkes arrived at 8 to warn her that she was to be re-arrested that morning and interviewed further.

This final interview, the longest of all four, began at 11.57am and lasted 33 minutes. Renno told Sheila that police officers had been to search her house and removed some of her clothing and four walking sticks. They had also interviewed Jane and Simon and found more 'discrepancies' – about the state of Aunt Flo's health and her mobility, about arrangements for her visit to 25 Fair Meadow, about the silver torch. The possibility of Aunt Flo's having stomach cancer is raised, then the subject of euthanasia.

'Were you ever under the impression that she was soon due to die?'

'No comment.'

'Mrs Bowler, do you believe in euthanasia?'

'No comment.'

'What I'm asking is why was Flo Jackson killed? Why did she have to die?'

'No comment'

'Were you jealous of maybe Jane's closeness to her?'

'No comment.'

'I can see no other reason why this lady should have to be killed.'

Booth develops this psychological guessing game: was Sheila perhaps angry and bitter that Aunt Flo lived to the age of 90 when her own husband Bob died at a much younger age? How can she have behaved so callously as to make biscuits when her aunt's body has been found in the river?

'You were walking around the house almost full of the joys of spring – totally detached.'

How, immediately after identifying the body, can Sheila ask 'will the local authorities pay for the burial?' Is she really this cold, callous woman, or is there something else, like money worries? 'We've heard that you're short of money. You're frowning. I mean if that's not the case tell us, tell us people are telling us wrong. We can only go by what people are telling us unless you tell us different, what are we to believe?'

How Sheila longed to talk about Bob's good pension, about her substantial £150,000 house with its mortgage fully paid up twelve years earlier, about her own reasonable income, about the £15,000 of savings she had in her bank.

But instead, as directed, she said, 'No comment.'

The evidence of the Greyfriars staff (that Aunt Flo was completely immobile) and of Judith Pearson and Christopher Beckett (the two passing motorists who thought the Audi was empty when they saw Sheila walking away from it) is now rehearsed. When Renno quotes Sheila's statements about the motorcyclists she can scarcely contain herself:

'You're shaking your head. Am I saying this wrong?'

'No comment.'

Booth describes a saloon car sighted at 10pm near the pumping station by Mr Giddings, the caravan park owner:

'You've closed your eyes very heavily there Mrs Bowler. Is that uncomfortable for you to hear?'

'No comment'

The interrogation ends with Renno describing Sheila's 'flippant' attitude, 'making biscuits as though it's [a] common, common occurrence to find out that your Aunt's just been found dead.'

Booth chips in:

'I think up until now you've sort of tried to detach yourself and close it out of your mind… you're not sitting there protesting your innocence. Even now you're not even looking angry, you're looking uncomfortable and embarrassed and maybe ashamed which I would expect. I'm sure you are ashamed and maybe you didn't intend for her to die. I don't know, unless you tell us we don't know.'

'No comment.'

'The time now is exactly 12.30pm' said Detective Sergeant Renno, 'and I'll switch the machine off.'

In one respect Russell Parkes's strategy had worked: Sheila was released pending further investigations. Perhaps if she been allowed to respond to police questioning Booth and Renno would, as Parkes warned, have 'tied her up in knots.' But she left the interrogation inwardly blazing with indignation that she had had to sit listening to such outrageously inaccurate speculations put to her by the police, whilst she was unable to say a word in her own defence.

Sheila was still almost speechless with rage as Parkes drove her back to Rye. Yet despite her resentment of the behaviour of Booth and Renno, she felt that because she had been released, the nightmare was now at an end. By the time Parkes's car drew up outside 25 Fair Meadow she felt confident enough to give the surprised solicitor a hug of thanks. She was later to write from Holloway that she had felt 'so grateful to be home' and 'really thought that was the end of it all.'

Just as she had embarked on the biscuit-making that so enraged Linda Booth, Sheila again immersed herself in practicalities. Years later she recalled her reaction.

'I had to dash to the bank to get money for Robin the decorator as he was going on holiday next day, then I popped in to see Anne [Wood, her close friend] in the shop – that's the Sue Ryder charity shop in Rye High Street where Anne worked. "Am I glad to see you!" she said. Then I went home and got sorted.'

Meanwhile in London Jane was trying to continue with her music examinations, without any idea what was happening to her mother in the police station. She tried all morning to telephone but was not allowed to speak to Sheila. The next exam was due to start at 2pm, so in desperation she went to find her tutor.

'He already knew my great aunt had been found drowned – my cello teacher had told him. Now I had to tell him that my mum was arrested on suspicion of murder. He was really sympathetic and told me I didn't have to go into the exam – they could give me an aggregate mark instead. But I wanted to do it. I thought it would take my mind off things.'

Jane went into the exam and somehow managed to finish it. When it was over she rushed out of the examination room to a telephone outside the students' common room and called Hastings police station. Mrs Bowler had left about three o'clock, they told her. Jane rang Fair Meadow but there was no answer: at this point Sheila must have been in the High Street talking to Anne Wood. Like her mother, Jane imagined that the release from the police station had put an end to this whole awful affair. 'I thought it was all OK now, so I was on a real high.'

When she finally spoke to her mother later that evening Sheila reassured her further. It was all over – everything was fine now and there was nothing to worry about. It seems both mother and daughter genuinely believed – naive as it may sound in hindsight – that 'this was the end of it all.' Sheila insisted there was no need for Jane to come home – she should carry on with her lectures, rehearsals and exams. Jane took her advice, completing her finals on 17 June.

And indeed, Sheila continued with her own life as usual too – with just one change. The day after Sheila was released from Hastings police station, Anne Wood pushed a note through her door offering to come back to stay with her on weekdays – an offer Sheila gratefully accepted. Anne's children, like Sheila's, had grown up and left home. She was working full-time in the charity shop during the day, but said she would enjoy Sheila's company in the evenings. She arrived that night and stayed till July, sleeping in Jane's bedroom. Anne would return to her own house in Icklesham at weekends when Simon came back to stay with his mother.

When half-term week ended the following Monday Sheila returned to her pupils at Battle Abbey, Bricklehurst Manor and Marlborough House and carried on with her teaching schedule for the next six weeks as if nothing had happened. The only sign that anything was amiss was the occasional unmarked police car patrolling in Fair Meadow, observed by some of Sheila's neighbours from behind their lace curtains.

But the police were continuing to pursue their investigations. On the day Sheila was released from Hastings police station, they were particularly busy. Detective Constable Poplett, who had arrested Sheila and interviewed many of the witnesses, took a statement from Sylvia Archer, a dispensing chemist, who came forward and said she drove past the stranded Audi. The Audi, she said, was empty and three people, two of whom she recognized as the Soans, were coming towards it. This meant her timing was too late to be of any help to the police case.

On the same day Detective Constable Rowley, Sheila's other arresting officer, was interviewing William Brien, an unemployed man in his mid-30s. He had spent Wednesday May 13 drinking in a Rye pub, consuming seven pints of beer. He left the pub at 9.45pm but missed the last train from Rye and decided to walk home. But he was too tired and fell asleep in a field on the Hastings side of Winchelsea. By this time he thought it was about 11pm but as he did not wear a watch he could not be sure. The only point in Brien's statement to interest the police was his failure to see any motorcyclists – but then he had drunk seven pints of beer.

Also on the 27th, PC Roy Panniers, a traffic officer stationed at Hastings, was asked to test-drive the route taken by Sheila on the night of 13 May when she drove from Mr Day's house in Cooden to the Ferry Hill junction. He recorded the distance as 16.1 miles and timed it as taking 31 minutes 54 seconds. A slight variation of the route was a little further – 17.5 miles – and this took Panniers 33 minutes and 42 seconds to complete.

The first journey began at 8.30pm, with traffic 'light to moderate.' The second journey began at 9.27pm and 'traffic was generally light.' PC Panniers adhered to all speed limits and never exceeded 50mph. Panniers may of course have been driving faster in his powerful police car than Sheila in her elderly Audi. He says he 'did not exceed 50mph,' suggesting that he did travel up to that speed for much of the journey. Nearly a year later, in June 1993, he was to do a third test-drive, taking 32 minutes and 18 seconds.

Sheila had said in the past that Aunt Flo disliked being driven at more than 40 mph. She was accustomed to driving elderly people around and keeping at a steady pace: Helen Goodwin was one of those who vouched for her being 'a good driver, not a fast driver.'

Another police officer called Harrison did a test drive of Sheila's earlier journey, from Greyfriars to Mr Day's house, a distance of 15.7 miles, and timed it at 34.5 minutes, not exceeding 40 mph.

These timings are crucial, because the police were plainly trying to prove that Sheila had ample time in the period between leaving Mr Day and arriving at the Soans' house to commit murder. If Mrs Dobson was right that she left Greyfriars at 8.03 she could reach Cooden about 8.40, according to Harrison's timings. She herself thought she was within five minutes of the Days' house at 8.45pm. If she left Mr Day soon after 9pm, on Panniers' timings she could have reached the Station Road junction at about 9.35. Mr Soan thought she arrived at his door between 10 and 10.15. The police calculated she could reach Winchelsea, drive off the A259, put Mrs Jackson in the river at the pumping station, drive back on to the A259, deflate the tyre and start off towards the Soans' house, all within this 25 to 40 minute gap. Though Mrs Dobson's time of 8.03 was accepted as correct because she was certain she looked at her office clock, there are in fact only two fixed points – exactly verifiable times – in the whole case: 10.21 when Britannia Rescue recorded Sheila's call; and 10.42 when Mr Soan's call to the police was logged.

On May 28 the police asked Mr Coulmanhole, the recovery truck driver, to help them with an experiment. He was shown a B registration Audi very like Sheila's and asked to watch while an officer deflated the front nearside tyre. He was told to stop the officer when the tyre reached the pressure level he had noticed on Sheila's tyre the night of May 13. When he stopped the process, the tyre pressure was found to be 10 psi. Photographs were taken of the tyre at every stage of the experiment.

Another statement, dated 12 June, was taken from David Price, a Home Office forensic scientist based at the Forensic Science Laboratory in Aldermaston, near Reading. He said that on 21 May he had received the front nearside wheel and tyre of an Audi 80, registration number WJK 714T. The statement rehearses Sheila's account of the problem with the car and its removal to her home by the recovery vehicle. Price continues: 'When examined by police officers the following day, the tyre was found to be almost flat and was then pumped up so the car could be driven to the police station.' Mr Price says he was asked to find out if there was any fault with the wheel and its Michelin MXL tubeless tyre. When he measured the tyre pressure on 27 May he found it to be 18.5psi and that the tyre was 'in good condition.' Having checked the whole wheel including the tyre, and found no damage of any kind, he describes how he reinflated it to the recommended pressure of 25 pounds per square inch and 'found no loss of pressure during a test over a 13 day period.'

In his opinion, says Price, 'the only way air was lost from the tyre was via the valve' which he found undamaged. He concedes that 'it is feasible that there could have been dirt trapped in the valve core prior to the police having reinflated the tyre and so it could have had a slow leak prior to coming to rest.' But if the valve cap was fitted normally, as it was when he received it in the laboratory, (though PC Reese, who had pumped up the tyre, said in his statement that he did 'not recall whether the dust cap was replaced on the valve') 'it would have prevented loss of air, even if the valve core had dirt in it.'

Price therefore reached the conclusion that 'the only way this tyre can have deflated is for air to have been let out of the valve at the point where the vehicle came to rest.'

This conclusion seemed to the police yet another piece of damning evidence against Sheila Bowler. But Price did not attempt to explain how it was that the pressure of the tyre when it first entered police possession was 15psi as measured by vehicle examiner PC Watson, but had now *increased* to a pressure of 18.5psi. Nor how it was that PC Watson recorded the tyre as being 'in poor condition' while Price had said the very opposite.

In early July Sheila and Simon went to London to attend Jane's graduation ceremony, held in St Marylebone Church opposite the Royal

Academy of Music. Princess Diana, troubled by her impending divorce, had cancelled her speech and everyone was disappointed. But while other families made the best of it and laughed and celebrated, for the Bowler family this was not a joyful occasion. Sheila felt upset for Jane, who had been awarded a lower second class degree. She had heard her preparing her examination piece, the Elgar Cello Concerto, and thought she played quite brilliantly. But obviously her written exams had let her down. Sheila thought Jane deserved a higher grade and was sure her result had been affected by the police questioning in the middle of the examinations.

The family joined the audience in applauding the address given by students' union president Aled Jones (who a few years earlier had found fame as the chorister in the hit record *Walking in the Air* from the film *The Snowman*). But they all felt overwhelmed with sadness. The rain poured relentlessly down and as they filed out towards the reception, Sheila, Simon and Jane remembered Bob's pride in his daughter's progress and wished he could have been there. The tension of the months since his death had taken their toll, and by the time the official photographer was ready to take graduation photographs, Jane was in tears and had to leave.

A few days later Russell Parkes told Sheila he was going on holiday and made an appointment for Friday 10 July for her to meet Dave Harding, one of the partners at Heringtons. Parkes had by this time spent many hours interviewing Sheila at her home, recording the interviews on tape. 'He said he wanted to know my whole life story, everything about me, so I told him all I could.'

In the two weeks when he was away, Parkes now said, Sheila might need another solicitor, just in case anything cropped up in his absence.

At around this time Sheila also consulted another lawyer – but not about police suspicions against her. Ever since Bob's funeral she had been growing increasingly uneasy as she thought about the way the hospital had treated him. At the time some of the nurses told her they had expressed concern at his rapid decline and felt action should have been taken more quickly to try and save him. Now Sheila's colleagues at Bricklehurst Manor advised her to consult a local QC, George Pulman, whose children attended the school. In fact Sheila knew him already – she gave piano lessons to one of his children. Pulman, a commercial silk, gave what advice he could, but was far more concerned when Sheila mentioned, almost in passing, her own involvement with the police. He told her that though she had been released after police questioning, this was not necessarily the end of the affair. Indeed, he said gravely, this was a matter to be taken very seriously. Sheila said confidently that her lawyers had everything in hand and Pulman recalls that she did not seem too concerned.

On Tuesday July 7, Detective Sergeants Renno and Booth once again travelled the route that Sheila Bowler said she had taken on the afternoon of 13 May. This time they had with them Mr David Wrighting, a civilian technician who was operating a video camera. Renno drove the car and Booth made a running commentary. The purpose of the video was to demonstrate that the route taken by Mrs Bowler was a very illogical one, if she was, as she had claimed, in a hurry to try and return Simon's shoes in Hastings on the way to teach at Battle Abbey. They could not know that Sheila's behaviour was so often illogical and impulsive. She had not worked out the most sensible route to Hastings: she had simply behaved like most women trying to juggle the needs of work and family. She had looked at her watch, decided she might have time for the errand, and shot off down Dumb Woman's Lane, only changing her mind when she hit a traffic jam.

Dr Michael Heath, the Home Office pathologist, spent Wednesday 8 July writing up his official record of the post-mortem he had carried out on Mrs Jackson on 14 May in the presence of five police officers. He noted that he had found 'bruising to the left and right upper arms which was consistent with having been caused by restraint being applied to this region from a hand grip.' He found 'extensive bruising and tearing of the muscles of the shoulder blades' caused, he concluded, by 'vigorous movements of the upper limbs whilst the victim was trying to save herself from the immersion process.' He found 'a bruise over the left hairline and outer aspect left eye which was consistent with having been caused by blows to these regions.' There was 'no evidence of natural disease that could have caused or contributed to death.' He recorded the cause of death as immersion – in layman's terms, Mrs Florence Jackson had met her end by drowning.

At 8am that same Wednesday morning, 8 July, two days before her appointment with Dave Harding of Heringtons, Sheila was up and about early as usual, though her friend Anne Wood was still upstairs in bed. Sheila was getting ready to go out shopping, then in the late afternoon she had her Battle Abbey lessons to teach.

The doorbell rang and as Sheila went to answer it she raised her hand to draw back the heavy velvet curtains covering the glazed front door. Through a gap in the curtains she could see that the two people waiting at the front door were David Renno and Linda Booth.

Sheila's hand fell from the curtain. She rushed upstairs to Anne and shook her awake.

'It's the police! They've come to get me again!'

George Pulman QC had been right. This matter was far from over.

Sheila rushed back down again and, composing herself as best she could, opened the door.

Anne hurried downstairs and appeared in the lounge in her dressing-gown, just as Booth and Renno were explaining that they needed Sheila down at the station for extra questioning about some new evidence.

'Good morning, Mrs Wood,' said David Renno as Sheila went off to make some toast to sustain her in the ordeal ahead.

Later Anne was to tell Sheila, 'I expect you wondered how they knew my name?'

Although Anne had not said anything to Sheila for fear of worrying her, the police had in fact visited her the previous afternoon when she was at home in Icklesham before returning to Rye to stay the night with Sheila as usual.

'They knocked on the door. I opened it and said good afternoon but I wouldn't invite them in. Renno said, "I believe you're a friend of Mrs Sheila Bowler. We're investigating the murder of Mrs Jackson, her husband's aunt." "I never met Mrs Jackson", I said, "And I know nothing about the case." Then they went away.'

Sheila gulped down some breakfast then got into Linda Booth's red BMW. This time she was driven further to Bexhill police station.

Parkes's colleague Dave Harding was summoned to the police station and introduced himself to Sheila.

'I didn't think we'd meet this soon,' he joked, trying to lighten the sombre mood.

At 10.09 Renno and Booth began their fifth interrogation. This was the longest of all and lasted 42 minutes. According to the verbatim transcripts of the taped interview, Booth begins by focusing on cheques signed by Aunt Flo, the earlier ones made out, significantly, to Bob and Sheila jointly. As Sheila had explained to Monica Steward, she and Bob sometimes paid the aunt's bills, and Booth now tells her the police have spoken to Steward and confirmed this. No doubt had Sheila been able to explain, she could have clarified any confusion in a matter of seconds. Later from Holloway she wrote, 'I was dying to say something all the time.' But as in the May interviews she followed Parkes's instructions and Harding must have agreed, for he took no action to change them.

Once again Booth challenges Sheila to explain the confusion over Aunt Flo's visit: the earlier arrangement for 6 May, the plan to visit Jane and the Bishop's Stortford friends, the failure to make up a bed, the refusal of the Home's offer of a zimmer, the 'imaginary' walking stick, the missing chrome torch, the failure to have the tyre checked, the opinion of the forensic expert that nothing is wrong with it – 'I mean, that is damning evidence.'

Booth tells Sheila she is a liar: 'I'm afraid that there is no nicer word that I can put.'

Interestingly at this point Booth still seems prepared to consider the theory that Aunt Flo could have walked to her death: 'All right then, let's go on the assumption then that your aunt has this surge of adrenalin that people talk about then. Old people sometimes have. And she's there herself. This half mile. This immobile lady has had this surge of adrenalin, which we accept elderly folk do in certain circumstances.' But Booth immediately rejects the theory on the grounds that the old lady could not have got that far in the twenty minutes or half hour that Sheila was away.

The tragic circumstances of Bob's death, and the possibility of Sheila's bitterness, are rehearsed once again: was something said on the journey from Greyfriars, asks Booth, 'that really you got quite angry and bitter about?... is there something that happened on that journey that you snapped on?'

'No comment.'

Booth now moves to alleged inconsistencies over timings and suggests Sheila is lying to try to shorten the period when she could have had time to put Flo in the river. She repeats the allegations of callous behaviour. According to Booth, WPC Ellis, the young officer who attended Fair Meadow on the morning of May 14, had steeled herself to deal with Sheila's grief.

'But she didn't have to. Within minutes you were up and carried on with your biscuits as if nothing had happened. Were you blocking it out of your mind?'

'No comment.'

The inconsistencies, says Booth, 'are quite monumental in themselves. They're not just little slight various [sic] on a theme, they are complete alterations.'

Nor, puts in Renno, has Sheila been very helpful to the police.

'In fact ... to say you were evasive was putting it mildly. I mean you weren't over co-operative and helpful to us to make yourself readily available to have the statement taken... Didn't you have to go and visit somewhere else?... In fact I think we took you to the railway station didn't we?' This was, claims Renno, a delaying tactic to give Sheila time to work out a better statement.

The motive, puts in Booth, was money.

'We see from her accounts that Mrs Jackson's funds were very quickly dwindling with the amount that she was having to pay at Greyfriars – something like £200, £250 [a week] was being paid for her keep there and her money was getting very very low. And we understand that there was quite a bit of pressure being put on you for the release of the flat.' Perhaps, concludes Booth, 'we shouldn't really be worrying ourselves. After all she was 90 odd wasn't she? She'd had a good life. She was gonna die soon. OK so no big deal. An old vulnerable lady – there was no reason why she should have died like that and you can give the answer as to why she did.'

'No comment.'

'Don't you think she deserves an answer from you as to why she died?' asks Renno. 'Don't you think you owe it to her? To let the world know why she died?'

'No comment,' says Sheila Bowler.

Once more Sheila was released and driven home. Once more she tried to carry on her life as usual.

Towards the end of July Barbara Jones, the last member of Greyfriars staff to see Aunt Flo alive, had two appointments with the police.

On the 27th, DS Renno and WDS Booth drove her to the spot on the hairpin bend where Sheila had parked the Audi. Then they drove on, turning right into Station Road, and continued till they reached the pumping station. Could Mrs Jackson have walked this far unaided?

No, said Barbara Jones, she could not.

Two days later, on the afternoon of 29 July, Renno and Booth took Mrs Jones on another trip, this time to see the recovery vehicle driven by Mr Coulmanhole on the night of May 13. Could Mrs Jackson have got up into that truck?

No, said Barbara Jones, she could not.

Was this further proof to indicate that Sheila Bowler knew Florence Jackson was dead before she called the recovery vehicle? That the question of getting the old lady up into the truck would never arise?

On the day Barbara Jones was viewing the recovery truck, Sheila was sitting on a train travelling from King's Cross to Royston in Hertfordshire. She was on her way to stay with her sister Mary and her husband Albert, to celebrate Albert's 81st birthday. The family celebrations were to be on Sunday 2 August, and Sheila wanted to arrive in good time the previous Wednesday.

That evening she realised she had forgotten to leave Mary's telephone number with Marie, her neighbour in Fair Meadow, so she rang and left a message.

On Thursday morning Marie rang in a great state:

'I'm sorry but I gave the Bexhill police your sister's phone number. They rang me up wanting to speak to you.'

Sheila immediately called Russell Parkes to find out what was happening.

'You're going to be charged on Monday with Aunt Flo's murder,' he said.

'But I'm not coming back till Monday,' said Sheila.

There was a pause at the end of the line.

'I'm afraid you must – we're due in Rye magistrates' court at 8.30am,' said Parkes.

Suddenly the reality of the charge struck Sheila, and as at the 'arresting speech,' her reaction was physical. She was to write later from Holloway, 'I started to shake uncontrollably, scarcely able to take in that such an injustice could be meted out to me.'

She phoned Jane who was staying in Buckinghamshire with her step-sister Elizabeth and told her what had happened. Jane said she would return to Rye the next day, Friday.

That Thursday Mary and Albert had planned a special day out touring round the part of Suffolk made famous by the painter Constable, and Sheila felt she must go along with them, not to disappoint Albert – especially now that she would have to miss his birthday celebrations on the Sunday.

'We had lunch at a hotel and a really nice cream tea but I couldn't enjoy any of it. All I could think of was the following Monday.'

She cannot remember how she got through the rest of her stay.

On Saturday Sheila travelled to King's Cross alone. She arrived in the early afternoon and was met by her step-daughter Elizabeth, who drove her to Rye and stayed with her, Simon and Jane for the weekend. Elizabeth, a lecturer on education, was horrified that her stepmother, who had always been so kind to her, so loyal to her father, and so dedicated to the care of his aunts, was being treated in this way.

On the Monday morning Russell Parkes arrived at 8am and explained the procedure. The police had told him they wanted Sheila at the police station first, and would then be driving her to the magistrates' court themselves.

By 8.30 they were at Rye police station where Sheila was fingerprinted again and had her photographs taken in a small room with a plain wall behind her – full-face and profile mug shots like any common criminal, though she was too dazed to notice much about the process. Then she was left in the room for about fifteen minutes with Sergeant Catt, whom she knew – his wife had made the loose covers for her sofa. Sergeant Catt looked embarrassed. His superiors made it clear it was not necessary to lock Sheila in the room.

Next she was taken outside to a waiting police car. There in the front, stony faced, sat Detective Sergeant David Renno and Woman Detective Sergeant Linda Booth.

Without a word Sheila got into the back of the car and they set off along Cinque Ports Street and under the ancient stone arch known as the

Landgate, near the spot where Mr Soan once had his barber's shop. Then on along Hilder's Cliff, with its panoramic view over Romney Marsh to the sea. A few early-rising tourists were strolling down the High Street, peering into curio shops, unaware of this piece of local drama. The police car turned left and up East Street, with its ancient beamed houses, to the town hall where the magistrates' court was in session.

Rye Town Hall is a noble building near St Mary's Church where Bob had been a churchwarden. Situated on the corner of Market Street, it used to be the old market hall, built on pillars to provide a covered area underneath for traders to sell their wares. This flagged courtyard is still known as the Butter Market. It was here each November that Bob and Sheila Bowler would distribute British Legion poppies to volunteer vendors – often shivering in the chill sea-mists swirling in across Romney Marsh. On that marsh, two hundred years earlier, a local butcher, John Breeds, was hanged for murder. When Jane was a child, the Town Clerk could sometimes be persuaded to open up the Town Hall attics so that local schoolchildren, shuddering with delighted terror, could see the iron gibbet still containing part of his skull.

Now, amazingly, the Town Clerk was ushering in Sheila Bowler, also set to face trial for murder.

She followed Russell Parkes upstairs to the first floor courtroom. They went through the splendid double doors into the elegant hall, its panelled walls surrounded by honours boards listing the names of all the mayors of Rye throughout its long history. In a small town like this one, the town hall has many functions to fulfil: magistrates may sit in session here, but the room is also used for social occasions. As Sheila sat down she recalled that the last time she was in the room was for a sale in aid of the Church of England Children's Society – a genteel English lady engaged in genteel charitable works.

She glanced over her shoulder. Behind her sat Jane and Simon, Elizabeth and her husband Vernon: they had come straight to the court while Sheila was at the police station. There too was Paddy Buxton, who as Vicar of Rye had, just a few months earlier, helped Sheila plan Bob's memorial service. Now that seemed like thousands of years ago. At the back of the hall sat some local restaurant owners waiting to apply for a licence to sell alcoholic beverages – a mundane local request in the midst of this nightmarish local melodrama.

Just before the proceedings began Parkes leaned over to Sheila.

'The police are going to oppose bail,' he whispered, 'but don't worry – it'll be all right.'

It had never occurred to Sheila till that moment that she could actually be taken into custody. Years later she was to write, 'It is impossible to describe how I felt – a sort of numbness and disbelief that this was happening.' As before, she had succeeded in detaching herself as far as possible from the proceedings, as if they were part of a hideous dream and she would soon wake up.

Before she had time to dwell too deeply on the prospect of prison, the three magistrates entered. The chairman of the bench took his seat in the great carved Mayor's Chair on the raised dais. Immediately Sheila recognized him: it was Alan Webb, who owned the sweet shop opposite the town hall, quaintly named, for the benefit of tourists, Ye Olde Tuck Shoppe. Jane and Simon, like all Rye children, had spent their pocket money there on sugar mice and licorice bootlaces. According to Sheila, Mr Webb seemed most surprised to see her there.

'I saw him stare at me and he looked startled.'

On Mr Webb's right was Mrs Jones, a former teacher: Sheila knew her too from work they both did for the annual Rye Festival of music and the arts. On his left was Mrs Osborne, the wife of a local builder, whom Sheila knew slightly. Magistrates, if they know the defendant, are supposed to declare an interest and withdraw. But in a small town like Rye, where everybody knows everybody else, this proves to be impossible.

A woman official from the Crown Prosecution Service read the indictment, that on the night of 13 May, 1992, Sheila Bowler, of 25 Fair Meadow, Rye, did wilfully murder Mrs Florence Jackson. As Russell Parkes had warned, Detective Sergeant Renno rose to say that the police were opposing bail.

The magistrates retired to consider their decision. It seemed to Sheila that they were out of the room for hours, though in fact after about fifteen minutes they returned. Mr Webb announced that they had decided to grant bail because of Mrs Bowler's family commitments. (She found this touching, considering her adult children had both left home and she had only her elderly ginger cat, Whisky, to care for!). Mr Webb asked Russell Parkes what sum he had in mind as surety. When Parkes suggested £2000, with Mrs Bowler's step-daughter Elizabeth standing surety, Mr Webb agreed that this was just the amount he and his fellow magistrates had had in mind. Bail in murder cases is by no means always granted, and to set so low a sum is extraordinary and surely gave some indication of Sheila Bowler's standing in the town of Rye.

As Sheila and her family left the court, they saw the police car parked immediately outside the Town Hall: 'All ready to whisk me off to prison!' said Sheila wryly as they drove back to Fair Meadow. She made everyone coffee – and suddenly remembered she had planned to return to Royston later that month for a few days' holiday. She drove back to the court with Parkes to ask the magistrates' permission. It was immediately granted.

That afternoon she contacted the schools where she worked and explained the situation. The three headmasters were all supportive and said they were happy for her to continue with her teaching. But within a few weeks, all three had written saying they had now discussed the matter further with their schools' governors, and felt this would after all be inappropriate. They all expressed their regret: the head of Marlborough House said Sheila's job would remain open for her once this business was all over. Dr Lewis at Bricklehurst Manor invited her to come and have coffee with him and his wife whenever she wished. On the one occasion when she did so, they sat chatting in the school garden. One of the youngest pupils marched up to her on her way to morning break. 'Mrs Bowler!' exclaimed the little girl, 'I thought you were locked up in jail!'

Sheila was now on an extended summer holiday, with no end in sight to this protracted nightmare. She tried to set about her household and charity duties as usual. She was now obliged to go along every Monday morning to Rye police station to sign her name as a condition of bail. One Monday she and Jane were on the way to a shopping expedition in Eastbourne when she realised with horror that she had forgotten to sign. They had reached Pevensey Bay and it was 11.45, just 15 minutes short of the noon deadline. They found a phonebox and telephoned Heringtons. Emma Kerr told them to get to Rye as soon as possible. She would phone the police station. The duty officer was very understanding: 'Try to get back here as soon as you can,' he said.

Sheila sped back to Rye, only just keeping the Audi within the speed limit. Though she arrived at the police station 45 minutes late, the officer did not seem to mind. Unlike DS Renno and WDS Booth of the Bexhill CID, the Rye police had known Sheila, as they knew most of the other Rye residents, for years. In the past, a policeman strolling round the town would often tease her about parking on a double yellow line 'just for a few minutes, officer, while I pop into this shop.'

Throughout that summer there were a number of occasions when she had to return to the magistrates' court on technicalities. After a visit to the court she would sometimes meet a friend for coffee at The George Hotel in the High Street, and once she saw the Chairman of the Bench, Mr Webb, there too. He nodded and smiled pleasantly. By the kind of coincidence that could only happen in small town like Rye, Mr Webb's son was later to purchase Aunt Flo's vacant flat in Ferry Road.

Ten days after Sheila was charged at Rye magistrates' court, a second post mortem examination was carried out on the body of Mrs Florence Jackson, this time at Eastbourne District Hospital Mortuary. The pathologist carrying out the examination at 2.40pm on Wednesday 12 August was Dr Vesna Djurovic, Senior Lecturer and Honorary Consultant in Forensic Medicine at Guy's Hospital Department of Forensic Medicine. She had been engaged by Russell Parkes to give a second opinion on the cause of Mrs Jackson's death. Once again, Detective Superintendent Foster attended the examination.

Dr Djurovic studied Dr Heath's first post mortem report, and a set of police photographs taken at that time. She reached the same conclusion as Dr Heath: 'Mrs Jackson died, most probably, as the result of immersion.' But, she added, 'The injuries to her head, abrasions to the back of her left hand and the deep bruising to the muscles of the shoulder blades could all be accounted for by the process of immersion'; while the bruising on her upper arms could have occurred 'even if she was only held firmly by the arms, for instance if she needed support.' Significantly, she emphasized that 'drowning is most often accidental... suicidal drownings are often relatively common. Homicide by drowning is rare.' Later she was to tell Sheila's lawyers that when she first examined the body she could not understand why this was ever treated as a murder enquiry.

On 1 September Tom Day was once again visited by the police. They brought with them a video of the *Lovejoy* programme Mr Day had been watching on the night of 13 May. They had discovered from a Mr Edward Bachell at the BBC's Investigation Unit that this particular episode of *Lovejoy*, called *The Italian Venus*, had begun at 1959 hrs 28 secs, and ended at 2051 hrs 31 secs.

They showed Mr Day the video, asking him to stop it at the point when he had switched off his television set. He said he recognized a scene when Lovejoy was talking to a woman, 'They were talking about a tray, I thought.' At this point, said Mr Day, he had switched off the television. This scene was just seven minutes and 30 seconds into the programme. Mr Day's recollection caused the police some problems: although it fitted in perfectly with the murder theory, leaving Sheila Bowler ample time to return to Winchelsea and put Mrs Jackson into the river, it could not be squared with the evidence of Mrs Dobson and the other Greyfriars staff that she did not even leave the Home until after 8pm.

On 24 September Jonathan Ashe, the police photographer, paid a visit to Mr Eric Garland, a specialist shoe repairer and fitter in Eastbourne. He accompanied Mr Garland to Eastbourne District General Hospital where the body of Mrs Jackson was still lying in the mortuary where Dr Djurovic had examined it. He was asked to measure her feet, then the size of the slippers retrieved from the scene of her death, then the distance from the end of the feet to the end of the slippers when fitted on. Still, it seems, the police were seeking to disprove the 'walking theory' by trying to show that the slippers would have been loose enough to fall off somewhere along Station Road.

For Sheila the waiting seemed to go on for ever. That September Jane had taken a live-in teaching job at Dover College preparatory school in Folkestone. She was not too far from Rye, but she was worried about her mother. She felt Sheila had never had time to grieve properly for Bob, and persuaded her to visit a local bereavement counsellor.

So Sheila attended counselling sessions once every week for the next three months. In October, on the 8th and the 22nd, appointments were made for her to visit Peter Haydn-Smith, a forensic psychiatrist, at his Hastings clinic to see whether she was fit to face trial. The report he sent to Russell Parkes recorded that he had no problems at all with her mental state. Dr Jeelani, in his capacity as Sheila's GP, was required for the same reason to give her a full medical examination. As he filled in the paperwork he fulminated to Sheila that this was all 'a load of rubbish, a waste of time.'

Sheila's friends rallied round as best they could. Anne Wood recalls, 'I kept thinking that as soon as the police found out a bit more about Sheila Bowler they'd realise how ridiculous their line of questioning was. As soon as they started to make a few enquiries about her they would realise it couldn't be her.' Even those who found Sheila difficult agreed. Biddy Cole, the aunts' neighbour who had witnessed Sheila's care over the past seven years, was later to say in a television interview, 'She was an irritating bossy lady, she talked like a machine gun at you. But between the arrest and the trial was the one time you didn't cross the road to get away from her. You felt she needed your support. If she'd wanted to bump off Aunt Flo why not do it when she lived next door?'

Christmas 1992 came and went, with the impending trial casting its long shadow. On February 4 Russell Parkes drove Sheila to a different magistrates' court in Hailsham, about twenty miles away, to appear before a stipendiary magistrate and face committal proceedings.

Here she met Charles Byers, the barrister Parkes had instructed. Sitting with Audrey Mummery, Audrey's husband Brian, Elizabeth and Jane (who attended all the hearings) Sheila heard counsel for the Crown attempt to read out the full indictment – though the stipendiary magistrate, Paul Tain, made several attempts to cut him short, saying it could be taken as read.

The case against Sheila Bowler, said Peter Clarke, prosecuting, was as follows: the body of Florence Jackson, aged 89, was found in the River Brede on the morning of 14 May 1992, near the road outside the town of Winchelsea. The river had a steep embankment and Mrs Jackson's slipper was found 400 yards from the car. 'Its position is pivotal to the case,' said the Crown counsel. He went on to stress the old lady's immobility, the refusal of Sheila Bowler to sign the property form, the Greyfriars arrears,

Sheila's suspicious behaviour, and the testimonies of two motorists, Beckett and Pearson, who said they saw the Audi empty. There were three alternative explanations for Mrs Jackson's demise, said counsel: one, that she walked to her death; two, that she was abducted and fell or was pushed into the river; three, that Sheila Bowler murdered her, missing the slipper left on the ledge because it was dark.

The first explanation, he said, was impossible, and like the second was contradicted by the two motorist witnesses. The third was the only remaining explanation.

'This defendant set about killing her aunt by taking her to the edge of the River Brede where there is a steep embankment and pushing her into the river to her death. This is not a case of it could be Mrs Bowler or it could be another person,' he said.

Charles Byers countered the charge: the whole case, he said, was based on supposition and conjecture. The ingredients of a *prima facie* case require both motive and opportunity. There was no realistic motive: Mrs Bowler was comfortably off, and there was evidence of her caring relationship with her husband's aunt. Nor was there opportunity. There simply would not have been time for Mrs Bowler to commit the crime in the way described. The motorists' evidence that the car was empty was faulty: the Audi had solid headrests and Mrs Jackson would have been invisible to passing drivers.

At this point the stipendiary magistrate interrupted testily: this was not a matter for him, he said.

Byers pressed on: Mrs Bowler would have to have carried out her plot by 9.50pm at the latest. She could not have got to Winchelsea in time, nor was there any forensic evidence to link her with the river. The case must be dismissed.

But the case was not dismissed. The magistrate decided there was a case to answer.

'The Galbraith test says in a given case, could a jury convict on the evidence given and I am convinced it could.'

He referred the case to the Crown Court.

At the back of the court, watching the proceedings with great interest, was Detective Superintendent Brian Foster, the officer in charge of Operation Dace.

The next stage was a Pleas and Directions hearing to fix the date of the trial. A few weeks after her Hailsham ordeal, Sheila was required to appear before another court at Hove, near Brighton. It was arranged that in this court room, on Monday, 28 June, 1993, just four months later, Sheila Bowler would stand in the dock and face trial for the murder of Mrs Florence Jackson.

Defending her would be Nicholas Purnell, QC, an eminent London barrister and former Chairman of the Criminal Bar Association, available to defend a woman in Sheila's financial situation only because of the Legal Aid system. Prosecuting would be another London silk, Anthony Glass, QC.

CHAPTER SIX

SCARLET LADY

On 28 June 1993 the elegant stone-built Crown Court in Lewes High Street was covered with scaffolding. While it was being refurbished the magistrates' court at Hove, further along the South Coast, had been temporarily upgraded to try more serious cases. Hove is a courtly older sister to brassy Brighton, and its court building stands in striking contrast to the faded elegance of its once fine terraces. It is an ugly 'sixties structure, three storeys high, with wide concrete steps leading up to aluminium and glass doors. The only ennobling feature is the enormous ornate coat of arms above the entrance, emblazoned with the legend *Dieu et mon droit.*

On the first day of the trial, the Bowler family set out at 8am from Rye. Jane drove her mother and brother to Heringtons' office at St Leonards-on-Sea, and Russell Parkes took them on to Hove. Sometimes other friends drove them. The second week Elizabeth took over as chauffeur.

Sheila was shocked to see press photographers crowding around the front steps:

'I had a great shock arriving at the court to be faced with a battery of cameramen as we entered. I just couldn't understand why so much publicity was accorded to an innocent person. I really believed, in spite of a lurking thought I could be convicted, that I would be acquitted. I had been primed by Mr Purnell at a meeting in London two months earlier that I would not have to say anything until the second week, and that on the first day I would be painted as the scarlet lady.'

Sheila was certainly not dressed to kill: for most of the trial she wore a sober navy blue jacket and skirt and a variety of plain light-coloured shirts. She said later she had no idea what to wear.

Some of Sheila's friends who attended were later to say she had chosen her court costume badly. The navy suit was meant to give the impression of a sensible professional: instead its sharp, rather masculine tailoring made her strong-featured face, already gaunt with tension, look harsh and forbidding. It is no surprise that journalists covering the case were soon to dub her 'The Black Widow.'

Following Sheila and her family up the steps of the court came Detective Sergeant Linda Booth, also smart – but much more 'feminine' – in a pale pink suit (as a detective she never wore police uniform). She was carrying two tyres wrapped in plastic sheeting; other officers carried four more tyres and the rest of the exhibits to be put before the court, among them Aunt Flo's slippers and her clothes.

The case of Regina v. Sheila Bowler was listed to be heard in Court One. The carpeted foyer looks more like a students' union entrance than a court of law, and the long narrow waiting area upstairs, also carpeted, is dotted with potted plants. At the far end is an area behind a trellis-like screen labelled 'Prosecution Witnesses.' Booth and Renno went and took their seats behind this half-partition which divides it from the area marked 'Defence Witnesses.' Sheila, Simon and Jane sat down in the Defence area, immediately in front of the door to the Court One public gallery. They were soon joined by the faithful Anne Wood.

At 10 o'clock Sheila and her family and Anne were summoned into the court room. Other friends were shown into the public gallery, leading straight off the waiting area. Sheila was directed up some steps into the dock, a large enclosed box with its top half encased in glass. This is designed to protect the court from dangerous outbursts by angry defendants, but it reaches only down to head height from the ceiling above and has strange circular apertures higher up – presumably for ventilation and increased audibility. Sheila was joined in the booth by a uniformed officer. 'He smiled and was perfectly pleasant. They were not always the same ones – some were women. I remember one male officer sat reading a whodunnit novel all day long.'

Simon, Jane and Anne were shown to seats on Sheila's right. The dock is immediately underneath the public gallery, so she could never see her friends there. The gallery has twenty-four seats and was usually full.

Sheila looked around. The morning sunshine filtered through the vertical slatted blinds on the tall windows. Somehow she felt no sense of occasion, no alarm. Everything just seemed so ordinary. Court Number One is hardly awe-inspiring. There is none of the panelled grandeur of the traditional courtroom. It is rather like a lecture theatre, with functional benches with foldback seats in olive-green leatherette, and long formica-topped fixed tables. The jury benches to the right of the dock are the same, but are supplied with paper and pencils. The only splash of colour comes from the red office-type swivel chairs on the raised dais for the judge and the court clerk.

Detective Sergeants Booth and Renno came in and sat in the seats below the dock on Sheila's left. At the front of the court, to the right, her Defence team – Nicholas Purnell, Charles Byers and Russell Parkes – were already deep in whispered consultation. Purnell had told Sheila that if she wished to communicate with him during the proceedings to correct any misapprehensions, she could do so by passing him a note via one of the ushers. In the event it proved difficult, from her glass cage, to attract the ushers' attention and she was only to do so on one or two occasions. She had been given a notebook and pencil and she confined herself to noting the name of each witness and the number of minutes they spent giving evidence. But she only managed this for the first few witnesses. Occasionally she scribbled a few comments, punctuated by an irate exclamation mark or two if something was completely wrong. But most of the time she found it difficult to listen very intently to the dream-like sequence of events unfolding before her eyes.

Alongside the Defence team sat the Crown lawyers: Anthony Glass, QC, his junior, Tom Kark, and a Crown Prosecution Service solicitor. Above them on the left was the witness box with a prominently placed microphone, and near it the press benches.

Before the proceedings could get under way, the jury had to be selected and sworn in. The clerk to the court called out twelve names and the jurors came in one by one and sat on the jury benches on the right of the court: 'When the jury was picked,' recalls Sheila, 'I was a little horrified to see how young some of them appeared. There were roughly equal numbers of men and women – slightly more men, I think seven men and five women. One of the men, a fair-haired young lad, only looked about 18. One of the women was wearing sunglasses, which I thought a little odd. She kept them on throughout the whole trial.'

When the jury had been sworn in, the ushers ordered the court to rise for the judge. At this point Sheila was surprised to be ushered out of the dock again: 'I had to go out of the courtroom while the judge entered.

Apparently Mr Justice Garland objects to the prisoner being there before him.'

The Honourable Sir Patrick Neville Garland was a tall, distinguished man in his mid-sixties. Returning to the dock, Sheila noticed that as he took his seat on the red swivel chair he placed beside him on the bench a small square of black cloth – a remnant, she supposed, of the days when murderers were executed and the judge would don a black cap before passing sentence.

As Purnell had predicted, Anthony Glass did indeed paint Sheila Bowler as a wicked lady. The case against her was outlined just as it had been at the court in Hailsham four months earlier. But now Glass, his tones grave and ponderous, his delivery slow, methodical and painstaking, painted a much more detailed and colourful picture. The murder, he said, was a cold, callous plot, driven by that age-old motive, greed. The Crown did not have any obligation to prove motive, but in this case the motive was clear. The prize, he told the jury, might not seem to them very great – Florence Jackson was not a wealthy woman. But, he reminded them lugubriously, 'Some people have murdered for half a crown.' There was no way the old lady could have got into the river except by being taken there: the Crown would bring witnesses to prove she was completely immobile.

The Crown would also prove that as well as motive, Sheila Bowler had plenty of opportunity to push Mrs Jackson into the river that night in May 1992. They would bring forward witnesses to show that Bowler drove Mrs Jackson on a detour so she could commit her crime under cover of darkness. They would bring other witnesses to prove that at the time she claimed the old lady was waiting in the car, she was in fact already dead in the River Brede and the car was empty. They would examine post mortem reports to show Mrs Jackson's injuries were consistent with being pushed into the river. They would bring yet more witnesses to prove that Bowler's behaviour on the night of May 13 and the morning of May 14 when the body was found showed her to be an unfeeling murderess who cared nothing for the fate of the old lady she had so callously dispatched. They would bring expert evidence to prove that her cover story about the tyre being faulty was a fabrication. She had let the air out of the tyre herself.

The alternative proposition, to be put by the Defence, was, frankly, ludicrous, said Mr Glass. If Mrs Bowler did not put Mrs Jackson into the river, it had to be some homicidal maniac who happened at that time to be on the loose in the Sussex countryside, just conveniently in the half hour when Bowler was away seeking help.

Purnell's response was scathing. On the contrary, he said, there was no realistic motive at all for Sheila Bowler to murder Mrs Jackson. Mrs Bowler was a respectable widow, well-provided for by her husband's pension and her own earnings. You could not, he said, call it a king's ransom, but it was adequate for the modest lifestyle this lady chose to lead. She had her own comfortable mortgage-free home and a small sum in savings. She had cared for Mrs Jackson, her late husband's aunt, for fifteen years.

Purnell's style was very different from that of his adversary Anthony Glass. Compared with the solid, bespectacled prosecutor who spoke so slowly and solemnly as if weighing his every word with care, Purnell was flamboyant, eloquent and confidently dismissive of the ludicrous charges that brought his client to court. He rehearsed for the jury the Defence put forward at Hailsham by Charles Byers, deftly countering one by one all the allegations made by the Crown. Quite simply, he concluded, there was no case to answer.

After the initial speeches by counsel, it was time for the witnesses for the Prosecution to come forward and give evidence.

The first evidence for the Crown was the reading of a statement by Sarah Silberston, the assessment officer in the Social Services financial section, supplying information about the Greyfriars arrears, and Sheila's refusal to sign the property form. Silberston's evidence was clearly designed to fix immediately in the minds of the jurors the motive for the murder – that Sheila Bowler's expected inheritance was in danger of ebbing away unless she took action to stop it.

The next plank of the Crown case was to prove Mrs Jackson's immobility, and to this end the Greyfriars staff were brought in one by one. First called was Deborah Freeman who said that Mrs Jackson was frail, quiet, sometimes confused and afraid of the dark. 'She had extreme trouble walking,' said Mrs Freeman, and since her accident she had never seen her walk unaided. She had taken her in her own car to a hospital appointment in January and had done up the seatbelt because 'she did not fully understand seatbelts plus her arm was in plaster.' Cross-examined by

Purnell she recalled that there was talk of a malignant growth and that the old lady was due for an exploratory examination. Purnell pointed out that she must have been mistaken about the plaster, as the accident was not until April. Freeman was asked to describe the circumstances of the fall. She said Mrs Jackson had fallen down a ramp. Was she being helped along, asked Purnell.

'No, she trotted along,' said Freeman.

'On her own?'

'Yes.'

The first day's hearing was over. Sheila and the family drove back to Rye, exhausted. There had been one opportunity throughout this stressful day for them to meet, but it had not been easy. At lunchtime they had decided to avoid the press by getting as far away as possible from the court and lunching at a pub on the sea-front, just one street away. But as they left the building the photographers were waiting and they had to run to escape them. Later Sheila was to tell friends: 'The awful picture of me that appeared in the papers next day showed me under great stress as we were all rushing to get away. Luckily the press didn't follow us to the pub, but it taught us a lesson. After that we always took sandwiches and drinks and sat in the car in the sunken court car park for lunch. It was protected by walls and bushes. We always knew the photographers were waiting just the other side of the wall, but they couldn't see us as long as we stayed in the car. The whole process was so tiring that we couldn't face cooking anything in the evenings. We would eat a bit of salad, or go and get fish and chips, and talk about that day's proceedings, then fall into bed.'

At the end of the first day – and every day for the next two weeks – the court would clear and Sheila would be free to leave the dock and join her family on the benches. Purnell, Byers and Parkes would join them for a consultation on the day's events and a discussion of plans for the following day.

That first day they were optimistic: Sheila was told to ignore the vilification of her character by the Crown – it was just part of their strategy and would get them nowhere: 'Now, in hindsight, it may seem extraordinary,' says Sheila, 'but I actually did ignore what was going on in that courtroom. It was as if everything I was hearing was of no consequence, as if it had nothing to do with me. From the very start I had been told the case would be thrown out and I felt the charge and indeed the whole story was so utterly ridiculous that it would get nowhere in a court of law.

'My lawyers agreed. A few months before the trial – it must have been around Easter – Russell gave Jane a lift to Rye station with her cello. She was always much more worried than I was, and she asked, "Mum will be all right, won't she?"'

Jane says Russell told her the police were very worried about the case and it would be thrown out. 'It's OK, there's no problem,' he said.

First to appear on the Tuesday morning was Joan Dobson. Sheila hardly recognized the Greyfriars Matron: she had had her hair done quite differently, and was smartly dressed in a grey suit: 'I could not believe the way in which Mrs Dobson, the matron from Greyfriars, presented herself. I think this was her big day.'

Mrs Dobson was asked by Mr Glass about the periods of respite care for Aunt Flo while Mr Bowler was alive, and how she found Mrs Jackson:

'She was a delight,' said Dobson. 'Despite being mentally frail she had a delightful sense of humour.' She confirmed the old lady's fear of the dark. Asked about mobility, she explained that before the fall Mrs Jackson could get around with a zimmer, but after the fall, in which she had sustained a black eye as well as a fractured wrist, 'she was not mobile without the assistance of at least one member of staff.' She had, said Dobson, 'lost her confidence completely.'

'Could she have walked in the dark night a distance of some eight hundred yards or thereabouts unaided?'

'No.'

In fact Mr Glass had exaggerated: the distance was 500 yards, not 800.

Now Joan Dobson was asked about the number of visits made by Mrs Bowler from the beginning of December 1991 until her aunt's death on 13 May 1992. Six times, said Mrs Dobson, according to the records.

Nonsense! scribbled Sheila in her notebook.

Purnell in cross-examination challenged Dobson on the number of visits – his client had made far more, he claimed. Mrs Dobson stuck to her estimate of six.

Purnell wanted to know how many times Mrs Jackson had fallen while at Greyfriars? 'Just once?'

'Just once,' agreed Joan Dobson.

Lynda Hanson, Mrs Jackson's key worker was in the witness box for a full hour, twice as long as Joan Dobson. Hanson was asked about a trip when she took Mrs Jackson in her own Ford Escort Cabriolet to see Dr Jeelani because of a rash. She had put on the old lady's seatbelt for her: 'I really did not give it a thought whether she would be able to do it or not. I just automatically assumed she couldn't.' She was then taken through her own notes, and confirmed that she had written, 'Flo needs to know someone is always around. She appears not to like to be on her own for too long.'

Purnell cross-examined Hanson on the notes, pointing out a great number of entries recording visits and telephone calls from Mrs Bowler dating back to August 1991 when Mrs Jackson and her sister Miss Gillham first entered Greyfriars for a period of respite care. He read aloud the records of the care given by both Mrs Bowler and her husband until the time of his death.

Hanson – who was, Purnell pointed out, the Greyfriars worker closest to Mrs Jackson – contradicted the evidence of her superior Mrs Dobson. Flo could, she said, get about on her walking frame after her accident. It took a while for her to gain confidence but eventually she was able to walk with a zimmer frame without being held by staff.

Now Purnell read aloud the Greyfriars record of Mrs Jackson's planned visit to Fair Meadow, then the report of the police visit to the Home at 11.05 on the evening of May 13: 'The police want to know who was in the car and how much help Flo needed to get in and out of the car. They were told by us that it was unlikely that Flo could walk away.'

Glass re-examined Hanson, emphasizing the old lady's immobility. How far could the old lady walk with Hanson's help? 'Perhaps two widths of this room,' said Hanson, glancing across the courtroom.

Anna McGlanaghy, the care worker who had dressed Mrs Jackson on the morning of 13 May, was even less optimistic. She could only walk about one length of the courtroom, she said, and it would take at least five minutes, or 'longer if she had to stop to have a breather. She did not actually walk – she just shuffled along.' There was little more she could add and after ten minutes she stood down.

Erica Britton, who had gone to fetch Mrs Jackson's coat and suitcase on May 13, also said she had difficulty in walking. She described how Mrs Bowler had collected the old lady, and how she herself had advised against taking the zimmer. She had not noticed a walking stick in the car. As Mrs Jackson left with Mrs Bowler, she heard Mrs Bowler say, 'Oh, come on,' the same, said Britton, 'as anybody would if you are trying to do something in a hurry.'

She thought Mrs Bowler had stayed at Greyfriars for about ten minutes.

Asked about the frequency of visits, she said Mrs Bowler would come about once every two months, but in cross-examination admitted that in her original witness statement she had mentioned far more visits than that. But, she said, Mrs Bowler did not stay very long because Mrs Jackson did not have much to say.

Barbara Jones was next to take the stand. Sheila knew Barbara quite well and felt sorry for her: 'Barbara Jones was shaking as she gave her evidence – it was obvious she was terribly nervous. When we went home that evening I told Jane I was sorry for her. Jane was furious at me for "sticking up for the enemy"'.

Jones's account of the evening of May 13 was similar to Britton's except that she emphasized that 'Mrs Jackson had said she was not going to make it.' *(Aunt Flo was always saying that about everything* wrote Sheila. *I always had to chivvy her along).*

But Mrs Jones's description differed from Britton's on one important point. According to Jones, she had asked Mrs Bowler if she wanted to take the zimmer frame, and Mrs Bowler had said, 'No, she won't need it.' In cross-examination Purnell reminded Jones of Erica Britton's advice not to take the frame, but she insisted that she remembered nothing of this exchange.

Jones was asked by Mr Glass about the two trips she had made with the police following Mrs Jackson's death: she had visited the pumping station and seen the recovery truck. Could Mrs Jackson have walked from the car to the pumping station?

'No, she couldn't,' said Barbara Jones.

Could she have climbed into the truck?

'No, she couldn't,' said Barbara Jones.

In cross-examination she re-emphasized Mrs Jackson's immobility. Despite her nervousness and her very quietly-spoken answers, Jones was questioned for half an hour, twice as long as Britton.

Joyce Law, who had packed Mrs Jackson's suitcase for the first abortive trip on May 6, was unable to be in court, so she was 'conditionally bound' in her absence, and her statement was read aloud. The court heard of her conversation with Mrs Bowler when she asked that Mrs Jackson's laxative medication be withheld as she had to drive her home. When Law remonstrated that the old lady needed the medicine, 'Mrs Bowler just laughed and the conversation was ended.' This testimony ended the Greyfriars evidence and left Sheila furious: so much of it was, she said, simply nonsense.

After lunch Tom Day took the stand – an important witness because he was the last person apart from Sheila Bowler to see Florence Jackson alive. Glass quizzed him about the reason for Mrs Bowler's visit. How did she know the protein supplement was ready for her to collect? Had she telephoned in advance? No, said Mr Day, though he had expected it to be sent that day. Indeed it had been sent, but for some reason it had not been left in the shed as usual. Sheila had said 'they had called on the off-chance the parcel would be there.'

Glass pressed on doggedly: But Mrs Bowler had said she was going to be in the area the next morning. Then why on earth make a special journey that Wednesday night? 'Did she give any explanation as to how it came about that she was popping in?'

'To the best of my recollection it was stated or implied that they were over in the Bexhill area anyway so they called in passing.'

Sheila made a note on her pad: *Knew Helen Goodwin's supply was running out and she wanted more. Had been to collect protein a couple of weeks earlier. Knew Days were due for another delivery about then. No need to phone.*

Day's evidence was also critical in terms of timing. But in the event it proved impossible to sustain. A statement was read from Edward Bachell, of the BBC Investigations Unit, confirming that the *Lovejoy* programme began at 1959 hrs 28 seconds and ended at 2051 hrs 31 seconds. 'So it began half a minute before 8 o'clock and ended just after 8.50,' summarized Glass. The police experiment whereby Mr Day was asked to stop a video of the film at the point where he switched of the set proved only that Mr Day must have been wrong. He said he stopped watching and opened the door to Mrs Bowler at 8.07 – an impossible time to sustain.

'What we *can* be certain about,' said Purnell scathingly in cross-examination, 'is that nobody, not Nigel Mansell or anyone else, could travel from Greyfriars to your house by road in seven minutes, could they?'

'Of course not,' agreed Mr Day.

Nor was the evidence of Mr Giddings, the owner of Ferryfields Caravan Park, as much help to the Prosecution as they might have expected. Asked about the car he had seen reversing away from the pumping station as he went to fetch his son from karate, at approximately five to ten, he said he 'thought it might have been a light grey, but I am not really certain.'

'Are you able to help us as to whether it had a boot or a hatch back?' asked Glass.

'No.'

Far more damaging for the Crown was Mr Giddings's sudden revelation, not mentioned at all in either of his two statements, that the mystery car had reversed out of the pumping station and he saw it in his driving mirror, following him as he drove off to the karate class in Northiam, *away* from the A259 junction. So it could not have been the Audi. Purnell in cross-examination pressed him on his timing. It was no longer approximate: 'I know exactly the time I left. I did it every week at five to ten.' 'On the dot?' ' Yes' 'With a sort of military precision?' 'Almost.'

The afternoon wore on and the sun cast longer shadows across the courtroom through the slatted blinds. Day and Giddings were each in the witness box for about thirty minutes.

Judith Pearson, one of the Crown's motorist eyewitnesses, was only questioned for fifteen minutes. Her evidence must have been even more disappointing for Glass: although it was clear that she had seen Sheila Bowler walking away from the car when she drove past – she was pretty sure it was 9.50 because she remembered the time she left a local restaurant – she now said she could not be sure whether or not the Audi was empty: 'I don't *think* there was anyone in the car, but I can't be sure.'

The next motorist witness, Christopher Beckett, was less reliable on his timings. On the way back from the Robin Hood pub in Icklesham he had seen the Audi and a lady walking away from it. But his description now, as in his statement, did not fit Sheila Bowler.

'Are you any good at describing ages of women once they get beyond about forty?' asked Glass.

Purnell objected: his learned friend 'must not proceed to question about something as important as description in a murder case by suggesting the witness may have difficulty in ageing a lady over the age of 40.'

Glass reworded his question: 'Can you help about the age of this woman?'

'As I stated previously, 45 to 50.'

Under cross-examination Beckett admitted that he could not remember whether or not he had looked into the Audi: 'It is not something I remember.' Although he was questioned closely for forty-five minutes – almost as long as Lynda Hanson – he would not commit himself further.

Harry Kershaw's evidence at first seemed more encouraging for the Crown. He and his wife were on the way back from the same pub in Icklesham as Mr Beckett, the Robin Hood, and had driven past the Audi on their way home: 'I slowed up as I went by, had a look in, there seemed to be nobody about, so we carried on home.' He had seen nobody about at all. But his timing, which he said he could fix fairly accurately at between 10.35 and 10.40, was either wrong, or Sheila and the Soans were already searching along Station Road. After ten minutes he stood down.

Sheila sat in her Tardis-like glass box and listened as witness followed witness throughout this second intensive day. There was still an element of fantasy about the occasion: 'The whole proceedings still had an unreal atmosphere but as the case unfolded and the Prosecution's case was demolished systematically by Nicholas Purnell I began to feel very optimistic.'

There was just half an hour to go before the court was adjourned. The last witness that day was Mr Soan the barber. He described Mrs Bowler's visit.

When she arrived, he told the court, he and his wife had been tidying up after some visitors left. They were the people who were going to move into his house, which he leased, and after they left he was chatting about them with Mrs Soan. He thought it must have been between 10 and 10.15pm. Mrs Bowler looked as if she had been hurrying to get there because her face was flushed. 'I said to her I am sorry to hear about your husband dying and she seemed up-tight.' Before that she had seemed calm, 'just like there was no problem.'

Sheila wrote down another note in her book: why had he omitted the discussion about his diabetes, and his uncomfortable relationship with his neighbours which was causing him to move? He had certainly spent a long time that night telling her about all his troubles, a conversation which had delayed her return to Aunt Flo. Maybe he found these things too embarrassing to mention in public.

Soan described Sheila's phonecall to the recovery firm and walking back to the car with her, seeing the flashing lights of the Audi. 'Did there come a time,' asked Mr Glass, 'when Mrs Bowler said something?'

'Yes, I suppose 25 yards or so from the car, and she said, "She's not there."'

'Were you able to see into the car at that point?' asked Glass.

'No, I could not see. All I could see were the hazard lights flashing.' He had, he said, been watching a big articulated lorry trying to negotiate the Audi.

Wrong, scribbled Sheila. They were nothing like as far as 25 yards away when she had noticed Aunt Flo was not there. *Only about a car's length,* she noted.

The front passenger door of the Audi was completely closed, said Mr Soan, and the old lady had gone.

Door on the latch, not tight shut, noted Sheila.

He described the search, and Mrs Bowler's words: 'She said that she couldn't have got far because she had difficulty in walking and she'd broken her wrist some little while before.'

'But you did not go down Station Road any further than you did?'

'Mrs Bowler said she couldn't have got that far because she could not without a zimmer or stick or something.'

Mr Soan, as befitted his former profession, was an inveterate chatterer but that day's session was over. He would have to continue his evidence the following morning.

When the court had been adjourned, Sheila said goodbye to Russell Parkes: this was his last full day in court. He had arranged to go on holiday to France and would not be attending the rest of the trial.

Wednesday was the last day of June, Day Three of the trial. Mr Soan was recalled for cross-examination about his part in the search for Mrs Jackson. He recounted it in graphic detail, ending: 'Me and my wife decided it was best to get help because prior to that Mrs Bowler said that when she left the car there was some motorcyclists that turned in or were on that corner of Station Road and we thought, well, the best thing to do was to get a bit more official help than we were.'

Next came the statement of Linda Brierley, read aloud. She was the shift controller, employed in Huddersfield by Britannia Rescue, who had been on duty on the night of May 13. Her statement recorded the call at 10.21pm from Mrs Bowler: 'I was also informed that Mrs Bowler had an elderly lady passenger with her. Because of that information I marked this job a priority.' She added that Mr Coulmanhole had asked for extra time to help search for the old lady, who had gone missing. Her statement confirmed that she had handed the tapes of the conversations to Sussex police.

The next witness after Mr Soan was Peta Cameron-Clarke, a short plump lady. She was wearing a floral skirt, recalls Sheila. 'She was asked about my earlier trip down Station Road and the phonecalls I had made to her. When she came down from the witness box she glanced towards Renno and Booth as she passed them and gave a little smile.'

Next came Steven Coulmanhole, the recovery vehicle driver. He was asked particularly about his conversation with Mrs Bowler as he drove her back to Rye that night. He confirmed to the court what he had said in his statement: Sheila Bowler had said she did not want to be rung up by the police in the small hours of the morning because she tended to wake up early since the death of her husband, and did not want to be woken in the middle of the night.'

In the dock Sheila sat fuming.

The police evidence – from PCs Millington, Doswell and Joyce, and from Sergeant Tickner, who had been in the police helicopter – was dealt with fairly rapidly. They were allowed to refer to their notebooks, and were questioned on certain parts, but their testimonies differed very little from the information contained in their statements. They simply told of their part in the search for Aunt Flo, though the jury heard PC Millington describe Mrs Bowler's 'total lack of concern for Mrs Jackson's wellbeing,' a view corroborated by PC Doswell's statement, which was read aloud in his absence.

Again Sheila felt intensely irritated: 'Of course I wasn't too concerned. I was sure she was going to be found – she'd just be wandering around somewhere, as old people do. I wasn't at all happy about leaving the search. I only did so because the police told me to.'

The statement of Mr Abnett, the sluice keeper, was read aloud, then Mrs Steward, Sheila's Battle Abbey colleague, was called to the witness box. She repeated what she had said in her statement about the two conversations she had had with Sheila Bowler in the staff room at Battle Abbey School.

'Is there anything else you can remember?' asked Mr Glass. Steward thought for a moment. 'Oh yes' she said finally, 'She did say that Hastings police haven't got a very good reputation.'

In the dock Sheila sighed. 'Thanks very much, Monica,' she thought.

Next came one of the Crown's most important witnesses, Dr Michael Heath, the Home Office pathologist who had carried out the post mortem examination on Florence Jackson. Mr Glass asked Dr Heath to take the jury through his report, and to produce the set of photographs of the process, Exhibit 44. The injuries, abrasions and tears to the clothes were examined in detail. Heath said death, in his opinion, was caused by drowning. But 'a bruise over the left side of the hairline and over the outer aspect of the left eye...might be consistent with having been caused by blows to these regions.' These, he agreed with Glass, could have been caused by a fist.

At the end of Glass's examination-in-chief of Dr Heath, Purnell asked permission to reserve his cross-examination 'until the jury and your Lordship have had the opportunity of seeing the scene.' He would, he said, prefer the doctor to visit the site in person, rather than simply viewing the video and looking at the photographs. Later in the trial this was proved to have been a stroke of brilliance on Purnell's part.

Dr Heath's evidence was adjourned until 2 July, the Friday of that first week, and the judge announced that the jury would be taken by coach that afternoon to visit the site in Winchelsea. He and the lawyers would join them there. The court was adjourned for lunch.

Emma Kerr drove Sheila from Hove to Winchelsea. They planned to have lunch in Rye, but it was the height of the tourist season and there was nowhere to park. So Emma waited in the car while Sheila dashed into the Swan Tearooms in The Mint – the winding street leading downhill from Rye High Street – and asked Robert, the proprietor, for some sandwiches. 'No time for your favourite bacon and mushroom toasted sandwich today?' he joked. Then they drove back to Winchelsea, parked in the layby opposite Tanyard Cottages, and ate the sandwiches.

They need not have rushed: it was some time before the coach carrying the jurors arrived and parked behind them. Then a large car drew up and parked in front of Emma's car. Out got Nicholas Purnell, Anthony Glass and their juniors, and a tall man Sheila thought she recognized. It turned out to be Mr Justice Garland – he looked quite different without his wig and robes. They all strode off in the direction of the river, except for Charles Byers, who came up and escorted Sheila and Emma to the river bank. They walked through a gate and across a field on the opposite bank to the pumping station.

It was a beautiful summer's day and the water of the River Brede sparkled and danced in the afternoon sunshine. Butterflies fluttered among the frothy white cow parsley flowers and sheep bleated across the peaceful Marsh. No scene could have felt less sinister. That morning something had inspired Sheila to forsake her usual navy blue suit for a bright red skirt and somehow, here on familiar local ground instead of in the Hove courtroom, she felt a surge of optimism.

Across the river the jurors were standing on the concrete slab next to the small red-brick pumping station, or plodding about in the long grass. One of the more intrepid male jurors clambered gingerly down the steep bank above the drainage pipe culvert and stood on the concrete ledge, peering into the water.

It seemed extraordinary to see the opposing QCs chatting together like old friends. It just showed that to the professionals, a murder trial was rather like a game of cricket. Sheila speculated that they had both been out to lunch with the judge before the Winchelsea excursion. She wondered if the jury had noticed all the details about the position of the Audi on the A259 the night of 13 May, and the point on the same road which she and

Mr Soan had reached when she said there was nobody in the car. 'He said we were just by the layby, 25 or 30 yards from the car. Of course nobody would have been able to see into the car at that point, but in fact we were much nearer before I realised that Aunt Flo was not there, and said so. This was not pointed out by anyone during the trial, but I did not say anything. I still felt very detached from it all as though it was all unreal and I had no part to play in it.'

Jane travelled home from Hove to Rye with Auntie Mary and Uncle Albert who had been in court that morning. Simon was not feeling well that day – it was the only day of the trial he missed. 'Auntie drives rather slowly,' says Jane, 'and by the time we were coming round the hairpin bend at the bottom of Ferry Hill, the jurors, the judge and the lawyers were walking all together up to Tanyard Cottages before getting back on to their bus. It seemed very strange to see them all out together like that, as if it was some sort of jolly coach outing. I felt very embarrassed and hoped they wouldn't notice us as we drove past.'

After about three-quarters of an hour the visit was over. The jurors trooped back on to the bus and Emma drove Sheila back to Rye. Sheila took the opportunity to do a little shopping: 'I was the luckiest because I lived so near. I went and bought some bread in the Olde Tuck Shoppe and met Mrs Webb, the magistrate's wife, who asked me how things were going. I said they were going very well. Then I dropped in to see Anne [Wood] at the Sue Ryder shop and she gave me a lift home.'

The next day, Thursday 1 July, began with police evidence about the tyre. PC Reese was asked about the time when he reinflated Mrs Bowler's nearside tyre in her drive at 25 Fair Meadow. He said he read the pressure as 17 pounds per square inch, attempted to reinflate it to 24-26 psi but could only reach 20psi. He disconnected the foot pump and must have replaced the valve cap, although he had no recollection of doing so. He confirmed that he had driven the car back to the police station, and that it had by that evening lost 5lbs in pressure.

Victor Booth, the scene investigator, described the part he had played in the police tests, including his reconstruction of the walk Florence Jackson would have to have made to reach the pumping station.

PC Derrick Watson, the Rye police vehicle examiner, told how he examined the Audi 'as a result of a request from scenes of crime officer Mr

Booth.' He confirmed that he measured the pressure as 15psi. Asked if the valve caps were missing, he referred to his report made at the time and said that if dust caps had been missing he would have recorded the fact because the form he was required to complete was designed to record anything defective or missing.

Detective Constable Poplett gave an account of how he had arrested Sheila Bowler, and the way she had reacted.

On the last day of the week, Dr Heath was recalled by Mr Glass who had a few more matters to put to him. Heath declined to speculate about the cause of a tear in Mrs Jackson's coat. There was a great deal of discussion about death by drowning, but attempts to pinpoint the time of death were hampered by lack of data about the depth and temperature of the water.

It proved invaluable to Nicholas Purnell that by the time he embarked on his cross examination he had made sure the jury had seen the steep river bank for themselves.

Heath said that Mrs Jackson's injuries could have been caused at any time within four hours of her time of death. Had her injuries been four hours old at the time the Prosecution alleged Sheila killed her (9.30 to 10pm) then clearly they would have been noticed by the Greyfriars staff and Mr Day – and Mrs Bowler could not have done the deed.

But Mr Purnell was more interested in how Aunt Flo could possibly have got into the water. The Defence had accepted Mrs Bowler's initial scepticism that the old lady could have walked to her death. Now it was up to Purnell to prove that she was *so completely* immobile that Sheila Bowler could not physically have got her into the water. He put it to Heath that, considering Mrs Jackson's immobility, 'it would be physically impossible for someone, short of being a gladiator or someone of that nature, to get a body alive or dead and hurl it out into the water?'

'That is correct,' agreed Heath.

Her injuries were inconsistent with having been pushed from the top of the bank, so what, Purnell asked the doctor, was the alternative?

'I am not saying it would be done in a few seconds, it would certainly take a few minutes. You could assist her down the bank,' said Heath.

Instantly Purnell poured scorn on the idea: 'Dr Heath, I suggest this is really in the realms almost of fantasy, but you are suggesting a superman. You remember how difficult it was to get down the bank yourself?'

Heath insisted that on the contrary a single person could have helped Mrs Jackson down that bank.

'What about a lady of 63?' asked Purnell.

'Yes' replied Dr Heath, 'My mother is 80. She could run up that bank.'

There was laughter in court.

'Dr Heath, forgive me,' said Purnell. 'This is a murder trial and you are an expert witness and my client is standing trial on a murder charge... Are you being facetious in your answer?.. We know this elderly woman had trouble with walking. Could anybody run up that bank? Could you run up that bank? Your mother at 80 could run up it?'

The exchange continued, lapsing into bathos as Dr Heath pointed on a photograph to part of the bank: 'My mother could from this part here in a couple of skips she could have been up it.'

'A couple of skips?'

'Yes.'

The judge intervened: 'We have left out that this was probably in the dark.'

'Pitch black,' agreed Purnell, using a little poetic licence. In fact there was 92 per cent moonlight on the night of May 13.

In re-examination Glass asked the doctor how easy it would be to get the old lady down the bank if she resisted. Then, said Heath, you would have to apply more force: 'What she had was just two blows to the head or two injuries to the head, one on the forehead and one on the eye. They may be "encouragement blows," if I can describe them as such.'

Dr Jeelani, GP to both Mrs Bowler and Mrs Jackson, took the stand as a witness for the Crown. He was asked about a report he made to the Department of Health and Social Security in 1990 about the mobility and general health of his patient Mrs Jackson. He replied that he had written that she had multiple falls at home and signs of brain failure, becoming slightly confused and disorientated. She had restricted mobility but was able to dress and undress, and was able to get around her flat. The report had been written to help her gain mobility allowance. In cross-examination he confirmed that she was incontinent and that Mrs Bowler had played a major part in the care of Mrs Jackson and her sister Miss Gillham.

Purnell focused on this valuable information: 'Mr and Mrs Bowler, throughout the time when you were treating Miss Gillham and Mrs

Florence Jackson, had always taken a very active and caring part in the care of them?'

'Yes,' agreed Dr Jeelani. 'It is only Mrs Bowler who drew my attention to them. They themselves could not ask for it. Yes, she played a very active role and I do not think they would have lived on their own without the help of Mrs Bowler, it would not have been possible, otherwise they would have had to be put into a nursing home a lot earlier.'

'It was Mrs Bowler who would alert you to the fact that the aunts needed attention?'

'Yes, several times there was a medical problem and she would do that.'

'And it was Mrs Bowler who would take an active part in their everyday living circumstances, buying them food and visiting them regularly?'

'That is correct.'

'She would look after their needs as best she could?'

'Very true.'

Purnell pressed his point home: 'Can you give us some idea over a period of how many years we are talking about?'

'From 1977 onwards.'

The next witness was heard very briefly: PC Roy Panniers confirmed what he had said in his statements, describing three timed journeys he had made in an unmarked police car between Bexhill and Winchelsea on 27 May and 11 June 1993, just seventeen days before the trial started, to replicate Mrs Bowler's routes on May 13.

He was followed by the last witness for the Prosecution to be heard that week. David Price said he was a scientist from the Forensic Science Laboratory at Aldermaston, where he had been working for the past twenty-two years, specialising in vehicle component failures. He had been called to give evidence on the nature of any damage to the Audi's front nearside tyre, which the police had asked him to examine.

His testimony began well, and by the time the Friday hearing was over, Glass had led him carefully through the complexities of his technical examination of the tyre. Mr Price said he found the tyre was in good condition with a pressure of 18.5psi. He was asked whether the air got out of the tyre on its own or whether it was let out. He said it must have been let out. He had been asked to consider all the possibilities: there was no puncture, there was no defect in the wheel itself, there were no signs that the tyre had ever been dislodged from the bead. There was no dirt between the tyre and the wheel. The valve was clean and there was no way for dirt to get in. Nor had the valve leaked: the state of the valve assembly was so clean that it must have had a valve cap on. Then Glass asked him to state his conclusion: 'My conclusion I can come to is that air was let out from this valve at the point where the vehicle came to rest.'

The first week of the trial had ended.

That day Sheila had departed from her usual practice and had driven the Audi to Hove, with Jane taking her own car. They had separate plans for the weekend. Jane wanted to stay at home in Fair Meadow, but Sheila and Simon planned to stay with Mary and Albert at Royston. They had attended the hearing that Friday and would travel back with Sheila. But in the event Sheila and Simon stopped for a few hours in Essex on the way to Hertfordshire. Susan Catmur, Sheila's childhood friend, was 50 that day and her family had arranged a surprise party.

Throughout the weekend the family discussed the trial so far. Albert said Purnell was a brilliant advocate and Sheila was obviously in good hands.

Simon and Sheila left Royston around 3pm on the Sunday. They wanted to attend Evensong at St Mary's in Rye. At church, where Simon was a regular member of the bell-ringing team, friends came up to enquire how the trial was going. Chris Davson, a pillar of the church, had a gift for Sheila. It was a pearwood cross on a leather thong which, he said, he loaned to people in need. The last person to have it was a young curate at Rye, James Gladstone, a descendant of the Victorian statesman. He had died of cancer in his thirties.

'I've got a feeling you might be needing this,' said Davson.

CHAPTER SEVEN

SENTENCE OF THE COURT

Monday 5 July was another fine summer's day: as the second week of the trial began, it looked as though last week's good weather was holding. The journey to court was now becoming almost routine. Sheila gazed through the car window as they drove through the lovely Sussex countryside. They passed the turning to Glyndebourne where she had once been treated to opera tickets ('I wasn't impressed – all that corporate entertaining!') and sped on over the rolling South Downs towards the coast. She still felt cocooned by the same sense of detachment that had sustained her for over a year.

At 10 o'clock the court reconvened. Once again Mr Price the tyre expert was called to the witness box, this time for cross examination by Purnell. Russell Parkes had told Sheila that the barrister had spent an entire weekend studying the tyre evidence, and now he set about demolishing the Crown's thesis.

Price's testimony fills no fewer than one hundred and fifteen pages in the transcript of the court proceedings. As the hours wore on, with the expert being recalled after the lunch break, it became so convoluted that, Sheila could not help noticing, the jurors looked increasingly confused and some looked very bored: 'One of the younger ones appeared to be nodding off and the judge kept glancing across at them – I suppose they must dismiss jurors who fall asleep.' But she was afraid to look at them too closely: 'Russell said to me before the trial, "Now you mustn't ogle the jury!"'

Nicholas Purnell's aim was to point out that all the tyre evidence was put forward on an entirely false basis, because Mr Price thought the tyre had been found completely deflated, and did his tests accordingly. Steven Coulmanhole, when interviewed by the police and asked to take part in the test, had concluded that the tyre, when he had to drive it onto the recovery truck, was inflated to about 10psi. But as Purnell pressed on, the evidence became almost incomprehensible in its technicalities.

In re-examination by Mr Glass, Price introduced a further proposition – that the air could have been let out at the scene by someone like a mischievous schoolboy. This led the questioning into so many further complications that the judge was moved to intervene: 'Does this really help us very much, Mr Glass?... It is rather in the realms of extreme hypothesis.'

The next testimony came from Jonathan Ashe, the police photographer, who described the videotapes and photographs he had taken of the body of Florence Jackson on the river bank, and of the section of river where her right slipper was found, the area around the pumping station and a number of tyremarks on the hardstanding next to it. He told the court about photographing the post mortem examination, then the Audi inside and out, and Victor Booth's walk along Station Road. He had also, he said, photographed a newly purchased pair of slippers, and had filmed Deborah Bassett wearing them to walk along Station Road – an experiment designed to show the wear on the soles of the slippers after the walk.

The last witness for the Crown that afternoon was Detective Sergeant Linda Booth and arguably she may have been the most important, because it was she who had taken such extensive notes so soon after Mrs Jackson's body was discovered.

Mr Glass began by asking Booth to produce a number of exhibits. The first was Exhibit LB/1: the pair of black patent shoes which Booth had obtained from Sheila Bowler – the ones Sheila produced on May 14 and said she was wearing the previous evening. Then Sheila's coat and skirt were produced – the reversible anorak with the imitation fur fabric lining was produced as Exhibit 77; the skirt was Exhibit 53.

Now Booth was ask to show the jury a further exhibit – the black and red shoes produced on the 20th May.

'At 13.45 in the afternoon did she produce to you a pair of black and red shoes which she said she was wearing on the night of the 13th?'

'That is right, my Lord,' replied Linda Booth, using the deferential language that police officers use in response to counsel's questions.

Next she was asked to produce the will of Florence Alexandra Jackson dated 11 December 1989, leaving all her property to Robert and Sheila Bowler or their children if they predeceased them.

Glass then took Booth through all the statements she had written up from the 'scribble notes' made on the days she spent with Sheila Bowler following Mrs Jackson's death. He picked out the salient points: the lack of food in the house on the night of the 13th; the failure to have a bed made up; Mrs Bowler's denial that her aunt-in-law was afraid of the dark; the power of attorney held by Mrs Bowler; the missing silver torch; the ushering out of the police officers from 25 Fair Meadow on the night of May 14.

He then read to the court the full statement taken from Sheila by Booth on May 20. It amounts to twelve and a half pages in the transcript of the trial, and reading it aloud enabled Glass to rehearse the bizarre tale once again before the jury.

Finally he asked Booth to describe the video, filmed by Mr Wrightling, a technician, in which she had made a running commentary. She explained that this was a film of a journey in a car driven by Detective Sergeant Renno along two different routes from Rye town to the junction of the A259. The first was via Dumb Woman's Lane and Station Road: it took eight minutes. The second was via Winchelsea Road travelling towards Hastings: it took four minutes, half the time of the first. Booth said the purpose was to compare the routes. The underlying purpose was of course to discredit Sheila's story of the impulsive detour to the Hastings shops.

Then the court was adjourned till the following day.

Next morning, Tuesday 6 July, video equipment was set up in the jury's retiring room so that they and the judge could watch Mr Wrightling's film. They also saw another video with some aerial shots. This shows the entire area of the incident, with close-up shots of the river bank, the spot where the Audi was parked, and the area near the pumping station where Mr Giddings said he saw the reversing car.

After the showing of the video, Purnell cross-examined WDS Booth, asking her the purpose of the filmed journeys. Booth explained that the route described by Sheila to go to Hastings and change a pair of shoes 'seems such an illogical route for one to take when in a hurry to try and change shoes before getting to school.'

Purnell agreed that the alternative route would have been four minutes quicker, but a more sensible comparison would have been made if the two journeys had been started at Mrs Bowler's home, and if they had been made during a school term rather than in August, when the traffic situation would be quite different.

Sheila felt even more irritated, and so did Jane and their local friends in the public gallery. Everyone seemed to be missing the point. It was perfectly plain that Sheila's left turn into Dumb Woman's Lane was nothing to do with a short cut, and everything to do with her sudden impulse to go and complain about Simon's repaired shoes. Anyone who knew Sheila Bowler could tell you she was an impulsive driver – she would shoot off half way across the county without a thought. But it was usually to help out friends or children, or do some act of generosity. She was also an inveterate complainer, as local shopkeepers knew to their cost. But there was no malice in her complaints: she was simply a meticulous perfectionist, a thrifty woman who liked good value for her money.

Next Purnell moved to discuss the timing of the uncautioned statements taken by Booth. The policewoman insisted that when she took the statement from Sheila Bowler on 20 May 1992 she was not being treated as a suspect.

Now Purnell turned to the 'lack of food in the house' evidence, linking it with Booth's comment about the cat's food being frozen and the fact that Mrs Bowler did not possess a microwave. He poured scorn on the inferences drawn by Booth:

'She does not have a microwave: you thought that was a significant point to note, did you?'

'Not particularly, no.'

'She then remarked she had absolutely no food in the house and would have to go to the pub. You asked to look at her food cupboard to see what she had?'

'No I didn't, no.'

As for Booth's obvious irritation about being hurried out of the house, he explained that Sheila had had a long and exhausting day, having police with her all the time, having to identify the body of Mrs Jackson at the mortuary. Was it surprising that she wanted to get rid of them and go out for a meal?

Next the Defence QC turned to the evidence about Sheila's failure to make up a bed for Aunt Flo.

'Mrs Bowler was asked by you what sort of sleeping arrangements she had made at Fair Meadow to accommodate Mrs Jackson and she said she was going to put her to sleep on a bed settee in the lounge.... When you were at Mrs Bowler's house how much of the house did you look at?

'On that day?'

'On any days.'

'I subsequently went and did a full search of the house in company with other officers'

'When you made a search of the house did you look for this piece of bedding equipment upon which Mrs Bowler said she was going to put Mrs Jackson to sleep?'

'No, I did not'

'It's a pity you didn't,' thought Sheila, 'because you would have found it in Simon's room – the old Relyon folding bed I got from my sister years ago.' But it was no use getting angry: there was nothing she could do. Shut in her glass cage, Sheila suddenly felt more detached than ever: 'I watched what was going on, and more and more I had the sense of unreality. I kept thinking, "All this has nothing to do with me"'

Finally Detective Sergeant Renno took the stand, explaining his part in the investigations, notably the interrogation and the drive, with Booth and Sheila, over the route she claimed to have taken.

By midday on Tuesday, Day Six of the trial, the jury had heard all the witnesses for the Prosecution.

Now Nicholas Purnell made an announcement. He wished to lodge before the court a submission of No Case to Answer. The judge said he would hear it, and asked the jury to leave. 'Take advantage of the fine weather while you can!' he told them. Sheila thought that was a bad sign: it sounded as if the jurors would be coming back soon to resume their duties. Everyone else remained in court.

Purnell launched into a forceful demolition of the Crown's case. He submitted, he told the judge, that during the course of the Prosecution's case 'the three pillars of my friend's scenario which he invited the jury to consider have imploded, if I may use that curious phrase, not by any forensic skill on behalf of the Defence, but they have simply subsided by reason of their initial implausibility under examination by reasons of the circumstances which have now taken up a week of your Lordship's time and the jury's.'

Both Beckett and Pearson, said Purnell, had collapsed; Heath's evidence about the injuries and the method of getting Mrs Jackson into the river had been literally laughed out of court, and the proposition that Mrs Bowler was heartless and cold to the old lady had been proved ridiculous, not least by Mrs Jackson's own doctor.

The *Lovejoy* evidence had also collapsed – according to Mr Day's timing the journey from Winchelsea to Bexhill would have to be done in four minutes. And the timing of the entire exercise was in dispute, apart from two fixed points – the conversation with the Britannia Rescue operator at 10.21 and Mr Soan's call to the police at 10.42.

The forensic testing had been remiss – 'no one has seen fit to measure the height of the deceased body; no one has seen fit to weigh the deceased; no one had seen fit to taken the temperature of the body on recovery; nobody saw fit to take the temperature of the water'– all standard practical steps in a murder case. The tyre test had been rendered useless by being based on a wholly false premise. This was not perhaps surprising: 'Nobody notes or photographs the state of the car at Mrs Bowler's house in the morning. By the time the car is driven to the police station the raw material on which the experts have to work has been subjected to two pumping-up exercises. No one knows whether there are dust caps on the wheel or not – that is the wheel which is then examined first by Mr Watson then by Mr Price.'

Purnell ended by asking the judge to direct the jury in accordance with the Galbraith test. This was the legal ruling used by the stipendiary magistrate at Hailsham to decide that there was a case to answer in *Regina v. Bowler.* Now Archbold's *Criminal Pleading, Evidence and Practice,* a weighty legal tome, was quoted to give the court the benefit of the full instruction. The Galbraith ruling says that a judge can stop a trial if there is *no* evidence that the alleged crime has been committed by the defendant; if the evidence is tenuous, the trial judge has two choices: he can either (a) conclude that 'the Prosecution evidence, taken at its highest, is such that a jury properly directed could not properly convict on it; or (b) he can conclude that there is enough prosecution evidence on which a jury could properly convict, then the judge should allow the matter to be tried by the jury.'

Mr Glass got to his feet to address the judge. He argued that part (b) of the ruling applied in this case. He argued the case so strongly, at such length and in such detail that Mr Justice Garland came to the conclusion: 'I think I shall tell the jury that they can go away for the day.'

The jury was summoned back and told that because the submissions were going on for so long, he intended to adjourn for the day. But, he said, he took the view that 'this is a case that should go to the jury.' He would give a fuller ruling when the court reconvened the following morning.

Next day, Wednesday 7 July, before the jury was called in, the judge gave his ruling: the case must go ahead, he said, even though it was based on circumstantial evidence. Mr Justice Garland gave his reasons: 'Mr Purnell submitted that the decision in Galbraith does not apply to a case dependent on circumstantial evidence. In my view it does. Consideration of circumstantial evidence involves a two-stage process. First, determining on the whole of the evidence what facts have been proved, and secondly deciding what inferences the jury are sure that they can draw from those facts; both are matters generally speaking within the province of the jury. There is in my judgement, on one possible view of the facts, evidence on which a jury applying the two-stage process could properly come to the conclusion that the defendant is guilty.'

Sheila's family and friends in the public gallery leaned forward to listen as the judge continued:

'Mr Purnell was able to construct a very persuasive argument on the differences between the Crown case as opened and the evidence as it now stands, adding that the defendant must have been prejudiced by being branded in the opening as a callous and cruel woman who killed for greed rather than see her inheritance disappear at the rate of some £250 a week. The Crown's suggestion that the only alternative to the defendant as the guilty party was that a wandering maniac abducted and killed the deceased pre-empted the proper approach to circumstantial evidence. I say that in my view the jury can ask the question, "If not the defendant then who?"

The judge went on to give a brief summary of the evidence so far, ending with the words: 'I hope this explains why in my view on the evidence as a whole at this stage of the case there are issues to be left to the jury. It is not for me on the evidence to pre-empt their functions.'

So Nicholas Purnell had failed to get the case dismissed. The trial must go on. The jury was recalled.

Now, at last, it was time for Sheila herself to stand in the witness box. She had half expected never to have to appear there, and now she felt herself terribly unprepared. Nicholas Purnell had decided she would have to take the stand because otherwise the jury would never have the opportunity to hear her deny the murder. But the Crown had painted a black picture, with witness after witness coming forward to give what Glass had interpreted as damning testimony. At the time it had seemed to Sheila that her counsel had demolished them all one by one, and his submission to the judge of No Case to Answer had, in her view, been masterly.

But now, as she walked up the steps and into the box, she knew that in spite of Purnell's best efforts, she was about to face a terrible ordeal. The judge had decided there was a case for her to answer.

Placing her left hand on the black, leather-covered Bible, she read from the card held up by the usher:

'I swear by Almighty God that the evidence I shall give shall be the truth, the whole truth and nothing but the truth.'

As Sheila read aloud the words familiar to everyone from a million courtroom dramas, that last word, *truth*, assumed a particular resonance in her mind. Her Methodist parents had always insisted on truthfulness; her Methodist friend Audrey Mummery had advised her to tell the truth and all would be well. Sheila knew she had done nothing but tell the truth from the outset of this nightmare and where had it led her? Like the phrase *Dieu et mon droit* on the coat of arms outside the court building, 'the truth, the whole truth and nothing but the truth' now seemed a hollow and empty maxim.

Purnell began by asking the judge whether his client could remain seated while giving evidence, as she had circulation problems in her legs. She recalls: 'I had asked my counsel if I might be allowed to sit as I was not sure how many hours I would be standing and my legs are painful after standing for a period of time. I suffered from deep vein thrombosis some years ago.'

Mr Justice Garland agreed. Sheila sat down.

First Purnell took her through the statement she had made to WDS Booth, almost line by line, giving her a chance to correct any misapprehensions. The jurors were each given a copy of her witness statement as an exhibit, so they were able to study in detail what she had said on May 14, 15 and 20.

Purnell dismissed the motive of money, inviting Sheila to tell the court about her reasonably comfortable lifestyle. She was asked about Florence Jackson's will: she said that in May 1992, before the old lady's death, she had no idea what was in the will – it could have been made in favour of Sheila's children or step-children or other relatives.

Next the Defence counsel looked at opportunity, framing his questions to show that there simply would not have been time for Sheila to carry out the murder.

Sheila gave her entire account of the events of May 13 without ever suggesting that Aunt Flo's death might have been the result of an accident. In fact Purnell's questions were designed to emphasize Mrs Jackson's complete immobility and to this end, Sheila's initial words to PC Millington that the old lady could walk, though not very far, were ignored.

By taking the line of *complete* immobility, the Defence suggested inconsistencies in Sheila's story.

Why, for instance, did she bother to bring a walking stick if she knew the old lady could not use one? How was she going to get Aunt Flo upstairs to bed, or even into the house if Simon did not happen to be at home? She was not asked how her aunt got into the river: it was not, after all, part of the Defence's brief to prove it. All she felt she had to do was to show that Flo's death was nothing whatsoever to do with her.

Now it was time for Anthony Glass to begin his cross-examination. The prosecuting counsel pursued ruthlessly the apparent inconsistencies in Sheila Bowler's evidence. During her own counsel's questioning, Sheila seems to have given a reasonable account of her actions. Purnell had taken her through the events of 13 May in calm chronological order, gently teasing out additional information that might be helpful to her case.

But Glass's strategy is quite different. Immediately he goes into the attack, no longer ponderous and plodding, but piling question upon question with lethal intensity, deliberately skipping from topic to topic so that Sheila becomes confused, angry and defensive.

Glass begins by forcing Sheila to concede, once and for all, that Flo, far from walking to her death, could not even have got out of the car on her own: 'As far as you are concerned, do you agree that Mrs Florence Jackson could not have walked to her death last night?'

'I did not think that she could have walked very far at all, if at all, from the car.'

'So on your evidence, Mrs Bowler, can we exclude that she could have walked down Station Road by herself and fallen in where her slipper was found in the culvert. We can exclude that, can't we?'

'Yes.'

Now Glass quickly offers 'the only explanation' for the old lady's death, forcing Sheila to accede: 'You knew that she must have been abducted, didn't you?'

'That seemed an explanation,' replies Sheila.

'It seemed the *only* explanation, didn't it?'

'Yes.'

'Why didn't you ever say to anybody: "My aunt must have been abducted. She could not possibly have got out on her own"?

'I don't know.'

'It is because you killed her, isn't it?'

'No it is not.'

So in the first few minutes of cross-examination Glass has limited the jury to considering two – and only two – alternatives: first, the unlikely possibility that a mystery abductor has appeared out of the Sussex countryside in the short time Sheila is away from the car, and done away with Aunt Flo. Or second, that Sheila herself has killed the old lady.

Now he sets out to prove that the latter alternative is by far the more likely explanation. He reminds the jury of the evidence of Mr Coulmanhole, the recovery truck driver, which painted a picture of a hard-hearted woman who hoped her sleep would not be disturbed by news of the old lady's fate. Why, he asks, had she told Mr Coulmanhole that she did not want to be rung up by the police in the small hours of the morning? Sheila denies saying this at all: that was not how she felt anyway.

He reminds the jury that she failed to take Aunt Flo's suitcase out of the car. When she arrived back at Fair Meadow that night, why had she taken her own briefcase out of the boot and left Mrs Jackson's suitcase behind? Was it because she knew Florence Jackson was dead and would not be needing it – because she herself had put her in the river?

'I thought she might need the case if she was found and had to be taken to hospital.'

Glass moves on to Sheila's working patterns, to her financial situation, then back to her work and how she would manage to accommodate Aunt Flo. Sheila becomes so confused and tired that often she seems to be giving her monosyllabic responses quite automatically without allowing herself time to think. Why else would she give incorrect answers to simple factual questions:

'Had she [Aunt Flo] been married?'

'No.'

Yet Sheila knew perfectly well that Aunt Flo was married late and widowed early in her life.

Every few sentences Anthony Glass re-implants in the minds of the jurors the notion that Sheila is a calculating killer with no warm feelings of affection for a defenceless old lady:

'You planned to kill her but got cold feet? On the day you found her in a pool of blood… you could not go to hospital with her because you had to go *shopping*. What was it that was so desperately important to purchase you could not go to hospital with her?'

Shifting his questions back again to the night of 13 May, he asks why, if Sheila was worried about her tyre, had she not had the car checked by her local garage or one of the other service stations? Why risk a long detour with an elderly lady in a car which worried her, with no spare tyre?

'My question, Mrs Bowler, is really did you think it sensible and safe to take Aunt Flo in such a vehicle for over 30 miles at night? Did you think that a sensible thing to do?'

'In hindsight, no.'

'From Greyfriars to home and safety was five minutes away wasn't it, in Rye?'

'Yes.'

In another confusing time-shift he returns to her movements earlier that day. Why the detour along Station Road past the pumping station?

'Were you doing a reconnaissance in Station Road on the afternoon of the 13th as to where Florence Jackson was to meet her death? Was that the reason?'

'Of course not.'

Relentlessly he picks up on other points: why had she told Mrs Cameron-Clarke and Mrs Steward about her anxieties over her tyre tracks which might be found in Station Road? Why had she given the police a second pair of shoes? Was it 'because you did fear that the shoes that you had first given might supply some evidence against you? Is that not the reason?'

'No it's not the reason.'

'Why didn't you ring the Days to see if they were going to be in and that the [protein supplement] had arrived?'

'I didn't consider that it was necessary.'

'Going to Mr Day's in Bexhill was your excuse to be out, wasn't it? So you could consume some of the light, because you planned to murder Aunt Flo when it was dark or just about dark. That is the truth of the matter, isn't it?'

'No, it is not.'

On and on go the questions, twisting and turning, ducking and diving, shifting and sliding, challenging and accusing.

Glass's techniques of pacing and control are masterly. Occasionally he slows his pace and adopts a more conciliatory tone, lulling his quarry into temporary complacency:

'My goodness, when you arrived at Mr Soan's house it was a matter of some urgency to make that telephone call?'

'Yes, it was.'

'Some people can go on a bit, it is difficult to stop them talking?'

'Yes'

'Do you put Mr Soan in this category?'

'Yes'

'And you had an emergency on your hands?

'Yes.'

Glass reminds the jury of Mrs Bowler's professional status. Her responsible job should be a point in her favour but he can also use it to underline the enormity of her alleged crime: 'You are quite an experienced person at dealing with people, aren't you, and making your point of view clear, that sort of thing as a teacher?'

'With children, yes. Mostly children.'

'Did you ever say to Mr Soan: "Look, I'm terribly sorry, but this is an emergency. I have got an elderly lady in the car, can I just straight away use your telephone?'

'Oh yes I did.'

'Did he let you use it straight away?'

'Yes, he did.'

'So we are talking about a minute or two before 10.21 that you get to his house, you make your point clear and you get to the telephone.'

'Yes.'

Glass permitted himself a tiny smile of triumph. His strategy had worked. Sheila Bowler in her confusion had fallen into the trap he had set. If she had used the telephone as soon as she got to the Soans' house, that meant she must have arrived just before 10.21. If on her own evidence she left Mr Day's house in Bexhill at 9pm and if, from the police test drives, the journey to the Station Road junction took only half an hour, what was Sheila Bowler doing between 9.30 when she arrived at the junction and, say, 10.15 when she rang the Soans' front door bell? Didn't that give her ample time to murder Aunt Flo?

The timing, says Glass, is critical in this case. He directs Sheila to one particular passage in her statement: why on 15 May had she failed to mention that on the return journey from Bexhill, she made a detour into the centre of Bexhill, to look for the shop Elan? She had only told detectives about this on 20 May. Hadn't she invented the whole detour because by 20 May she had realised that timing was becoming an important issue? Sheila's answer is that she had forgotten all about it. After all, she had not stopped at the shop – she had just noted it in passing to check its location. Glass makes her explanation sound like a lame excuse.

He presses her further about her visit to Mr Day. Mr Day had said in his statement that she had 'stated or implied' that they would be over in the Bexhill area the next day anyway so they would call in passing. Why, he asks, bother to go that night? 'If you had in any event intended to be in Bexhill on the 14th there would have been no reason at all to be in Bexhill on the evening of the 13th, would there?'

'No.'

'Do you see the point?'

'Yes.'

'Do you agree with me?'

'Yes.'

What speed was she driving, wonders Glass: 'Aunt Flo said I was driving too fast, so I slowed down to 40. Even that was too fast.' Was the trip a chore, he asks. No it was not, says Sheila indignantly: Aunt Flo did not get many opportunities to get out. The drive to Bexhill was not a chore, it was very pleasant. She explains why she had to stop the car: 'Aunt Flo had begun to rub her stomach which suggested that she was in pain. She had been to hospital for exploratory examinations and I pulled her up under the arms.'

Yet again she is asked about the timing of the arrival at the Soans: this is a point the jury must not be allowed to forget.

'I arrived at the Soans' house at 10 past 10. Bexhill would only be a five minute detour. I drove slower. As I said, Aunt Flo does not like driving fast.'

'Would the journey from Bexhill to Winchelsea have taken an hour?'

'I would not have thought it took an hour.'

It took far less, says Mr Glass, especially if Sheila left Tom Day's house, as he says she did, soon after the *Lovejoy* programme started. Even if she left later, at sunset, which that night in mid-May was at 8.43, she would still have had ample time to return to Winchelsea and commit the crime.

Now the prosecutor moves to the behaviour of the tyre. Why, if she was worried about the tyres, had she not gone into a service station and had them checked? The car had behaved similarly before but it had righted itself, explains Sheila.

Glass is incredulous: 'It must have gone through your mind, Mrs Bowler, from that very afternoon, that you could have a serious problem with the car that day, bearing in mind the driving you planned for it?'

'I was concerned.'

'Why on earth didn't you do anything about allaying your concern when help was available? Why didn't you do anything at all?'

'I planned to do it the next morning.'

Why, asks Glass, had she pretended that the valve caps were missing, when an experienced police vehicle examiner said they were not? 'Are you really saying, Mrs Bowler, that the police have supplied a couple of dust caps?'

'There were no dust caps on those two nearside wheels.'

Back he comes to the central issue before the jury, the issue they must never be allowed to forget: 'I'm going to suggest, as you appreciate, the Crown's case is that you did away with Florence Jackson that night and you did away with her at the pumping station, didn't you?'

'No.'

'And you did away with her in such circumstances that she left her slipper behind at the point where she went in, didn't you?'

'No, I did not.'

'I come back to the point I made. She couldn't have just walked off with the killer, could she?'

'With help maybe.'

'Taking five minutes to go the distance of this court. Are you honestly saying that you think as a realistic possibility that she walked off with the killer?'

'No, she couldn't have walked.'

What about the testimony of her former teaching colleague Mrs Steward? Why had Sheila brought up in a casual conversation the subject of her tyre marks being found down Station Road? Because Mrs Steward had said nothing at all to make her mention the tyre marks. Was it because she was beginning to get worried about what might be discovered as a result of forensic examination?

Half way through the cross-examination the court adjourned for the lunch break: 'The cross-examining went on past the lunch break,' she recalled years later, 'and I was not allowed to associate with anyone. So between one and two o'clock I sat in solitary confinement (at least from any family or friends or my counsel) in the foyer of the court, and ate my sandwiches.'

There was one small table in the cramped tea bar under the stairs. She was still sitting alone there eating her lunch when someone tapped her on the shoulder. It was David Turner, a clerk at the Rye branch of Heringtons. Coincidentally his wife had taught Jane at Rye primary school. 'I hope it all goes well,' he said. Then two ladies approached and wished her luck.

'We've been sitting in the public gallery,' said one. 'You mustn't think we've got a sordid obsession with murder cases,' said the other, 'it's just that we're very interested.'

Hovering about nearby she saw Detective Superintendent Brian Foster. He had attended the court every single day to check on the case's progress. He had spent long months of investigation on Operation Dace, and now his efforts were coming to fruition.

Back in court that afternoon Glass pursued his cross-examination ever more persistently, picking up points from Sheila's written statement.

Why, he demands, had she repeatedly refused to sign the property form to release Aunt Flo's house for sale and pay the Greyfriars fees?

'At that stage,' said Sheila later, 'I experienced a complete loss of memory and in order to play for time I asked for the question to be repeated. Even so, it did absolutely nothing to revive in my memory the reason why I had not signed the property form. So I ended up giving only the original reason, which was that Bob said before he died I was not to sign it, rather than the reason my solicitor John Sperring had given in his statement to the police, which was that the form was not legally binding and was therefore pointless – although that might have given the Prosecution the opportunity to say that if I had signed it no harm would be done.'

Back once more to the tyre. Why on earth, asks Glass, his deep voice full of melodramatic incredulity, had Sheila not decided to drive slowly along on the damaged tyre – which was not after all completely deflated, just to get a bit nearer Tanyard Cottages and further away from the corner? 'Trying even very slowly to get there?' Surely this would be preferable to leaving an old lady in the dark near a difficult corner for an uncertain time? Why hadn't she done that?

'Why did you not at least have a go at driving that car with Aunt Flo in it very slowly along the road so you would not have to leave her in the dark on the road in the car on her own? Why did you not try it, Mrs Bowler?'

'I don't know. I just felt the tyre was too flat.'

'You didn't try it, did you?'

'No.'

Why had she left Florence Jackson in the car when everyone at Greyfriars said she was afraid of the dark – she liked the light on, she liked the curtains drawn.

Sheila says these views of Aunt Flo were exaggerated. She never said she feared the dark – she just didn't like the idea of people peering through the window at her. Of course she hadn't liked leaving Aunt Flo alone in the car, but she didn't seem to mind, and Sheila didn't think she would be away long. She had 'half run' till she found the lights on in the Soans' house.

Why, asks Glass, did Sheila not tell her daughter, who was fond of her great aunt, that the old lady was coming to stay?

Sheila replies frostily that Jane lived in London and in any case she was approaching her music degree exams. She would hardly be likely to come down to Rye in such circumstances.

'The point I am making is this, that it was rather an event in your life and an event in Flo's life. On each of the two occasions you never mentioned it to your daughter, do you see the point? The point I am making is this: you didn't tell your daughter about Aunt Flo coming because you knew Aunt Flo was not going to live beyond the night that you collected her. Is that not right?'

'That is not true.'

As Glass's questions continue relentlessly for another hour and a half, jumping about in terms of time and place, calculated to confuse, the trial transcripts show Sheila becoming more and more tired and muddled: 'I felt absolutely numb, as question after question was fired at me I really wondered what the point was of making me repeat information that was to be found in my statement. I was so scared of saying too much that I often just answered yes or no, and failed to qualify one or two comments which I realised, too late, could have gone in my favour in the jury's eyes.'

Anthony Glass's final question was designed to damage any remaining vestiges of Defence evidence showing Sheila as a dutiful, caring niece to her husband's elderly aunts:

'You have heard from the police about the inquiries they have made. Have you put any advertisements in any newspaper *yourself* or anything like that to try and see if any person saw this elderly lady being abducted from a car on the main road and put into another car that night, have you done anything?'

Nicholas Purnell objects: 'This defendant had a solicitor, as my learned friend knows, on the 20th May!'

'I do know,' persists Glass. 'Have you *yourself*, was my question, done anything like that, have you put in an advertisement?'

'No'

'Have you *yourself* made any enquiries to see if anybody saw such a happening?'

'No.'

'Because you would know it would be a quite hopeless exercise, wouldn't you, as you did away with her at the pumping station.'

'I did not.'

At 3.30pm Sheila Bowler stood down and returned to the dock.

There was time for just one more witness that afternoon. David Brown, a local farmer, was the first Defence witness called. His function was to raise in the jury's minds the possibility that Mrs Jackson was murdered by an 'unknown abductor.' He repeated what he had said in his statement: he had been driving along the A259 from Rye to Hastings when a car coming from the opposite direction had come round the Strand Bridge bend at high speed, cut straight across his path and headed off down the road to Winchelsea Beach. It was travelling so fast and so dangerously that he remembered thinking, 'They must have done a bank job.' He particularly remembered that the car had one odd-coloured door.

Mr Purnell then asked Mr Brown to read the date on the top of his statement. He read aloud that it was May 18. But, he protested, this was not the date the statement was taken. Although he had contacted the police on May 14, immediately he heard the news of Mrs Jackson's death, and they had promised to come and take a statement, he had to telephone them twice more, and it was in fact two weeks later before they finally arrived to take the statement.

The implication was that the police, having decided from the outset that a murder had been committed and that Sheila Bowler was the culprit, were not interested in pursuing any other avenue that might scupper their theory.

Mr Glass poured scorn on Brown's testimony. There were, he pointed out, no banks in Winchelsea to rob, and this theory of an unknown abductor was quite fantastic.

The second Wednesday's hearing was over.

Sheila's step-daughter Elizabeth attended the court each day that second week of the trial. She told Sheila that evening that her testimony in the witness box had started well, but that she seemed to lose confidence as the hours went on and began to sound very unsure of herself.

'She told me she could see the adrenalin draining away,' recalls Sheila. 'Elizabeth was right. The cross-examining continued for about another hour and a half after lunch, by which time I really felt I had given an appalling account of myself, though the family tried to say I had done well.' (When Russell Parkes visited her later in Holloway Prison, he told her that Nicholas Purnell had said she was one of the worst witnesses he had ever encountered.)

So that evening Sheila was particularly surprised to receive a phonecall from France. It was Russell Parkes in Brittany ringing from a local shop. He had sneaked out secretly, he said, because his wife objected to his working on holiday. But he had just spoken to Charles Byers and was confident of victory: 'I've got the champagne on ice!' he told Sheila.

Thursday, July 8, was the penultimate day of the trial. By this time the case had attracted a great deal of publicity in both national and local media and each day more and more photographers appeared at the court. Friends reading the newspaper reports and watching the progress of the trial on the local television news were becoming more and more anxious. Of course, everyone expects the opening days of a trial to look gloomy for the defendant, as the Crown paints a black picture. But now the Prosecution witnesses had had their say.

Mrs Daisy Wood followed David Brown as the second motorist brought by the Defence as an eyewitness to support the 'unknown abductor' thesis. When she entered the witness box Sheila recognized her from earlier that morning. She recalled seeing her sitting in the 'Defence Witnesses' section of the first floor lounge, a small, grey-haired woman 'who looked as though she didn't want to be there.'

Mrs Wood was clear about the timing of her sighting of the stranded Audi. She was driving from Hastings towards Rye when she passed 'a family size car.' She did not see any lights of any kind on it. She said she arrived home at 10.45 by the clock and she knew the journey took 12 minutes, so she would have passed the car at 10.37, before the arrival of

Harry Kershaw, who had said he saw nobody around at all. She said she saw beside the parked car 'what looked like a group of people, definitely one or possibly two, they were either helping someone into or out of the car.' She could not say if they were male or female.

Mr Glass dealt with Mrs Wood's evidence just as summarily as he had dealt with Mr Brown's. It was perfectly obvious, he said, that the people she saw were no unknown abductors but the search party - Mr and Mrs Soan and Mrs Bowler herself – gathered around the car.

The final witness for the Defence was Mr Sperring, Sheila's solicitor. He was asked by Mr Purnell about Florence Jackson's financial situation. He said Mrs Jackson had a state pension and occupational pension from her job in the Foreign Office, which could have been supplemented by an attendance allowance. Purnell put it to Sperring that if the flat was sold, the money could have been invested and the interest added to Mrs Jackson's income. He agreed. Sperring gave a valuation on the Ferry Road flat of about £35,000. He confirmed that Mrs Bowler had come to consult him about a property form she had been asked to sign and he had told her it had no legal force and she need not sign it.

As she watched the solicitor step down from the witness box, Sheila felt a wave of panic sweep over her as she sat helpless in her glass box. So was that it?

'I had a real shock when in the second week the Defence witnesses came and went almost without trace,' Sheila was to write later from her cell in Holloway prison.

But for their part Nicholas Purnell, Charles Byers and Russell Parkes were satisfied that the glowing testimonial from Dr Jeelani, who was, after all, a witness for the Crown, would be quite strong enough to convince the jury of Sheila Bowler's good character.

Next came the closing speeches for the Crown and for the Defence. Whereas in the opening speeches the Crown has the advantage of placing the allegations firmly in the jury's mind, the Defence counsel is able to deliver his closing speech last and hopes effectively to refute all the Crown's allegations.

Anthony Glass's closing speech methodically considered all the evidence piece by piece. Bowler was, he said, inspired by the 'age-old motives of greed and money.' It was clear, he concluded, that Mrs Jackson had been driven around for nearly two hours as Sheila Bowler waited for darkness to fall so she could carry out her wicked plan to expedite the old lady's death and prevent her £35,000 nest-egg (the estimated value of Mrs Jackson's flat – though it would later be sold for just £18,000) being eroded any further by nursing-home fees. On Dr Jeelani's evidence there were times when the old lady was not really orientated – she did not know where she was.

She had gone down that bank with Sheila Bowler because this was somebody she knew and trusted. That was how she had gone to her death in the River Brede – this frail, 89 year old lady who was afraid of the dark.

There was nothing at all wrong with the Audi's front tyre, Glass went on – a forensic expert had proved that. In any case, if there had been, why did she not proceed to drive, very slowly, along to Tanyard Cottages?

Plenty of passing motorists had come forward and two had made statements to police at the time saying they had seen the car and it was empty as Sheila Bowler walked away from it. That was because by that time Mrs Florence Jackson had been drowned in the River Brede. That was why Bowler had not bothered to take the zimmer frame from the Home; that was why no food was ready for supper; that was why no bed was made up; that was why she had not even bothered to take the old lady's suitcase out of the car. She knew none of these things would be needed – because Mrs Florence Jackson was already dead in the river.

Had Bowler shown any remorse or grief? On the contrary, she had told the recovery truck driver she did not want to be woken in the night. Even when she heard the news of the old lady's death, what had she done? She had carried on making biscuits and seemed to the woman police officer to be full of the joys of spring.

'A couple of blows and a shove cruelly ended the life of Florence Jackson,' concluded Anthony Glass. 'They were acts of calm, cool and cruel deliberation.'

Now it was Purnell's turn to convince the jury. He scornfully dismissed all the Crown's points: the motive, the opportunity, the method. He drew the jury's attention to tests which would have been invaluable had the police seen fit to carry them out. He contrasted them with pointless tests which had been undertaken, but which had added nothing to the case. For instance, there had been no attempt to make a forensic examination of Mrs

Jackson's clothing – in particular the torn sleeve of her coat and the shoulder of her petticoat – which might have led to the discovery of an unknown abductor.

There was, he said, no forensic evidence whatsoever to link the defendant with the river bank or with the violence inflicted upon Florence Jackson: no tyre marks, no footprints, no weapon, nothing found on defendant's clothing or shoes, and nothing in the car.

Sheila Bowler, he said, was being asked to prove her innocence, instead of the Crown having to prove her guilt. He would not, he said, specifically deal with Mr Price's evidence about the tyre, the wheel and the valve – enough time had been wasted on that already. But, he warned the jury, they should be sceptical about its credibility: for instance, PC Watson, who examined the tyre the day it was removed from the Audi had thought it was in poor condition, but Price said it was in good condition with adequate tread and little damage. He reminded the jury about the pressure measured as 17psi by PC Reese who tried and failed to pump it up to 25 or 26 psi, making do instead with 20; then the pressure had dropped to 15 psi by the time it was measured by PC Watson at the police station less than a mile away, and finally 18 psi by Mr Price.

On the timing on the evening of May 13, Purnell said it was simply too tight, bearing in mind the difficulty of moving Florence Jackson and what Sheila Bowler would have had to do to get her into the water. 'Here we have an immobile old lady, dark rough ground and a very steep bank – it is impossible.'

On Glass's sinister interpretation of Mrs Bowler's failure to remove Mrs Jackson's suitcase from the car, Purnell said that if she had, she might have been accused of removing the contents of the car, which after all was quickly removed to the police station.

On Mrs Bowler's failure to creep along by the kerbside on her deflated tyre, Purnell said that would have been dangerous enough to cause an accident.

He concluded by asking the jury to remember that here they were dealing with an elderly widowed lady of 63. When they went off to consider their verdict, they should take into consideration her age and her likely fate if they returned a verdict of guilty.

At the end of that day, Sheila, Jane, Simon and Elizabeth met Nicholas Purnell and Charles Byers as usual to discuss progress. Purnell announced that he would not be in court for the whole time on the following day. He had to attend an important meeting in London: he sat on the Lord Chancellor's Advisory Committee and he could not miss it. But there was no need to worry, he assured Sheila. She would be in the capable hands of Emma Kerr and Charles Byers.

Although Sheila thought this rather strange, in one sense she found it reassuring: it meant there was nothing to worry about: 'After the closing speeches on Thursday of the second week I really thought there would be no problem in my being acquitted as there had not been any proof of my involvement – no surprise to me!'

Friday, July 9, dawned warm and sunny yet again. To Sheila and the family it seemed their year-long nightmare was almost at an end. 'The last day,' Sheila told her family as they set off for Hove. 'At least now we're on the very last lap and it'll soon be all over.'

'The last day, Friday, was a real scuffle to get into the court past the press,' recalls Sheila. 'Simon was wonderful and cleared the path for me.' The photographers gathering at the stark concrete entrance shuffled back as Simon, a large man, sometimes clumsy because of his very poor eyesight, cut a swathe through their midst: 'Look out, here comes The Bodyguard!' they joked.

Mr Justice Garland began his summing up by pointing out to the jury that it was their duty 'to consider a period of about two-and-three-quarter hours on Wednesday 13 May of last year between about 8 o'clock and quarter to 11.' Then he described the events leading up to the death of Mrs Jackson. As both the Defence and the Prosecution had accepted that Mrs Jackson was immobile, it is hardly surprising that the judge concluded, 'She could not have got out of the car by herself; at best she could only have walked slowly for a very short distance with somebody helping her.'

'The case that we are dealing with,' he went on, 'is murder. In this case the issue is straightforward enough and there is no difficulty about it. The issue in this case really is, was it the defendant or somebody else?'

He agreed that 'with hindsight we may feel that it would have been beneficial if more tests had been carried out.' But in their absence the jury's duty was to look at the whole of the available evidence and draw their conclusion from that: 'When you ask yourselves what conclusions you are sure you can draw you are entitled to ask if anyone else could have done it. You have to exclude the possibility of an unknown abductor before you can draw an inference of which you can be sure.'

He reminds them to give weight to Mrs Bowler's good character, not least because of her age. They are entitled to take into account that anyone who has reached this age without committing any offence (they must disregard a minor road traffic offence) is less likely to commit so serious an offence as murder now. They should not hold it against her that she elected to remain silent during police interviews because that was anyone's right. They should draw no inference from it.

Next he summarizes the evidence. The tyre evidence he dismisses in one sentence: 'The evidence of the tyre tests has turned out to be of no use at all.' Similarly, the Prosecution witnesses Pearson and Beckett turned out not to be sure whether or not the Audi was empty when they passed it. Likewise, 'it became abundantly clear that Florence Jackson was not put in the river by a couple of blows and a shove from the top of the bank.'

So far, so good: Sheila and her supporters were encouraged.

But, went on the judge, 'a great deal of evidence remains, including that of the defendant herself.' He would divide it up into a number of topics: motive; the purpose of the journey to Bexhill and back; the tyre and the behaviour of the car during the journey; the timing, which was important; how and where Florence Jackson was killed; the defendant's behaviour, and finally 'the role of the unknown abductor.'

A few significant remarks were noted by Sheila's team as helpful to their case. There was no evidence at all, said the judge, that the defendant knew what was in Mrs Jackson's will – the jury had a copy as an exhibit and could look at it, but they must remember she knew nothing of its contents. Dr Jeelani had 'presented the defendant and her late husband as supportive and caring people who enabled Flo and Lil to go on living in their own flat.'

Mr Day's words 'stated or implied' had led Mr Glass to overstate his case: there was nothing to prove that Mrs Bowler had any fixed plan to be at Bexhill on the morning of May 14. Indeed, Mr Day had been wrong on several counts: 'He is clearly terribly wrong about the *Lovejoy* timing,' just as 'he was also wrong about the conversation with Mrs Bowler. The *Lovejoy* video was not played over to him until three-and-a-half months later.'

Running through the complicated timing evidence of the motorists brought as eye-witnesses by both Defence and Prosecution, Mr Justice Garland asked, 'Is it impossible to reconcile all this? Are you left in doubt by it all?'

Dr Heath, in cross-examination by Mr Purnell, had been 'led into what can only be described as a wholly unrealistic speculation. It was quite clear that [Mrs Jackson] could not have been pushed from the bank anywhere without this being obvious from examination of her body or her clothing. So, as [Dr Heath] finally agreed, she must have gone in from the top of the culvert and that is where her slipper was found. There are difficulties and Mr Purnell reminded you of them. There is a steep bank from the top of the bank to the top of the culvert and we have all looked and one of you tried it.'

The taking out of the briefcase from the car might be explained as a matter of habit, and the conversation with Mrs Cameron-Clarke about tyre-marks might be explained because that lady said she had herself raised the subject. The failure of Mrs Bowler to tell her daughter about her great-aunt's visit could have been explained by the imminence of the girl's music exams.

The summing up so far seemed fair and rather in Sheila's favour. But then the judge turned to the theory of the 'unknown abductor,' supported on the Defence side by the evidence of the torn clothing, the failure to eliminate fingerprints, the car seen by Mr Giddings turning at the pumping station, the car recollected by Mr Brown which looked as if it had come from a bank job, and the red car coming up Station Road stopped by Mr Soan.

But, he went on, 'Is it really credible, that someone quite by chance would abduct and immobilize an old lady at a busy spot where the traffic moves slowly, with the caravan site on the other side of the hedge without losing one or both of her slippers, taking a walking stick which was of no use to her and the torch when the owner of the car with its flashing hazard lights might reappear at any minute?'

Lastly – Mr Justice Garland's voice was grave – 'We know, and there is really no dispute about it, that Florence Jackson was unlawfully killed by drowning. Somebody murdered her by putting her in the river. Why did the defendant never tell the police that Florence Jackson could not have got out of that car by herself and make it clear that it was not a missing person situation but an abduction? The defendant says she did not tell the police because nobody asked her. Ask yourselves – why not save the police and the dog handlers, Mr and Mrs Cameron-Clarke, Mr and Mrs Soan, Mr Coulmanhole all running around looking? It was put to her, "Why not try to drive slowly on that tyre.. to get a bit nearer Tanyard Cottages and further away from the corner, rather than leave the old lady in the dark near a difficult corner for an uncertain time?" Nobody suggested, as Mr Purnell seems to think, that she should drive in such a way as to cause an accident.'

The judge ended by warning the jury not to be influenced by sympathy for the defendant on account of her age: 'and please do not be deflected by consideration of what as a matter of law would be the consequences of a verdict of guilty. Mr Purnell frankly should not have referred to it, you must put it out of your minds.'

In other words, the jurors were forbidden to think beyond the verdict they gave that day. They were to put out of their minds any ideas about what might happen to a woman like Sheila Bowler if they found her guilty of murder.

When Mr Justice Garland had finished his summing up, he addressed a few final words to the jury about technicalities such as electing a foreman, taking with them the exhibits of the case and the procedure if they wanted to see other artefacts, for instance Mrs Jackson's clothes. If they wished to see any of the videos again they could come back to open court. He asked them, 'as a final matter of law' to try to arrive at a unanimous verdict.

At 11.17am on Friday 9 July the jury retired to consider their verdict in the case of Sheila Bowler and the courtroom was cleared. Sheila, Simon, Jane and Elizabeth left the court and climbed the steep stairs to the first floor lounge. From the public gallery came Susan Catmur, Jane's friend Mary Anne and her grandmother Mrs Jones, and Hilary Jones, Jane's cello teacher. They all sat down in the 'Defence Witnesses' area. At first nobody knew what to say.

Finally the reality of her situation had dawned on Sheila: 'The judge's summing up appeared fair until the end. I could not believe my ears, and I really knew from that moment that I had no chance.'

Charles Byers joined them. He remained optimistic: 'In spite of that Charles Byers said not to worry too much, as the further away the jury got from the summing up, the more they were likely to forget it. We tried to keep our spirits up during the interminable wait.'

Linda Booth and David Renno stood talking in the 'Prosecution Witnesses' section. At the other end of the lounge a number of journalists were milling around.

Jane began to cry: 'Don't let that lot see you crying,' admonished Sheila. The journalists appeared to be out of earshot – until someone noticed a wire leading from a black bag on the carpet. A microphone had been left strategically placed near where they were sitting. Simon went and asked an official if there was somewhere else they could sit. They were shown into a small room leading off the lounge area.

Someone had brought sandwiches and they pecked at a few, but nobody had any appetite. Susan Catmur suggested a game of consequences – a bizarre suggestion, but then the whole situation was bizarre. They all joined in.

The waiting went on and on. An usher came in and told them crossly that they were not allowed in that room at all. This room was for barristers only, he said sternly. They left and returned to the public lounge.

After three long hours, at 2.20pm, they were recalled to the court. But the usher assured them this was not to hear the verdict. While they and the jury were out, there had been a technical development. The jury had sent a note to the judge asking a question, and the judge had discussed his answer with counsel. By this time Purnell had returned from his meeting and he and Byers compared their notes with those made by Glass, Kark and the judge himself.

The jury were recalled and the judge read out their note: 'On what part of the journey on 31st May from Greyfriars to Bexhill or from Bexhill to Station Road did Mrs Bowler assume that she was going at 40 miles an hour?' The judge explained that everyone had compared notes and had produced the following amalgam: 'She did not go out very often at

Greyfriars. The drive to Bexhill was very pleasant. Flo never liked travelling very fast. Then either: "I was travelling no more than 40", or "I slowed to 40. Flo said even then wasn't I travelling rather fast." That, he added, was from Greyfriars to Bexhill.

The jury retired again and the court was again cleared. This time a room was found for the Bowler party and they were allowed to wait in privacy. Three more times they were called back on technicalities or jury questions – though for a while, sitting in their private room, they could not be located by the court ushers.

The second recall was to hear a discussion between counsel and the judge about hotel accommodation being available if the jury could not reach a verdict and the court had to return on Saturday. (In 1993 jurors were not allowed home for the night if they were in the middle of trying to reach a verdict. Now the rules have changed and they are permitted to return home.) The hotel booking would have to be confirmed by 5 o'clock so the judge had decided to bring the jury back at 3.30pm and say that 'they must not feel under any constraint of time, but if they feel that they are not going to reach a verdict in the next quarter of an hour then they are to say.' He added: 'The prospect of a re-trial is absolutely horrendous.'

The third recall was to hear the judge respond to another question from the jury. They wanted to know more about the evidence of Mrs Pearson and Mr Beckett – what they saw or did not see, and the timings. Once again Purnell and Byers conferred with counsel for the Crown to supply as exact an answer as possible from the notes they had made.

At 3.15 the jury returned to court and the judge read out the answers given by Pearson and Beckett, ending with Beckett's words, 'I can't be sure there was no one in the vehicle.' He asked the foreman if he wanted any of the passages read again and the foreman said he did not. The jury retired again at 3.20pm.

At 3.50, the fourth recall, the jury were summoned back to court to be given the majority direction, and once again the whole court was reconvened.

The clerk to the court asked the foreman to stand. 'Mr Foreman, will you answer my first question Yes or No. Have you reached a verdict upon which you are all agreed?'

'No,' said the foreman.

The judge explained that a majority verdict was one where either ten or eleven of the jurors agreed with one another on the defendant's guilt or innocence. If the jury could not reach a unanimous verdict, a verdict where they all agreed, then he could accept a majority verdict of 10 to 2 or 11 to 1. If they could not manage that within the next hour, hotel accommodation had been reserved for them to stay overnight, but the hotel had to be told before 5 o'clock. They must go away, and if by 4.50 they thought they would need more time the following day, Saturday, they must tell the jury bailiff and it would be arranged.

Sheila was feeling less and less hopeful: 'By this time I was beginning to feel really spaced out. I hardly knew what to think.'

At 3.52pm the jury retired to consider their verdict once again.

At 4.24pm they told the jury bailiff they wished to return to the courtroom.

Sheila and the family were summoned back to the courtroom for the last time. Yes, said the usher, the jury had reached their verdict.

Sheila stepped back into the glass-covered dock in trepidation: 'When Charles Byers came and called us back to court for the verdict I knew immediately the jury filed back in, by the grim look on their faces, what the verdict was.'

'Would the defendant please stand,' said the Clerk to the Court.

Sheila got to her feet.

'Would the foreman please stand.'

The foreman to the jury stepped forward.

The clerk addressed the man solemnly: 'Mr Foreman, will you please answer my question Yes or No. Have at least ten of you agreed upon a verdict?'

'We have indeed,' replied the foreman in a subdued voice.

'Do you find the defendant guilty or not guilty?'

'Guilty'

Sheila gasped and swung round to look at her children. Jane burst into tears.

'So' went on the Clerk, 'You find the defendant guilty. Is that by a majority of 10 to 2, or 11 to 1?'

'11 to 1' said the foreman.

The Clerk repeated the verdict: 'So you find the defendant guilty by a majority of 11-1?'

'We do,' said the foreman.

Byers and Glass said they had nothing to add.

Mr Justice Garland pronounced his final words in the trial of Mrs Sheila Bowler: 'There is only one sentence the law permits me to pass in these circumstances and that is one of life imprisonment. I make no comment on the circumstances of the case.'

Left to right: Simon, Jane, Aunt Flo.

Left to right: Jane, Aunt Lil, Sheila, Simon, Aunt Flo.

The trip to Oberammergau. Left to right, Aunt Flo, Aunt Lil, Sheila, Jane.

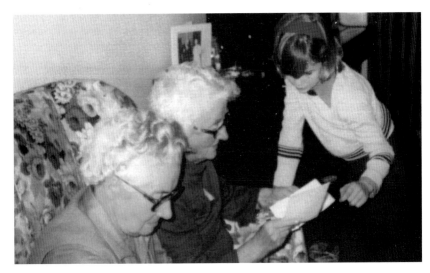

This picture, taken in 1977 shows the aunts as part of the Bowlers' happy family.
The picture shows, left to right, Aunt Lil, Aunt Flo and Jane, aged 8 years.

Aunt Flo in the Bowlers' garden sometime in the late 1980s.

The last picture of the Bowler family, August 1991, taken in Vienna (where Jane was playing with the East Sussex Youth Orchestra) before the sudden death of Bob in January 1992. The picture shows, left to right, Bob, Jane and Sheila.

25 Fair Meadow with the Audi.

The pumping station and the culvert showing the steep bank of the River Brede where the right slipper was found.

SHEILA BOWLER

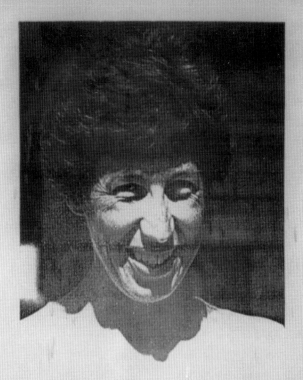

1255 DAYS

The poster designed by Sophia Borthwick for the candlelit vigil.

Sheila uses the prison bag to patch up her greenhouse.

Christmas Eve 1997, with Jane.

Christmas Eve 1997, with Tim and Tinker.

Sheila with cards from well wishers: February 1998.

Sheila with her 'Welcome Home' cake.
Left to right: Angela, Jane, Simon, Sheila and Tim.

CHAPTER EIGHT

HOLLOWAY

HMP Holloway: Monday 12 July 1993: 'When the word "Guilty" was pronounced my only feeling was disbelief – I could not believe that I had been convicted of a crime I had not committed – when all I was doing was a good turn to an old lady. My main emotion was one of utter disbelief and a feeling of being stunned that such a miscarriage of justice could be brought about by our so-called fair legal system. With the same numbness I felt when I was arrested I turned and was taken out of the courtroom. My last view of the court was Jane in tears with Elizabeth's arm around her.'

Sheila was taken down into the depths of the court building by two officers and locked in a cell. All her belongings were taken away from her – her handbag, her engagement ring – though she was allowed to keep her wedding ring, wristwatch and the £30 in cash she had with her. The family were not allowed to come and say goodbye: the only visitors permitted were Sheila's lawyers: 'Charles Byers and Emma Kerr came down to the cell to see me. Clearly they did not know what to say. The best Byers could think of was, "At least you won't die in there." Perhaps he meant I would get out on appeal, but that was not the way I took it.

'Then I was taken out through a dingy back exit leading into the car park. A taxi had backed up close to the door – I could hardly think at all, but I remember being surprised it wasn't a police car – and I was hustled into the back. As we drove out of the car park a host of press photographers were waiting at the exit. They pushed their cameras right up to the windows and I dreaded the photos they might publish next day.

'Then I was whisked away to Holloway, with the photographers running behind, still trying to take pictures of me. I was seated between a male and a female officer. They talked among themselves as if I was invisible.'

The taxi arrived at Holloway about 7.30 in the evening. Throughout the journey Sheila had in her mind the vision of a dark and lowering Holloway Prison. As a little girl she remembered passing its forbidding gates. But that was the old Holloway: it was demolished and rebuilt during the 1970s and '80s and the modern red-brick building is very different. In any case, the taxi was at the back entrance before Sheila even realised they had arrived.

She was taken to a desk and handed over to the reception officer. At that time of night the reception area was almost empty with just a couple of other women there. Sheila was too stunned even to take in what they looked like. First she was strip-searched by two female officers. This degrading process, which involves stripping, standing naked before prison officers and turning around (euphemistically called 'doing a twirl' by women prisoners) is now routine for all new prisoners. It is part of the Prison Service's long-standing battle to try to prevent drugs being smuggled in: 'Of course it was degrading, but I was too stunned and tired to care.'

She got dressed again: 'You can't wear those clothes in here – they're quite inappropriate!' snapped one of the officers, staring at the smart white blouse and dark navy skirt Sheila had worn in court. Sheila explained she had no other clothes with her, but would get her daughter to bring some in next day.

An inventory was made of her few remaining belongings, most of which had been taken away at the court. She was told to hand over her money: from now on it would be doled out to her weekly in the form of credit for goods in the prison canteen, known as 'private spends.' No prisoner is ever allowed to possess cash.

The woman officer seemed to soften slightly: 'Have you ever been in prison before?' she asked.

'No, I haven't,' said Sheila.

'Then let me give you a word of advice,' said the officer. 'Don't trust anyone in here: some people may seem very nice but they'll be trying to get round you.'

She gave Sheila a bedding roll containing two sheets, a pillowcase, a towel and face flannel. She was also given a nightdress – an old-fashioned long-sleeved garment made of flowered flannelette – a bar of white soap, a toothbrush and toothpaste.

'I'm sorry, you're too late for supper,' said the officer. Sheila was offered a glass of water and a bread roll, which she declined.

Then a prison doctor took all her health details, and told her she would be taken to the medical unit. Sheila wondered why this was necessary.

She followed another officer through a series of locked gates and along low-ceilinged cream-painted corridors to the medical unit. Although she was unaware of it at the time she was being taken to C1, Holloway's notorious psychiatric wing, housing some of the most desperately mentally ill women in the prison system. As Sheila was to write later in her diary, 'I was now a "lifer" and all life-sentenced prisoners are taken to C1 on admission: you are watched in case you are tempted to damage yourself, because this is the medical wing.' 'So-called,' she added in parenthesis. Sheila had automatically been designated a suicide risk.

Anyone unfamiliar with prison life is immediately struck by the extraordinary levels of noise in prison buildings – the echoing slamming of heavy doors and the jangling of keys, unmuffled by curtains or carpets; the blaring tannoy announcements, and, above all, the constant shouting and screaming as officers bawl out orders and prisoners yell back at them and at each other.

Holloway is no exception. Though by the time Sheila arrived, the eight o'clock 'bang-up' deadline had passed, and all the women were locked in their cells. Sheila heard them continuing their conversations, their shouts and raucous laughter echoing through the barred windows across the enclosed yard. Others yelled abuse at passing officers through the door hatches.

Sheila was put in a dormitory with four metal beds, one in each corner. Though each bed had a pinboard above it, the entire wall surface was covered with photographs and magazine cuttings. The heavy door slammed shut and the officer's keys jangled as they turned in the lock.

Sheila turned to face her new room-mates. They were all years younger than her – closer indeed to Jane's age. Two of the girls were very overweight with poor skin and unkempt hair. Sheila later found they were on heavy tranquillizing medication.

'They totally ignored me and I tried to detach myself from the whole situation – I felt we were in completely different worlds.'

The third woman spoke to her: 'She told me I'd better put my shoes on top of the cupboard or the cockroaches would get in them. I looked round and I could see that the room was filthy. Sure enough I saw four large cockroaches coming in through the window. My bed was in the corner nearest the outer wall. C1 is on the ground floor and outside in the exercise yard was all manner of filthy rubbish which attracted rats and cockroaches.

'I was still finding the whole situation very unreal: I felt I was being treated as the lowest form of humanity. Holloway was the saddest place I'd ever come across – so many youngsters, really only children.

'One of my room-mates spent the whole time yelling out of the window at a friend across the yard. The other kept banging and kicking on the door shouting things like, 'Gimme a light.' The third kept throwing a chair around. They seemed so frustrated, like animals in a cage. I just wanted to escape from it all, so I made my bed, got under the bedcovers, covered my head with the blanket and was so exhausted that I fell asleep straight away.'

The prison life of Sheila Bowler – Prisoner Number TV3389 – had begun.

Sheila was later to say that during the four years she spent in prison, she would wake every morning thinking she had had a nightmare, and would lie still, waiting to wake up. Maybe in a few minutes she would hear the singing of birds in her neat garden, the early greetings of her Rye neighbours, the muffled bells of St Mary's echoing across Romney Marsh.

Instead, this first Saturday morning, 10 July 1993, she woke to hear snatches of shouted conversation from outside her barred window. When she later began to make notes recording her experiences, she jotted down what she recalled:

Conversation floating past my window

'I was haemorrhaging so bad down the block they're givin' me tablets to stop it but I ain't taken them 'cos they're only coverin' up 'cos they was in the wrong puttin' me in there!'

'Got any bacca you can send round?'

'I want my fuckin' parcel or I'm gonna whack one of you twats!'

All new prisoners are allowed one 'reception' telephone call at the prison's expense, and when the dormitory was unlocked at 7.30am Sheila asked if she could make a call home. One of the officers took pity on her and after breakfast – bread and margarine with marmalade – she allowed her, most unusually, to phone from her office.

Back at 25 Fair Meadow Jane picked up the telephone: 'The first thing that struck me was the background noise. Though Mum said she was ringing from an office, there was still a lot of yelling and screaming and the echoing sound of banging doors. It sounded like Bedlam, but Mum was amazing. She was trying to tell me what time I could come and visit, and what clothes she wanted brought in. But there was such an uproar I could hardly hear a word. In her best schoolmistress voice she suddenly shouted out to the other women, "Will you *please* be quiet, all of you!" I was terrified – at that stage I didn't know the first thing about prisons and I thought she'd get a knife in her back!'

Sheila told Jane that she would be allowed to come and visit at 10.30 that morning, and read out a long list of items she wanted brought in.

As soon as she had put the phone down, Jane woke her step-sister Elizabeth and they filled Sheila's large white suitcase with all the toiletries they could find, and all the clothes Sheila had requested. There was very little time to spare if they were to make the long drive from Rye in time for the start of the visit.

It was Jane's job to navigate but by the time they reached the convoluted one-way streets of North London she was so distraught she found it almost impossible. She had never map-read in London before, and found the streets around King's Cross terribly confusing. She felt shaky and slightly nauseous, and began to panic, thinking they would miss the visit altogether.

'Elizabeth and I were both so upset, and in a terrible state when we finally dragged the suitcase into the prison entrance. We went up to some prison officers behind a glass screen, and the first thing we were asked was to show our visiting order. Nobody can visit a convicted prisoner unless the prison has issued an official form, but of course we had never heard of such a thing. The officers went away and muttered among themselves, and it looked as if we wouldn't be admitted at all. Then I heard one of them say, "I suppose we can't turn them away as it's their first visit." The warder at the gate pressed a button and these huge double glass doors slid open. We went through and found ourselves in a smoky, crowded waiting room and we sat down with the suitcase and waited. Nobody told us what to do.

'After a while we realised what other people were doing, and we were told to empty Mum's suitcase into a grey metal tray which slid through a hatch behind a glass panel. You had to speak through a microphone to the officer behind it. I emptied everything into this tray, but almost immediately the officer shoved it all back at me and told me the few things Mum was allowed to have.

'We had to sort everything out and put most of it back into the suitcase to take home again. It was so humiliating having to go through Mum's personal belongings – her underwear, her toiletries – in front of everybody else in the waiting room. Nobody spoke to us – they just stared. Elizabeth and I were both getting more and more distraught. In the end two men sitting waiting, who both seemed stoned out of their heads, took pity on us. One of them said, "Cheer up, the first visit's always the worst." It was a nice thing to say but it made me cry even more.'

All the banned items had to be stored in lockers before Jane and Elizabeth were given a 'rub-down' search and told to climb the steep stone stairs, clutching their locker keys and the few pence allowed to buy refreshments.

Upstairs in the visits room they found Sheila sitting at a table right at the front – one of several specially set aside for 'reception visits' for new prisoners – looking remarkably composed. As usual she was concealing her own feelings – partly because this strategy of detachment had got her through all the crises of the past year, and partly not to upset her daughter and step-daughter still more. She looked just as smart as she had in the Hove courtroom – she was still wearing her white blouse and dark navy skirt, and indeed, she told her daughters, on her way to the visits room one of the prisoners thought she was an officer and asked her permission for something.

The visit lasted one hour, and at the beginning Jane was very tearful. She could not find a paper tissue, and was very touched when one of the prisoners serving refreshments from a kiosk came out and gave her one. But by the end she left resolving that she would do her utmost to help her mother. Sheila must not stay a minute longer than necessary in what she was already describing as 'this hell-hole.' Sheila's lawyers had immediately begun discussing an appeal against her conviction, and Jane privately determined that by the time the next visit was due she would have tried to hurry the process forward.

Sheila's early phonecall to her family on Saturday morning was the first of many that day. In fact that first weekend, 10 and 11 July, the telephone hardly stopped ringing at 25 Fair Meadow as friends and acquaintances rang to comfort the family. It was left to Simon to answer the calls – Jane was too distraught by the ordeal of visiting her mother in Holloway.

We made one of those calls, late on the Sunday evening. Our daughters had been Jane's contemporaries at Rye primary school. With Sheila we used to share the regular Friday evening car runs across the Marsh to the old Hastings swimming baths on the sea-front where our children all had swimming lessons.

We had moved about thirty miles away to Staplehurst in Kent eight years before Sheila's troubles began, and the girls had lost touch, though we would occasionally bump into Jane when we re-visited Rye's picturesque tourist attractions with overseas visitors. Though we were aware of the accusation against Sheila (we had met a Rye acquaintance on a train a year earlier and heard the gossip) we had, like most of those who knew Sheila, dismissed the police allegations as ludicrous.

So we were horrified when we turned on the early television news that Friday evening, 9 July, and saw Jane walking in tears down the steps of Hove Crown Court as her mother faced life imprisonment for murder.

On the Saturday morning, while Jane was setting off to visit Sheila in Holloway, we were sitting in our kitchen reading the newspaper headlines. THE AUNT, THE BLACK WIDOW, AND A MURDER MOST ENGLISH, said the *Daily Mail*.

PIANO TEACHER GETS LIFE FOR AUNT'S MURDER was *The Telegraph's* headline. The next evening we rang the Fair Meadow number and left a message for Jane: 'Why don't you come over and see us when you feel up to it,' we suggested, 'and tell us the whole story, in case there's anything we can do.'

By the time she got the message, Jane was beginning to recover from the Holloway nightmare and was wondering which way to turn. Russell Parkes was still on holiday in France, Jane knew no other lawyers, and the message reminded her that her primary school friend's grandfather was a well-known lawyer. Perhaps his son* would know something about the law.

---

* Tim Devlin, a former *Times* journalist, was not a lawyer, but he knew something about miscarriages of justice. His father, Patrick Devlin, was a law lord who had played an important part in the campaign for the release of the Guildford Four. Lord Devlin was now

Sunday 25 July, two weeks later, was unseasonably damp and dreary as Jane sat in our living room for four hours and told us about this extraordinary case, starting with her mother's late-night telephone call on 13 May 1992 and ending with the dreadful moment more than a year later when Sheila was sent to prison for life.

We taped our conversation with Jane and transcribed it in a document which ran to thirty pages. A week later Jane returned carrying a bundle of witness statements which she photocopied for us in our office.

These documents, together with Jane's account of the case, and our previous knowledge of Sheila's character, convinced us that here indeed was a gross miscarriage of justice. Two points struck us most forcibly. First, we had always known of Sheila's passionate commitment to Jane's musical career. It was inconceivable that she would ever commit such a terrible crime, but it was doubly impossible that she would choose a time in the very middle of Jane's music degree finals to do so. Secondly we knew Sheila Bowler as a perfectly intelligent woman. The cold, calculating plot she was supposed to have hatched was so riddled with pitfalls that no-one with the slightest degree of intelligence could ever have thought it would work.

We were not of course lawyers, but we had a close relation we could consult. Our first port of call was our brother-in-law, the Appeal Court judge, Sir Paul Kennedy, who made it clear he could not look at an individual case, but could give us general legal advice. A prisoner would only be granted an appeal if the grounds were strong enough, he told us. Obviously the best hope was to find fresh evidence to support the appellant's case, and he agreed with our idea of trying to involve the local newspapers in a campaign to seek information and support.

As an embryonic campaign to support her case started to take shape, Sheila began to telephone us regularly, as often as her limited budget of phone cards would allow (we heard years later that she used to take her

very ill (he died the month after Sheila's trial) and could do nothing to help. Tim had set up a public relations agency which he ran from home, and one of his clients was The College of Law which trains solicitors and barristers, so he had many contacts in the law. Angela, a former teacher, was now a partner with Tim in the consultancy. Coincidentally she had spent the last few months before the trial visiting prisons as part of the research for a book, *Criminal Classes,* on the links between educational failure and criminality. So she was familiar with the kind of world Sheila had entered.

special prison phonecards into the bath with her in case they were stolen. 'They were my lifeline,' she said).

In one of these conversations, in early September, Sheila took our advice to begin keeping a diary of her life in prison. It might be useful when she was released, we thought, to be able to prove the physical and mental hardship she was having to suffer as a result of this terrible miscarriage of justice.

With remarkable stamina, she managed to write up the diary almost daily for the four years she spent in prison, apart from a few months when she was too ill or depressed to do so. The diary is neatly written in blue ballpoint pen in Sheila's upright, well-formed handwriting on a series of lined A4 jotter pads. It is a fascinating record of the response of a middle-aged, middle-class, educated woman to a new, sad and sometimes brutal world. All prisoners are to some extent affected by the paranoia that infects all total institutions like prisons, and when she posted each episode of the diary out to us, Sheila would always leave the top sheet of A4 paper blank so that it was not too obvious to any prying eyes that she was keeping a diary of her prison life.

Like all prisoners, Sheila had some particularly bad moments. One of the first came at the beginning of September – the weekend when Bob would have been 74. Prison officers recognize that birthdays and other special days are difficult to cope with – they have even invented the phrase 'anniversary syndrome' to describe the phenomenon. Sheila deals with her grief as best she can, noting it in her diary with characteristic euphemism:

Sunday 5 September 1993

'Tap runs on easily for all sorts of reasons, I guess not least as it was Bob's birthday yesterday. Didn't mention it to Jane and Simon today as I thought it might upset them too much.'

She was still recovering from a fall which left her with a black eye and a badly strained shoulder: it was to cause her trouble for many months, but she manages bravely to joke about it: 'I fell last Sunday after slipping on some water outside the kitchens and gave my head a bad crack, rendering me almost senseless. I think more attention would have been taken if I was out for the count! The doctor examined my eye which was almost shut when he saw me, looked at my swollen hip, put me on the couch, waved my legs around, then sent me back to the unit prescribing Panadol if I needed it. The doctors here are pathetically ineffective. This was the same doctor who, on seeing me when I entered this unit, asked if I had come to accept my situation. He seemed surprised when I said No. I remarked that as I had done nothing wrong I was never likely to accept my sentence.'

Sheila had been moved from C1 when it became clear after a week there that she was unlikely to want to harm herself. She was moved on to another wing, C5, the unit where most of the Holloway kitchen workers, mainly the more mature women, are held. Now she had her own cell. Paradoxically perhaps, 'lifers' are the aristocrats of the prison system, mostly respected – and sometimes feared – by other prisoners and, as a concession to their very long sentences, allowed a few more privileges. One of these is a room of their own.

As well as keeping up her diary, Sheila had to work hard to reply to the dozens of letters she was now receiving each week from friends and supporters, never fewer than half a dozen every day. Sheila kept all the letters from the four years she was to spend in prison, and counted them on her release – they ran into thousands.

Susan Catmur, the daughter of Sheila's old piano teacher Mrs Vines, wrote to her every other day. Sheila still has 737 of her letters. The loyal Anne Wood sent a postcard or letter every week with cheerful chat and Rye gossip. There are 210 of them. Carol Brigham, with whom Sheila used to have coffee some mornings before going to see to the Aunts, sent encouraging maxims: 'Carol says if Terry Waite can do it [prison] under such dreadful conditions, she is sure I can. But I don't think I am in the same category as Terry! Difficult to keep motivation going, would be easier if I *knew* the time span was only another ten months.' In fact, nearly four years on, Sheila was to meet Terry Waite when he came to join the Easter celebrations at Holloway in 1997 and judged an Easter bonnet competition.

At this early stage in her sentence, Sheila was allowed a one hour visit every fortnight, and like most prisoners, lived for that hour, though as she wrote early on, it was a mixed blessing: 'Feel very cheered since visit this afternoon. But after ten days have passed, the next four days seem interminable.'

Many prisoners, friendless and estranged from their families, have no visitors at all. For Sheila it was very different. So many people wanted to visit her that it proved difficult to fit them all in, even though three visitors are allowed on each visit. Her family of course were her priority, but there were dozens of friends who continued to visit regularly throughout the whole four years of her imprisonment. Very few had ever set foot in a prison before, and found the experience a real eye-opener. One, a woman magistrate, arrived without any form of identification and was mortified at being made to walk a mile to the nearest bank and get a print-out of her bank statement before being allowed in. Others, like Canon David Maundrell, who had conducted Bob's memorial service, and the Reverend Paddy Buxton who had helped organize it, were luckier. As Sheila's religious advisors they were allowed special chaplaincy visits outside regular visiting hours:

Monday 6 September 1993

'David Maundrell came to see me this afternoon. I am able to receive him in the chaplain's office as opposed to the large visiting area. What a luxury to tread on a carpet!'

Sheila's diary also makes fascinating reading because it charts a spiritual, emotional and sociological journey. For the first few months it shows that she is able to stand aside from prison life and maintain the numbed detachment that enabled her to survive arrest and trial. Although she goes through the motions of daily prison routine, she is still the outside observer, looking with pity at the other prisoners.

That Monday in early September 1993 she wrote in her diary: 'I could weep at the sad spectacle they presented yesterday in chapel. Most of them are between 17 and 23 – most on drugs, and many with several children. I have never seen such a dejected group of human beings. They are here for minor offences (apart from drug-dealing) such as non-payment of poll tax or TV licence. No way should they be locked up as they are: it only magnifies their deep sense of guilt and inadequacy. Not nearly enough suitable treatment is available.'

Sheila has never found it easy to express her emotions – this was one of the reasons she aroused police suspicion in the first place – and her diaries are never self-indulgently introspective. But just occasionally, hidden in her accounts of the humdrum routines of prison existence, a sentence or two reveals like a flash of light the reality of what she is feeling. The day after David Maundrell's visit, two months after her conviction, her anger makes her eloquent:

Tuesday 7 September 1993

'Can always find things to do but nothing takes away the immense feeling of solitude and rage I feel, isolated as I am from the world. Do wish I didn't feel so miserable when I wake in the morning. It's not so bad once the day gets going. Dreamt last night an officer came and asked me if I wanted to go home. Just don't know how I can stand this for so long. Motivation is so difficult to keep going and it is only nine weeks since I came here. It might as well be 9000 weeks.'

In fact at this stage Sheila had no idea how long her sentence would last. In spite of the view of the then Home Secretary, Michael Howard, that 'life should mean life,' few prisoners actually stay in prison until they die. Howard introduced the distinction between mandatory and discretionary life-sentences, and Sheila was in the latter category. A 'tariff' system sets the length of the sentence, taking into consideration the recommendations of the trial judge. But it would be another three months before Sheila would hear her fate.

Meanwhile, she tried to recreate in Holloway a life as similar as possible to the life she had left. In the evenings, locked in her cell from 8pm to 8am, she took up knitting again, while on her battery radio she listened to Radio Four, specially the music programmes, plays and news and current affairs to keep her in touch with the world outside. She listened to Choir Girl of the Year and the finals of the Leeds Piano Competition. By mid-September the batteries were running down.

Monday 13 September 1993

'I should have got some batteries today at canteen – we are not allowed to have them sent from outside – but I have only got £5.80 a week at the moment which includes my OAP's allowance of £3.25, and I must buy fruit and tea, talc and deodorant.' Mindful of the pennies, she changed her newspaper order from *The Independent* to *The Times* 'as it is now only 30p.'

Sheila had always made sure she and her family ate well with plenty of home-cooked food, fresh fruit and vegetables. The prison food was unspeakable, and the last meal of the day was served at 4.15pm.

Tuesday 14 September 1993

'Ghastly supper – three fish fingers (highly suspect), black potatoes (refused). Best thing were the peas (not mushy for once), then semolina (ugh!) Rock cake for supper at seven with a cup of tea. Terrible lunch yesterday of fish which was covered with batter and very dry because we had come up very late from the gardens. Supper not much better – dried-up meat pie, been in hotplate from 3.15 to 4.15.'

In fact towards the end of her fourth year in prison, Sheila was to elect to become a vegan in the hope of gaining a little extra nutrition. In Holloway vegans receive a 'special vegan pack' consisting of a small bag of muesli, a bag of nuts, three oatmeal biscuits and a spoonful each of marmite and peanut butter, unceremoniously smeared into polystyrene cups.

Through the grapevine of Rye people who visited Sheila in Holloway, news of her awful diet reached Robert, proprietor of the Swan Tearooms in the Mint, where she used to enjoy a toasted bacon and mushroom sandwich. She was also fond of meringues and Robert asked if he could bake her a special batch and send them into the prison. Sheila could imagine the Governor's reaction! But the gesture was typical of many kind offers from those who knew Sheila well.

The gossip continued to buzz in Rye and Winchelsea and many people remained convinced that Sheila Bowler must be guilty. In an area full of retired people brought up to believe in the infallibility of British justice, it seemed impossible that eleven of the 'twelve good men and true' on the Hove jury could have made the wrong decision. In a miniature version of the Civil War, families were divided by their views on Sheila Bowler. In Rye polite society, hostesses decided that – like politics, sex and religion – the subject of Sheila Bowler was one best not discussed at the dinner table. But people who knew her well could never accept the myth of the cruel, callous murderess deservedly locked up for life.

Meanwhile, far away from the Rye arts and music festival she had once helped to organize, Sheila joined the Holloway chapel choir and was one of the few prisoners who attended regular practices, though she found it difficult to memorize the words of the hymns: 'My brain, I fear, is becoming atrophied already!' She was indignant at the ways some of the prisoners behaved in chapel:

Wednesday 15 September 1993

'Very rude people at the back when a representative of the Mothers' Union stood up to speak. I helped the chapel-cleaner, a lady from Mauritius, prepare tea for twenty-nine people. Some of them behaved like animals and were taking eight biscuits at a time. They know nothing about manners!'

All prisoners when they first arrive are 'fitted for work' – allotted some kind of job, unless they are young offenders under school-leaving age, in which case they have to attend full-time education. As luck would have it, Sheila was given work that she found reasonably conducive: she was sent out to work on the Holloway gardens, which at least gave her a breath of fresh air daily and a chance to enjoy the late autumn sunshine. Characteristically, she set to work with a vigour unfamiliar in Her Majesty's Prisons:

Thursday 16 September 1993

'I have been set to weed round the very tall Queen Elizabeth roses. They are about six or eight feet tall and many of them have gone past it and produced hips. So I have taken it upon myself to prune them as well. I don't think the officers mind what I do as I never hang around.'

It was not long however before Sheila's sharp tongue got the better of her: 'The gardens officer in his usual bumptious way called a *pieris* a *spirea* and when I pointed out his mistake he said "Just testing!". He couldn't remember the name of the *choisyia* and was even more surprised when I told him it was called Mexican Orange Blossom.'

Next day (was the officer taking his revenge?) her work changed:

Friday 17 September 1993

'My chief job is now clearing the leaves, which is rather like clearing the Forth Bridge, and 'wombling,' which is the prison name for collecting the mounds of rubbish that is chucked out of the windows. (Remember the Wombles of Wimbledon Common?) We have to put plastic things in one bag, other rubbish in another, and believe it or not we have to empty them at the end of the day and make a list of the contents!'

Monday 20 September 1993

'Ghastly afternoon. Home Office chap turned up and we had to turn out the rubbish we had collected and assemble it in lines on the lawn so a photograph could be taken of it. Then in the pouring rain we had to put everything back in the bags. We were soaked and then had to spend an hour waiting in the gardening shed. I shall be eaten up with rheumatism by the time I get out of here.'

She was also given an additional task: 'I have been asked to care for Thomas, the Holloway garden cat, feeding and brushing and combing him each morning.' Thomas was some compensation for her beloved Whisky, the big ginger tom pining away back at 25 Fair Meadow. But getting access to the prison cat was not always easy: 'On a wet morning when there is no gardening this is a problem as I have no red band yet.'

Prisoners regarded as trustworthy were given a red wristband to wear, which allowed them to move more freely round the prison. It was at that time a piece of red cloth with a plastic insert containing the prisoner's photograph, job description and the areas of the prison in which she was allowed.

It was not long before Sheila became 'a redband.' At the end of September she wrote: 'One good thing happened today. I was told I had been granted a red band which gives me more freedom and hopefully will allow me into the church when I am free, to play the piano.' Soon she was practising regularly on the chapel piano: 'Managed a good 30 minutes' practice before work this morning and this afternoon.'

Some officers were kind, perhaps in deference to Sheila's age and her polite behaviour:

Wednesday 22 September 1993

'A really nice officer let me have a bath at 4.30 today when we came up early from the gardens. Then she said I could sit and watch the TV. What a treat to see a bit of news uninterrupted! She didn't lock me in until 8pm. It was so peaceful – I felt almost human again.'

She went to classes in aromatherapy and reflexology: 'Didn't learn much but will try not to be too hasty and will give it another go next week.'

But despite these valiant efforts, her diary still records her loneliness and depression:

Sunday 3 October 1993

'Feeling of depression almost unbearable. My mood swings are most unlike me. Will I ever get out of this hell-hole? I think the worst emotion is loneliness, which is worse than boredom.'

Every month or so, Sheila would surreptitiously post us the latest section of her diary. We typed each episode onto a computer disk. We found it fascinating – and worrying – to trace how Sheila was adapting to prison life, and how the subtle process of institutionalization was taking place. Every prisoner to a greater or lesser degree is subject to this process. It begins with small concessions to the practical necessities of daily life. Jane had brought Sheila a Monet poster:

Monday 4 October 1993

'Put up the poster Jane brought me on Saturday. I never realised before what a good adhesive toothpaste is.'

Far away from Ahmet's Bexhill hairdressing salon she found a new way to stay smart: 'A young prisoner cut my hair very well in return for a £2 phone card.'

The adaptive process is reflected in subtle changes in the language the prisoner uses. Sheila was soon writing about 'bang-up,' 'room-spins,' and 'private spends' as naturally as any old lag. Most significant is the shift in interest away from outside people and events towards a concern with prison affairs.

Sheila was no exception. Although she kept constantly in touch with family and friends by letter and telephone, and still enjoyed Rye gossip, she now began to take more interest in the other prisoners, and her diary begins to record their problems, and the endless frustrations of prison life. Her visitors noticed that while they gossiped about their own affairs, Sheila's eyes would stray around the other tables in the visits room: was Maureen's son visiting her today? Whose baby was that on Mary's lap?

At the end of September, after Sheila had been in prison more than two months, staff directly responsible for her were asked to contribute to an allocation report, giving their views on which prison she should move to from Holloway, which is mainly a remand prison, though about ten of its 500 women are lifers. From these confidential reports, made available to Sheila years later, it is clear that she had made a good impression in the ten weeks since she arrived at Holloway.

Her personal officer, responsible for her individual welfare, commended her for keeping herself busy, and said she was 'an intelligent, polite and mature woman who has not been a behavioural or discipline problem to any of the staff.' He recommended she should remain at Holloway because it was the most accessible to her daughter and partially-sighted son, and to her solicitor. He added: 'Sheila is very confident that she will be released from prison in about a year's time following a successful appeal. I would be concerned for her emotional wellbeing should the appeal not go as she expects it.'

The Church of England chaplain agreed, saying that he was concerned about her age and health. He added: 'Sheila maintains her innocence and is placing a great deal of hope on her appeal being upheld. She has an excellent relationship with members of staff and is trusted by them. Her relationships with other prisoners is also good. She has a quiet, pleasant demeanour. There is a great deal of sympathy for Mrs Bowler in Rye and concern at her conviction.'

On October 11 Sheila began a new job in the prison library, though she kept her garden job on Saturday mornings. She embarked on a course to prepare her for the work:

Wednesday 14 October 1993

'Have done homework tonight but have not studied *The Basics of Librarianship* very thoroughly. Very difficult to concentrate this evening as the racket outside is ghastly with shouting and screaming going on across the square.' Perhaps because of the stress, or maybe from eyestrain from cataloguing new books, she was suffering from one of the migraines which were to plague her for the next four years. Nevertheless she set about sorting out the library as she had the flower-beds and found the work made the days pass more quickly: 'Library badly organized and very dirty. Quite tricky classifying the non-fiction books with the Dewey numbers. Terribly noisy in the library tonight – smoking and drugs being handed around.'

In mid-October London Weekend Television featured Sheila's case in the *Casebook* slot of their *Crime Monthly* series. This reconstruction of the events of May 1992, made with the co-operation of Sussex Police, showed the Pooh-sticks experiment, with police officers floating the walking sticks, and Superintendent Brian Foster congratulating his officers on the success of Operation Dace in securing the conviction of an evil murderess. At Holloway the prison officers watched with interest. One of them taped the programme and allowed Sheila to watch it the following day.

Monday 18 October 1993

'Still reeling from the appalling LWT programme. The woman portraying me was nothing like me and appeared as a broken, dowdy, sour-faced widow eking out a meagre existence on a widow's pension by teaching at home.'

We had also watched the film and afterwards discussed it with Jane and Simon. Other friends of the Bowlers telephoned LWT, outraged by the programme. The producers replied that the *Casebook* feature was always the police interpretation of a recent case and as it was only a 15 minute slot in a one-hour programme, could not go into great detail. Nevertheless all the supporters who watched it felt strongly that Sheila was going to need all the support she could get in the face of this kind of adverse publicity.

Next day, when Sheila telephoned in some distress, we asked her to start compiling a list of everyone she could think of who might join a supporters' group. Sheila's lawyers were working on an appeal application, but there was no guarantee that permission would be granted, or that the appeal, if allowed, would be successful. It might be necessary to send a petition to the Home Secretary. That evening we sat down and began composing a letter, the first of many addressed to The Friends of Sheila Bowler. The campaign had begun.

CHAPTER NINE

BULLWOOD HALL

Despite the recommendations made by the officers and chaplain that Sheila should be allocated to remain at Holloway, the authorities decided that she should move to another prison, and after four months she was sent to Bullwood Hall in Essex.

However grim the conditions at Holloway, Sheila, like most other prisoners in her situation, was alarmed at the prospect of change. In spite of its large, volatile and constantly shifting population, Holloway has one major advantage – it is easy to reach by public transport. Bullwood Hall, like most of the other fifteen women's prisons, is isolated in the middle of the countryside, and Sheila realised that Simon, partially-sighted and unable to drive, would find it difficult to visit so often. Also Bullwood, once a girls' borstal, is now one of two high-security prisons, apart from Holloway, holding women who have committed very serious offences. The other, Durham's notorious H wing, then held Myra Hindley and Rosemary West, and it was some comfort to Sheila that at least she was not being sent there.

Bullwood Hall is a squat red-brick building surrounded by what David Jessel was later to describe as 'a vomit-coloured fence.' In the spring of 1992 Judge Stephen Tumim, then Chief Inspector of Prisons, had visited the prison with an inspection team and the prisoners told him of a harsh and inhumane regime. They were locked in most of the day and the food was appalling. Tumim left, promising to take action, but when October came and the Home Office had still not published his report, the women went on a five-day hunger strike and the prison received a lot of press attention. In December the report was published and the prison announced a new regime starting on January 3, 1993. Some changes had been made to improve conditions. But by the time Sheila arrived, nine more months had passed and standards had slipped again. Exercise was limited to three-quarters of an hour each day, there was more lock-up, the food had deteriorated, and the education department had declined, with many of the teachers absent and fewer prison officers on duty to supervise classes.

Sheila was driven to the prison one afternoon in early November and was allocated to the induction unit, Jay Wing.

Tuesday 9 November 1993

'It is ghastly – 12 mini-rooms each about 12 foot high and only 9 foot by 8 foot. It is cold – the walls are cream-painted brick – and there is constant piped music – much too loud. Must get some earplugs or it will drive me crazy. Horrible feeling of claustrophobia. Window in my room is six foot from the ground and that is the only daylight we have on this wing.'

One of the first prisoners Sheila met was Sara Thornton, who was already well known to the media because of the high-profile campaign to free her. Years later her conviction for murdering her husband Malcolm was quashed and she was finally released after a re-trial. Now Sara came up to Sheila: 'I've been waiting for you!' she said. Sheila noted in her diary, 'Sara had watched the case and said it was obvious I was innocent. Then she ushered me into her room, which she called 'campaign headquarters' and entertained me with a song she had written to be played on her guitar. She looks ill – she is very underweight.' She was probably still recovering from a hunger strike to draw attention to her case.

Sara had made life difficult for some of the staff and they felt she was a publicity-seeker and a disruptive influence on other prisoners. Sheila was fascinated, years later, to read one of the confidential reports made by the Lifer Governor in the January following her meeting with Sara, by then 'shipped out' to a different prison:

'Bowler was adamant that she would not serve the life sentence imposed. She stated that if the appeal system failed, then the pressure groups would finally force her release. One is mindful of the information that Sara Thornton might have passed on to her whilst still here at Bullwood Hall. If that is the case,' adds the report waspishly, 'then I would suggest that Bowler takes notice of the fact that Thornton is still in prison.'

During her last few weeks in Holloway, Sheila had struck up friendly relationships with three other prisoners – a woman and her daughter, and another older woman. Now she was in a prison where she knew no-one:

Monday 15 November 1993

'Missing them all very much. Very lonely. It is hell on this wing. Today a youngster had a cassette handed in and she has been playing it at full blast ever since. I tried to counteract the noise by watching a 1952 Joan Collins film – without much success.'

At Holloway Sheila had experienced relatively little animosity from other prisoners. With its 500 prisoners it is the largest women's jail in western Europe and has an amazingly rapid turnover: two thirds of the prisoners stay there on average just 28 days. As her prison reports show, Sheila identified a few maturer women she could get on with, and left younger women to their fights and drugs. But at Bullwood Hall, which holds about half the number of women, the atmosphere is much more claustrophobic. The prison used to run its own farm, and prisoners were allowed to work in the surrounding fields tending the animals. But Michael Howard's crackdown on prison security, following several high profile escapes by male prisoners, had a devastating effect on women's jails, as they were subjected to the same security measures. Now Bullwood Hall women have to remain within the cramped confines of the prison building – so it is not surprising that tensions run high.

At first, Sheila had to steel herself against whispered insults. Like those convicted of offences against children, prisoners who have attacked defenceless old people come low in the prison pecking order and sometimes have to be segregated for their own safety: 'One of the women has been making up all sorts of dreadful things about me. She was heard telling someone I was suffering from rigor mortis.'

Another woman hissed, 'Bloody murderer' under her breath as Sheila passed. A third sneered at her middle-class manners, 'Who does she think she is, Lady Diana?' Once she discovered that insulting grafitti had been scrawled all over the identity card on the outside of her cell door. She dismissed it in her diary as school-girl stupidity: 'Silly billies, putting remarks on my cell card.'

But the insults were not always so easy to bear: 'Don't know how to take this confined situation for so long.'

Sheila was not alone in being insulted by other prisoners: older women are in a minority in a prison population whose average age is much younger than the population outside, and many experience difficulties with the volatile and noisy behaviour of girls in their teens and early twenties. Sheila was the oldest woman at Bullwood Hall and she tried to sit at the same table as women in their forties and fifties at mealtimes: 'We have had to move our table to the end as we were being bombarded with chips one side and doughnuts the other.' With typical understatement she adds: 'Find some of company at meals a bit much sometimes: so glad to be locked in at eight.'

The only way to get through her sentence was to throw herself into as much activity as possible, just as she had taken part in town life in Rye. She attended evening classes in computing and aromatherapy – when they were not cancelled because of staff shortages. Her migraine returned with a vengeance and the toothache that had begun at Holloway now became severe. She put in another application to see the dentist but it took two more weeks of pain before she managed to get the tooth filled.

Every incoming prisoner is given an induction assessment, and the (unsigned) document, available to Sheila only years later, is perceptive: 'Sheila presents as a strong, independent and assertive individual with inner emotional resources. The strain of the trial and her imprisonment have taken their toll. Despite apparent outside support I have questions as to how easy she will find it to ask for help or support. It would automatically be assumed that with her abilities she could cope. Staff in all departments need to guard against such assumptions. Some difficult times may well lie ahead. The anniversary of her husband's death will certainly be a difficult period, as will the anniversary of her arrest, conviction and imprisonment. Further problems may arise if outside support declines and obviously should her appeal be unsuccessful, she will need considerable support. Under those circumstances the future that she would face would probably seem bleak.'

Had Sheila been able to read this report at the time it was written, she would probably have dismissed it with a curt, 'Nonsense!' She would also have been amazed to read in the same report that 'it was felt at one point at Holloway that she was depressed and as a result a Suicide Risk Form was completed.' 'I would never think of taking my own life, whatever happened to me,' she has said many times over the years. 'My faith in God is too strong.'

After a few weeks things began looking up. Sheila heard from her lawyers that she had definitely been granted leave to appeal, and that legal aid had been allowed to fund it. The news gave her a spurt of renewed energy:

Tuesday 16 November 1993

'I jogged 21 rounds of the netball courts in exercise this morning. It was a beautiful bright sunny day.'

It is not surprising that other prisoners, slouching around smoking roll-ups, stared at her in amazement. Within a week or two they had nicknamed her Supergran!

She was also moved to Swan, the lifers' wing, in a room upstairs at the end of a corridor:

Wednesday 17 November 1993

'Much happier as I can see out of the window to the woods, although the fence spoils the view.'

When she arrived, she had been allotted a job in the laundry – work she found very hot and tedious, with long periods of inactivity. The laundry women washed all the prison's bed linen and the white uniforms of the kitchen women, as well as the personal laundry for each wing, which would come in on allocated days. The kindly laundry boss was a prison officer liked and respected by all his workers, who nicknamed him Mr T.

Then, out of the blue, she was given one of the most coveted jobs in the prison.

Wednesday 17 November (cont.)

'Was surprised to be offered a job in Visits, involving handling cash and being in charge of the cash box to be brought back to Swan wing at lunchtime.'

But next day, in a typical piece of prison inefficiency, she was told that the job offer was a mistake – her predecessor had been sacked but was now to be reinstated.

In mid-December the wing officers brought in boxes of Christmas decorations and the women began stringing paper chains from wall to wall. On the 15th, Sheila recorded the preparations dismally in her diary:

Wednesday 15 December 1993

'Wing being decorated. Can't understand how people can be so jolly. Maybe if I wasn't here for life I would feel differently.' At the end of the entry she adds laconically, '7pm. Just heard my tariff is *12 years*. What a Christmas present! Wish I could go to sleep and wake in two weeks' time.'

We asked lawyer friends about the tariff. They explained that the tariff system, giving prisoners the right to appeal, had only been introduced in the last twelve months and nobody at that point had much experience of it. They advised Sheila to appeal against the twelve year tariff set for her, an action which would not in any way compromise her separate appeal against conviction. She should maintain her innocence, say she was a victim of circumstantial evidence and was not in any way a danger to the community. She set about writing the appeal letter.

Sheila had already made up a list of about 200 people who might wish to help in a campaign to free her, and in early November Jane had signed the first of the letters mailed out from our office to the group now officially christened The Friends of Sheila Bowler, letting them know the prison address and asking them to support Sheila, initially by sending her a Christmas greeting.

Five days before Christmas Sheila wrote of her delight:

Monday 20 December 1993

'Cards and letters still rolling in – incredible. Have as many as if I were at home.'

A week later she added: '204 cards have arrived for me – my room is getting to be called The Royal Mail. It doesn't make me very popular with the officers as all the cards have to be checked for drugs!'

Still, Sheila had no enthusiasm for this first Christmas behind bars. She did her best, reading the lesson at the carol concert ('Was exceedingly nervous. Salvation Army gave rousing accompaniment'). It was hard to feel festive.

Sunday 30 January 1994

'Very bad about writing diary. Patchy. Perhaps lack of time plus long periods of desolation and depression. Christmas seemed to go on for ever. The Prison Service did their best to make it a festive occasion but I had no heart for it.' Sheila had had her 64th birthday on January 3rd. She did not even bother to mention it.

The week before Christmas Sheila was offered a new job – that of Administration Orderly. On December 20 she began. Although her duties involved little more than cleaning, she told friends it made a lot of difference to be walking on carpet and hearing people having normal conversations – a far cry from the bellowed interchanges between prisoners and their guards:

'Have been asked to clean out boardroom and two toilets and sweep passages. Everything below par cleanliness-wise. Could spend a whole day cleaning one of the loos! Boardroom very neglected.'

She also made coffee for the Admin staff and – in a valiant attempt to inject a little efficiency into the Prison Service – she typed out an *aide-memoire* of their requirements, starting with the Governor. The list is a fascinating vignette of Sheila Bowler's reaction to prison life:

Strength of Coffee required for Admin Staff

Mrs Butler	*White, 3/4 spoon*
Mr Blackman	*Black, 1 spoon plus a little more depending on size of mug and strength of coffee + dash milk*
Mr Galloway	*Black – 1 heaped spoon*
Mrs Bright	*White – 3/4 spoon, milky and not too hot!*
Mr Hart	*Very strong tea*

One of Sheila's duties was to take the Governor's coffee into her office, and it was her custom to listen to see if the Governor was on the telephone before knocking and entering. One day, after she had been doing the job for about a month, she had her ear to the door for just this reason when a woman senior officer appeared on the corridor and stared at her angrily.

That lunchtime the SO called her over. Standing beside her was Sheila's personal officer, with particular responsibility for her behaviour. 'The SO interrogated me in front of everyone on their way to lunch, accusing me of eavesdropping at the Governor's door. "I shall be speaking to the Governor about this!" she threatened.'

That afternoon, in a ghastly travesty of a boarding-school carpeting before the headmistress, Sheila was summoned to explain to the Governor, who finally said she believed her. But she was nevertheless dismissed from the job. Sheila was mortified by the indignity: 'I just could not believe it!' she wrote furiously in her diary that night.

But her ignominious dismissal turned out to be a blessing in disguise, for it meant she was now transferred to work in the visits room. This was the job she had lost after just one day because of administrative bungling, but now she had been reinstated and she was to keep the job for over a year. Prison reports made at the time noted that she was 'polite to staff and visitors, keeps the stock up to date and is a conscientious worker.'

The year 1994 began with Jane Bowler feeling a little more optimistic. We had been contacted by the Channel Four programme *Trial and Error* about Sheila's case. The programme is made by Just Television, and Chris Mullin MP is on their advisory board. Two of his Sunderland constituents, the parents of Jane's friend Sophia Borthwick, wrote to Mullin, who notified the programme's producer. Coincidentally, Walter Merricks, another Just TV board member and a high-ranking officer of the Law Society, had been contacted by his father, a Winchelsea resident who had heard of the case from Anne Wood. The organisations Liberty and Justice have a close working relationship with *Trial and Error* and had also been in touch after hearing the background from letters we wrote to them. In January one of the programme's researchers, Sue Walker, made an appointment to come to Kent, meet Jane at our house and hear about Sheila's case.

The morning of Saturday January 29 was icy cold and as bad luck would have it our central heating had broken down. When she arrived around noon, Sue found us huddled with Jane round the gas fire in our living room, surrounded by papers about Sheila's case. She listened as Jane once again told the whole story, sitting on the same chair as on that wet July afternoon six months earlier, when her mother was first sent to Holloway.

Sue interrupted only occasionally to check the details of the extraordinary tale, commenting that on the face of it the prosecution case seemed to be 'full of holes.' When the story was told, she said she had three points to make. She wanted to emphasize, she said, that her programme was approached by hundreds of prisoners alleging miscarriages of justice, and researchers could only undertake to investigate a tiny fraction of them. They would have to look in great detail at Sheila's case before they even considered interviewing her. Secondly, the producers reserved the right to cease their investigations at any point if there was the slightest suggestion that the prisoner was after all guilty. Third, they never took on a case until after the first appeal had failed. We all nodded agreement.

Later, Sue was to tell the programme's producer that as she heard the story unfold, she was secretly becoming more excited by the minute. An experienced researcher who could trust her own judgement, she was privately convinced that here indeed was a genuine miscarriage of justice.

Just over two weeks later, Sue travelled to Bullwood Hall with producer Steve Phelps, whose father lived in Hastings and was already concerned about the case. Prisons are not very welcoming to TV programme-makers, so they went as ordinary visitors on a visiting order Sheila had sent them in advance. That day, February 15, there had been a heavy snowfall and the journey through the Essex country lanes was a nightmare, especially as their hired car broke down.

Tuesday 15 February 1994

'They arrived very late at 3.30 and all we had was a very rushed 15 minutes. It felt like being in the witness box again!'

Rushed or not, Phelps and Walker had satisfied themselves that Sheila's was a case worth investigating. So concerned were they that they took the unprecedented step of embarking on a full research programme *before* the case reached the Court of Appeal.

Sheila's diary entry recording the visit of the television researchers was the first after another long gap. Like many people both inside and outside prison, she found those weeks early in the new year particularly desperate. Not only was this her first Christmas in prison – it was only the second in thirty years without Bob.

On January 27 she had been assessed by the Lifer Board. The Lifer Governor read through the reports contributed by all who had dealings with her: her personal officer, works officer, education staff, lifer liaison officer and the Church of England chaplain. All said she was a conscientious worker who stood out from most other inmates because of her education, background and age. All mentioned the extent and strength of her support in her own community. All expressed their fears for her should her appeal fail.

The chaplain mentioned the unfortunate incident outside the Governor's office which caused Sheila to lose her job: 'I have found her to be a very hard worker (the Governor's corridor with all its windows has never looked better!) and I know she has been very upset by the "events" which means she will no longer be able to work there. I have sympathy with her for when I have knocked on the Governor's door it is not at all easy to hear if there has been a reply.'

Throughout the Christmas period we had been in correspondence with Charles Byers about Sheila's case. We reported that Lord Justice Kennedy had expressed doubt about the success of any appeal, unless strong fresh evidence could be found, because appeal courts are reluctant to interfere with the decisions of juries, especially juries that have reached such an overwhelming majority verdict as at Hove.

We had also, we told Byers, corresponded with Alistair Logan, the Guildford solicitor who had worked with Lord Devlin to free the Guildford Four. He had agreed there was a pressing need for new evidence to suggest that the original jury's verdict was unsafe. And we had spoken to Sydney Kentridge, the distinguished South African lawyer, an old friend of the family, who had expressed his concern about the case.

We arranged to go with Jane Bowler and George Pulman, QC, the local barrister who knew Sheila, to meet Charles Byers and Nicholas Purnell, to see whether we could help to find fresh evidence.

A meeting was arranged for mid-February.

At the beginning of February Sheila had made her first close friend at Bullwood, a Nigerian woman we will refer to as B. At last she had met someone equally well-educated, and they would do crosswords together. B had defended her against the rumour-mongers, and now it was Sheila's turn to offer support when in early February B's brother died, followed a week later by her father. Sheila wrote at length about the matter in her diary:

Thursday 17 February 1994

'Very traumatic, especially as in B's culture the eldest daughter is supposed to take on the responsibility of burying parents and B cannot be there. B even more distressed yesterday morning as the officers gave her a room spin, [search] saying they believed she had a mobile phone in her room. It turned out that one of the nurses had mistaken the aerial of her radio for a phone and reported her.'

It is well-recognized by prison staff that while male prisoners tend 'do their bird,' leave their problems at the prison gate and keep themselves to themselves, women tend to bring their problems about family, housing and money into jail with them, and are often much more supportive of each other. But sometimes the burden of taking on another prisoner's problems is too great to bear, and Sheila felt herself under even more stress than usual:

Tuesday 22 February 1994

'B still very depressed and it is having a bad effect on me.' A visit from Jane plunged her once more into misery. She wrote in her diary: 'Really looking forward to darling Jane's visit this afternoon and she was so miserable and unhappy. She was very upset about nothing in particular – perhaps because she was alone and didn't have to keep up appearances. How does God expect me to bear this pain and anguish? God please keep all my family safe while I am in this hell-hole.'

This entry is followed by another lapse, this time of about five weeks. Sheila seems to have lost the motivation to record her dreary daily routine.

B was moved to an open prison and despite the burden of her problems, Sheila missed her terribly.

Good Friday, 1 April 1994

'Desperately lonely without B, although we did not always see eye to eye. We did not always talk a great deal but we always knew we were there for each other.'

We had written to Sheila on 21 February, saying that the meeting at Nicholas Purnell's chambers the previous week had been amicable and constructive. At this point Purnell felt the best strategy was to pursue and further strengthen the defence given at trial: that Aunt Flo had been so completely immobile that no one person, especially a lady of Sheila's age, could have got her into the river unaided. He suggested engaging the services of a medical expert to go to Holloway and examine Sheila with a view to proving she would have been physically incapable of such an act. The expert would also be asked to visit the Station Road site to see the spot where Mrs Jackson met her death.

George Pulman said he knew an expert in orthopaedic medicine who might take on this work. He also made an appointment to visit the Winchelsea site himself. The lawyers felt that a video reconstruction of the events of May 13, possibly on the second anniversary of that night, might help the cause in the Court of Appeal. They felt that the argument of 'lurking doubt' would be strengthened by the television programme. On these terms they agreed to meet the *Trial and Error* researchers.

The Easter holiday weekend seemed 'even longer than Christmas' to Sheila.

Monday 4 April 1994

'Seem to get more and more depressed each morning when I wake. How I miss my home and friends.' Sheila filled the time as best she could, knitting toys – Goldilocks and the three bears – for a charity stall at Colchester Zoo run by one of the women officers. She joined in bowls and snooker competitions ('did away with a couple of hours') and went to the gym for aerobics classes. One bright spot was a letter from Chris Mullin MP, asking for a progress report on her case. She replied immediately, giving him an account of the meeting at Purnell's chambers and answering some detailed questions he had asked about the case.

On March 29 she had heard from Jane, who had met Sue Walker and David Jessel in London: they had already made an initial visit to Rye, and intended to start filming the reconstruction the following week.

On 7 April we drove to Bullwood Hall to visit Sheila to report on the progress of the campaign. Sheila's diary that evening reveals how nine months in jail had led her to accept aspects of prison life that would have shocked and horrified her at the outset:

Thursday 7 April 1994

'Lovely to see Angela and Tim today. It is Angela's 50th birthday. They brought me five lovely Black Dragon lilies. There was trouble at the gate which delayed them coming to the visits room. A girl in Osprey Wing had tried to cut her throat but I don't know if that was the cause of the delay.'

For a woman as meticulous and industrious as Sheila, the inefficiency and unnecessary bureaucracy of the Prison Service and the apathy of its inmates was particularly irritating. Her 'coffee list' for the Admin corridor was one of many attempts to impose her own high standards of order and neatness on the shifting chaos around her. But throughout her diary her frustration is evident.

One of her duties as visits orderly was to make sure there were enough snacks and drinks in stock in the small refreshments kiosk – not an easy task:

Friday 8 April 1994

'Chaos reigned at visits on Thursday because insufficient stock left after

Tuesday so after the first 15 minutes of the visit there were few refreshments left.'

Another time she put in an order for more insulated beakers for hot drinks:

Tuesday 19 April 1994

'I asked three times in the last two weeks for more beakers and none were forthcoming. I asked an officer to ring the canteen and remind them. I heard her remark about me on the phone, "I know she's a silly cow!" The whole system seems geared to winding prisoners up to see how far they can go before we snap. They'll have to wait for ever to get the desired result from me!' And, she adds tartly: 'I really don't know the answer for the prisons – I think it would be a good start if the officers were more disciplined themselves!'

She quotes an example: 'The noise on the wing was unbelievable this evening – guess who was on duty – Miss X and Miss Y. They made it sound as if we had some mentally deficient people on the wing. In the process of playing pool Miss X broke a pool cue and managed to hit Miss Y with one of the remaining pieces!

'Forgot to mention the disgraceful behaviour of Miss X on another evening. She stuffed herself with lasagne liberally covered with mayonnaise and then proceeded to indulge in some very vulgar behaviour. The wing is always very noisy when she is on duty. She then started to fool around with darts. Most of us sensible ones stood out of the way or went to our rooms. There is so much metal and brick around the place it would not have taken much for a dart to ricochet on to somebody and maybe cause serious injury. At 7.20 Miss X was violently sick and had to be taken off duty and we were locked in early at 7.40 instead of 8 o'clock.'

Sheila was also shocked at the waste of resources: 'Can't understand why a water-softening plant is needed for the visits complex. Sure the prison could run on half the cost when considering the wastage.'

Perhaps the authorities took her advice: a few months later the prisoners serving refreshments were replaced by second-hand vending machines which were perpetually out of action. Sheila commented waspishly: 'No provision made for catching spills from drinks machine. Nobody yet knows when I am to be made redundant as visits orderly.' [She was not].

Meanwhile there were other petty economies: 'Toilet rolls are now issued individually as the wing got through three months' supply in three weeks. We are issued two each about every other week and a box of tissues once a month. I have a bad cold – the first in four years – and have used almost a whole box today!'

Sheila's own language was becoming less ladylike by the minute. When reprimanded by officers she writes furiously:

Thursday 19 May 1994

'I felt like telling them to "stuff it" but that would have counted as being un-cooperative and gone down on my report.' She begins quite casually to spatter her diary entries with words and phrases like *grass* (informer) and *Co-D* (co-defendant) that would raise eyebrows at any genteel Rye coffee morning.

The apathy of the other prisoners continued to irritate her:

Tuesday 24 May 1994

'C helped me clear up the visits room this morning. It took her two and a half hours just to vacuum the carpet. In that same time I had cleaned the loos, babies' changing room, reception area, corridor entrance and small visits room!'

It seems the prison authorities took full advantage of Sheila's willingess to work hard, despite her age. The confidential reports they made at the time reveal they were also aware of her need to keep busy. She would sometimes be asked to spend all day returning to her old tasks on the Administration Corridor. Maybe the Admin staff wanted their windows cleaned properly again, and their coffee made just as they liked it! Just as she had done after Bob's death and again after Aunt's Flo's, she threw herself into these practical tasks with the energy of a woman half her age. It made the time pass and there were other compensations: 'They are extremely kind to me in Admin and speak to me as though I am a human being.'

That June the weather was very hot, Swan wing was unbearably stuffy and again Sheila was plagued by migraines:

Tuesday 7 June 1994

'Felt really exhausted all day, found step aerobics very tiring – sure it is partly due to lack of essential vitamins and emotional strain of course – I really feel *anno domini* is setting in apace. Am very tired and wonder how I would ever be able to run a house again.' But she managed to enjoy watching a few of the Wimbledon tennis matches, especially an exciting one where Navratilova was beaten by Martinez.

In mid-June she was cheered to hear that Nicholas Purnell, Charles Byers and Russell Parkes had seen a preview of the *Trial and Error* film and were impressed enough to ask the producer for some of the material to use for her appeal:

Friday 17 June 1994

'At least they think it is fairly certain I will get out on appeal or get a re-trial. Trying not to get too excited. Do wish I could go to sleep and wake up just before the appeal.'

In fact the lawyers now seemed willing to consider putting forward the possibility of accident in the Advice on Appeal document they were preparing. They decided it would be wise to interview and 'proof' as expert witnesses some of the interviewees filmed for the television programme: Professor Archie Young, of the Royal Free Hospital, the UK's top geriatrician; Professor Bryce Pitt, a professor of the psychiatry of old age, and Lucy Rees, Senior Physiotherapist at the Conquest Hospital, Hastings. They also suggested re-interviewing Dr Jeelani on the question of Mrs Jackson's mobility.

Meanwhile prison staff were trying to prepare Sheila for the possibility of defeat in the Court of Appeal. She was interviewed by a probation officer for her six-monthly review to be held on 26 June – another of the regular reports made on all LTIs – long-term inmates.

21 June 1994

'He fired questions like, "If your appeal fails, how will you feel?"' That night she wrote in her diary: 'Feel it is so destructive. Cannot give up hope although at the back of my mind cannot shut out the possibility of failure.'

Meanwhile Sheila's personal officer – the prison officer responsible for her individual welfare – asked her if she would accept the idea of a lesser charge such as manslaughter. (It is not uncommon for life-sentenced prisoners to be advised to change their plea in this way on appeal): 'I said I could never admit to a crime I hadn't committed.'

Reading through these prison reports now, nearly four years later, it is clear that staff were becoming increasingly worried about the high hopes

Sheila was pinning on a successful appeal. Indeed, the Lifer Liaison Officer went so far as to note: 'Our main area of concern is if she loses her appeal, it is believed that she will be an extreme suicide risk. This is based on what she says in that to her, a life sentence means she will die in prison due to her age. All staff who deal with her are aware of these thoughts and the necessary preparation has been made if failure of the appeal is the outcome.'

Her personal officer agreed: 'Sheila doesn't think she could bear it if her appeal is dismissed. Due to her age she says she will die in prison.' There are hints of Sheila's growing frustration: the officer adds: 'Sheila regards her peers as naughty schoolchildren and she misses the stimulation of intellectual conversation she is so used to. She states she finds it difficult to accept staff, some of whom are half her age, telling her when to get up, when to eat, etc. But she realises that she has to accept this.'

The Anglican chaplain noted that 'she has begun to relate well to my Methodist colleague, the Revd Teresa Rutteford, and we are aware that should the Appeal fail she will need a great deal of support. I am hopeful that her strong faith in God will sustain her in the coming days whatever the result of the Appeal.'

The education officer said Sheila attended evening classes on two evenings a week, in computer studies, word processing and aromatherapy, and that she took her studies seriously, got on well with other inmates, and helped to settle new students into class. The PE instructor noted that 'she is keen to play indoor bowls but sadly there are not too many others interested. We shall have to persevere.'

Another concern was Sheila's refusal to take part in any 'offence-focused work.' This was unsurprising, as she steadfastly maintained she had committed no offence at all. But the training of those who work with prisoners requires them to ensure that their charges face up to their offence. 'Tackling offending behaviour' has been dubbed 'the dreaded TOB' by Chris Tchaikovsky, Director of the support group Women in Prison and herself an ex-prisoner. It is meant to be a central plank of what is known in the Prison Service as 'throughcare.'

A medical officer complained about Sheila: 'She has not caused any problem to the system but does not seem to have accepted her offence or sentence. I feel that it is unlikely she will do either – it would also seem unlikely that she will cause any major problems, which may make staff unlikely to rock the boat. But I feel that she must be encouraged to talk about the offence and her feelings – but this will require a concerted effort from all disciplines.'

No such effort seems to have been made. It was by this time generally known in the prison that a television programme about Sheila's case would be shown in September, followed shortly, it was believed, by her appeal hearing. Until then, any further action was put on hold.

A Polish prisoner, G, arrived from Holloway and soon Sheila struck up a friendship with her. G kept a budgerigar called Bombel in her room (all lifers can keep caged birds if they wish) and Sheila promised to look after it for her when G returned to Holloway at the end of June for three weeks on 'accumulated visits' – the system whereby prisoners far from their families are sent to a prison nearer home and allowed visits from people unable to travel so far.

Tuesday 28 June 1994

'G has taken off for Holloway this morning and I am in charge of Bombel. Terrified he is going to pine away and die. It is now 8.30pm. He has been out of his cage most of the day. Last night I was very worried he would not be able to breathe after I covered the cage with two towels as instructed by G so ran along to ask F who assured me he would be OK.' F was a prisoner who had been jailed for plotting the murder of her husband. She seems to have known how to care for budgerigars, but Sheila was still worried. 'I kept peering under the towel to make sure he was still on the perch and not lying inert on the floor of the cage. Today F gathered some grass for him when she was out on exercise.'

Bombel survived his holiday and Sheila missed him when he returned to his owner's cell:

Monday 18 July 1994

'G arrived back from Holloway at lunch time with bad reports of situation there. Strange now Bombel has gone. Time still dragging unbearably. Very depressed,' she wrote.

The next morning she was woken early:

Tuesday 19 July 1994

'Terrible confusion in trying to get me unlocked and down to Admin by

7.50am in preparation for the visit of the Director General of Prisons, Derek Lewis. Visit seemed to go well – I had to stay in Admin all morning.'

Friends continued to visit, though the journey to Bullwood Hall was much longer for most of them. Inevitably it was harder for Simon to visit. He had been able to manage to reach Holloway by train and tube, but now he had to rely on local friends to drive him to Essex.

Jane of course was Sheila's most regular visitor and she often cut a strange figure waiting in the queue outside the prison gate, clutching her cello in the fibreglass case bought for her by Flo and Lil so many years ago. She would sometimes be on her way to play at a rehearsal and the instrument was too valuable to leave in the car, The gate officers would smile to themselves as they stashed it away in their kiosk for Jane to collect on the way out.

One afternoon a friend came with her daughter and new baby granddaughter – Sheila felt it was wonderful to see such a small baby, though she felt the visits room was uncomfortably hot.

Canon Maundrell, who had visited Sheila regularly in Holloway, once had to walk the three miles to the prison from the railway station in the nearest village, Hockley. Both he and Paddy Buxton, the Vicar of Rye, would have a word with the prison chaplains during their visits. One of these noted in his regular report to the Lifer Board: 'I met both the present Vicar and his predecessor who came in to visit her on separate occasions. From what I heard there is a lot of sympathy for Sheila and concern about her conviction.'

Many other friends and supporters sent letters and the few gifts Sheila was allowed. Cut flowers had been permitted at Bullwood Hall since Sara Thornton ran a successful campaign for the women to have them – though later some prisons, including Holloway, banned them because addicts used them to get drugs smuggled in, hidden in the stems or blooms. Sometimes, Sheila wrote, 'my room looks like Covent Garden!'

Her favourite parcels contained tapes of classical music, though her friends soon discovered that they had to be sent in a transparent case that the officers could open up. For her birthday we had given Sheila a subscription to a monthly music magazine which she looked forward to with relish. Some friends gave her the gift of their own labour, painting her house and keeping her garden in order: 'Liz and Murray [Johnstone] are angels and have gone to Fair Meadow and repaired my fence.'

At about this time we had another reason to visit Number 25. The Crown Prosecution Service wanted access to the garage where the Audi was still kept. They needed to take some measurements, they said, and we were the only people who seemed to be free that day to let them in.

When the appointed day arrived it turned out to be a very windy morning. A car drew up outside the house and out got the CPS solicitor and Dr Roger Lewis, an expert witness for the Crown on the behaviour of geriatric patients. The woman solicitor was carrying a piece of paper with instructions about the data they needed. As they headed for the garage, a sudden violent gust of wind seized the paper and swept it high in the air and away over the red roofs of Rye to Romney Marsh and beyond it the sea. We could not suppress a smile. Perhaps, after all, the gods were with Sheila Bowler!

Sheila also kept in constant touch by telephone, especially with elderly friends who could not travel to the prison. One of these was Helen Goodwin, the lady whom Sheila had taken to buy the wedding hat.

Sunday 24 July 1994

'Had quite a long chat with Helen. She appears to be missing me a great deal, especially as I have not been available to shop with her for clothes for her latest excursion to a wedding.'

We would always eat breakfast with the telephone on the table, knowing that soon after Sheila's cell was unlocked at 7.30am we could expect a call for an update on the campaign. Throughout the four years of her imprisonment, Sheila was to ring us almost daily, as she did so many of her other friends.

At the end of July it was our turn to thank Sheila for a gift: Jane had arrived on Tim's 50th birthday with a large cardboard box. 'This is nothing to do with me,' she said, 'You can blame Mum.'

In the box was a splendid chromium-plated toaster. During the making of the *Trial and Error* film we had gone to 25 Fair Meadow to let the film crew into the kitchen, and on the phone to Bullwood Hall that evening were able to reassure Sheila that her kitchen was being kept tidy in her absence, and that we particularly admired her shiny chrome toaster. Now Jane had brought along an even more splendid version of the same model.

We later discovered that the day after our chat with Sheila, the owner of a small ironmonger's shop opposite Battle Abbey received an unexpected phonecall: 'It's Mrs Bowler here,' said a disembodied voice, 'I want to order a toaster for a friend of mine.'

The man almost dropped the receiver: 'But – Mrs Bowler – I… I thought you were in prison!'

'So I am,' snapped the voice, 'but that doesn't mean I can't buy a gift for a friend!'

More and more people were being imprisoned, as Michael Howard's 'Prison Works' policy was enthusiastically implemented by the courts. During the period Sheila was in jail, the women's prison population was rising at twice the rate of the men's, and conditions worsened because of overcrowding and cuts in expenditure. Throughout the long hot summer of 1994 Sheila reported 'unrest on the wing,' and more and more 'room spins' as officers tried to track down the increasing number of drugs illegally brought into the prison: 'I hate my belongings being disturbed when I am not there. It's as bad as a burglary!' The problems increased as the year wore on:

Tuesday 23 August 1994

'Yesterday there was a strong smell of 'hooch' [illegally distilled alcohol, made in prison with yeast, sugar, fruit and rice smuggled from the kitchens] in an upstairs bathroom and some of the women looked distinctly red in the face. Discontent all round as the incoming phonecall equipment had been fitted but no box yet. So when the calls started coming on Wednesday night there were great ructions. Two young officers should have been aware of the risk of not taking control of the situation straight away. Result was near riot with lots of screaming and shouting and some of the inebriated rushing up and down the wing. Three were taken to the block [punishment cells]. The following morning we were all locked in and had room spins, and apparently they did find some hooch in one of the rooms.'

More trouble was to come when, after a lot of money had been spent installing the equipment, incoming phonecalls were banned – another result of Michael Howard's stricter security measures.

On Tuesday September 20, *The Times* printed an article on its law page: *What Happened to Aunt Flo?*, by Tim Devlin. It was illustrated by a large photograph of the old lady with a smaller inset picture of Sheila. The article outlined Sheila's case and the concern raised by it. That evening Channel Four screened the powerful *Trial and Error* film about Sheila's case: 'Film received great acclaim by everyone, even officers and tutors who come into the education department from outside.'

Overnight Sheila had become a prison celebrity.

CHAPTER TEN

BLACK FRIDAY

We were all invited to a London studio to watch the screening of the film. Afterwards everyone was jubilant. The case for Sheila's innocence had been put so forcibly. Surely now the appeal was heading for success.

At the party after the viewing, Michael Mansfield QC, a veteran of many fights against miscarriages of justice, came quietly up to speak to Jane. 'I just wanted to say,' he warned, 'that it may take more than one appeal to get your mother released.'

When the excitement of the *Trial and Error* programme had died down, Sheila was now faced with a very difficult decision: should she change her Defence team? As preparations for her appeal continued, it was becoming clearer that the most likely explanation for Aunt Flo's disappearance was that she had wandered off on her own and fallen to her death in the river. All the research carried out by the television team had pointed to that explanation. All the experts they had consulted thought this was a distinct possibility. There was nothing physically wrong with the old lady's limbs, and in her confused mental state she might well have followed some unknown impulse, left the car and walked off.

As Sheila's trial lawyers had run the defence that walking was an impossibility, and had afterwards sought to bolster this theory still further, it was a little difficult to see how this same team could now with credibility propose the walking theory as the main plank of an appeal against conviction.

Through David Jessel and Steve Phelps, Sheila and her family heard about another solicitor, Ewen Smith, of Glaisyers, a Birmingham firm. He had worked with the television team on other cases. He recommended one of the barristers who had also worked with *Trial and Error*. David Martin-Sperry, of 1 Crown Office Row, a set of chambers in the Temple, had successfully led the appeal of Mark Cleary, the subject of an earlier programme, who had been released after ten tragic years of wrongful imprisonment. Now Sheila had to consider changing her legal team.

Monday 26 September 1994

'Have had a dreadful weekend trying to make a decision. My bed has been chaotic each morning – looked as though I had fought the entire prison! At last, made decision that I must change counsel.'

The following Friday she sent off a letter to the Registrar of Appeals requesting the change.

Friday 30 September 1994

'So I have taken the leap and just trust that I have done the right thing. Time drags badly. Just hope legal aid will be transferred.' Her personal officer had to be told, and repeated her earlier advice: 'She said I must be prepared in the event of a re-trial that I may be offered the "opportunity" of pleading guilty to a manslaughter charge! In other words, pocket my pride in order to get off earlier, as at a re-trial where I pleaded not guilty to murder, I might still get a guilty verdict! I could never confess to something I had not done, and in any event there would be no grounds as I am innocent and not nuts!'

A week later she received a letter from Nicholas Purnell wishing her well in her change of lawyers. But at the beginning of October a further problem arose.

Monday 10 October 1994

'Had a blow today: Master McKenzie [Michael McKenzie, QC, Registrar of Criminal Appeals] now apparently requires fresh evidence before granting me permission to change counsel. Maybe I shouldn't have changed – all sorts of doubts crossing my mind. Feel depressed and quite vulnerable as I don't have anyone at all representing me just now.'

The following week she was encouraged by the success of another Bullwood Hall lifer's appeal. J was released to spend Christmas with her family. When the news reached the prison, Sheila wrote: 'J's 14 year-old daughter said she would lock her mum in her room the first night out, just to make her feel more at home!' Sheila allowed herself the dangerous luxury of imagining for a moment how Jane would react if her mother should be released on appeal.

Meanwhile there was a prison drama which was to have serious consequences for Sheila and the other women prisoners.

Thursday 20 October 1994

'P went on temporary release to see her son in South London, accompanied by two women officers. While they were at the house, P did a runner. Everyone wondered what had happened when she had not arrived back at 8pm. The officers are in big trouble from the powers that be.'

The escapee was re-arrested after a few days and sent to Holloway. On 9 November she was returned to Bullwood Hall and Sheila commented: 'P's escape while on a day out has not done anyone any favours. Everyone going out of the prison – to hospital, court or whatever – must now be handcuffed. In fact, even if you need to go to the loo, a chain is extended under the door.'

Sheila was describing the practice of shackling, which was not to be discovered by the media for another year when ITN showed secretly filmed footage of a Holloway woman shackled to prison officers just one hour after giving birth. Another result of increased security was that prisoners could no longer receive any visitors in their cells:

'David Maundrell came last week. We are not allowed to entertain anyone in our rooms, not even the prison chaplain or any minister. Can't think why, especially as my room is immediately opposite the office and I always leave the door open. Instead I went with David to the chapel. We were locked in at 1.45pm today. The new rule is that all rooms must be spun [searched] every 28 days so we have to be locked in. This is the price we pay for inmates at men's prisons escaping.'

The entry ends on a more upbeat note: 'The real excitement of the week was hearing my legal aid had been transferred to my new solicitor, and my new counsel thinks my appeal might be heard before Christmas.'

But as the weeks passed it became clear that the appeal would not now be heard till the New Year. A new leading QC had to be instructed and the choice was an important one. Then a date must be found when the new barrister was free.

The barrister finally briefed by Ewen Smith of Glaisyers was Gordon Pollock, QC, the distinguished commercial silk. Pollock was chosen at the suggestion of Richard Ferguson, QC, then Chairman of the Criminal Bar Association, and the head of junior counsel Martin-Sperry's chambers.

The new leading counsel was a colourful character who rode round in full leather gear on a powerful motorbike. Rumour had it that he was a millionaire: he had certainly achieved media fame a few months earlier, defending the record company Sony against the rock star George Michael. The decision to brief him for the Bowler appeal raised some eyebrows in legal circles. As Sean Webster, a legal journalist, was later to write in *The Times* [25.9.95]: 'The involvement of Mr Pollock, a leading commercial silk who does not normally handle crime, was another cause for bitterness. He was seen by some as a hired gun brought in by the Defence because he was outside the Criminal Bar fraternity, and would not pull any punches.'

Whatever legal wrangles were going on behind the scenes, Sheila could think of nothing but the Appeal. It seemed amazing to her that she was approaching her second Christmas behind bars.

Tuesday 6 December 1994

'Have had the Christmas tree on the wing for several days but I shall be very glad to see it go on Twelfth Night as it means my appeal will be nearer. How the days drag and how miserable I feel. This Christmas seems even worse to get through.'

On December 8 there was another prison review of her situation, and the Head of Residential governor read through the reports, noting that 'the date of the appeal is still unknown but it is expected to be heard towards the end of January 1995. With regard to the appeal, the recent TV programme, along with added investigating impetus by her barrister, appears to have given her an increased hope of success. It is quite obvious to staff that there is very little else going on in her mind. She was informed that whilst keeping an optimistic view she must allow for the appeal being upheld. If this is the case then Sheila will require immense support. It is still the opinion that she will be a High Risk potential suicide case. Therefore the following months would create a lot of anxiety amongst staff, as it is the general opinion that there would be no real warning of suicide.'

He added that her 'prison behaviour remains exemplary. Sheila still maintains her dignity, appearing to be more comfortable in her surroundings now that there are a few more older women on the wing. It is also worth noting that with the acceptance of prison life she acknowledges the authority of officers. This she frequently challenged in earlier days, mainly due to her age and former occupation.'

The governor concluded: 'It will be a relief for all once the appeal has been heard and we each know our destiny.'

On Christmas Day the prison once again tried its best to cheer up the prisoners:

Sunday 25 December 1994

'Breakfast of sausage, fried bread, solid scrambled egg, tomatoes and bread, marg and marmalade. Had lovely flowers from Jane, Tim and Angela and the music of *The Piano* film from Jane. Hankies from Simon. Managed a quick phone call to Si and Jane. Heard the greetings tape from Sue before breakfast.' [Susan Catmur had taped Christmas messages from her own family and some of Sheila's other friends, for Sheila to listen to on Christmas morning]. Church at 9, badly attended as most hadn't read the notice. Very loud reggae music most of morning so opted to watch *Dr Doolittle*. Forgot to say I had a call at 8am from J [the lifer whose appeal had been allowed in October]. She appears a little lost since she was released – I'm sure it will take a long time for her to adjust to normal living. Lunch not actually served on our plates till 12.20 so a terrible job to finish by 12.40 when we were locked in. Seems a very long day. Reggae music blasting out all evening. I seem so far away from reality this Christmas. Why is it the days seem to get longer?'

Sheila marked the beginning of 1995 by printing the date in large letters:

SUNDAY 1 JANUARY 1995 – HOORAH!

'At last '95 has dawned. Perhaps things will now move a little quicker. Had a call from Jane to say she is picking up Professor Archie Young and Ewen Smith a week on Monday to take them to Winchelsea to see the river, so that is a step in the right direction. Have an inkling the appeal might be before the end of January. The sooner the better I guess – but am I scared!'

Just over three weeks later she heard from her solicitor that the most likely date for the appeal would be 20 March:

Wednesday 25 January 1995

'Surely my appeal will not be carried on to the next legal term? A blow today as we have been told that after this week we can only use £11.25 of our private spends for phonecards. This means my calls will have to be reduced by 50%. This is the result of men prisoners spending so much each month, such as £400 or more on phone cards and luxury foods! The quicker I get out of here the better. I have now annoyed Miss Y. This officer is all of 22 and she told me off because I dared to look around to see if there was a pen on her desk before asking if I may borrow one. Apparently I should ask first. The next time she calls me Sandra instead of Sheila I shall feel tempted to retaliate. VERY FED UP TONIGHT!'

By mid-February she was feeling even worse. Ewen Smith had visited the prison:

Thursday 16 February 1995

'Very, very fed up as Mr Smith said on Tuesday that the first date the QC is available for my appeal is 10th April.'

However, preparations for the appeal were proceeding steadily. David Martin-Sperry had drafted a Grounds of Appeal document, which began with the assertion that 'the Defence at trial wrongly conceded that Florence Jackson was murdered.'

The grounds relied on calling two areas of fresh evidence: the expert evidence that Mrs Jackson could have walked away from the car and accidentally fallen to her death in the river; and evidence from character witnesses, none of whom had been called at trial to mitigate the vilification of Mrs Bowler's character by Greyfriars staff and other Crown witnesses. The document set out to ask the Court of Appeal to receive evidence which might have been called for at trial, and because this line was taken, some criticism of Nicholas Purnell was unavoidable.

Professor Young, having now visited the Winchelsea site, was asked to consider each stage that Mrs Jackson would have had to follow in order to reach the river unaided. After the visit he had attended a conference with the lawyers and concluded that had the old lady stayed on the metalled road to the pumping station, she might well have been able to cover the distance without falling. He particularly emphasized that there were many well-documented examples of elderly people achieving extraordinary physical feats while under stress. He also examined the Greyfriars records and found that Mrs Jackson was not nearly so immobile as the trial jury had been led to believe. He set about preparing his report.

It is standard practice, when cases go to appeal, that if any criticism is made of trial counsel, the Registrar for Appeals sends the new grounds of appeal to this first counsel to give him or her a chance to make comments. Sheila was sent a letter asking her to waive her privilege – in other words, to agree for Nicholas Purnell to be shown this confidential document. She wrote back immediately to her new lawyers, agreeing to this procedure.

It was however many weeks before Purnell was to receive the new Grounds. There were two reasons for the delay. First, Sheila's counsel assumed that the Registrar of the Appeals Court had the duty to inform her previous counsel that he had been criticised. But in fact the Registrar was later to maintain that this was not his duty.

Second, the death of Professor Young's father in Scotland led to a long delay in the delivery of his final report, which in turn delayed the sending of the Perfected Grounds of Appeal to the Registrar. Nicholas Purnell did not receive them until the beginning of April. He was therefore forced to respond to the criticisms the document contained without reference to the transcripts of the case, which he did not have time to obtain.

It was a delay which was not helpful to the outcome of Sheila Bowler's appeal, and indeed it led the Bar Council to clarify the rules on Appeals. It subsequently ruled that it is the duty of Counsel to inform their predecessors of any criticism in good time so that they are able to make an informed response. The case of Sheila Bowler was now becoming a talking point in the small enclosed world of the London Bar.

The February entries in Sheila's diary become shorter as her nerves become more frayed. As her appeal draws nearer, after the seemingly interminable wait, the prospect of a chance of freedom unsettles her, and other worries press upon her.

Friday 17 February 1995

'Had my most sleepless night ever in prison as I knew Jane was driving home from teaching in Harpenden in terrible gales and rain on the M25.'

Saturday 18 February 1995

'Sat in TV room for short while then someone came in and said I was sitting in their seat. Felt like replying, "I didn't know we had our own personal chairs!' Sick of being treated as though I am an idiot. Don't know how I shall cope with the outside world after this.'

But just over a week later she heard the best news in almost two years:

Monday 27 February 1995

'At last definite date for appeal – 10th and 11th April. What a relief – don't know whether I feel more anxious or excited! Frantic phone-round.

Have contacted about six people and hope to get in touch with and write to 19 others. Feel very optimistic just now and think that surely my good luck I have been blessed with so far will last, plus the good work and advice from all. Discovered that prison transport is going private from 1st April which means I must go to court from here with no Bullwood Hall officers that I know. I will have to go in a Securicor sweatbox [secure van divided into separate cubicles].

Sunday 19 March 1995

'Mr Smith and Mr Martin-Sperry came for visit on March the 9th. They were not impressed as it took them 40 minutes to gain access, then they were thrown out after an hour and a half. Of course no refreshments were available as the vending machines were not working. We had our visit in a room off the visits room. Luckily I had managed to provide tea, coffee and biscuits. M-S said he couldn't drink coffee without sugar, but he lunged into the biscuits, particularly the chocolate ones, with great vigour! Very useful meeting – no promises but they are obviously working hard and think a re-trial is a great possibility. Only three weeks and one day to Appeal Day. Am engulfed with a mixture of fear, anxiety and excitement.'

The local Rye newspaper, the *Rye Observer*, printed news of the impending appeal, beginning, '*Supporters of Sheila Bowler are confident she will be free by Easter.*' Jane gave an interview to the paper, telling readers the date of the appeal and encouraging supporters to attend the hearing. In the bullish feature, headlined, '*Daughter leads fight for Mum's Freedom: Supergran coping well with prison,*' Jane said that the attitude of other prisoners had changed drastically following the Channel Four documentary the previous year: now they were all rooting for the woman they had nicknamed 'Supergran.'

On April 3, a week before the appeal was due to begin, Nicholas Purnell sent a document to the Court of Appeal, with copies to the Prosecution and Defence lawyers. Under the heading *Observations* he defended his strategy at Sheila Bowler's trial, saying that far from rejecting the possibility that Florence Jackson's death was an accident, this defence 'was left open until the weight of evidence at trial of her immobility was such as to make the theory unsustainable.' In other words, he had himself become convinced by the evidence heard at trial that Mrs Jackson could not have walked to her death.

These *Observations* directly contradicted the 'walking theory' which was the main plank of the appeal. The document must have been fresh in the minds of the appeal court judges when, just seven days later, they sat to consider the case of Sheila Bowler. Purnell was well aware of the damaging effect they were bound to have and expressed his regret. In paragraph 11.2 he wrote: 'It is, therefore, a matter of considerable personal regret to me that I should be put in the position of making these observations which cannot assist Mrs Bowler.'

While Nicholas Purnell was penning his *Observations* and their lordships were perusing them, Sheila Bowler was waiting in prison, full of hope. She was mistaken in thinking she would be taken straight to court from Bullwood Hall. On Friday 7 April she was moved to Holloway. She left Bullwood Hall 'after being strip-searched by two particularly obnoxious officers' and arrived back at Holloway at 4pm. The driver of the prison van had great trouble changing gear and got lost several times, but Sheila was glad of a chance to look at the scenery:

Holloway: Saturday 8 April 1995

'Yesterday's drive: after passing the church where Bob and I were married just over 33 years ago we traversed the weirdest route imaginable to London.'

At Holloway she was strip-searched again and – by this time too late for tea – offered 'a meal of cold congealed scrambled egg and soggy chips,' which she declined. '8pm last night found me at last in a dorm on C3, the reception wing. Blankets and bedcover are not clean and very thin.'

Conditions had deteriorated in the sixteen months or so since she was last at Holloway, though it would be another eight months before the new Chief Inspector of Prisons, Sir David Ramsbotham, would walk out of the prison in disgust at what he found there.

Same Day: 4.25pm

'My worst fears about coming back here have now been confirmed. Holloway is now dirtier than ever, the food worse and the locking in cells much more frequent, especially at weekends. Warned by the other girls in the dorm that baths and a phone call are now practically impossible. There are often fights over the phone. I was awake at 4am drinking tea out of my small flask – the larger one I had at Bullwood isn't allowed here as it won't fit through the door hatch to be filled with hot water by the wing cleaners when we are locked in. A lot of other items allowed at Bullwood are banned here, like my powder compact and round-ended scissors. Don't know how I can iron my clothes for court, as getting to the iron is almost impossible. I won't be allowed out of my cell for a bath on Monday as J was before her appeal. That concludes today's episode – except to say that Jane and Sarah must be about to embark on the concert just about now.'

The great church of St Martin in the Fields, Trafalgar Square, was packed for the concert that Saturday evening. The programme for this romantic spring concert by the Belmont Ensemble, held by candlelight, was a popular one, and tourists wandering in from the London streets joined regular concert-goers on the oaken pews. One of the highlights of the evening was the Vivaldi *Double Cello Concerto,* played by Jane Bowler and her friend Sarah Harrington. Only a few of the audience – *Trial and Error's* Steve Phelps, Sheila's sister Mary, Anne Wood, one or two other Rye friends and ourselves – were aware of the poignancy of the occasion. Jane's London debut in this particular piece, one of her mother's favourites, had been arranged months earlier, with the help of the singer Rebekah Gilbert-Dyson. Rebekah, whose husband Peter is the Belmont's conductor, had been a school friend of Jane's in Rye. They planned the concert to celebrate Sheila's freedom.

But Sheila was still locked in a cell on the other side of the city and within 36 hours would be standing in the dock appealing against her life sentence. As the concerto ended and the audience burst into applause Jane, radiant in her emerald green silk dress, came forward to receive a bouquet of her favourite white lilies that Sheila had ordered. But as she read the card and made her exit, Jane was in tears.

The following afternoon we sat with Jane and Sheila in the Holloway visits room. Maybe this would be her last day in prison, and Sheila was giving us detailed instructions about her possessions. As we left Holloway that day, we walked out onto Parkhurst Road carrying all the items Sheila wanted taken home, stashed in two enormous transparent sacks, stamped in blue with the letters *HM PRISON SERVICE* and a large heraldic crest. There were some raised eyebrows and puzzled stares on the return journey to Kent as passengers alighted at Sevenoaks and Tonbridge.

The spring sunshine was dazzling next morning as we made the return train journey from Kent with Simon. The fair weather seemed auspicious and we approached the great Gothic law courts, the Royal Courts of Justice on the Strand, in good heart. Outside the courts we met Jane and the host of supporters who had gathered there.

A few weeks earlier we had mailed out another letter to The Friends of Sheila Bowler. The list had grown since the *Trial and Error* programme and Sheila had received even more Christmas cards than in 1993. This latest letter was to let everyone know the date of the appeal, and to ask them to come along to the court and support Sheila. Some were familiar faces – friends from Rye, Sheila's piano pupils, elderly music teacher colleagues and Jane's young friends from the Royal Academy. Others were strangers who had seen the television programme and read about the case in the press. David Jessel, Steve Phelps, Sue Walker and other members of the TV team were also present.

At 9.40 a prison van lumbered along the Strand and in through the ornate side gates of the Law Courts. Sheila peered out of the darkened windows: 'What a joy to see the normal world again, even the sights of North London!' she wrote that evening in her diary.

Monday 10 April 1995

'The journey to the Court of Appeal took only 20 minutes, though I felt lucky to get there at all because the hassle getting out of this place was incredible. Nobody remembered to wake me, though of course I was up, washed and dressed long before 7am. Two pieces of white bread were pushed through the hatch with marge, two sausages and a tea bag, sugar and no water. At 7.30 I was taken down to Reception down four flights of stairs and subjected to another strip search – bra up and pants down – talk about humiliating – I wondered why I'd dressed in the first place. About 30 of us waited in a noisy holding room till we were herded into sweatboxes. When we reached the Law Courts I noticed a few press people outside the main entrance, and a Rye photographer – but we were swept through the side gates and I had to be handcuffed to enter the building.'

Just before 10am Sheila's supporters filed through the security checks into the echoing marble halls – a Dickensian scene with appellants and lawyers standing in huddles and families sitting on stone side-benches until it was time to ascend the steep staircases to the courtrooms.

The appeal was to be heard in an august – but surprisingly small – courtroom panelled in oak and lined with leather-bound legal tomes. The court ushers, garbed in black academic gowns, were soon telling the crowd of more than eighty supporters that the courtroom was full, and it was some time before they could be persuaded to open the public gallery upstairs.

The press benches were packed: Joe Weber from the *Brighton Evening Argus* had followed this case through the trial at Hove; now he sat next to reporters from *The Times, Guardian* and *Independent.*

Behind the Crown Prosecutors sat two familiar figures, Woman Detective Sergeant Linda Booth, and Detective Sergeant David Renno, still 'Badger' to the Bowler camp, his black hair with its distinctive white streak slicked back. They sat stiffly, looking straight ahead, occasionally exchanging a few words.

A hush fell on the courtroom as the ushers gave the order, 'All stand' and their lordships entered: Mr Justice Latham, Mr Justice Morison, and – most senior of the three – Lord Justice Swinton-Thomas.

Through a narrow door on their lordships' left entered Sheila Bowler, smart in the blue jacket and pale pink shirt Jane had brought to the prison the day before, and flanked on either side by prison officers. The clerk to the court asked if she was indeed the appellant, Sheila Bowler. She replied quietly that she was, then took her seat in the dock, looking pale and drawn but managing a smile across the court at her family and friends.

That night in her diary she wrote: 'Lovely to see the court crammed with supporters. Even so I felt very isolated and lonely to hear the proceedings grinding on as though I was completely invisible.'

To the eighty or so supporters watching the proceedings from the back of the courtroom, there seemed to be two appeals in progress. As in a play in the theatre, there was a major plot and a sub-plot. The subject of the major plot was Mrs Bowler and the subject of the sub-plot was Nicholas Purnell. But on that first day the sub-plot seemed to be at the centre of the court-room stage.

In opening his submissions Gordon Pollock lambasted Mrs Bowler's previous Defence team in strong terms rarely heard in an English courtroom, where the posturings of bewigged barristers in mannered antiquated language seems to many onlookers an expensive waste of time. Mr Purnell, said Pollock, was seriously at fault in not obtaining a report from an expert in geriatric behaviour to show that Mrs Jackson's death might have been accidental. All that Mr Purnell would have had to do was to show that this was a possible explanation for her death. The standard of the Defence representation, argued Mr Pollock, fell substantially below what was required.

He strongly called into question the claim by Purnell in his *Observations* that he had kept the possibility of accidental death open until the weight of evidence at the trial was against it. This was simply untrue, said Pollock. In fact this possibility had been abandoned on the very first day of the trial. He called Purnell's *Observations* 'disingenuous' and 'deliberately misleading.'

It was strong language from a leading commercial silk pitching into a leading criminal silk. Pencils scribbled furiously on the press benches: wrangles among top legal eagles make good copy.

Next Pollock criticised Purnell for failing to call three character witnesses (Mrs Biddy Cole, Mrs Susan Catmur and Mrs Helen Goodwin) who would have helped counter the attacks on Mrs Bowler's good name.

Moving on to the main plot, Mr Pollock asked their lordships to admit new evidence by Professor Archie Young of the Royal Free Hospital. He would tell the court that Mrs Jackson could have got out of the car and walked to her death – immobile as she may have seemed.

It was strong stuff. Pollock eloquently asked their lordships to imagine the old lady, frail and confused as she may have been, undoing the seat belt, opening the door of the car, stepping out on to the dark pavement, and journeying along the tarmac road and down the lane towards the river.

At the end of the first day, Sheila's friends felt elated as they gathered in the George pub across the Strand. Mr Pollock had done well. And now Sheila herself was more sanguine. That evening at Holloway she wrote up the day's events in her diary:

Monday 10 April 1995

'I could deduce no conclusions from the first day but I thought Mr Pollock was very good. After the morning's session I was taken from the dock back down two flights of stairs for lunch: choice of sausage casserole, all-day breakfast or vegetable tortilla. Opted for the latter but could not eat it as it was practically all pasta, few vegetables and literally floating in fat. I just had a cup of sweet coffee to keep my strength up.'

Tuesday dawned – another lovely spring day. But this day was not to be so sunny for the Bowler Defence team. Gordon Pollock was able to produce, like a rabbit out of a hat, photographs of the soles of Mrs Jackson's stockings which seemed to show holes in the heels – a sign surely that she must have walked along that road to her death. In the public galleries eighty heads nodded vigorously. The judges were not impressed: indeed, later investigation following the appeal revealed that the 'holes' were merely a trick of the light.

Just before lunch a court usher went up to the judicial dais and handed the judges a newspaper cutting. It was a small piece of paper, measuring roughly seven inches by five inches, and it was written by Robin Young, *The Times* reporter who had covered the case on the previous day.

'INCOMPETENT DEFENCE BLAMED FOR WIDOW'S MURDER CONVICTION' read the headline.

Again their lordships were unimpressed.

During the afternoon Gordon Pollock's evidence began to falter and David Martin-Sperry was criticised by Lord Justice Swinton Thomas for not giving Mr Purnell due notice of the grounds of appeal which criticised him. There was much talk, unfathomable to those on the public benches, of certain sections under certain rules of certain Acts, all of it concerning the conduct of one barrister towards another. Lord Justice Swinton-Thomas referred once or twice to the appellant, mispronouncing her surname, as he had throughout the whole appeal, so that it rhymed with 'howler.'

In the dock Mrs Sheila Bowler frowned and looked puzzled. Once or twice she glanced sideways at her supporters and raised her eyebrows. They frowned back, shrugging their shoulders. What had all of this talk of the rights and privileges of lawyers to do with proving the innocence of the woman in the dock? What had it to do with their friend, the forgotten protagonist, sitting there disconnected from the charade unfolding before the spectators' eyes?

Now it was the turn of Anthony Glass to bend their lordships' collective ear. Confidently he poured scorn on the 'walking theory.' Then he took the court through a litany of the improbable steps which Mrs Jackson would have had to undertake to get to the river bank.

Listed one after the other in Glass's ponderous tones, the stages did indeed sound highly implausible. They included undoing the seat belt with her right arm in plaster; opening the heavy metal car door; getting out of the car on her own; collecting the walking stick, which, said Glass, she was not in the habit of using; remembering to close the car door behind her; walking the distance of 500 yards without falling or being observed; and all the while keeping tightly grasped in her left hand the paper tissue which Mrs Bowler had given her in the car, and which was found still in her hand when her body was pulled from the river. All these actions, Mr Glass reminded their lordships, would have to have been undertaken in the dark and in slippers which were substantially too large for her deformed feet.

Mr Justice Latham, seated on the right of Lord Justice Swinton-Thomas, now intervened. Until this point his interjections had suggested that he might be more sympathetic than his colleagues to the Bowler cause. 'Of course,' he said, Professor Young's evidence is 'theoretical' – he never saw Mrs Jackson alive.' Meanwhile Professor Young waited patiently outside on one of the wooden benches in the long marble corridor, where he had been sitting all day.

The turning point of the hearing came when the judges announced, towards the end of that afternoon's session, that they intended to retire for a short while. They returned after fifteen minutes and told Pollock they had decided they were not prepared to hear Professor Young's evidence. Mr Pollock sat down, deflated. Swinton-Thomas ruled that it was now time to adjourn the court for the day.

The supporters left the court in deep gloom, wandering back down the stairs and into the echoing great hall. The afternoon sunshine outside was still dazzling, but it did nothing to lift their mood.

As she sat in her prison cell that night, Sheila's spirits were low too:

Tuesday 11 April 1995

'Terrible ending to the afternoon with everyone looking grim when the judges decided (after adjourning for about 15 minutes) that Professor Young's evidence was not to be allowed. Mr Smith came to see me and said, "A bad day." He explained that he could only offer a glimmer of hope and if the appeal was dismissed there was nothing that could be done. I was rather confused as this does not seem to be the view expressed by others.'

Sheila's diary entry does not convey the true extent of the depression she felt that dreadful night. Convinced now that the appeal would be dismissed the following morning, and that she would be condemned to a further ten years in prison, she wrote a letter addressed to Simon and Jane.

Tuesday 7 pm

'Darling Si & Jane

I am now back at Holloway. The others are at a karaoke evening. I remade my bed. Perhaps I had better leave it as it is tomorrow, ready for tomorrow night.

I can't think how you are feeling tonight, apart from sheer desolation. Mr Smith thinks there is only a glimmer of hope for tomorrow – at least it is a glimmer. I cannot think why God is putting us all through this dreadful trauma – perhaps it is because of some terrible misdeeds of a past life. Whatever happens you must keep the flag flying for however long it takes.

Mr Smith is convinced you and Simon can keep the home going, but he is saying nothing further can be done for me. There's always Chris Mullin.

You must always remember that I love you both very much and please, please, please both of you the best thing you can do for me is to get on with your lives, and remember that I shall look forward to coming out to a very lovely son & daughter, even more grown up and maybe an additional family! This is I know, looking ahead a bit. I'm not pretending this will be easy at all, but I know you have the strength to cope with it, & I am exceedingly proud of you.

All my love

Mummy xxx

Perhaps a miracle may happen.

PS. Mr Smith says he has no idea what Tim will say to the press except an impassioned plea on TV or in the press for someone to come forward with perhaps having seen something that night.'

Sheila had no envelope so she folded the two pieces of lined A4 paper and addressed the outside to Ewen Smith, with the request, 'Would you please give this to Simon and Jane.' The next morning, when Ewen Smith came to see her in her cell beneath the courtroom, she handed him the letter.

The third bright Spring day of the appeal was, surprisingly, much more relaxed. Gordon Pollock went through the remaining grounds of appeal. First he dealt with the matter of the tyre. He argued that the trial judge should have put more emphasis on the police evidence that there had been a measured decrease in the tyre pressure. It should have weighed more strongly in Mrs Bowler's favour.

Secondly, he argued that the judge's summing up was unbalanced to the disadvantage of the Defence and that the judge was wrong to tell the jury that Mrs Bowler in the witness box enjoyed no special advantages. It was an abstruse point and probably lost on Sheila and most of her supporters. The day ended with Lord Justice Swinton-Thomas announcing that he had decided to reserve judgement in this case until a later date.

Sheila returned to Holloway. Though she felt rather deflated, the atmosphere in the court had seemed more positive, and that evening she felt less depressed:

Wednesday 12 April 1995

'The court started at 10.45 with Gordon Pollock still fighting on. I really thought it was just a case of going through the motions so that after lunch the judges would announce the case would be dismissed. About 3pm all was finished except for the judges' decision – but they decided judgement would be reserved for a later date. At least there seemed some hope left, especially when Gordon Pollock came to see me afterwards and said, "A brighter day."

After Monday's high hopes and Tuesday's gloom, the judges' decision to reserve judgement left Sheila's supporters with a sense of anticlimax. Jane and Simon had received their mother's letter and Jane was moved to tears. 'Surely,' she said, 'this delay must at least mean a re-trial. The judges couldn't be so inhuman as to keep us waiting then dismiss the appeal.'

Across the Strand opposite the Royal Courts of Justice, The George pub is a picturesque half-timbered hostelry. The carved beams of its facade show poachers chasing geese – scenes of rural crime and punishment, dating from the time when London was bordered with green fields. The George's former landlord sought out those green fields himself: by an extraordinary coincidence he left London to run The Top 'O the Hill pub in Rye at the corner of Fair Meadow, the inn where Detective Sergeants

Renno and Booth dropped Sheila and Simon for their meal on the evening of 13 May 1992.

The George's bar staff must have witnessed many a scene of joy or despair as appellants and their families celebrate or drown their sorrows. Sheila's supporters, gathering there that Wednesday afternoon, felt more as if they were in a state of limbo. But the *Trial and Error* team were cautiously hopeful, and David Martin-Sperry was even more positive. Their optimism was to carry Sheila's family and friends through to Judgement Day.

Back at Holloway Sheila was too busy over the next few days coping with the realities of prison life to have much time to brood on the possibility of a grim future behind bars. She now found herself sharing a dormitory with a drug-supplying prostitute and a heroin addict suffering severe withdrawal symptoms. Her 'private spends' had not been transferred from Bullwood Hall and because it was Easter weekend there was no work and no chance to earn more cash.

It was hard for her to share her family's optimism:

Easter Monday 17 April 1995:

'Am already trying to fight off thoughts of a possible permanent return to Bullwood Hall. Wish I could get my spirits up. My cold has now developed properly. I must keep positive with my thoughts on the possibility of a re-trial. Only a miracle would produce a 'walkout' now.'

Her main aim was simply to get away from Holloway:

Tuesday 18 April 1995

'I have badgered the office about going back to Bullwood Hall and at last was told this morning that I would go tomorrow.'

Despite the bullying that occurs in any prison, especially now that drug-use is so rife, women prisoners are usually much more supportive to one another than men and Sheila certainly found this to be true:

Sunday 30 April 1995

'It was a relief to arrive back at Bullwood Hall. Was greeted affectionately by most on Swan [the lifers]' wing. But strange as it may seem I felt very depressed.'

One reason was the loss of her old job. Prison jobs are not held while appellants go to court: 'I must now wing-clean, my original jobs having been given to someone else. I shall be well qualified to be a lavatory attendant at Charing Cross Station by the time I get out of here! My cough is worse – sure I am being subjected to passive smoking.'

But Sheila was furious when a routine visit to the prison psychologist led to a report to the lifers' governor that 'she was afraid there was a danger of me harming myself. I was not pleased about that comment as nothing would ever be further from my thoughts.'

Tuesday 2 May 1995

'Had to spend the morning wing-cleaning. Bathroom in a bad state with vomit on the floor. Think it was caused by cocaine that came in on visit yesterday. Of course the wrong two girls were strip-searched afterwards. Three others were absolutely stoned in the evening and the girl whose visit it was couldn't even find her mouth at tea-time. She looked absolutely dreadful as though she was retarded. I never thought to be mixing with such a collection of people! When I arrived back on the wing there was a message to ring Ewen Smith: Judgement Day [the delivery of the judgement at the Court of Appeal] is on Friday!'

That evening she added: 'Not impressed with the senior officer this evening. He came into the office and said, "Have you told Sheila that Friday [the Appeal Court judgement] is cancelled?" I was shocked and asked if that meant I was to phone my solicitor in Birmingham. "That won't be necessary," he said, shrugging his shoulders. I asked him if it was a wind-up, to which he laughed. How insensitive can you get? I told him he could have no idea what I am going through just now but he should try to develop some sensitivity and a little imagination!' Am now trying to plan tomorrow – will I be taken to court from here on Friday?'

Thursday 4 May 1995

'Heard I am leaving at 7.45am tomorrow. Locked in at 5.45 tonight so plenty of time to sort myself out. At the moment feeling rather too hopeful – dangerous!'

A smaller band of supporters returned to the Royal Courts of Justice on Friday 5 May to hear the judgement, but there were still enough to fill the public benches downstairs in the courtroom. When the court rose at the judges' entrance, Sheila's lawyers exchanged worried glances with the *Trial and Error* team: only two of the judges – Morison and Swinton-Thomas were present. Old Appeal Court hands like David Jessel and Steve Phelps knew this was significant. No bail order can be granted unless all three judges are in the court. A re-trial was the best that could be hoped for – and for a re-trial, the original conviction would have to be quashed and bail given.

Lord Justice Swinton-Thomas cleared his throat to deliver the judgement. The courtroom was still: Sheila and her supporters listened intently as he sketched the background of the case. Everyone waited for any indication of what his decision might be, hoping against hope that in a few minutes the anxious grey-haired lady in the dock would be walking free from the court.

Swinton-Thomas began by covering the first two grounds of appeal: first, that the Defence counsel at trial had wrongly conceded that Mrs Jackson had been murdered; second, that the Defence were wrong in failing to seek medical evidence. Mr Pollock, said Swinton-Thomas, had made very serious criticisms of the original Defence team.

When Swinton-Thomas moved on to discuss Professor Young's evidence, the hearts of Sheila's supporters sank. Professor Young, said the judge, did not even have transcripts of the evidence of the trial.

It was becoming perfectly clear which way the judgement would go. Jane, sitting next to us, looked across at her mother. Sheila sat perfectly still, her eyes closed.

It was plain that their lordships shared the views of Mr Glass. It was, said Swinton-Thomas, quite incredible that Mrs Jackson could have got out of the car. Against Professor Young's theoretical evidence must be set the evidence of the care workers who looked after Mrs Jackson and knew her so well. Against it must be set the evidence of Dr Jeelani. He had said on oath that Mrs Jackson was a 'persistent faller.' Finally Swinton-Thomas read out to the hushed courtroom Mrs Bowler's own evidence: " 'I do not think she could have got out of the car by herself".'

'The conduct of the Defence is not strictly relevant to this Appeal,' Swinton Thomas had said at the outset. But taken page by page in the stenographer's transcript, one quarter of the judgement was devoted to clearing the name of Nicholas Purnell.

Mr Purnell, said Lord Justice Swinton-Thomas, had managed to a great extent to undermine the Prosecution's case. Insofar as it was necessary for the Defence to put forward any theory for the cause of Mrs Jackson's death, he had rightly decided that the 'unknown abductor' was a more promising theory than the idea that this frail, immobile and frightened old lady could have walked alone to her death.

Nor were their lordships persuaded that Mr Purnell had made an error in not calling character witnesses. After all, eloquent testimony as to Mrs Bowler's good character had come from Prosecution witnesses such as Dr Jeelani. Swinton-Thomas called for a set of professional rules* governing barristers who wish to criticise their predecessors.

The judgement continued just a few minutes longer as Swinton-Thomas demolished the remaining grounds of appeal: one by one they fell like a pack of cards. Now Swinton-Thomas read out his last chilling paragraph:

'Finally, in the light of the way in which this appeal has been put, we should say that we have stood back and viewed the totality of the case and the totality of the appeal and have asked ourselves: Are we satisfied that this conviction was on the evidence safe and satisfactory? If we answered that question in the negative we would have no hesitation in allowing the appeal. However we answer the question in the affirmative. Accordingly the appeal must be dismissed.'

'All stand' said the usher. Swinton-Thomas got to his feet and the usher pulled back his chair. The court fell silent as Mr Justice Morison followed him out of the courtroom and Sheila was led away by the officers. Jane's muffled sobbing was the only sound to be heard as, shaking their heads in disbelief Sheila's friends and family filed out, one behind the other.

Most of the journalists hurried away without a word. Only a few – the *Telegraph* reporter Kathy Marks, and Joe Weber, the local Sussex journalist – hung behind offering their commiserations. Elderly women supporters

---

* A few months later these new rules were indeed produced by the Bar Council, the barristers' representative body. The seven-point guidance document was published in *Bar News* in December 1995 and became enshrined in the pages of Archbold's *Criminal Pleading, Evidence and Practice*. The Bar Council ruled that 'counsel newly instructed must promote and protect fearlessly by all proper and lawful means his lay client's best interests without regard to others, including fellow members of the legal profession,' provided any allegations against former counsel were properly made. Former counsel must be given plenty of time to respond, and must be allowed to ask for further time if necessary. Then newly instructed counsel must have an opportunity to make his own response.

wept quietly. Nobody knew quite what to do. Someone found a notepad and people began scribbling messages to Sheila: her lawyers alone were permitted to visit her in the cells and could take the notes to her.

'Don't give up,' 'We'll keep fighting for you,' 'It's not all over yet,' said the notes, but there was a hollow ring to the words.

At last it was time to leave the court and Jane and Simon had to face the cameras at the gates.

Next day the headlines proclaimed the stark reality: *'Woman loses appeal over aunt's death,' 'Aunt's killer loses appeal hearing,' 'Judges turn down appeal by woman who drowned aunt.'* But most of the reports carried vows that the fight would go on.

'We remain convinced of Sheila Bowler's innocence,' David Jessel told Kathy Marks of the *Telegraph*. 'We don't walk away from these cases and we will fight on.'

CHAPTER ELEVEN

STRANGERS AND FRIENDS

After the devastating news of 5 May, Sheila's diary falls silent. She would somehow have to survive the remaining nine years of her sentence. For the next six months she found it impossible to do much more than exist for one day at a time.

Her family and friends felt equally numb and close to despair. Everyone was well aware that once an appeal has been dismissed, the chances of having it returned to the Court of Appeal are minimal, requiring a demand from the Home Secretary himself that it should be looked at again. Sheila wrote us a letter on May 8:

Three days since Black Friday

'In spite of huge support how on earth would the judiciary be able to order a re-trial? My optimism is severely shaken though I know the fight is going on out there.'

Bullwood Hall staff had been prepared for a bad result, and a confidential report by the prison forensic psychologist the following month revealed that 'the multi-disciplinary team was sufficiently concerned to open an F2052 SH on Mrs Bowler.' This is the official procedure for identifying and monitoring prisoners at risk of self-harm or suicide.

The psychologist commented: 'Prior to her recent unsuccessful appeal my interviews with Mrs Bowler have focused on her concerns regarding her grown-up children and her release campaign. These concerns have tended to overshadow Mrs Bowler's own emotional adjustment to her situation. Indeed, Mrs Bowler's coping strategies appear designed to leave her as little time as possible to dwell on her own internal life. Mrs Bowler has indicated that stoicism is a long-standing characteristic of her coping style. These strategies have enabled Mrs Bowler to deal effectively and constructively with her situation. However, since the failure of her appeal these strategies have been severely challenged. The fall of her appeal has in her own words "devastated" Mrs Bowler, and her coping style, that barely acknowledges her own feelings, is taxed by the increasingly pressing need for her to address her emotional response to her situation.'

In a separate report, a probation officer noted that 'Sheila is also proud of her ability to cope and so was rather put out when the F2052 SH was raised in mid-May. But having had the opportunity to talk through the reasons for raising it, she has accepted that it was done with her welfare in mind.'

The probation officer also noted that 'Sheila's outside support, to my knowledge, remains strong at present, but this may be something which will need to be monitored as time goes on, particularly as Sheila finds this support vital to her survival in prison.'

If prison staff thought the support for Sheila would now drain away following the failure of the appeal, they were wrong. Those who had witnessed the fiasco at the Court of Appeal in person, or had read about it in the press, were all the more determined to continue the fight, though they were realistic about the enormity of the task ahead.

At this stage, the best hope for the campaigners seemed to be to galvanize into action the ever-growing body of supporters. Only with their help could the campaign continue.

Audrey and Brian Mummery wrote immediately to the organisations Liberty and Justice, asking them to look again at Sheila's case. And twelve days after the judgement was delivered, we pulled ourselves together and mailed out another letter to the Friends of Sheila Bowler, this time signed by us and containing an envelope with a Freepost address to encourage people to respond. We began with the good news of *Trial and Error's* continuing belief in Sheila's innocence, and the team's determination to find a way of proving it. We went on to outline four ways in which supporters could help continue the campaign for her freedom.

First we asked for character references for Sheila from those who knew her well – some of whom would have first-hand experience of her long-term care for Aunt Flo.

Secondly we explained that the case could not be returned to the Court of Appeal without fresh evidence: we asked local people to report any piece of information, however trivial, related to the case.

Third, we asked for case histories to support the theory that Mrs Jackson walked to her death: 'We need as many examples as possible of the kinds of things that elderly people are capable of doing under stress.'

Finally we stressed the importance of maintaining a high profile for the campaign with publicity in local and national newspapers, and asked supporters for any other ideas. The letter ended: 'Sheila, as many of you will know, has suffered a real setback with the failure of the appeal. But amazingly she has pulled herself together again and is regaining her strength to go on with the fight. Please continue to give her your support so that in the end we shall all have the satisfaction of seeing that justice is done and an innocent woman set free.'

Almost immediately the letters began flooding in – so many of them that the postman would push then in elastic-banded bundles through our letterbox. They formed a veritable *This is your Life* collection testifying to the good character of Sheila Bowler.

Predictably the first batch came from people who knew Sheila well, some since childhood. Several ladies in their eighties told how they had known her since birth, and spoke of her loyalty in keeping in touch over the years. Mrs Beatrice Prebble wrote to Jane: 'I have known and loved your mother since she was born and I am quite certain in my own mind that she is incapable of doing such a thing.' Miss Audrey Hunt, a singer, had enjoyed many musical evenings with Sheila when they were in their teens and had found her a loyal friend for the next fifty years. There were many more letters in the same vein.

Then there were those who remembered Sheila from her student days, like Mrs Winifred Vines (mother of Sheila's faithful friend Susan Catmur) who taught her piano as a teenager, and Miss Olive Rees who had been her music teacher forty years earlier: 'She was bright and intelligent, and worked with determination to succeed and obtain her degree. She had an attractive personality, was sensible and I was always prepared to write on her behalf if she applied for a new job.'

Anne Somers met Sheila as a fellow student at Trinity College of Music in 1952:' We have remained friends ever since – she is a generous, kind and thoughtful friend. Sheila would pour her considerable energy into helping to solve any problem, whether it was transporting our belongings from Bayswater to Romford in 1957, or searching for a teapot I needed on Christmas Eve 1992.'

Teaching colleagues and employers added their testimonials: there were letters from serving and retired heads and deputy heads, including June

Parker, former Head of Battle Abbey School. Many teachers and secretarial staff from Sheila's former workplaces vouched for her reliability and high principles. All expressed their horror at her imprisonment. 'Shocked,' 'astounded,' 'incredulous,' 'horrified,' 'appalled' were the words they used.

The former Head of English at Battle Abbey School went further: 'If this death is indeed a complex plot, then it is so full of holes that it must have been devised by someone very stupid. Sheila is not a stupid woman. Most importantly I know how concerned and proud she was about Jane's musical career.'

Sheila's piano and cello pupils added their voices, speaking of her patience and support. Many young musicians, friends of Jane's, described how they had benefited from Sheila's hospitality over the years.

More recent friends wrote of Sheila's thoughtfulness and loyalty: 'She was a staunch friend and so very reliable.' Many recalled 'simple caring actions' – the offer to lend a cot for a grandchild; the support when relatives were ill, 'always bringing us a flower or a little plant for the garden'; her devotion to her own family 'she adored both her children; she was an extremely caring mother'; 'her family came first.'

Women who had worked with Sheila over the past twenty years in local charities said she was 'honest, kind and unstinting in her work.' On the NSPCC Committee she was 'most hard-working and dedicated. She did all the arduous and heavy jobs'; 'she always helped and found time to help others.' At the Royal British Legion she 'worked hard for the Poppy Appeal, not just on the day but for weeks before and weeks after.' The picture that emerges – of a woman of enormous compassion, duty, consideration and loyalty – is hard to square with the picture painted by the Greyfriars matron and her staff, and the police who had investigated Mrs Jackson's death. They depicted Sheila as harsh, cold and unfeeling, and ultimately cruel and calculating.

But even her staunchest supporters, who knew her well and did not for a moment doubt her innocence, were frank in their letters about her sometimes tactless ways: 'She did not suffer fools gladly, and perhaps her manner might seem abrupt at times. But that could not denigrate what I feel is a straight and honest character.' 'Sheila has a very unfortunate manner which many people find off-putting, but her innate kindness and reliability has never been in question in my mind. I find the accusation against her to be totally out of character.'

Canon David Maundrell wrote praising Sheila from his retirement house in Chichester, but added: 'Sheila has a blunt and at times even rather abrasive way of saying things, which some people find off-putting at a first meeting. And she does not easily show her feelings. Those who know her well accept all this as part of the way she is made, and know her to be a good, honest and trustworthy person, and a good friend.'

Sheila's step-daughter, Elizabeth, wrote movingly about her step-mother's loyalty to her father Bob and her daily care for his aunts over many long years: 'Hers is not a passionate, extrovert nature, but once a commitment has been made she will dutifully carry it out.' But, she went on, 'It could be said of my step-mother that she is her own worst enemy in this appalling situation. She has a pride and reserve which prevents familiarity with others, she views the world from a privileged stance and can be intolerant of people whom she perceives to be less able than herself. This should not imply that she is capable of murder.'

A significant batch of the letters took up the theme of Sheila's exceptionally devoted care for her family, particularly her dedicated daily attendance on Bob's elderly aunts. Mrs Rene Skinner wrote from Bristol to say she had known Flo and Lil in their youth and visited them at Sheila's home in Rye on many occasions: 'I was always invited for a meal and a happy evening, and I know Sheila was constantly in touch with them later. I have never – and I mean never – heard them say anything but nice things about her. She does not deserve to suffer in this way.'

Helen Goodwin, the elderly lady whom Sheila took to buy the wedding hat, wrote: 'Sheila was unstinting in her devotion to Bob's two aunts. She never forgot them. I used to meet both of them as they made their way on one of their trips to Rye and one of their pet topics of conversation was how kind Sheila was. They thought Sheila was the most wonderful person on earth.'

The aunts' neighbour, Biddy Cole, reiterated her belief that 'Sheila is one of the last people in the world to have acted in this way or even to have considered such an action. She struck our family as a very caring carer who really was extremely fond of the old ladies. In all the time they lived next door I never once heard her shouting at them, despite sometimes having to clear up very distasteful messes. I would describe her as kind, caring, surprisingly tolerant and extremely conscientious of the responsibilities she had undertaken for her husband.'

Others wrote of Sheila having to rush off 'to call in to do whatever necessary for the old lady's needs and make sure she was comfortable. I believe she went every day and I always admired her dedication'; 'She visited the aunt all the time and always tried to get the best care for her'; 'I am sure it was because of Sheila that both aunts were able to stay in their own homes for so long.' A bus driver from the village of Ore recalled helping Mrs Jackson on to his bus, accompanied by Mrs Bowler. He remembered the older lady as rather cantankerous and bossy: 'Mrs Bowler's voice had no forceful or authoritative tone to it. It was Mrs Jackson who dominated Mrs Bowler on my buses, while Mrs Bowler said nothing.'

Some of the correspondents referred specifically to Sheila's relationship with the Greyfriars staff. It was, they said, her very dedication that led her to speak frankly in Aunt Flo's defence – in the same way that she had annoyed the primary school teachers when she spoke up for Simon.

In terms of the next stage of the campaign, the most fascinating batch of letters were from people with first-hand knowledge of caring for the elderly. Many of them were complete strangers who had seen the *Trial and Error* programme or read about the case in the newspapers. They told stories remarkably similar to that of Sheila and Aunt Flo. They told of leaving seemingly immobile relatives unattended, and returning to find them missing. The phrase 'There but for the grace of God...' was frequently quoted.

One of the most moving letters was an anonymous one, from a man of 90: 'I remember still vividly the day when I came home and my mother was not there. She was bedridden, suffering from cancer of the ovaries, and could hardly see. But she went by bus from Bayswater to Richmond to commit suicide by drowning. She was saved but died soon afterwards in a hospital in Richmond. The police interviewed me, being sure I had taken her to Richmond and pushed her in the water. How could she have got there in the physical state she was in? The police put me under house arrest and would not even let me visit my mother in hospital. The enquiries went on and proved I could not have been there. This happened 50 years ago and I still have nightmares.I cannot tell you my name because I could not face to be involved in this terrifying matter again.'

Several people described relatives with Alzheimer's disease who seemed only able to shuffle along, but were found 'marching down the road,' or 'jumping out of the chair' to the amazement of carers – only to have forgotten a few minutes later that they had ever moved at all. The commonest motives were the need to find a bathroom, or the sudden desire for a cup of tea or a favourite food, and compelled by these urges, infirm people could negotiate apparently insurmountable obstacles. One woman's dying bedridden mother was found downstairs in the kitchen declaring she was going to make scrambled eggs. A 90 year old immobile blind lady was discovered raiding the larder when her nephew returned unexpectedly from work.

Many were seen 'rushing' along, abandoning their zimmer frames or walking sticks. Howard Hickman, a Rye man who drove Greyfriars residents to Magdala House, the day centre attended by the aunts, recalled one elderly man picking up his zimmer and hurrying from the car because it was raining heavily. Mrs Courtney-Bennett, another Rye resident, described how her 92-year-old father, bedridden for months, suddenly decided to change beds in the middle of the night: 'To do this he had to remove from the spare bed various packed boxes and large cases of papers, books and clothes, as well as a heavy television – all of which he managed without damaging anything. He died a few days later.'

A woman wrote from York describing pushing her 97-year-old grandfather in a wheelchair round a hospital because a fall had left him unable to walk: 'I stopped to talk to someone in a side ward, leaving him just outside the door. When I returned, after only a few seconds, he had gone. The ward sister went mad, insisting I had left him somewhere. He was found wandering around, walking, on the other side of the hospital. All I can say after reading Sheila Bowler's story is There but for the Grace of God go I!'

In some cases the distances travelled by seemingly immobile people were comparable with Aunt Flo's alleged walk from Sheila's car to the River Brede. A Macclesfield woman was found by police wandering up a hill in

Stockport, six miles away, saying she was going to visit her mother. Her daughter-in-law wrote: 'At the time we felt very harassed by the police because they didn't appear to believe us. I often wonder what would have happened if she had not been found. I feel we would have been under grave suspicion of harming Mother.'

A Lincolnshire man described how his mother, suffering from dementia and able to move only in a wheelchair, walked alone out of a nursing home, through two yale-locked doors and into the street, where she walked a further 750 yards to reach her son's TV and radio shop.

Another severely handicapped lady in her eighties walked a quarter of a mile across 'a solid sheet of ice' to join her daughter at a relative's funeral: 'When we came out of church imagine my horror to see my mother amongst the mourners. I could never imagine how she had negotiated that treacherous stretch of ice that day.' Several people described elderly parents who had walked long distances back to their old homes, sometimes in their nightclothes, sometimes even carrying a suitcase. They had often managed to escape unnoticed from care homes.

Another significant group of letters came from professionals in the field of geriatric care: doctors, nurses and careworkers in homes for the elderly. Many told similar stories of patients in their care. A social worker told of a housebound lady suffering from dementia who had managed to take a train from Milton Keynes to Brighton, via London, without a ticket, and then walk to her death in the sea: 'Everyone in that case said they had believed such actions impossible without help. Yet she did it!'

Like the family carers, the professionals testified that sudden and unexpected mobility by infirm and demented geriatric patients is a very well known phenomenon to those employed in caring for them. A typical letter was the one from Mrs Hazel Webb: 'I am an REN and work in the Nursing Home sector caring for the elderly. I can assure you that residents who "cannot walk" are frequently found down the corridor, in the bathroom or even down the road. One outstanding case I frequently quote is of an elderly resident who needed two nurses to help her transfer from bed to chair, and walk a little way with a zimmer. One afternoon she went missing and was found by police two hours and two miles later, sitting on her own doorstep.'

Dr John Finch, a Southampton GP with forty years' experience of treating the elderly, wrote saying he was 'very disturbed by this case. I venture to suggest that if the court had heard testimony from half a dozen experienced nurses selected at random from homes for the elderly, they would tell you, if they were truthful, that it happens surprisingly often that frail patients wander to unexpected places, though up until then they have been considered incapable of such activity.'

Of particular interest was a long and detailed letter from Beverley Kite who runs the Carers' Association. She had already contacted the Alzheimer's Disease Society and was to continue her active support for the campaign to free Sheila.

We typed up all the letters and filed them in a steadily growing dossier. We replied to each letter-writer personally, asking their permission to add their names to the list of Sheila's supporters, which now numbered well over five hundred. We also asked people for one further favour: would they be prepared to send a letter to their own Member of Parliament, asking for representations to be made to the Home Secretary, Michael Howard, about Sheila's case?

The response was extraordinary. Within a few weeks, supporters were sending copies of the replies they had received from their MPs, sometimes enclosing copies of correspondence with Timothy Kirkhope, Parliamentary Under Secretary of State at the Home Office, whose job it was to deal with letters to the Home Secretary about alleged miscarriages of justice. The letters were standard replies, summing up the bare facts of the trial, the appeal and the reasons for its dismissal. All the letters ended with the same words: 'As you will appreciate, it is not for the Home Secretary to review the decisions of the courts or to seek to substitute his judgement for that which the courts have reached on the evidence before them. However, I can say that we will look with care at any representations which those now acting for Mrs Bowler may decide to submit, to see if there are grounds upon which it would be right for the Home Secretary to refer the conviction to the Court of Appeal.'

Media interest in the case continued. Jane travelled to Birmingham to appear on the television breakfast show *Good Morning with Anne and Nick,* where her beauty and obvious sincerity struck home to viewers who responded in their hundreds. She recorded an interview for the *My Story* programme on the now defunct Viva women's radio station. On October 15 the *Sunday Express* ran a long feature on the case, written by Jay Iliff in its *Classic* colour magazine; the following week the *Mail on Sunday* published a full length interview with Jane by Jemima Harrison, accompanied by a large photograph. Again, readers were moved by the plight of the lovely young musician, whose promising career had had to be put on hold as she fought for her mother's freedom. More and more letters – some from overseas – fell through the our letterbox in response. One of the most moving was a letter from Mrs Daphne Tebbs, who said she had attended the St Martin in the Fields concert with her sister from America, little realising, until she read the *Mail* article, that the attractive young cellist was in the midst of such awful stress. Most of the new letters – Mrs Tebbs's included – contained accounts of the extraordinary feats of the elderly. All were typed up and added to our database.

Many writers, often pensioners themselves, sent small sums of money, postal orders, or stamps, to help with the campaign. These were all sent to Sheila to help her maintain her supply of phonecards and her ever-increasing postage costs as she struggled to keep up her correspondence with well-wishers.

A regular correspondent was a Hong Kong resident, a lawyer called Peter Surman. He told us he was reading an old copy of *The Times* and noticed Tim's article, entitled *What happened to Aunt Flo?* while on a plane to New Zealand. He had been intrigued by the case ever since. Mr Surman shared Sheila's love of music and would write telling her about the music scene in Hong Kong. Later he was to write fascinating accounts of life in the city as the handover to China approached, and each Chinese New Year he would send her a special Chinese calendar. He later moved to Fiji and continued his correspondence there. His letters allowed Sheila some form of mental escape for a few moments as she read them in her tiny prison cell.

One day that October a letter arrived from one of Sheila's NSPCC colleagues Tessa Potts. In a telephone conversation arising from the letter, Mrs Potts suggested arranging a meeting between us and members of Greyfriars staff (whom she knew well through her work with the Home's League of Friends) on the 'neutral ground' of her own home. The residential home had now been closed down and was up for sale, and she thought some of the staff might be willing to help us.

Seated around Mrs Potts's tea-table in her neat Winchelsea parlour one late October evening, we met Mrs Valerie Nye, the former deputy at Greyfriars, and Mrs Annie McGlanaghy, the careworker who had dressed Mrs Jackson on the day she went missing. Mrs Nye confirmed that soon after Mrs Jackson's death, she had received a memo from Social Services directing that no staff should answer any questions about the case, but that all enquiries should be directed to the County Hall press office. However, as she was now retired, she felt able to speak informally. Other members of staff were more reticent. Although Greyfriars had closed, most of them had been redeployed in other council-run establishments and felt the Social Services veto still applied to them.

The first topic of conversation was an attempt to clear up a confusion over the photograph of Mrs Jackson's slippers as it had appeared in police records. Sheila remembered that the old lady wore men's brown and white checked slippers bought for her by Bob, whereas the slippers shown on the photograph were black. According to a report by Mark Webster, a forensic expert employed by the Defence to check any damage to the stockings and slippers, these black slippers were size six.

The two women expressed surprise. Annie McGlanaghy recalled dressing Mrs Jackson in the checked slippers on the morning of May 13. She had gone off duty at 1.30pm so she supposed someone could have changed the slippers. But there was no way, they both declared, that Mrs Jackson's feet would fit into such a small size – she would need size seven or eight at least. Her deformed toes needed that length to be comfortable. Mrs Nye promised to check with other former staff in case something had been spilt on the slippers before Mrs Jackson went out with Mrs Bowler.

As for Mrs Jackson's mobility – the ladies were adamant that she could not have walked to the river without assistance. They both stressed her fear of the dark, and remembered how she would ask for the curtains to be drawn together 'when it got dark, about this time of day.'

Next morning Mrs Nye rang us. She was, she said, 'devastated.' She had spoken to other care workers, and one of them – who did not wish to be identified – admitted she had changed Mrs Jackson's slippers because just before Sheila arrived, the old lady, as usual incontinent, had had an accident and the checked slippers were soaked. Mrs Nye was most upset: the size six black slippers, she said, 'must have been crammed on her feet.'

We were interested in this revelation for two reasons: first, the slippers would have been too tight across the width to fall off during Mrs Jackson's walk from the car to the river. They could not have been so tight as to be painful: there is no record in the statements of Mrs Britton or Mrs Jones, the two care-officers who helped her into Mrs Bowler's car, of any complaint from the old lady. Nor did she mention tight slippers to Mrs Bowler. But the looseness of the slippers had been an important point in the Prosecution's favour at the Hove trial. It had been alleged that if the old lady had walked to her death, the slippers would have fallen off and been found on the road, not on the river bank.

Secondly, the careworkers had strongly confirmed a fact known from the outset, but never fully developed as evidence helpful to Sheila's defence. The old lady was indeed incontinent – supplying a powerful motive for her to wish to leave the car in a hurry. This could also provide an explanation for the towel Sheila had seen pulled across the gear stick towards the passenger seat. The incontinence issue had certainly been explored at trial, but had not been developed as a incentive for walking, because that was not the line taken by the original Defence team.

The *Trial and Error* team had vowed to continue their support of Sheila Bowler and they were as good as their word. This case was unprecedented in that they had made a programme before the dismissal of the appeal. Now they decided to take an even more unusual step: there would be a second programme, to be screened in November that year.

The centrepiece of the film was to be a gathering of Sheila's support group at the Rye Lodge hotel, an old-established hostelry on Hilders Cliff, looking out over Romney Marsh towards the sea. The date set was 31 October, Hallowe'en, and we told Jessel we had our doubts whether elderly supporters would brave the 'trick or treat' youngsters or the chill mists sweeping over the Marsh.

We were mistaken. The 'Friends' turned out in force, filling the basement bar room as the cameras moved from group to group and people spoke movingly of their belief in Sheila Bowler's innocence. Andy Hemsley, the chief reporter on the local paper, the *Rye Observer,* was there covering the story. Throughout the campaign he printed articles about Sheila's case and helped to keep the issue alive locally, even when all hope seemed to be lost and there were many who doubted Sheila's innocence and were content to see her locked away.

A few days later Simon and Jane received a phonecall from Ian Newton, a forensic psychologist who had worked as a Medical Research Council officer at Manchester University medical school, at the North West Injury Research Centre. He had seen an article in the *Daily Mail* about the case and was surprised to hear that the appeal had been dismissed. He offered to look at the papers of the case and give us his views. He was particularly interested in the post mortem photographs:

'At first sight the injuries appeared slight and were not those that might usually be associated with assault. I sought a further opinion from Professor Michael Horan, Professor of Geriatric Medicine at Manchester University. He was a former colleague of mine at the injury unit and, I discovered, a colleague of Professor Archie Young who was already assisting the Defence team. I asked him how old the injuries might be. He said he thought they were at least one hour old. Dr Heath had said at the Hove trial that he would place them at some point "within four hours of the time of death." If indeed the Mrs Jackson's injuries had been four hours old, then the Greyfriars care staff, Mr Day and indeed Sheila herself could not have failed to notice them, and Sheila would be in the clear.'

Newton also consulted Dr William Lawler, a very experienced Home Office forensic pathologist: 'He agreed that the injuries were not typical of assault injuries. Had there been a violent assault, he said, then bruising would have appeared much earlier.' The experts Newton consulted agreed with him that the marks on Mrs Jackson's forearm, said by Dr Heath to be finger grip injuries, were too light to be the kind of strong grip marks caused, as Heath had suggested, by someone restraining the old lady before pushing her into the water.

Another expert in his field, a Glasgow scientist, also made contact. He had developed an intriguing theory on the reason for the leakage of air from the Audi's tyre. In lengthy and usually late-night telephone calls to us and to junior counsel David Martin-Sperry, he would explain in enormous detail, incomprehensible to the non-scientist, exactly how in an older car, the metal rim of a tyre can become separated from the rubber treads when a motorist is negotiating a steep hill or going round a sharp bend. His ideas, like the hundreds of others coming in from all over the country, were typed up and duly submitted to Sheila's solicitors.

A campaign as grim as this one certainly needs its lighter moments. At about the same time a sleuth of quite another kind appeared on the scene. Miss Isabel Joseph, an elderly lady living in Norfolk, announced that she had seen all the publicity and had decided to take up Sheila's case. Her past experience qualified her well for the task, she said, because she had been among other things a private investigator and a journalist and had many contacts in the media.

On her ancient typewriter Miss Joseph compiled a series of polemics, written in *Sun*-style hyperbole, demanding that Sheila's case be overturned. The first was illustrated with a photograph of Sheila, captioned: 'FACE OF DESPAIR: ELDERLY WIDOW WRONGLY ACCUSED!' Opposite was a picture of Mrs Jackson headed: 'GUTSY AUNT FLO! GROSS MISCARRIAGE OF JUSTICE!'

Miss Joseph announced her attention of going right to the top. She claimed to be working in close and constant collaboration with such dignitaries as John Mortimer, and she sent her pamphlets to (among others) Margaret Thatcher, Betty Boothroyd, Terry Wogan, Judge Pickles, Cliff Richard, Gillian Shephard and Mrs Norma Major (who did indeed send Miss Joseph a courteous reply, asking for further details to put before her husband, then still Prime Minister).

Miss Joseph then embarked on a barrage of telephone assaults which must have sent her phone bill into the stratosphere and brought Bexhill CID, Glaisyers solicitors and the Home Office almost to their knees.

Many of Sheila's supporters were sceptical, especially when this latter-day Miss Marple demanded that Sheila should employ the services of a hypnotist, and came up with the idea that low-flying swans had moved Aunt Flo's slipper to its final resting-place on the pumping station ledge. She also suddenly remembered – severely stretching the credulity of Sheila and her family – that she had been a great friend of Aunt Flo's in her youth in London's East End.

But everyone had finally to admit it was Miss Joseph who set up such a rapport with the faceless bureaucrats at the Home Office's C3 Division that one of them came personally to visit the River Brede in Winchelsea. This official was to return to the Home Office to deal with the case even after C3 was disbanded and its work handed over, in 1996, to the Criminal Cases Review Commission – a tribute to Miss Joseph's dogged persistence.

There were other unusual letters – one from a qualified graphologist who offered, free of charge, to analyse Sheila's handwriting and help to prove her innocence. Another came from a company offering lie-detector tests. A third correspondent requested exact details of Sheila's time and date of birth so that he could work out her astrological chart.

Predictably perhaps, letters came from other prisoners, some claiming that they too were victims of miscarriages of justice.

Meanwhile back at Bullwood Hall, there were very few lighter moments for Sheila. The wing seemed noisier than ever: she asked for ear-plugs to be sent in but they were banned. She wrote to us, 'I am getting a greater and greater antipathy towards being locked in every day, especially with the way in which some of the officers summon us to our rooms. There is a desperate shortage of staff. I feel very depressed – everyone is working so hard for me out there and I can do nothing. Get panic-stricken and wonder how I will cope if no 'hard' evidence is discovered and I have another nine and a half years to go.'

The screening on November 9 of a second *Trial and Error* programme on the Bowler case came just in time to cheer Sheila and her supporters at the lowest point of the campaign. David Jessel launched a fearless and blistering attack on the workings of the Court of Appeal, its refusal to admit expert evidence and its sidelining of the appellant in favour of a legal wrangle.

More and more letters came flooding in from viewers, giving the campaign a much-needed boost.

CHAPTER TWELVE

ANOTHER CHRISTMAS

The constant stress, noise and poor diet was beginning to take its toll on Sheila's health. Towards the end of November she took up her diary writing again, inspired by negative rather than positive motives.

24-25 November 1995

Have been motivated to continue as Tuesday last week I was taken ill and feel I should record the events in case I may be taken ill again and there will be no accurate record of what happened.'

There follows a detailed account of what seems to have been a slight stroke: 'I started to fill in a VO [visiting order] for Jane when I lost control of my left hand. Then as I was walking to breakfast carrying my jar of marmalade in my left hand I immediately dropped it on the landing. I managed to get downstairs to the wing office, felt faint, then collapsed on the floor with my left hand, arm and leg paralysed. My speech was slightly affected and I started retching.'

She was taken to the surgery on a stretcher, where her blood-pressure was found to be higher than usual, then to the medical wing where she slept until lunchtime. She spent the next few days resting, and returned to work on Friday.

'I still felt I wasn't able to control my left hand properly to write, and it wouldn't do what I told it at the piano.' She returned to work, and the doctor saw her again and arranged for her blood pressure to be taken at the same time every day, but in fact the attention she received over the next few weeks was patchy to say the least.

Sheila's friends were alarmed and a number of them wrote separately to the Home Secretary, to Anne Widdecombe MP, then Prisons Minister, to the Director-General of the Prison Service, to the Prisons Inspectorate, to the Governor, Chaplain, and Chair of the Board of Visitors of Bullwood Hall, and finally to Jacqui Lait, then Sheila's local MP.

We wrote to Michael Howard mentioning the dossier of evidence being compiled on the case: 'We hope this will convince you to refer the case back to the Court of Appeal. But inevitably this process is going to take time – time which in view of Mrs Bowler's age and health, may prove crucial.' The letter ended: 'There will be a public outcry if this lady's health is seriously impaired in prison, or worse still if she dies, and is then proved (as we are confident that in time she will be) to have been completely innocent. We feel we must warn you now of her plight.'

Yet another Christmas was approaching: more cards than ever were sent by Sheila's supporters but Christmas Day itself seemed even bleaker – Sheila hardly mentioned it in her diary. Meanwhile Ian Newton was continuing with his investigations, and on December 28 he came to dinner with Jane and Simon at 25 Fair Meadow to meet us. Jane had made a delicious beef stew (after frantic phone consultations with her mother) but her guests' enjoyment of it was somewhat hampered by Newton's graphic explanation of the technical details of death by drowning. In the end we persuaded him to wait until after the coffee was served.

Two days later Newton visited Sheila in prison. He said later: 'I was impressed by her lack of evasiveness and her openness. Together with the other evidence, I thought that she was a most unlikely murderer.'

Sheila for her part was impressed by Newton's professionalism and dedication – especially as his input was made entirely without any form of payment. He explained his views to her and later to us:

'Aunt Flo's mobility had become the key issue of the medical evidence. It was this aspect that was puzzling. Usually in the individual who is immobile, and particularly the elderly, there would be some evidence of muscle atrophy or muscle wasting. From my recollection of the autopsy photographs there was no such atrophy or other evidence of musculo-skeletal disease which would account for Aunt Flo being unable to walk.

'Another issue was her mental capacity: although there appeared to be some evidence of impaired mental function, she was by account reasonably *compos mentis*. There were also the additional factors that she was apparently afraid of the dark and the fact that she was on diuretic medication. Either or both might have provided an imperative to leave the vehicle, possibly to go to the toilet.'

In the year 1996 Michael Howard's 'Prison Works' policy was reaching its zenith. The emphasis was on containment rather than rehabilitation and women's prisons continued to suffer from the intense security measures imposed on men's jails.

As well as having to endure the general decline of the prison system, Sheila had her own problems: her shoulder was still giving her pain nearly two years after her fall at Holloway and in early February she was taken for treatment at Southend Hospital: 'Very humiliating being dragged through hospital manacled to an officer.' The experience must have been almost unbearable for a fastidious woman of 66.

Back inside the prison van the rules could be relaxed a little and the officer driving the van was prepared to chat. Sheila stared out at the back streets of Southend and spoke wistfully of her home in Rye near the coast, and how she longed to see the sea again. In one of those flashes of humanity rarely seen in prison life, the officer made an unscheduled detour along the seafront. Sheila gazed through the van window at the great winter waves crashing in on the beach, and breathed the salt sea air once more. Then the van turned back towards the prison and her tiny barred cell.

That same month, in her report for one of the regular review boards, a Bullwood Hall probation officer recommended that it was time to consider a move of prison for Sheila. One of the criteria she emphasized was Sheila's need to maintain proximity to her supporters: 'She appears to have enormous support from friends and neighbours who write regularly. It is clear that this support is very important to Mrs Bowler and has helped her to maintain a positive attitude to her situation. Prior to Mrs Bowler's appeal, it was felt that perhaps the support she relied upon might dwindle somewhat if the appeal was unsuccessful. However, since the dismissal of her appeal, this support has endured.'

If campaigners against miscarriages of justice are ever in any doubt about the value of their efforts, they should be encouraged by the reaction of prison staff in charge of Sheila Bowler. The knowledge that there were hundreds of people outside fighting her cause undoubtedly impressed them enormously. Other reports refer to 'enormous external support'; 'the many people who are working on her behalf'; and the 'incredible amount of support both from her family and her many friends.' The Lifer Governor in his summary goes further, and acknowledges the steadfastness, integrity and restraint of Sheila's supporters. He refers to the 'pressure group of people from her home area who fight her corner with gusto, her case being examined by television at one stage. I must add this has no effect on the prison and any infrequent contact is always polite and proper.' But, he adds, 'A move out of area would really be a cruel blow, and one could predict an uproar from many outside. If her conviction stands Sheila will, through age, quickly become a problem and an establishment with appropriate accommodation with medical services will be essential.'

For the time being, however, Sheila remained at Bullwood Hall. She was a little cheered at the prospect of an important meeting of the campaign leaders, the TV team and her legal advisors.

The meeting was finally fixed for Sunday 3 March at the London studios of Just Television, the production company that makes *Trial and Error*. Hosted by producer Steve Phelps, it was attended by David Martin-Sperry, Ewen Smith of Glaisyers and his assistant solicitor Helen Barton, Ian Newton, Jane, Sheila's close friends the Mummeries, and us.

The central item on the agenda was how the Home Secretary could be persuaded to refer the case of Sheila Bowler back to the Court of Appeal. The lawyers confirmed that the Home Office's C3 division, acknowledging the enormous pressure upon them from MPs and members of the public, were eagerly awaiting a document containing new grounds of appeal so that they could take things forward.

There was some urgency in the matter: C3 was due to be replaced that year by a new body, the Criminal Cases Review Commission, specifically set up to look into miscarriages of justice. Home Office civil servants were anxious to clear up all the outstanding cases on their books before handing over.

But there were still grave doubts about the contents of the draft grounds of appeal. Did the document contain enough fresh evidence? Was it wise to repeat the earlier criticisms directed at Nicholas Purnell which might, after all, have lost the first appeal?

The rest of the meeting consisted of a brainstorming session, with everyone putting forward possible ideas. Ian Newton presented his own commentary on the autopsy photographs. Steve Phelps suggested that the issue of hypothermia in the elderly should be examined: it was a strange phenomenon, he said, that just before death from hypothermia occurred, the sufferer became very hot. This could explain why all the buttons on Mrs Jackson's coat, cardigan and dress were found to be undone.

But he felt that the key to this mysterious case lay with the Greyfriars staff. Ewen Smith said he had repeatedly sought to interview them, but had been unable to get permission from East Sussex Social Services.

We handed over to the solicitors our bulky dossier of case histories recording the extraordinary feats of infirm elderly people, for inclusion in the material to be sent to the Home Secretary. We had also prepared a file of letters about Sheila's good character, for the same purpose.

Audrey Mummery expressed grave concern about her friend's deteriorating health. She had been working constantly on Sheila's behalf since the failure of the appeal, liaising with Helen Barton, who had taken a personal interest in Sheila's case and had put in an enormous amount of work on it. Audrey had produced a detailed analysis of the timings of the events of 13 May 1992. She had persuaded Sheila to draw from memory a map of Greyfriars, showing just how far the careworkers had had to walk to collect Aunt Flo's coat, suitcase and medication.

Audrey had concluded that whatever Joan Dobson had said about looking at her clock, Sheila could not have left the Home as early as three minutes past eight. Now Audrey undertook to approach all those people willing to stand as character witnesses should a second appeal be granted. She would ask them to submit full character references to be sent to Ewen Smith.

Everyone left the meeting briefed, like Audrey, with appropriate tasks to perform to keep the campaign afloat.

At the beginning of May 1996, Sheila was moved back to Holloway for what is known as the 'second stage' of her life sentence. All sentenced prisoners serving over twelve months, and all young offenders, are given a sentence plan, compiled in consultation between themselves and prison staff. A copy of Sheila's own sentence plan at this time contains the following recommendation: 'We strongly feel that she should move onto a second stage establishment. It is not felt she requires the degree of physical security offered by Bullwood Hall. That said, a move out of area would be seen as extreme. The external support system that has evolved and her strong family connections are recognized as being extremely important to Sheila. We would therefore ask that Holloway or Cookham Wood be considered.'

Despite Sheila's earlier anxiety to leave Holloway and return to Bullwood Hall after her appeal failed, she now considered herself lucky to be back in central London: at least her family and friends would find it easier to visit her.

The Holloway officers who recognized Sheila greeted her warmly. One of the female senior officers on 'the Fives' – the fifth floor of the prison – had not met her before, but when she eventually arrived on A5, the drug-free wing, she came up to her and said, 'You're Sheila Bowler, aren't you? I've heard all about your case and I think it's disgusting you're in here.'

Conditions were supposed to have improved slightly in Holloway since the famous walk-out by Sir David Ramsbotham just before Christmas 1995. He and his deputy Colin Allen, himself a Holloway governor in the late 1980s, refused to carry out their inspection until conditions had improved. They spoke of their disgust at the infestations of rats and cockroaches, the food rotting in plastic sacks, and the long hours when women remained locked inside their cells. Three weeks later the prison was in the news again over the shackling scandal. Now there was a new Governor, Michael Sheldrick, and at least the prison was said to be physically cleaner.

The officer escorting Sheila from Bullwood Hall promised she would go straight to a single cell on A5. But she was in fact at first taken to a room on another wing, D3. The wing itself was generally clean, but her own room was not: 'At least I have a single, although filthy. (So much for the supposed clean-up). Decided it wasn't worth cleaning as I am expected to move out soon – what chance! Have been told to ask each morning if there is space on A5.'

She was moved to C4 wing the following day, then to a single room on A5. She applied for a transfer to D2, the 'privileged wing,' which houses only about 17 prisoners, and where there is no lock-up during the day. There are other advantages, such as access to a washing-machine – a rare privilege for prisoners.

Sheila's application was successful after only a week, but the decision proved to be a disastrous mistake. She found herself sharing a dormitory with three other women who, she soon realised, were openly hostile. She began washing her face in a bowl in the basin and was told this was unhygienic: 'We don't wash our faces in there!' In the evening one of the women brought in a large frying pan full of food (one of the D2 privileges is for prisoners to cook for themselves) and very obviously invited her two room mates to share it, deliberately leaving Sheila out.

When Sheila tried to read herself to sleep they demanded that she switch out her bedside light as it was keeping them awake. When she woke early and began writing a letter they told her angrily that the rattling notepaper had woken them up. The following day Sheila requested an immediate transfer, which she was allowed: 'I'm not at all surprised,' said the wing officer. 'Nobody lasts long in that room.'

Fortunately a Senior Officer allowed her back on to A5 and eventually to C5, which houses mostly kitchen workers and is a fairly orderly and quiet wing.

Sheila soon began work in the prison library and once again had to apply for a 'red band' to enable her to move more freely, collecting books from the book bins. These are large 'postboxes' with a letterbox and a padlocked lid, made at another prison. When prisoners have finished with their library books they can post them through the top and the library orderly will go round collecting them.

By this time the 'red band' had become a plastic security badge bearing the prisoner's photograph and number: when Sheila first entered prison it had literally been a red cloth band tied around the wrist.

The librarian was pleased to have someone prepared to work and able to understand the cataloguing system. 'For a prison library containing about 10,000 books and reputed to be the best prison library in Europe,' noted Sheila, 'the staffing situation is bad.'

Her aim was eventually to try to get the job of Chapel Orderly so that she might once again have access to a piano. In fact it would be many months before she achieved her ambition. The prison chaplains, much as they admired Sheila's fortitude, were worried that the chapel work involved moving a lot of chairs around, and this might be dangerous for Sheila in view of her recent slight stroke.

The anti-drugs measures were making life more and more unpleasant for non-drug-using Holloway prisoners. Visitors could no longer bring in flowers because drugs had been smuggled within their stems. Now they had to be ordered by telephone from one of two specially appointed North London florists, at a minimum cost of £15, putting them beyond the reach of most families. Magazines could not be brought in either – drugs had been smuggled in between their pages, or the pages themselves had been impregnated with LSD.

At Bullwood Hall Sheila had been allowed to receive commercially produced vitamin pills, purchased at high street chemists or from her usual health-food suppliers, and sent in by her friends. At Holloway they were banned, despite persistent representations from her supporters that her age and worsening health should be considered.

As part of the new measures to control drug use, the prison appointed a band of specially trained officers known as the DST – Dedicated Search Team. They were to be seen standing round the visits room wearing their distinctive red tee shirts with a logo of three black letters, 'D.S.T,' and their black trousers. Going round the prison some of them carried small metal boxes like ladies' vanity cases. These were tool-kits containing implements to unscrew or prise open hiding places for drugs or 'hooch.' Holloway visitors were now subjected to much more rigorous searches by officers checking for drugs. As well as the routine 'pat-down' search they would have to open their mouths and turn their heads from side to side, lifting up their hair if it was long. Jackets and scarves had to be removed and left in lockers, and sometimes searching officers made visitors undo their bootlaces or remove their shoes. Sniffer dogs followed them up the stairs and along the corridor to the visits room, and Sheila's Rye friends with their sheltered lifestyles would often be horrified to witness the forcible and sometimes violent removal of a visitor suspected of smuggling in drugs.

The strip-searches grew more frequent as the Prison Service tried to crack down on drugs being smuggled into jail. The Dedicated Search Teams have earned themselves the nickname 'squat squads' because of an unpleasant practice where they require women to remove their underwear and squat over a mirror so that officers can see whether they have concealed drugs inside their bodies. Sheila wrote furiously in her diary that she would rather be sent 'down the block' than submit to such humiliating treatment – and indeed she never had to suffer it.

But she was outraged when she turned up for work at the library one day to discover that the DST had rampaged through her carefully ordered shelves, leaving books strewn round the floor with their cards tossed aside. Even worse, they had wrecked the little library courtyard with its pond and potted plants, tearing up paving stones in their continuing hunt for hidden drugs. Sheila railed angrily against this institutionalized vandalism. How, she demanded, could the young offenders be expected to behave properly if they were set this sort of example?

The week beginning 13 May 1996, the Holloway women listened for news of Sara Thornton's re-trial, starting that day in Oxford. Her original murder conviction was finally changed to manslaughter and she was released, having already served a six year sentence.

That same day, May 13, was the fourth anniversary of Aunt Flo's death. It was also the date of the annual 'fish-and-chip-run' of the Sussex bikers' clubs. Jane had decided to go along and see if she could find out any more information from bikers who might have joined the run in 1992. None of us were of course aware at that time of the police's investigations. Had Jane known they had discovered details of the two clubs meeting that night, her task would have been easier.

With two girlfriends she drove through the pouring rain to the Promenade Fish & Chip Restaurant on Hastings sea front where the bikers regularly met. With her she took a batch of leaflets headed *WEDNESDAY 13 MAY 1992, FISH & CHIP RUN*. The text, above a photograph of Jane herself, sought information from anyone who may have taken part in the event four years earlier and might remember important information.

Nervously the three girls went into the chip shop and approached the hefty leather-clad bikers, explaining their quest and handing out the leaflets. To their relief the bikers were most helpful. But, they explained, there were only about a dozen of them there that night. Four years ago the chip run had been very popular because it was a bright sunny day. Tonight was a wash-out. Jane drove home dejectedly, the sodden leaflets littering the boot of her car.

Meanwhile her friend Rebekah Gilbert-Dyson set about contacting all the motorcycle magazines. She submitted an article she had written about the events of 13 May 1992, asking if any of the magazine readers could help solve the mystery of Aunt Flo's death. But sadly there was no response.

Indeed, the watchword for that summer of 1996 seemed to be stagnation. We spent a fortnight's holiday in Ireland in late July and returned to find that very little seemed to have happened. In August an official from C3 – probably goaded into action by the redoubtable Miss Joseph – got in touch with Sheila's lawyers asking what progress they had made. It was felt that C3 officials were still trying to close their files on outstanding cases in advance of the new Commission – though that body's inauguration had been delayed by controversy over the appointment of its Chairman. The media had discovered he was a high-ranking member of the Freemasons.

Sheila began to feel less stoical than usual as the August heat set in and her migraines worsened. For the first time ever she began to suffer from eczema. Conditions at Holloway were worsening, there was more and more 'bang-up' in cells, and there was even a minor riot:

3 August 1996

'I am writing this at 10am Saturday. We have been locked in since 12.15 yesterday and we discovered this morning that the cause is a missing pair of scissors. Whole of prison locked in until they are found so you can imagine the racket being produced from all the rooms – screaming, shouting, banging of windows; sheets and clothes of all sorts being sent out of the windows alight, which set fire to some of the trees. The officers, as well as continuing their search, are now employed directing hoses on the areas outside the windows. Even mattresses and blankets have been thrown, in addition to the usual food, sanitary towels, plastic cutlery, bowls, plates and cups. There is now furniture being broken and thrown out of the windows. We were told at breakfast as it was handed through the hatch that the last time something was missing all inmates were locked in for four days. Bright prospect, especially as Simon and Susan [Catmur] are visiting Tuesday.

... It is now midday and I have just been strip-searched and had a room-spin [search]. Apparently it is a pair of scissors and a knife that are missing from the craft workshop. If the officers had done their job properly there should have been nothing missing as the class finished yesterday morning and they should have checked.'

That summer Sheila had another worry to contend with. She had become friendly with a woman prisoner in her mid-fifties, who shared her love of music. The woman was suffering from a hernia and for twelve weeks throughout that summer and autumn, her condition became worse and worse. She vomited after every meal, fainted frequently and lost two stones in weight as she waited weeks for a hospital appointment. Eventually she was in such pain that the prison took the unusual step of allowing Sheila to sleep for a few nights on a mattress on the woman's cell floor to give her support. But Sheila was losing sleep and was in danger of becoming ill again herself. Eventually the woman had a four hour operation.

Sheila had become so demoralized by prison life that she had no heart to continue recording its daily miseries. She stopped writing her diary and instead began writing to her lawyers, explaining how it felt to be incarcerated in a place like Holloway at the age of 66.

In a letter to Ewen Smith at Glaisyers, dated 11 August 1996, she wrote: 'My frustration with my situation increases daily, especially with the present state of the Prison Service with low staffing levels and much locking in. Between 8pm Friday and 8pm Saturday we were unlocked for four hours only and today, Sunday, there has been no exercise. Apart from going to church we have been out of our cells for only three hours. We are often subjected to the indignity of a strip-search and a room spin. No joke at my age. Officers feel very insecure which in its turn reacts on us in a very unfavourable manner.'

The lawyers replied confirming that a submission to the Home Secretary had been drafted, asking him to recommend a new appeal. David Martin-Sperry had sent the draft document to the eminent QC George Carman, famous for high-profile cases including the spat between cricketers Ian Botham and Imram Khan. He was subsequently to win Richard Branson's appeal in the Camelot National Lottery case. In October he replied with a written opinion to be included in the material sent to the Home Secretary.

In it he said he found the history of the case of Sheila Bowler gravely disturbing: the only realistic alternative to the defendant's guilt – that it was a tragic accident in which the deceased had walked to her death – had never been put before the jury. Thus Mrs Bowler did not receive a fair trial on what should have been the real issue in her case, simply because the real issue was never tried. It was his view that the conviction of Mrs Bowler was unsafe and there may well have been the most grave miscarriage of justice in this case.

Another important development that month was the arrival of a report commissioned by Sheila's solicitor from Professor Peter Vanezis, Regius Professor and Head of the Department of Forensic Medicine at the University of Glasgow. He had been approached earlier by Ian Newton who had outlined the pathological aspects of the death of Florence Jackson, and he had read the two post-mortem reports carried out by Dr Heath and Dr Djurovic and studied all the photographs of the body and the site where it was discovered.

Although Professor Vanezis agreed with the factual aspects of the earlier reports, he felt that many of the injuries were consistent with falling onto rough ground, possibly in the process of falling into the river. Like Ian Newton he found no signs of muscular atrophy or atrophy of the limbs caused by disuse, and concluded that 'this lady was quite capable of walking.' He saw no reason why she could not have 'wandered from the car and stumbled down the steep bank to drown in the water.' There were no pathological signs of a struggle against an assailant, nor that she was led to the water's edge and pushed. Finally, he pointed out, as Dr Djurovic had done, that homicidal drowning is extremely rare in the UK: most drownings are accidents or suicides.

Ever since the failure of the first appeal, David-Martin Sperry had been attempting to contact Dr Jeelani in Rye. From a reading of the transcripts of the Hove trial, he felt that Jeelani had appeared uncomfortable as a Prosecution witness and had stressed Mrs Bowler's dedication in caring for her husband's aunt. Perhaps he would be able to shed more light on the true extent of the old lady's mobility. But although he left message after message at Jeelani's surgery, there was no response: perhaps the doctor wanted nothing more to do with the case – or perhaps he had never received the messages.

Then one Friday in early November Martin-Sperry managed to discover Jeelani's mobile phone number and left a message there. The following morning the doctor returned his call. Far from showing any reluctance, Dr

Jeelani said he would be delighted to make a further statement about Mrs Jackson, and to attend court and give evidence if necessary. He had plenty more to say about the old lady's mobility and Mrs Bowler's care of her, but at the trial had never been asked the right questions. He had been worried about the case ever since.

Jeelani made a detailed statement which was sent to counsel on November 11. It was obviously a significant addition to Martin-Sperry's set of submissions to the Home Secretary. The doctor wrote that he would assess Mrs Jackson as fairly mobile, and thought it quite possible that in a confused state she could walk quite long distances. The fact that she was in a wheelchair at Greyfriars was more for convenience than out of necessity. Because of the regular meals and medication given her at the Home, she would have been even stronger and he would not have been surprised at the proposition that she could have removed her seatbelt got out of the car and wandered off. He expanded on the great dedication and care shown to the old lady by Sheila Bowler. At the trial he would have wished to expand more on all these areas had he been given the chance.

Within the next few days, David Martin-Sperry's document was completed and sent to the Home Office, asking the Home Secretary to refer the case of Sheila Bowler back to the Court of Appeal. The document was divided into ten sections.

The first gave the background to the case and its *dramatis personae;* the second gave a timetable of events leading to Mrs Jackson's death and the discovery of her body; the third described the police investigation; the fourth outlined the preparation for trial, with the Defence acceptance that Mrs Jackson was incapable of walking, and the failure to take statements from the character witnesses who volunteered; the fifth described the trial leading to the guilty verdict; the sixth described preparation for appeal by trial counsel, and the effect of the television programme; the seventh described preparation for appeal by the new legal team; the eighth considered the effect of Nicholas Purnell's *Observations* on the appeal; the ninth describes the appeal hearing and dismissal; the tenth and last part listed post-appeal developments, including expert evidence from Professors Young, McLennan and Bryce Pitt; Doctors Djurovic, Porter and Jeelani and the physiotherapist Lucy Rees; evidence from Greyfriars staff and from a leading nursing expert; anecdotal evidence on the extraordinary exploits of elderly infirm people; evidence of the statistical frequency of accidental drownings among the elderly; evidence about the injuries and finally character evidence from a number of potential character witnesses.

Now it was just a question of waiting for a response from the Home Office.

It was almost Christmas again – Christmas 1996 – Sheila's fourth in captivity.

With no news of any second appeal being allowed, it became increasingly difficult for the campaigners to maintain media interest in Sheila's case. People in prison can easily feel they are forgotten, and as much to boost Sheila's morale as to arouse journalists' attention, Jane and her friends hit upon the idea of holding a candlelit vigil in the days leading up to Christmas, to coincide more or less with the application to Michael Howard. At the beginning of December they circulated an invitation to Sheila's friends and supporters, asking them to attend a vigil on December 15 outside the Royal Courts of Justice in the Strand, the scene of such sadness the year before.

Sophia Borthwick, whose parents had first alerted their Sunderland MP Chris Mullin to Sheila's plight back in 1993, produced enormous placards bearing Sheila's photograph and the legend 'SHEILA BOWLER – 1255 DAYS.' (The task of counting the days fell to Rebekah Gilbert-Dyson!) With the permission of the police they were displayed tied to the barriers outside the entrance to the Courts. Each was lit by a small candle. The whole Borthwick family travelled from Sunderland specially to attend the vigil.

As the winter evening darkened, dozens of supporters, many of them young students or musician friends of Jane's, gathered around and stood holding their candles in solemn silence. Susan Catmur moved quietly among them with a cassette recorder, taping Christmas messages to Sheila. Mrs Daphne Tebbs, who had been in the audience at the concert at St Martin in the Fields, was there with her sister and American brother-in-law.

On Christmas Day in Holloway, Sheila listened to the messages on the cassette. They were the only bright spot in a grim day. Later she wrote to us, 'Christmas very bleak – no sense of Christmas at all except at the church – and even there it was very noisy. Meals were a disaster – there were only five of us in the dining room. There was no attempt at any sort of competitions, such as table tennis or pool such as they had at Bullwood Hall. All the decorations etc were only approached in a half-hearted manner. I wasn't much help myself.'

In early 1997 Holloway was in the news again when journalists discovered that Roisin McAliskey, the pregnant daughter of former MP Bernadette Devlin/McAliskey, was being held there without charge while awaiting extradition to Germany for attempted murder and possessing explosives. Her case quickly became an international *cause célèbre*. Her mother and the few other visitors she was allowed described their shock at her solitary confinement for much of the day, and deplored threats that her newborn child would be immediately removed from her.

Roisin was on A5 wing, and Sheila recalls seeing the young woman going to and from the surgery, which was on C5, to collect her medication, always guarded by two officers.

Sheila described her with pity: 'She was very small, under five foot, with short straight light brown hair, and huge eyes, which I always felt had a hunted, bewildered look. She usually wore a denim maternity pinafore dress over a tee shirt, and she seemed to walk with difficulty. If you spoke to her she would smile and reply pleasantly, but she seemed rather reluctant to speak to people. I thought she must be very lonely. She was locked in her room the whole time – she never came to association [the time each evening when prisoners are allowed out of their cells to 'associate' with others on the wing] or to meals. The officers must have taken food into her cell.

'Two officers stood outside her door day and night, and she was made to keep the light on twenty-four hours a day so they could look in and see what she was doing. My room faced out over the flat roof of the visits room and on that roof there was a security camera perpetually trained on Roisin's window. Later on she was pushed in a wheelchair because her legs were swollen. Then one day I saw her being wheeled to the lift being taken to the mother and baby unit.'

Whenever Roisin had reason to be taken from the prison, for instance for a checkup at the Whittington Hospital in North London where her baby was eventually born, all the other women in the prison would know because they all had to be locked in.

'Then one day somebody threw a parcel over the wall of the prison and everyone thought it was a bomb because Roisin was in the prison. All the women in the rooms opposite mine were moved out in case this bomb went off. I don't know what it was but it certainly wasn't a bomb. I saw Roisin as she was going off to have her baby and I wished her luck. I felt very sorry for her.'

Roisin remained out on bail after the birth and did not return to Holloway. Instead she was sent to the mother and baby unit of the Maudsley psychiatric hospital, suffering from post-traumatic stress disorder, and remained there while the courts wrangled about her extradition. (In March 1998 she was finally told by Jack Straw she could go free, but her solicitor Gareth Peirce said she was so unwell that she was unable to take the news in).

Sheila also caught a glimpse of Rosemary West when she was moved to Holloway from Durham's H wing for a short time for accumulated visits. One of Sheila's visitors had been asked by a group of press photographers outside if she could find out when West was arriving, but in fact her arrival was delayed to avoid publicity. A few days later Sheila saw her looking out of her window when she walked through the prison grounds on her way to the chapel.

Sheila had finally achieved her ambition to become chapel orderly and every week, as the chaplains had feared, she insisted on moving every one of the 150 chairs and polishing the floor underneath. One day she shifted a heavy wooden lectern and strained her back. But there were compensations: now at least she had access to her beloved piano, and the humane conversation of chaplain Leah Kerns. For a few minutes each day she could forget the misery of her existence as she played Debussy and Brahms.

(Later that year she helped the chaplains prepare for the Easter services. She described to friends a moving ceremony on Maundy Thursday when two of the chaplains washed the feet of some of the women prisoners in the chapel. But touching as Sheila found the ceremony, she could not resist a characteristically tart comment about the state of her carefully polished floor when the service was finished!

On Easter Monday Terry Waite came to judge the Easter Bonnet competition and Sheila remember her friend Carol Brigham's comments years earlier when she compared his imprisonment as a hostage with her own situation.

The following month his former boss, the Archbishop of Canterbury, came to visit the prison. Sheila was impressed by Dr Carey: 'We had a short service in the chapel with the Governor and other dignitaries, but the Archbishop really wanted to talk to the women. He didn't dress up in his robes – he just wore an ordinary suit. He had brought his wife with him and they insisted on going to the wings that people really ought to see – the psychiatric and medical wings, and the wing where the pregnant women are held.').

As she waited for some development in her case, Sheila continued to keep herself occupied as far as she could. She attended the meetings of the newly instituted Lifers' Group, at which the small number of women serving life sentences sought better treatment. Sometimes the lifers were allowed to air their grievances to guest speakers to their meetings, such as Frances Crook from the Howard League, Sir David Ramsbotham, and Simon Creighton from the Prisoners' Advice Service. They voiced their objections to newly sentenced lifers being placed on the medical wings – as Sheila had been placed on C1 back in 1993 – and asked for extra visiting orders and more activities to break the monotony of their long years in jail. They asked to be given paint to decorate their rooms.

They also asked permission to send for vitamin supplements direct from the manufacturers, so there could be no risk of using them to smuggle in drugs. Sheila felt strongly about this. Ever since she had been moved from Bullwood Hall she was still being refused her health-food supplements, and she had been waging a long campaign, involving the prison healthcare centre and the Board of Visitors, to have them returned in view of her age and recent poor health. What particularly galled her was that she had commissioned one of her supporters to buy a large quantity of the supplements, and now felt herself unnecessarily out of pocket.

Indeed, throughout the whole of her time in prison, Sheila kept a careful check on her finances. In a neat blue exercise book, ruled in five-millimetre squares, she drew up four neat columns, headed Date, Receipts,

Expenditure and Balance. The sums of money listed are minuscule (the average prison wage is around £10 a week) and it is touching to read, under Receipts, the small amounts (£5 here, £10 there) sent in by generous supporters to help with Sheila's supply of phonecards and stamps. Indeed, though officers accuse prisoners of complaining constantly, the only Request and Complaint form Sheila ever filled in was about the loss of a book of first-class stamps ('A parcel was handed in on a visit containing three pairs of socks and two books of ten first-class stamps. I discovered one of the books of stamps was missing. Both books had my name and number on the back').

She was also allowed another exercise book, one with an orange cover. (It is amusing to read the legend on the front page, ungrammatically headed INSTRUCTIONS FOR PRISONER'S NOTEBOOKS. Inmates are warned that the book 'will be withdrawn if it is misused in any way likely to affect security, good order or discipline, or if it contains material likely to jeopardise national security or encourage the commission of crime.' If they wish, prisoners may take an exercise book home with them on discharge, says the printed rule, but only if they submit it 28 days in advance to the prison governor with an application to keep it, and only if it contains 'nothing about staff, inmates, or matters relating to crime, including escape plans'.)

In the orange exercise book Sheila lists, by the month, the thousands of letters and cards sent in by supporters, neatly crossing them out when she has replied. The cards alone number 1,794. Conscientious as ever, even under the stress of prison life, she said later that she found herself under constant pressure to keep up with this enormous body of correspondence. But she felt that people who were so kind as to write deserved a reply – and they usually got one.

One of the more unlikely greetings cards Sheila received was a cartoon from another prisoner, the self-styled Charles Bronson, said by the media to be the most dangerous prisoner in Britain (the following year he had seven years added to his 25 year life sentence for a very serious hostage-taking incident). The cartoon demanded freedom for Sheila and thanked us for our part in the campaign.

While Sheila was struggling to maintain contact with her supporters, we felt we should mail them another update letter. There was precious little news to tell, but perhaps there was further help the campaigners could give. On 1 February 1997 we mailed out a letter thanking those who had attended the candlelit vigil, and all the hundreds who had sent Christmas cards to Holloway.

'As you know,' we wrote, 'the vigil was held to coincide with an application sent to the Home Secretary by Sheila's lawyers, asking him to refer her case back to the Court of Appeal. We were told to expect a decision early in the New Year.

'A whole month has now passed without news, though the lawyers have been told a decision is imminent. Meanwhile Sheila's health has not been at all good. For the first time in her life she is suffering from eczema, and her migraines are worse than ever before. Both these conditions are known to be stress-related. Sheila's powers to resist illness are lessening, not least because she is now prevented by tougher prison security measures from receiving the vitamin and mineral supplements she has taken for years. On 3 January this year Sheila had her 67th birthday, and we are increasingly concerned that unless speedy action is taken, her health will go into a decline that may be irreversible. This is an appalling prospect for a woman we are all convinced is entirely innocent.'

The letter ended with a call to arms: 'We are therefore asking you to write once again to your MP, expressing your concern about Sheila's case and asking him/her to write to Timothy Kirkhope, Parliamentary Under Secretary of State at the Home Office. We are told that he will be dealing with Sheila's case once the papers have been sent to him. We are very worried that she may be forgotten in the run-up to the General Election.'

Once again the supporters rallied round. Once again they sent back copies of their letters and the replies. The Sheila Bowler files now filled the whole of a large filing cabinet in our small office.

CHAPTER THIRTEEN

COURT NUMBER ONE

The last Friday in February 1997, we were celebrating our thirtieth wedding anniversary on the island of Tobago. The holiday was almost at an end and we were returning to our apartment after a pleasant evening meal when the owner approached us with a fax from England. We opened the envelope in some trepidation, worried that it might contain bad news about the family.

It was from our secretary, Alison. 'Jane asked me to tell you,' she wrote, 'that the Home Secretary has referred Sheila's case back to the Court of Appeal.'

On the balcony looking out over the gently lapping Caribbean, we drank Sheila's health with a glass of rum punch. It was certainly a cause for celebration, but champagne was not yet quite in order.

On our return a few days later we were able to read for ourselves the letter sent from the Home Office to Master McKenzie, the Registrar of Criminal Appeals. It was dated 26 February 1997. We read the first paragraph several times – it seemed almost too good to be true: 'The Secretary of State has decided today, under section 17 (1) (a) of the Criminal Appeal Act 1968 to refer to the Court of Appeal the murder conviction of Mrs Sheila Bowler.' The letter went on to give a summary of the case and the first appeal.

It was clear that Dr Jeelani's new statement had been of the most vital importance: 'The Secretary of State has not found this an entirely straightforward matter to decide in the light of the appeal judgement in May 1995. Dr Jeelani's new evidence, however, has led him to the conclusion, on balance, that it would be right for the Court of Appeal to have another opportunity to consider the safety of the conviction.'

In the light of this stirring news, media interest was suddenly revived in the case of Mrs Sheila Bowler. In early February the journalist Grania Langdon-Down went to visit Sheila in Holloway and wrote a feature for *The Independent,* illustrated with a smiling photograph of Sheila, Bob and Simon on their last holiday together. The article was headed: *I didn't kill her. Let me out, or I'll die in prison.*

Another woman journalist, Christa d'Souza, was shocked by the Holloway visits room. In March she wrote a three-page spread for the *Sunday Express* with a picture of Jane outside Holloway and extensive quotes from Sheila: "'It's dangerous to be optimistic. What if the worst happens? I don't know. How can I *possibly* tell?" A flicker of desolation crosses Sheila's blue eyes. "I shall probably just carry on as I am now, despairing inside!'".

The next task was to find a new senior barrister to run the second appeal as leading Counsel for the Defence. Ewen Smith decided to invite Jeremy Roberts, QC, a distinguished criminal silk with a fine track record, to take on the case. In a way it was a surprising choice: Roberts was primarily a Crown Prosecution Service barrister and at the time he accepted the brief, was engaged for the Crown in the appeal of the Bridgewater Four against conviction. The Bridgewaters were released in late February amid great jubilation among the women in Holloway and several of them told Sheila she should have nothing to do with the lawyer who had prosecuted them.

Sheila felt no such compunctions. If he can get me out of this place, she thought, I won't be complaining. By coincidence, a few years earlier, Roberts had crossed professional swords with Nicholas Purnell in the long-running Blue Arrow case, and had been victorious.

The appeal was fixed to run for three days from Monday 21 July 1997. We mailed a letter off to the Friends of Sheila Bowler, asking them to come along and support her as before. This time the hearing would be held before the highest judge in the land, the Lord Chief Justice himself.

On July 1 the new Anglican chaplain at Holloway was asked to contribute to Sheila's six-monthly 'review board' – the regular assessment given to all life-sentence prisoners. He commended her work as chapel orderly and concluded his report, 'Sheila is, in my experience, a very sincere and honest woman and is either innocent of the crime she was sentenced for or is one of the most calculating women in the entire prison system. I find it very hard to believe she is the latter.'

By this time, many of the Holloway prisoners and prison officers had become convinced of Sheila's innocence. The Wednesday before the second appeal, we went to Holloway for what we hoped was a final visit. Jane met us at the gate with a parcel of clothes for Sheila to wear at the appeal. She would be visiting her mother on the Sunday, but Sheila wanted the clothes well in advance 'so I can get them un-creased.' The prison had bent the rules in her favour – strictly speaking extra outfits are not allowed when women go off to court. But as we handed in the clothes to the visits auxiliary, he summoned us into his office for a chat: 'That old woman should never be in here,' he said. 'We all of us think she's innocent. She's a lovely lady.'

At the refreshments kiosk in the visits room we went to buy Sheila her usual treat – a KitKat chocolate bar. The visits orderly, an African deportee, clasped our hands in hers: 'We all hope Sheila walks free on Monday,' she said, 'but really we don't want her to go – she's so kind to everyone.'

With us at Holloway that day in mid-July was Clare Longrigg, the *Guardian* journalist. She had almost fallen foul of the sniffer dog on duty that day. The dog-handler told her to stop and stand still as it snuffled excitedly round her feet. Would she be dragged off for a strip-search, giving *Guardian* readers a unique insight into prison life? But the officer let her pass. 'The dog must have smelt my cats,' she said, as they joined Sheila at Table 22 at the back of the visits room. Like the other women journalists before her, Clare was shocked at Sheila's situation and remained for a further hour after we had left. The next time she would see Sheila Bowler, Clare would be on the press benches at the Court of Appeal and Sheila would in the dock, a silent and powerless witness as others decided her fate.

On Monday morning, Sheila's supporters turned up in force yet again outside the Royal Courts of Justice. Most confessed to a chilling sense of *déjà vu* and a feeling of trepidation. This time there was far more press interest in the case: we were filmed leafing through an enormous file of letters from the hundreds of people all over the country who had written to us recounting the exploits of elderly relatives. Journalists had by now dubbed this 'the people's case.' We thanked reporters from the *Express* and *Mail:* the articles those papers had printed produced hundreds more case histories.

Once more, Kathy Marks was on the press benches. She had reported the first appeal for the *Daily Telegraph* but was now working for the *Independent.* Clare Longrigg was there of course, and Julie Gatenby, the GMTV producer. She hoped that if Sheila's conviction was quashed she would appear on the television breakfast show next morning. But all the journalists respected the wishes of Jane and Simon to remain silent at this tense time, and did not badger them for comments. In the TV and radio interviews we were cautiously optimistic. But like everyone else we knew the appeal could go either way.

Court Number One, the Lord Chief Justice's Court, is the finest in the Royal Courts of Justice. It is grander than the other courtrooms, with its ornate gallery, stately Gothic carved panelling, and gilt-emblazoned coat of arms behind the judges' bench. Aloft there is a domed window affording a few glimpses of sky in this enclosed chamber. Here, possibly more than anywhere else in the land, you cannot help feeling some sense of the majesty and grandeur of the law of the land.

But like the other courts, Court Number One is not designed for mass protest, and the black-gowned female usher raised her eyebrows as more and more supporters filled the corridors outside the first floor room. Although their manners were impeccable, some were very determined indeed to get a seat. One lady had travelled from the north of England and booked two nights in a hotel on the Strand. She had never met Sheila Bowler in her life but she was a long-standing supporter who knew about the ways of the elderly. We had had hundreds of phonecalls over the years, and had listened to tales astonishingly similar to Sheila's own story. Now we met many of the supporters face to face.

Among those who came up and introduced themselves were Susan Caddick and her sister Sandra, who had travelled all the way from Merseyside. Their brother Eddie Gilfoyle had been the subject of another *Trial and Error* programme and, like Sheila, had had his first appeal dismissed. Another was Dorothy Cooksey from Manchester, leader of the campaign to free Susan May, a life-sentenced prisoner in Durham's notorious H wing. Susan had written extensively to us, always protesting her innocence, and though we did not know the full background of her case, we found it very disturbing. Susan had spent a night at Holloway when her own first appeal was dismissed a few months earlier, and wrote to say how supportive Sheila and the other Holloway women had been as she struggled back from the depths of despair.

Some supporters were obliged to wait outside for lack of space, but they soon developed an *ad hoc* rota system so that everyone would get a fair chance to witness at least part of the proceedings. As at the 1995 appeal, people from every walk of life, from students to pensioners, sat together united in their support for the woman in the dock. Others had been called as witnesses. They could not enter and had to remain outside in the draughty marble corridor. Biddy Cole waited there, as she had waited at the last appeal, joined by others already 'proofed' by Glaisyers.

On this occasion, unlike the last appeal, the expert witnesses were allowed into the court to listen to the proceedings. The tall, upright Scot, Professor Archie Young, his beard a little greyer after two years, but looking as resolute as ever, was joined now by two other experts – Dr Denham, another distinguished geriatrician, and Lucy Rees, the senior hospital physiotherapist who had appeared in the second *Trial and Error* programme. On the second day Dr Jeelani joined the expert witnesses, confident that at last he would have the opportunity to give a full account of Mrs Jackson, her mobility, and her relationship with the woman now in prison for her murder.

We were delighted to meet Beverley Kite, of the Carers' Association, for the first time. We had had many telephone conversations with her and Beverley was ready to give her testimony about the mobility of elderly people. We also met for the first time the doughty Miss Isobel Joseph, AKA Miss Marple, a diminutive figure with short white hair.

Another long-standing supporter was Ray Hine, who prided himself on his astrological predictions. At lunchtime on the second day of the appeal he strode up to Anthony Glass as the Crown Prosecutor left the court, and tapped him firmly on the shoulder. The QC spun round, and Sheila's supporters could not suppress a chuckle as Hine demanded to know the date of Glass's birthday. 'He was so surprised that he gave it to me,' said Hine later. 'Are you going to put a hex on him?' someone asked.

But that first morning nobody felt like joking as they took their seats on the ancient wooden benches.

Sheila could be seen hovering just outside the tall oaken doors, smiling and chatting to two prison officers. She was wearing a short-sleeved floral dress and looked pale, though quite composed. As she entered the dock, she smiled across at the public benches. The warmth of the support was almost tangible and the campaigners hoped the judges would be aware of it.

'All rise.'

The Lord Chief Justice of England, Lord Bingham of Cornhill entered, flanked on his left by the Honourable Mr Justice Dyson, and on his right by the Honourable Mr Justice Mantell. In his position as presiding judge on the Western Circuit, Mantell had achieved nationwide prominence as the judge at the trial of Rosemary West.

David Jessel and Steve Phelps, sitting once more beside the Defence team, pointed out another distinguished figure seated at the front of the courtroom to one side. This, they told us, was Sir Frederick Crawford, newly appointed head of the Criminal Cases Review Commission. They speculated that he had come to observe Sheila's appeal because it was a test case which might have implications for the CCRC. Since her first appeal the law had been changed, giving powers to the Court of Appeal to admit new evidence for consideration, even if this evidence had been available at the time of the original trial. It was a change that would prove to be in Sheila's favour.

There on the Crown benches sat Anthony Glass, QC, prosecuting this case for the third time. Behind him once more sat his junior, Tom Kark, and the same array of CPS solicitors. Yet again David 'Badger' Renno sat beside them.

The clerk to the court turned to face Sheila.

'Are you Sheila Bowler?'

'I am.'

As at her first appeal, those were the only two words Sheila would ever be allowed to speak before this court.

Lord Bingham, a spare, ascetic-looking man, began the proceedings without delay.

Jeremy Roberts QC rose to his feet. Gentle and diffident in style, he spoke in an exceptionally quiet voice, and many of Sheila's supporters were later to complain that they could not hear everything he said, especially as the old wooden benches creaked loudly every time anyone leaned forward to listen. But Roberts was addressing his remarks to the bench, not to the court.

The reason for the appeal was, said Roberts, 'by the Home Secretary's reference.' (Michael Howard, the Home Secretary in question, had by now been replaced by Jack Straw in the incoming Labour government two months earlier).

First, said Roberts, he would sketch the story of the case and explain where things went wrong. But before that there were two procedural matters to be dealt with. Should Nicholas Purnell be called before the court?

Mr Glass thought he should be.

'But we are not making any criticism,' emphasized Roberts. 'Those representing Sheila Bowler at the original trial did not know of other evidence available. If they had they would have run it.'

The Lord Chief Justice was firm: he preferred to press on with the case: 'The Home Secretary referred this case back to us. This requires us to allow the appeal if we think the conviction is unsafe, so it is better to concentrate most significantly on that possibility. So we would not be assisted by going into Mr Purnell's ideas. He may have been right, he may have been wrong. It could be that he was not at his best. The much more fundamental question is whether this verdict is unsafe.'

On the public benches Sheila's supporters exchanged relieved glances. At least this appeal, unlike the last one, would be about the appellant in the dock.

Lord Bingham immediately impressed everyone present in the court with his formidable grasp of the case. He leaned forward, his keen eyes fixed on Roberts, his chin cupped in his right hand, and listened intently to every word as Roberts pinpointed the location of the events of 13 May 1992 on aerial photographs, then went on to describe those events.

Occasionally Bingham would scribble a note, occasionally he interrupted to correct Roberts:

'On the evening of 13th May Mrs Jackson had a fracture to her left wrist,' said Roberts.

'Her *right* wrist!' said the Lord Chief Justice.

'Sorry, my lord – her *right* wrist.'

At every opportunity, Roberts made the point that he was not blaming the original Defence team for anything. The police had asked the careworkers at Greyfriars if Mrs Jackson could have walked to her death. They then 'concluded that they could rule out the possibility of Mrs

Jackson moving off on her own, therefore she must have been put in the river by someone else. We can see why the police behaved as they did: Greyfriars staff and Mrs Bowler herself said they did not think Mrs Jackson could walk.'

If, however, the police had consulted a doctor specialising in geriatric medicine, such as Professor Archie Young (an expert interviewed by a television programme) and Dr Denham (another expert brought in by the new Defence team), 'they would have been advised that it was not impossible to walk 500 yards and that elderly people can do it if motivated. We say that Mrs Jackson was left on her own in the dark in the car and this was a powerful motivation to get out. She was confused, she wandered off and fell in the river. We cannot exclude this possibility.'

There was no forensic evidence at all, went on Roberts, to connect Mrs Bowler with the site: 'Sweepings were taken from inside Mrs Bowler's car and compared with soil samples of the site: they did not match. Casts of the Audi tyre were taken and compared with tyre tracks at the site: they did not match. Nobody noticed any dirt on Mrs Bowler's hands: there would have been dirt had she let air out of the tyre. No passing motorist saw her do any such thing.'

'Finally,' said Roberts, smiling towards Mrs Bowler in the dock, 'there was no powerful motive for this highly respectable woman of 62 suddenly to become the murderer of an elderly lady whom everybody said was a lovely old lady, whom Mrs Bowler had cared for for many years. The only motive for this extraordinary transformation would be to avoid the depletion of the value of Mrs Jackson's flat which was her only asset. Mrs Bowler could inherit this in the will – indeed she did inherit it. But she did not know that she would.' This was not a plausible motive, he said, for this cold calculating murder.

'Another point I mention because it adds to the implausibility. Mrs Bowler's daughter Jane, who was 22 at the time, was following in her mother's footsteps as a musician and was studying the cello at the Royal Academy of Music. She was very fond of her great aunt, and Mrs Bowler was hardly likely to choose to disrupt her final exams and therefore her career.'

The entire trial and the subsequent appeal were rehearsed, ending with the refusal of the judges at the first appeal to hear expert evidence: 'They said they were not persuaded by the accident theory. Now your lordships can look at the case afresh because of the Home Secretary's decision to refer it back to you. We now have Professor Young and a second opinion who has come to the same conclusions. There is also a collection of reports by members of the public. They are not experts and are of no value on their own, but the two professors have seen them and although the layman finds these incidents surprising, the experts say, "They do not surprise us. We are familiar with these incidents."'

A slight frisson ran through public benches as people nudged each other and nodded: most of them were in court for just that reason. They knew only too well what elderly people can do.

Lord Bingham leaned first to his right and spoke to Mr Justice Mantell, then to his left and spoke to Mr Justice Dyson. The court waited in silence as they deliberated among themselves.

At last the Lord Chief Justice nodded: 'Yes, we will hear the evidence.'

The sigh of relief from the campaigners was audible. Sheila, her head and shoulders just visible above the pulpit-like dock, allowed herself a faint smile at Jane and Simon.

Roberts hoped their lordships might also be persuaded to read for themselves the testimonies sent in by members of the public. No, said the judges, they would receive these through the expert witnesses called by the Defence.

'We would also like to call Dr Jeelani,' Roberts pressed on. 'He feels he could have said a lot more at trial if his opinion had been asked.'

'We can allow that,' said Lord Bingham.

There was just one more request. Roberts cleared his throat: 'I ask whether your lordships and Mr Glass feel we should have character witnesses.'

The Lord Chief Justice gave a dismissive wave of his hand in the direction of the dock: 'This is a lady of complete respectability, recently widowed. There is no need for us to hear character witnesses and it would be a travesty to re-open this. That Mrs Bowler is of good character is common ground so it is not necessary.'

Sheila's friends and supporters nodded. Yet wasn't it the strangest situation that here they all were once again, contemplating the trial for murder of a lady whom everyone, including the most senior judge in England, now agreed was of impeccable character and complete respectability? Several of them admitted later wondering whether the Law really was an ass.

'And now,' said Jeremy Roberts, 'I would like to call my first expert witness.'

Anthony Glass got to his feet. He felt that the other expert witnesses should now leave the court: 'This happens, my lord, in ordinary criminal trials.'

Lord Bingham retorted sharply: 'I am surprised you use the term "ordinary criminal trial." I have never heard of such a suggestion! These are witnesses of the highest possible standing and they must be allowed.'

Professor Archie Young walked down from his place on the public benches and climbed the steps into the witness box.

'You are the Head of the Department of Geriatric Medicine at the Royal Free Hospital, University of London, and an honorary consultant physician there?'

'I am.'

Roberts took the professor through the notes made by Greyfriars staff about Mrs Jackson. Young's testimony continued after the lunch break. He concluded, he said, that it was perfectly possible for Mrs Jackson, finding herself in a very different situation from her room at Greyfriars, to have left the car and walked to her death.

'You have gone through the bundle of letters from members of the public where old people have done things that sound impossible?'

'Yes, among frail elderly people in the community. But I see so many of them that I would not even remark upon it to my colleagues.'

In his soft Scottish accent, the professor read two or three examples from the letters before him. Cross-examined in detail by Anthony Glass he maintained his composure: 'If she did this walk, it would be one of these extraordinary feats?' asked Glass.

'One of these *commonplace* extraordinary feats.'

Dr Denham confirmed everything that Professor Young had said: 'I could tell you about disabled people who have walked for half an hour.'

'How can this happen?'

'Motivation – we can only guess why. Old people wander off and when we ask why there are a variety of answers.'

'But this happens?'

'Oh yes, it happens.'

At the end of this first day, Sheila returned once more to Holloway in a Securicor van, lugging into it the three huge plastic bags which contained all the possessions she had accumulated over the past four years. Appellants invariably have to endure this clumsy process. Each morning they take the bags to court, each evening they bring them back into prison. It is difficult to see what else can be done – after all, the appellant might 'walk' – or the appeal might be dismissed immediately. She will then have to face the ignominy and desolation of returning to jail and unpacking the bags in her cell. This is exactly what had happened to Sheila that Black Friday in May 1995.

The other Holloway prisoners greeted Sheila, wanting to know all about the day. Her closest friend, one of the kitchen workers, was given a blow-by-blow account. They were joined by officers who had been listening to news bulletins all day, 'In case you walked today.'

Next morning, a new face appeared among the crowds of supporters queuing up to get into Court Number One. People stared a little at the attractive young blonde woman in the smart yellow suit. Some tried to engage her in small-talk as they waited. She replied politely but seemed evasive.

This was a prison officer who had taken a special interest in Sheila's welfare. But prison officers are forbidden to maintain any personal contact once prisoners have left their charge. Sheila had continued writing cards and letters to the officer, who later told us that she had followed Sheila's progress with great interest, but was not allowed to respond in writing. 'But I felt I had to come today,' she confided.

Sheila was late arriving at court that morning – there had been some hiccup in leaving Holloway. In Court Number One the proceedings had been under way for several minutes before the Clerk to the Court pointed out that the appellant was not yet in her seat.

Lord Bingham glanced impatiently towards the dock: they would just have to proceed without her, he ruled. It was only a few minutes more before Sheila arrived, but her friends and family privately noted the extraordinary vagaries of a legal system that could so nonchalantly dismiss the feelings of the person standing in the dock, whose whole future, whose very life, might be at stake.

Dr Denham was ruthlessly cross-examined by Anthony Glass, and seemed less positive than the day before. Glass discovered that he had not been shown the post-mortem reports written by Dr Heath and Dr Djurovic, and used this omission to weaken Denham's evidence. Sheila looked worried and her supporters shifted uneasily on the creaking benches.

Next Mrs Lucy Rees was permitted to take the stand and make a statement (provided, said their lordships, that she did it quickly). The court heard that she was the Senior Physiotherapist at the Conquest Hospital, Hastings. She gave her view that care staff in homes for the elderly have very little idea of the true capabilities of old people. She had come across frequent cases of elderly residents getting out of care homes and walking long distances. 'It is not at all uncommon.'

Dr Jeelani cheered everyone up. An ebullient character dressed in a dapper cream-coloured suit, he endeared himself to the court by frankly admitting that he had exaggerated Mrs Jackson's immobility in the report he had written for the DHSS on 10 February 1993. 'When I wrote, "unlikely to improve", you have to realise it depends on the context in which I wrote it. I wanted her to get that allowance.'

The Lord Chief Justice nodded kindly: 'You had to make those notes to maximise her mobility difficulties. That was very clear to us.'

'Yes. Mrs Jackson – she had the *structure* for walking – I never treated her for arthritis or anything, and she was not as confused as all that. I *wanted* that report to look bad.'

He said he had seen Mrs Jackson once at Greyfriars. 'She was in a wheelchair and she left the attendant and walked up to a table and back to get a knife and fork... She would go shuffling along like this...'

Dr Jeelani emerged from the witness box and demonstrated to their lordships a shuffling walk, one foot sliding along in front of the other. There was laughter in court.

Back in the witness box the doctor was unstoppable: 'A lot of my patients walk from nursing homes. I ask them what they are doing. They say they are looking for their mother – even though their mother has been dead for fifty years!'

After the lunch break, Glass's cross-examination of Jeelani took him into the complexities of cardio-vascular disease and the effects on mobility of 'mini-strokes.' The doctor was unfazed by the QC's scepticism:

'You have made a number of witness statements. Why have you never mentioned this in detail?'

'One, nobody asked me. Two, I have been *dying* to tell everyone.'

'If you had seen her get out of her chair and collect a knife and fork and walk back to her chair, why did you not say so before?'

'You are splitting hairs. I am a doctor not a lawyer. What I have told you is the *exact truth!*'

Dr Jeelani stood down. Sheila's supporters felt like giving him a round of applause.

Now Mr Glass called Dr Roger Lewis, a consultant physician and honorary lecturer at Guy's Hospital since 1978. Dr Lewis, said Glass, had written a report in April 1995 in preparation for the last appeal, but it was never used. Lewis, unlike any of the Defence expert witnesses, had the advantage of having visited Greyfriars and interviewed the staff. From his studies of their reports and Mrs Jackson's hospital records, he had concluded that she had significant dementia and was 'a non-mover.' Mr Glass questioned him closely:

'What about the state of her feet?'

'They are non-walking feet. They are smooth, with hammer toes and there is a lack of abrasions. Her slippers are very large and if she goes over any uneven ground then they slip off and trip her over.'

We recalled the phonecall from Mrs Nye, the Greyfriars deputy matron: she was 'devastated,' she had told us, to discover that an anonymous member of her staff had exchanged Mrs Jackson's large men's slippers, on which she had urinated, for a much smaller pair that – although still far too long – fitted snugly across the breadth of her feet.

'What about Mrs Freeman's evidence about her "trotting"?'

'That word has to be taken in context: I wouldn't take "trotting" with its literal meaning of high stepping.'

In his cross-examination Jeremy Roberts began by tackling Dr Lewis on the method whereby Mrs Bowler was supposed to have got Mrs Jackson into the River Brede:

'You've been to the scene, you've looked at the river embankment. What do you say about the suggestion that the old lady was *led*' – Roberts's voice was sharp with incredulity – 'was *led down the bank by a 62 year old lady?* Surely you would concede that such a postulation is absolute rubbish?'

Lewis frowned: 'It's certainly steep and very uneven: it would be difficult to do.'

'Realistically, it's a non-starter!'

'I can't say that.'

Roberts persisted: 'The Prosecution theory is that Mrs Bowler led the old lady down the bank, persuaded her down there, then tumbled her in. Are you *seriously* suggesting that this is a possibility?'

Lord Bingham leaned forward: 'Mr Roberts, I don't think that is any way to address a professional man like Dr Lewis. Would you rephrase the question, please?'

'I apologize, my lord. Dr Lewis, are you saying that you can see Mrs Bowler over there' – Roberts nodded towards the dock – 'can you see her leading this old lady down that steep bank? Can you envisage it?'

Lewis seemed to falter: 'What actually happened in that situation... I have not been considering that part of it. But could she get from the car to the pumping station?'

'Dr Lewis, are you not qualified to consider also whether someone could help a geriatric patient get down a steep bank?'

'I *can* give some opinion. It is extraordinarily difficult to be certain. She was not that heavy. One could help her with a strong arm – or two.'

'Are you saying it is possible?'

'It is not implausible.'

Roberts referred the doctor to the hundreds of case-histories sent in by members of the public, but like the judges, Lewis refused to consider them. They may be interesting stories, he said, but nothing at all was known about the medical condition of the elderly people described. Unless he was in possession of such medical records, any comparison between their cases and the case of Mrs Florence Jackson was meaningless.

Next Roberts explored the question of motivation, leading the doctor into complex speculation about thought-processes of the elderly and confused, and exploring the minutiae of Mrs Jackson's putative journey.

Judge Mantell grew impatient, intervening when the speculation reached the tissue found clutched in Mrs Jackson's hand: 'If she was using her hands to help lever her body out of the car, that would require her to open her hands.'

People in the public benches were becoming restless – all this speculation seemed to be getting nowhere. Jeremy Roberts drew his cross-examination of the doctor to a conclusion: 'If I asked you the same question as I asked Professor Young – what would you say if you were shown the car and told this story – you'd have to say "This is an extraordinary example of what elderly people can do", wouldn't you?'

'I'd say, "I can't believe my eyes" – because of the sequence of events involved.'

Lewis stood down, and the second day drew to a close. Just before the court adjourned, Roberts made one more attempt to persuade the judges to read through the file of hundreds of letters from members of the public recounting similar amazing feats by elderly people.

He was roundly rebuffed: 'We have declined to receive them in evidence,' said the Lord Chief Justice sharply. 'We are receiving evidence through the doctors.'

The court was adjourned.

As Sheila left for Holloway, and the supporters milled around in corridors, Jane remained in her seat in the courtroom. She began to weep quietly. This was the third time her hopes had been raised. Twice they had been dashed. Now it seemed to be happening all over again.

On the third day of the appeal, Wednesday, 23 July, Jeremy Roberts opened the proceedings with a summary of the case for the appellant. Yet again he ran through the events of 13 May 1992 and Sheila and her family wondered how many more times they would have to endure the sorry tale.

Now and again the judges intervened to ask for clarification. Mr Justice Mantell peered at one of the photographs and thought he could discern a lighter coloured area of grass on the bank where Mrs Jackson was said to have gone into the water: 'There *is* a discernible track in the grass,' agreed the Lord Chief Justice, 'but it could be caused by someone carrying out duties at the pumping station.'

Roberts spent some time trying to establish the exact timings of events that evening, then moved to Dr Lewis's evidence. Lewis was, said Roberts, 'espousing the wholly incredible idea that Mrs Bowler could have led this old lady down the slope to the top of the concrete and pushed her in... He is trying too hard to rescue the Prosecution case by espousing this part.'

'Are you being fair to Dr Lewis?' snapped Mantell. 'He is not espousing the Prosecution case. He is looking at material evidence and is not being drawn into any hypothesis.'

Politely but forcefully Jeremy Roberts challenged the judge: 'He did, my lord. When I asked him to consider this matter he did advance the suggestion that this is in his view something that could have happened.'

The supporters exchanged nervous glances. Was Roberts about to antagonise a powerful senior judge?

Mr Justice Dyson mediated in placatory tones; 'In response to your question he gave the answer that he had not considered the matter.'

Roberts moved swiftly on to Mrs Bowler's character: 'She is a lady who does not show her emotions very easily. She was brought up in a strict Methodist family. She gets on with life in a matter-of-fact way. She was the same when her husband died. She did not cry. She did not break down. She feels you must get on with your life.'

He drew his case to a close: 'Our general message is that there is a lurking doubt if nothing more – though we say there is a great deal more. There was no credible motive to change this respectable caring widow of 62 into a cruel cold-hearted murderer. There was no forensic evidence to connect her with any such crime. The two ways she is supposed to have done it – either pushing Mrs Jackson from the top of the bank or leading her half way down – both were impossible. Surely it is an extraordinary story – but we suggest that the Prosecution's case is more extraordinary.'

Anthony Glass doggedly rehearsed the Prosecution evidence yet again: 'Does the fresh evidence render the verdict unsafe?' he asked their lordships. Though he now conceded that the 'no food in the house,' like the 'no bed made up' evidence was 'not much of a point' he maintained that the Crown had presented a strong circumstantial case against the appellant: 'We say this conviction is safe.'

The court was adjourned, and Lord Bingham told counsel that it would reconvene at 10.30 the following morning for the judgement.

At least this time, thought Sheila on her way back to Holloway, we won't have weeks to wait.

On the morning of Thursday 24 July even more photographers and television cameras had arrived outside the Royal Courts of Justice. The strange story of Sheila Bowler and her elderly aunt was now familiar to the media, and the opening of the appeal had been carried on national news programmes. Meridian Television, covering the South-East region, had run detailed updates on each of the three days of the appeal. Each evening, we would return home to be besieged by telephone calls from supporters unable to attend the court hearing, and wanting the latest news.

That morning Sheila was despatched early from Holloway and treated to a tour of legal London as the security van – or 'sweatbox' as she had now learned to call it – dropped Holloway women off at the Old Bailey and other courts. As the driver reversed, he backed into a pillar at the back entrance to the Bailey and Sheila was thrown forward and given a nasty jolt. There are no seatbelts in the sweatboxes, though prisoners often have to travel long journeys on the motorways. Nobody came to check on the remaining passengers, each locked in her own tiny one-seat compartment. 'I could have broken my neck and nobody would have noticed,' thought Sheila.

The tension in Number One Court that morning was palpable as the Lord Chief Justice cleared his throat and began reading the judgement. Everyone listening knew that by the time he stopped reading, the fate of Sheila Bowler would be sealed, one way or another.

Again there was an unnerving sense of *déjà vu* as Lord Bingham read aloud the main points of the case. Just as in May 1995, spirits sank lower and lower as he rehearsed the case for the Prosecution, and were then raised as he gave the case for the Defence. The Lord Chief Justice's voice, professionally neutral from the experience of decades, coolly intoned the familiar facts and fictions in the story of Sheila Bowler and Florence Jackson.

Sheila's supporters felt anything but cool. Angela Devlin had spent the last three days taking verbatim shorthand notes of the case but now her hand shook so badly that she had to set her pen to one side. The elegant, carefully constructed phrases, products of one of England's finest legal minds, rang out through the hushed courtroom.

The miraculous words, when they came, caught people almost unaware. 'And therefore we have decided, somewhat reluctantly, to quash this conviction.'

'YES!' There was a whoop of joy from the back of the court as Simon half rose to his feet. 'Yes! *Yes!!*' Lord Bingham's words continued without pause as clapping erupted along the benches and Jane, like many others, wept tears of joy and waved and smiled at the woman sitting stunned in the dock.

The lawyers were leaning forward, straining their ears as Bingham continued impassively reading the judgement. Their lordships had decided it would be right that a re-trial be held promptly, within the next four months if that were possible.

The supporters' joy was momentarily tempered. People dabbed at their eyes, not sure whether rejoicing was yet in order. Then Jeremy Roberts got to his feet, professional to the last, to apply for bail. Was his client free to go home, he asked the judges. The court was silent once more as Sheila sat upright in the dock to hear the Lord Chief Justice's reply. Afterwards nobody could remember his exact words, but he seemed to waving his hand airily, saying this was a perfectly respectable widow – of course she could go home to her family.

For just a minute or two longer the court remained quiet as the judges left. Then the wonderful reality began to hit home. Friends and strangers hugged each other, wept, laughed and cheered together. All the years of waiting were over. All the years of campaigning had succeeded.

Sheila Bowler was free at last – at least until the verdict at her re-trial.

CHAPTER FOURTEEN

ALMOST FREE

On Saturday 26 July 1997 Sheila Bowler sat in her daughter's London flat, a free woman once more. On the table was a tape-recorder and Sheila was speaking into the microphone. She had kept up her prison diary for four long years. Now was the time to start her diary of freedom.

Saturday 26 July 1997
It felt very strange in the court room when the result of the appeal was announced. There was general jubilation, with shouts and Simon shouting out, 'Yes!' Jane was in floods of tears sobbing her heart out – it reverberated round the whole court room. Angela was frantically trying to mop up the mascara streaming from her eyelashes!

For myself I just felt very stunned. I just couldn't believe it.

We walked out of the courtroom, it seemed like ages afterwards. We had various things to go through before I could go home. My counsel came down to see me and there was general thanks all round. I was given a piece of paper to help me make an announcement in front of the press.

I found it very interesting when I had to collect the money I'd brought into prison with me from the court office. The officer there was suddenly terribly concerned about the security van which had backed into a post on the way to court in the morning. Had I been hurt when the van backed into the pier, he wondered. My goodness, I thought, this is a sudden change!

When all my bits and pieces were finally gathered together I was escorted through yet another corridor to a small room. Simon and Jane came in and there were hugs and kisses all round. I was very surprised that I wasn't myself absolutely collapsing into floods of tears. But I was just so stunned I didn't really feel it was happening to me at all.

The really unexpected bit was walking out into the entrance hall of the Royal Courts of Justice. It was absolutely magnificent and huge. I suppose it's because it's ages since I've been in such a magnificent building.

And then I had to go out and face the press. That was pretty daunting.'

Most of Sheila's supporters were already outside waiting. They had left family and close friends their moments of privacy together. But the moment Sheila emerged blinking into the dazzling sunshine that July morning, it seemed she suddenly became public property.

Although we have spent years of our professional lives working with the media, we were not fully prepared for the amazing barrage of photographers, reporters and TV cameras that faced Sheila as she walked tentatively down the steps, clutching Jane's hand on one side, Simon's on the other. There were shouts and cheers and a round of applause. 'Give Mum a big kiss, Jane!' 'This way, Sheila!' The flashbulbs clicked and the barriers looked like collapsing as the crowd pressed forward. Large furry microphones were thrust out and a hush fell as Sheila put on her spectacles to read a short statement thanking all her supporters, and especially Ewen Smith, David Martin-Sperry and the *Trial and Error* team, for all they had done. There was a kind word for us too. 'I have been told I must not say any more as there is to be a re-trial,' she said finally, 'But at least now I have a chance to prove my innocence.'

The pressmen rushed away to catch their early deadlines and Ewen Smith ushered Sheila back inside the court until the crowd outside had dispersed. Standing in the echoing marble halls of the Royal Courts of Justice, perhaps inevitably Sheila's first thoughts were for the women she had left behind at Holloway and Bullwood Hall – both prisoners and staff. We rang the prisons and left messages with the gate officers.

Sheila's closest friend in Holloway, the kitchen worker who had shared her hopes and fears each night during the appeal, told us later how the news of Sheila's release had been received in the prison:

'All us kitchen girls had the radio on all morning. Sheila told us the night before that she had to be in court by 10, so we thought we might hear what happened on the 11am news. But of course that was too early – I think the judge was still reading it out then. I went on working but all I could think about was Sheila. Then about 11.45 the prison officer on duty told me a call had come through for me. To be honest it didn't occur to me it was anything to do with Sheila. I thought it was someone from my own legal team.

'But it was one of the C5 officers who was very fond of Sheila. She was there when Sheila came in four years ago, and now she was sobbing her heart out on the phone. She said, "It's Sheila!" – and then she couldn't say anything else for a minute and as she was crying I thought the appeal had been thrown out. Then she said, "She's out! It's a re-trial!"

'We were all over the moon and we listened to it ourselves on the 12 o'clock news. Then we all had to watch the Channel Four news and we had to laugh because all the girls were missing their favourite soaps, waiting for Sheila to come on the news. Somebody said, "This is Sheila's revenge – she always used to hate the soaps and now she's stopping us watching them!"'

We had all got together and collected Sheila's large prison bags full of her belongings, and as David Jessel and Steve Phelps took her and Jane off for an interview for that evening's Channel Four News, the rest of us repaired in a series of taxis to The Grapes in Narrow Street, a Docklands pub close to the Thames, for a celebration party. A *Daily Mail* reporter managed to follow us with a photographer and in a good natured gesture bought champagne and waited patiently till Sheila appeared, still clutching Jane's hand as if she could never let it go. She posed for photographs but not with the champagne. 'Let's keep that till after the re-trial!' she said.

It seemed everyone wanted to hug Sheila and hold her hand, as if to make sure she was really there with them. Sheila's prison diary had repeatedly mentioned the feeling of unreality that came over her in waves throughout her four years in jail. Now some of that unreality seemed to pervade the party that sunny Thursday afternoon in London's Docklands – ironically just a street or two away from Alpha Road where Aunt Flo had spent her childhood. But now the unreality had a touch of magic about it. David Jessel opened the *Daily Mail* champagne and proposed a toast: 'To the Witches of Winchelsea!' he laughed.

At last it was time for Sheila to leave. She was looking terribly tired and needed time alone with her family.

Next day she recorded her reactions on tape:

'We came back to Jane's flat with Naomi [Elizabeth's daughter] and Jane's friends. I think the overriding feeling was that I was still so stunned I couldn't believe it – and I felt desperately, desperately tired. In spite of that we all sat up talking – I expect I was doing most of the talking – until round about ten past, half past one.

'I felt very, very tired and went to bed but I couldn't sleep of course. My mind was going round and round the events of the day. Then I decided I was hungry, so I got up and crept outside to Jane's kitchen and ate some cake. I felt really wicked walking through a door that was actually unlocked in the middle of the night. I went back to bed and started to read. It was four o'clock. I thought I really must be going mad – there must be a time warp here somewhere. I think I must have dropped off for a while. About 6 o'clock I was awake again and Jane's friend came and sat on the end of the bed and we were talking away. It all seemed very, very unreal.'

Sheila looked round for the clothes she had brought back in the prison bags. They were nowhere to be seen. Jane had taken them all away to wash. She said they still had the smell of prison about them.

'Elizabeth was coming back from Paris on Friday on Eurostar and Naomi, Jane and I decided we would go and meet her. We went off at four o'clock. Jane was very worried that I wasn't going to be all right coping with walking to the station and getting on the tube. She said, "You know it's going to be rush hour when we come back." I thought, "Well, I don't know – it doesn't seem to worry me too much, you know, so let's try it."

Of course we were all very, very tired still and I felt very odd walking out of this house and – well, I suppose it was partly because I was so tired but my body just wasn't feeling right, walking out in the road like that.

'In fact I coped with the traffic very well. Jane kept pulling me back from crossing the road when she thought I shouldn't be. Anyway we got to Waterloo, lots of people of course, but I really wasn't worried about that. We met Elizabeth and there was great excitement all round. In the end she went off with Naomi and Jane and I came back here. We were both so desperately tired and the phone just never stopped ringing with people congratulating us.'

Back in Kent our phones had been ringing constantly too, ever since the news of Sheila's release had hit the headlines on Friday morning. All the nationals carried the story. The *Daily Mail* rewarded its young reporter's persistence with a full page story, headlined, *My chance to prove that I'm innocent*. Sheila had told him that friends had looked after her house and garden while she was in prison: ' Now I want to get on with the garden myself. I'm sure there is some weeding to do.'

One of the phonecalls to us was from a member of the Holloway Board of Visitors, who was on holiday in France. A friend had telephoned her with the news and she was thrilled: 'I've worked at Holloway for years and years,' she told us, 'and I've never seen a woman so obviously innocent as Sheila Bowler.' When Sheila finally got home to Rye, she found phone messages waiting from her from two of the Holloway chaplains whose support she had valued so greatly during the long dark years.

Meanwhile Sheila was still finding life outside prison very strange indeed. Prisoners reaching the end of a long sentence are usually given some kind of preparation for release, however rudimentary. But successful appellants against conviction are inevitably plunged straight into the outside world. Sheila's voice on tape is full of stunned incredulity:

'That Friday, the day after I was released, I felt like going for a walk along the river near Jane's flat. Jane was very worried that I'd get lost. She couldn't come with me because we'd agreed to babysit for the couple whose house she lives in, and the children were asleep. So she made me take her mobile phone with me.

'As I wandered along beside the Thames, I noticed a rosemary bush with some branches spreading over a garden fence on to the riverside path. I bent down to pick a sprig of rosemary – but at that moment the mobile phone rang! It was only Jane checking to see if I was all right, but I jumped a mile! I thought it was the police coming to arrest me for stealing the rosemary, and I was all ready to say I was allowed to, because it was growing over on to the path.

'Then as I was sitting down back at the flat, I heard a van door slam outside. That made me jump a mile, because it sounded just like the doors of a prison van slamming.

'At last I think it's sunk in that I am actually free of the prison, although it's not final yet – it won't be, until after we have a re-trial.

'I suppose it's inevitable that I can't have been out of prison this length of time without thinking about what's going on way back there. I just can't get over looking at my watch occasionally and thinking, "Oh well, in half an hour I'm going to be locked in until quarter to two." It's incredible, because by now we'd just be getting let out at 2 o'clock in the afternoon – if we're lucky. And of course because it was raining I thought, "Well, there probably won't be any exercise today, so it probably means they're going to keep us locked in a bit longer." I just can't get over programming my activities to the times when we were just going to be out of our cells in Holloway Prison.

'I forgot to say that when I arrived here on Thursday evening it was an absolute luxury to lie in a bath and not be screamed at by somebody else who decided they wanted a bath as well, or that I had pushed in the queue and taken my bath before someone else should have been there. And not having to watch out in case there's any nasty creepy-crawlies walking around the edge of the bathroom. Because it was pretty disgusting on the wing I was in at Holloway. They hadn't even decorated the bathroom, though it was the room that needed it most because the ceiling was all black and the emulsion was peeling off the walls. It was *disgusting*.

'It's really lovely to eat what I like and when I like, but I really find that my stomach can't take very much food at the moment. I suppose it's not in too good shape just now.

'Simon phoned several times since I came back here and this morning he was saying that half of Kew Gardens seems to have arrived at the house. It's incredible – I shall just never be able to get over the amount of support I've had from everybody during the last four years.'

Sheila spent Friday and Saturday in London, then on Sunday she planned to return home to Rye. She said would like to drop by and see us on the way home. She wanted to see the toaster she had given us when she was still in prison. We joked that we would have to polish it, knowing Sheila's high standards.

That morning a *Daily Express* reporter contacted us. Could he have an exclusive story of Sheila Bowler's return to Rye? The Lord Chief Justice had made it clear to journalists attending the appeal hearing that reporting should be restricted to what they heard in court: anything more would be prejudicial to the re-trial. But the *Express* man was sure a feature article about Sheila returning to her old home would cause no problems. We suggested a compromise. Sheila would not like her privacy invaded at home, we said, but we would ask her permission for the journalist to come along to the celebration tea party at our house and interview her there.

We had advised Sheila from the very outset that she should have nothing to do with 'chequebook journalism,' and indeed she and her family treated with revulsion any idea of profiting from this sorry story. None of them would accept one penny for speaking to the press or television. But they all agreed that the media had helped Sheila so enormously that she owed them a debt of gratitude. We also all felt strongly that the public ought to be made aware of how such a terrible miscarriage of justice could occur, and how long it had taken, despite the support of the media, to right a dreadful wrong.

It was a brilliant July afternoon when Sheila arrived at our house with Jane. Sheila's sister Mary and her husband Albert had driven them from London. Soon afterwards Simon joined them from Rye. They were happy to speak to the *Express* reporter and he arrived with a photographer who set about converting our bathroom into a darkroom and plugged in a computer system to send the photographs direct to the newspaper. Sheila was photographed strolling round the garden ('That bush could do with a trim'), tucking into a cream tea, and blowing out the four candles on a Welcome Home cake – one candle for every year of lost freedom.

Next day she rang us from her house in Rye. She was, she said, 'Getting sorted.' It had been wonderful to come back and find so many flowers and cards. But now there was so much to do to 'get everything straight.'

'The roses haven't been pruned and they've got blackspot. In the kitchen I can't find anything. Everything's been put everywhere – though I'm not really complaining. I wanted to wear a mauve dress today to go out shopping for the first time in Rye and I was trying to find the shoes that matched it. I couldn't find them anywhere. In the end they were on a rack in Bob's wardrobe.

'When I went out to Rye today we parked at Budgens [the supermarket]. As I was at the cheese counter an old lady came up to me and I couldn't for the life of me remember her name. In the end she had to tell me it, and she said how glad she was I was out. A few other people came up to me as well. Everybody I spoke to was very nice.

'I went to the Swan Tearooms in the Mint for lunch. Robert was thrilled to see me. I thanked him for his offer to send me meringues in Holloway and he asked me what I wanted today. When I said a toasted bacon and mushroom sandwich he said, "She had the same the last time she was here!" That was four years ago!

'When we went round the shops I did get a bit lost: I wanted to find Boots and it had moved while I was away. I did feel rather funny then, as I was standing in the street looking for it!'

Later, at the end of August, she told us, in one of her regular phonecalls, that she was now able to recognize that her behaviour on release was her own particular response to her long incarceration:

'I think I was slightly manic because subconsciously I kept thinking that I had to do things immediately, or they wouldn't get done before I got locked in again. I had to make myself realise that I'd got all day to do things. I could pick up the phone when I wanted to, and I could even look things up in the phone book, or ring directory enquiries. You just can't do that in prison, and they haven't even got a phone book in the office.

'Oh dear – just as I was saying that to you I nearly stopped myself, because as you know, every phonecall in the prison is monitored, though obviously there are some prisoners they watch more than others because they think they are troublemakers.

'I still keep thinking of time limits, and I worry that things have got to be done *right now*. The kitchen drawer sticks. I shall have to get a man to do it. The oven door doesn't shut properly – there must be something wrong with the insulation.

'I must have a new washing line. Some of the spokes on my whirligig one are so rusty I might as well get a new one. And the washing machine's just not doing its job properly. Jane bought it new while I was in prison so that's just not good enough! If they can't make it work properly they can replace it with another one.'

Fussy, meticulous, Sheila returned to her old shopping haunts and became once again every shopkeeper's nightmare. The new whirligig washing line was changed not once but twice. The new telephone was returned because 'it didn't have all the bits I wanted on it.' It was fascinating for us, hearing these household traumas day by day, to speculate how different things might have been if Bexhill police had asked Sheila's friends, rather than those who did not know her well, about the kind of woman she was.

Worst of all in Sheila's eyes, her beloved garden was a mess. Despite the best efforts of loyal friends to keep down the weeding, Sheila was back on the warpath, the scourge of weeds, pests and rampant vegetation: 'I've chopped down all that *pyrocanthus* and cut it up in pieces to burn it. But my roses still need pruning.'

A pane had broken in the roof of the greenhouse. With characteristic pragmatism, Sheila patched it up with one of the strong transparent prison-issue bags in which all her possessions had come home. 'Shame to waste it, and it does the job well.' Emblazoned with the royal crest and the words HM PRISON SERVICE in bright blue letters, the bag stood out a mile in the neat Sussex garden. We recalled WPC Ellis who had removed her uniform epaulettes to avoid gossip from the neighbours. What did the neighbours think of Sheila now?

One of them, an elderly lady, rarely manages to get out and about.

'I could take you out on a few trips' offered Sheila.

'Please, mum,' said Jane, 'wait till the re-trial's over, then you must promise me never to take old ladies out at night again as long as you live!' Sheila laughed and agreed.

So Sheila Bowler slotted back again into her pre-prison life in the pretty Sussex town.

Not quite. Although most people welcomed her back and would stop for a chat (though it was whispered that fifty per cent still thought her guilty) Sheila would find that prison had wrought radical changes in her approach to life. She had become more tolerant and also more sceptical. No longer did she automatically condemn those whom the courts had sentenced. Four years ago she would have dismissed all prisoners as scourges of society from whom the public ought to be protected. Now she knew better.

In late August she returned to Holloway prison to visit her kitchen worker friend. It felt very strange indeed going up to the main entrance on foot, rather than through the side entrance in a 'sweatbox.'

'One of the gate officers recognized me but nobody told me what to do in the visits room and of course I didn't know the rules from the other side of the fence!'

It was extraordinary to feel so totally at sea in an establishment where she had spent so many months. She found herself just as ignorant of the procedure as Jane and Elizabeth that terrible Saturday morning in July 1993.

'I stayed sitting in the foyer on a bench until I saw visitors going in through the double glass doors and realised I had to do that too. Then inside the waiting room I watched a man getting filthy clothes out of a filthy bag. He had something in his mouth and I thought he was probably bringing in drugs. I guessed the next door we'd be going through and went and sat near it. The female officer doing the searching recognized me and asked who I was going to see.

'When I got into the visits room I automatically went and sat on the blue chair – the one meant for the prisoner having the visit, instead of one of the three red chairs meant for the visitors! It felt very weird because we were sitting at Table 22. I was at Table 22 when Jane came to visit me the day before the appeal.

'The officers who recognized me were pleased to see me. One senior officer, a woman, told me she was driving along in her car when she heard about my release on the news, and like Simon in the court, she shouted out, 'YES!'

On another occasion, we accompanied Sheila to visit a different prisoner. We couldn't help noticing how Sheila seemed to relax when she entered the visiting room and became animated when hearing all the prison gossip. The officers who had known her joked and laughed with her like old friends: 'She loves it here so much I think we'll lock her back up!' said one of them as Sheila darted into the refreshment kiosk at the end of the visit to talk to the prisoner serving teas, and could hardly be dislodged when all the other visitors had gone.

Later that autumn, when the kitchen worker friend was released to a bail hostel, Sheila went to visit her. We met the two women for lunch and Sheila's friend described what it was like being the only woman in the hostel with 24 men, including three paedophiles and several other sex offenders. Sheila felt shocked and sad for the woman. They spent the rest of the day shopping, though the woman had no money as her benefits would not come through till the following week. She admired a smart lime-green suit and immediately Sheila offered to buy it for her – one of those flashes of generosity familiar to people like Helen Goodwin. The bailed woman declined – she had nothing to offer in return. But she knew Sheila wanted a ginger kitten to replace her beloved Whisky, who had achieved his five minutes of fame by appearing on *Trial and Error* but who had died while she was still in prison.

The woman offered Sheila a kitten just born to her daughter's cat. Sheila was delighted. 'But,' said the friend, 'we've had to promise her we'll take it back next year if... well, if the worst comes to the worst.'

On the weekend of 6 September, Sheila prepared to travel with Jane to Scotland to visit one of her daughter's friends:

'I couldn't think what to pack in my suitcase. After four years in prison, I just couldn't fathom out what you would need to go away for a normal weekend. It was the same with handbags when I was first released. I just hadn't got a clue what you should keep in a handbag! You don't exactly get to carry handbags in prison!'

At the friend's home in Glasgow, they all watched Princess Diana's funeral on television together on the Saturday. Although Sheila was still on bail, the Lord Chief Justice had told Jeremy Roberts he made no objection to her travelling around the country to stay with family and friends. But that Monday, 8 September, she had to be back in London, to face Pleas and Directions at the Old Bailey. It seemed like a poignant re-run of that weekend back in 1993 when she had had to return to Sussex for the same purpose.

The hearing, before the Honourable Mr Justice Blofeld, was inconclusive: Anthony Glass and his junior Tom Kark were both away on holiday and the barrister appointed from their chambers to attend the hearing had not brought the indictment. The judge was irritated and directed them to return in 28 days. Sheila's nightmare was still not yet over.

In late September Sheila heard that a date had finally been set for her re-trial. It was listed to begin on 12 January, 1998, and would be held at the Central Criminal Court at the Old Bailey. It was expected to last at least three weeks. Sheila hoped this meant no stone would be left unturned in the battle to clear her name. On October 10, for the first time, she was delighted to compose and sign the first letter she had ever written directly to The Friends of Sheila Bowler. It thanked them for their continuing support and announced the trial date.

At about this time, we received two interesting letters about the case. One was from a Kent woman whose mother-in-law had been at Greyfriars at the same time as Aunt Flo. Like Sheila, she had felt concerned at the way the old lady was cared for. Like Sheila she had taken her elderly relative out in a car and, convinced by Greyfriars staff that she was immobile, had left her alone. The old lady had left the car and walked a considerable distance to join her daughter-in-law.

The other letter was faxed by Sara Thornton, now living quietly in the Midlands, but ever aware of the need to fight against miscarriages of justice. The fax was headed *101 ways of dealing effectively with a re-trial,* and in it Sara explained that she was one of very few people to have been through the re-trial process. She wanted to give Sheila the benefit of her experience and the fax was full of valuable suggestions.

For instance, Sara stressed the need for Sheila to go through all the trial witness statements and write down her own comments. Sheila took this advice, examining in particular detail the transcripts of the police interrogations, and supplying the answers she might have given had she not been advised to say 'No comment' to each one.

Sheila also worked closely with us on our research for this book. The exercise was an invaluable one in terms of the forthcoming re-trial, because Sheila had to recall in great detail everything she could remember about the events of the case, from the moment she collected Aunt Flo on Wednesday 13 May 1992 – events on which she knew she would be closely questioned once again by prosecutor Anthony Glass.

As part of the research Sheila drove us in the same old green Audi along the route she had taken that fateful Wednesday afternoon. We drove past the aunts' flat in Ferry Road and out onto the route Sheila normally took to Battle Abbey. About three-quarters of a mile from the flat, a road sign shows there is a small left turn. This is Dumb Woman's Lane, and it was at this point on the afternoon of 13 May 1992 that Sheila had glanced at her watch and decided she would have time to rush off to Hastings to change Simon's poorly-repaired shoes and buy the sheet music. Now she took the turning again. Along the lane there is a fork: you can choose to go right along Float Lane which leads to the village of Udimore; or left along Station Road. Sheila took the left fork, as she had done back in 1992.

We drove on past the pumping station on our right – hardly noticeable as it is set back off the road – and tried to establish just where Sheila had stopped to check on her tyres when the car felt bumpy. It was difficult to remember after five and a half years, but she thought she would have waited till the road widened with a layby on the left hand side, just before Ferry Bridge ahead.

Then we drove up Ferry Hill, reversed in one of the streets in Winchelsea, and took the Audi back down that steep gradient. We asked Sheila to try and recall exactly where she noticed the car's steering worsening. She drove slowly down the hill and was able to indicate the spot where the car really began handling badly. Then we rounded the hairpin bend at the bottom and established the place where she thought she had parked that fateful night.

We all got out of the car and tramped along the route Aunt Flo was supposed to have taken. It seemed extraordinary to us that, five years after the incident, Sheila was still not at all clear where the body was found, nor the exact position where the old lady's right slipper was discovered on the river bank.

Next we drove on through the Sussex countryside, along the route Sheila had taken every day to her trial, to look again at the court at Hove. The building was still in use as a Crown Court and a friendly police officer allowed us to peer through the glass door at the court room.

'It looks much smaller now, with nobody in it,' observed Sheila.

She showed us the sunken car park where she and her family had eaten their lunch, screened by trees from the intrusive press photographers. At that moment a large 'sweatbox' drove in, backing right up to the rear entrance. Sheila instinctively felt sorry for the invisible prisoners behind the black window glass.

As we drove back through Hove, an orange warning light flashed on the car's dashboard. The indicators had failed – or at least they seemed to be working only intermittently. The Audi was now eighteen years old and though the shiny green bodywork was still immaculate, the car was showing inevitable signs of age.

'I must get my garage to do something about that in the morning – unless it rights itself,' said Sheila crossly.

'Let's drive straight to a Hove garage and get something done about it *now !'* we begged.

On the road back we stopped at a wayside pub, The Green Man at Ringmer, between Hove and Lewes. As we sat eating prawn sandwiches, Sheila said sadly, 'Bob and I had lunch together in this pub just three weeks before he died. What on earth would he have thought about what's happened since?'

The trip ended with a detour to see the aunts' first house in North Salts, followed by tea in a Rye tea-room. Sheila appeared not to experience even the slightest feeling of unease as she sailed through Rye in her well-tailored jacket, full skirt billowing, head held high. Jane told us later that personally she hated going to the town centre now – she was sure everyone was staring at them. But Sheila refused to be cowed. Half of Rye might still believe her guilty, even after the Lord Chief Justice himself had quashed her conviction, but she had done no wrong at all and there was nothing to be ashamed of.

The rest of the afternoon was spent at 25 Fair Meadow checking through the chapters of this book, with Sheila adding in details here and there. We were taken upstairs and shown the old-fashioned Relyon contraption that Sheila had planned to make up into a bed for Aunt Flo if she could not get up the stairs. It was not surprising it was not immediately apparent to WDS Booth during her search of 25 Fair Meadow. It looks more like a large brown leatherette zippered suitcase than a bed of any description.

In the garage we saw Aunt Flo's suitcase, still sitting undisturbed after more than five years. It felt strange and sad to look at its meagre contents: the white lacy cardigan, the white vest and pants, the blue nightdress with lace yoke, the blouse and peculiarly lurid green skirt. Sheila was scathing: 'That's not her skirt and blouse! She'd never have worn anything like that, nor would they have fitted her – she was quite large really. What induced them to pack things like that! You can see what I had to put up with!' In a neat blue flowered toilet bag was a red plastic comb, a face-cloth and a bar of soap. Sheila closed the case, zipped it up and returned it to its black plastic bag. 'I suppose I'll be able to throw that away one day,' she said, 'but not till everything's all over.'

Throughout the whole period between Sheila's release and the start of her re-trial, a team from Just Television, makers of *Trial and Error,* visited her frequently to film a fascinating 'fly on the wall' documentary of her reactions to this limbo-like state of semi-freedom. They planned to intersperse the footage with a parallel account of her lawyers' deliberations – the first time television cameras had ever been allowed to film inside an English barristers' chambers in the run-up to a murder trial. The team accompanied Sheila to Canterbury when she went to collect the new ginger kitten; they filmed her and her family decorating the Christmas tree.

One Saturday morning they filmed an important conference held at the River Brede pumping station site, when Jeremy Roberts and his new junior counsel, the distinguished Birmingham barrister Patrick Thomas, met Ewen Smith, Dr Vesna Djurovic, Dr Denham and forensic expert Mark Webster. They crossed the field and stood on the river bank opposite the pumping station, where some of the jurors had stood during the trial visit four years earlier.

As they discussed possible ways in which Mrs Jackson might have fallen down the steep bank, there was a gurgling sound in the tunnel beneath the concrete parapet where the slipper had been found. Suddenly a great rush of water came bubbling out of the channel, churning up the gently flowing waters of the Brede. The automatic pumping station had kicked into action, and for the first time it was plain to all the onlookers how easily Aunt Flo's body could have been swept the 20 yards downstream, until it was snagged on branches overhanging the bank. Her other slipper must have gone floating on unimpeded, to be found three days later in the reeds far away down the river. Perhaps the walking stick travelled on, over the top of the sluice gates and away out to sea.

Christmas was fast approaching – Sheila's first for four years as a free woman. She confided to friends that although she would try to make an effort for the sake of the family, privately she dreaded the festive season: as soon as it was over, she said, there would be nothing between her and the re-trial. The television crew filmed her putting up Christmas cards from hundreds of well-wishers. On Christmas Eve we joined the family for a candlelit dinner and tried to talk about anything other than the case. But it was always there in the background like a dark cloud hanging over us all.

There was in fact just one more celebration to come before Sheila and her family and supporters had to face the rigours of the re-trial. For her mother's 68th birthday in early January, Jane had prepared a special surprise. She had organized a repeat performance of the concert at St Martin in the Fields, Trafalgar Square, which Sheila had missed as she sat in her cell in Holloway Prison on the eve of her first appeal in April 1995.

Once again the great church, magical by candlelight, was packed with tourists who applauded enthusiastically as Jane, this time partnered by her friend Helen Edgar, played the Vivaldi *Double Cello Concerto*, once again accompanied by the Belmont Ensemble.

Jane's friends in the audience noticed how the years of anguish had wrought a change in her. Though she had lost none of her beauty there was a new strength in her features and a new determination in her playing. And as Jane rose to take her final bow, there were no tears now as her mother stepped into the aisle to present her with her favourite white lilies – this time in person.

The final weekend before the re-trial began, Sheila busied herself doing the ironing, getting ready suitable clothes to wear in court. Crossly she rejected the bright scarlets and turquoises she loved in favour of dusty pinks and greys. It seemed ridiculous to us all that a woman appearing in a court of law should have to tailor her appearance to fit conventional stereotypes of 'fragrant' womanhood favoured by the judiciary. But by now we had all learned the bitter lesson that telling the truth is simply not enough to win a case.

Tinker the ginger kitten was taken to a local cattery for the duration of the trial – and maybe beyond, who could tell? We paid one last visit to Fair Meadow with yet another batch of good luck cards from well-wishers. Before we arrived, in a typically generous and impetuous gesture, Sheila had dashed off in the same old green Audi to the Swan tearooms to buy a box of Robert's magnificent cream cakes as a final gift for us and our family. Some strangers taking morning coffee came up to wish her well. The TV team arrived to film a few final scenes before Sheila set off on the Monday morning to stay in Jane's London flat.

Sara Thornton faxed a final message to Sheila: 'There aren't many women in this country who will fully appreciate the awful process you are about to undergo. I want to give you the advice I wish someone had given me. Keep reminding yourself that you are a wonderful, brave woman, with many friends and admirers who will all be praying for you. That was the only thought that gave me comfort.'

In twenty-four hours' time the long period of waiting would be over, and Mrs Sheila Bowler would be standing in the dock at the Old Bailey, where for centuries rogues and vagabonds have stood trial, once again facing a charge of murder.

CHAPTER FIFTEEN

TEARS AT LAST

On the morning of Tuesday 13 January 1998 the re-trial of Sheila Bowler opened at the Central Criminal Court, Old Bailey, in Court Number Three. It began a day later than expected because of delays in other cases. There was mild media interest, but two other high-profile cases (the Docklands bombing case and a schoolyard rape case) attracted more attention. The alleged IRA involvement in the Docklands bombing meant that every morning around 9.30 half of Newgate Street was closed while three police cars, blue lights flashing, accompanied a secure prison van into the court, and dozens of armed police officers lined the street where once stood the old Newgate lock-up. It was an intimidating experience for Sheila's friends and supporters arriving early to queue for the public gallery.

On the press benches were the *Guardian, Independent* and *Times* journalists who had visited Sheila in prison and at home, reporters from the local TV channels, and a large contingent from *Trial and Error.*

Above them in the public gallery were some of Sheila's friends who were allowed to stay, even though they would later be called as character witnesses, and more *Trial and Error* researchers and journalists.

Court Three, in the oldest part of the building, is a panelled room not unlike those at the Royal Courts of Justice in the Strand where Sheila's two appeals were heard. But it is more cramped, for the dock takes up easily one-third of the floor space. Sheila, smart in blue jacket and pink-and-white striped frilled blouse, took her place there, accompanied by a female Securicor guard who, as she listened to the case, revealed that she had been an under-matron at Battle Abbey School while Sheila was teaching there.

The court rose as the judge, The Honourable Mr Justice Wright, entered, a genial-looking man in his sixties. Sheila's supporters – especially Jane's fellow musicians – found it somehow encouraging that his *Who's Who* entry listed music among his recreations.

The jury – six men and six women – entered and were sworn, and Sheila was called to the front of the dock. The woman clerk rose to her feet:

'Sheila Bowler, please stand. It is alleged that on the night of 13th May

1992 you did wilfully murder Mrs Florence Jackson. Sheila Bowler, are you guilty or not guilty?'

'Not Guilty.'

From the outset it was clear that the atmosphere of the re-trial would be very different from that of the original trial in Hove. The judge's smiling geniality set the tone. He told the jury that this was a case with an unusual history. Mrs Bowler had been convicted of murder in 1993 but her conviction had been quashed by the Court of Appeal because of new medical evidence which the first jury had no opportunity to hear. This, he said, was a completely fresh, new trial and they must not attach any weight at all to the fact that the earlier jury had convicted.

Jeremy Roberts made it plain that his own style would be equally courtly. As in the Court of Appeal, he appeared not to be directing criticism at anyone.

In such a civilized setting it therefore seemed doubly chilling to hear the Prosecution case rehearsed once again, especially after the relative normality of Sheila's last six months as a free woman. In his opening speech Anthony Glass summarized the key points of the Crown's case – the condition of the tyre, Mrs Bowler's apparently unfeeling behaviour and the alleged motive of money. But this time he appeared to be simplifying his case to a single major issue: was Mrs Jackson – elderly, frail and infirm as she was – capable of walking the quarter of a mile from Mrs Bowler's car to her death in the River Brede? 'Because,' he solemnly addressed the jury, 'that is the stark issue on which your decision is required in this case. This is a case of murder or nothing.'

The Prosecution's case was hampered by the absence of four important witnesses. Mr Soan had died suddenly at the age of 58 just days before the re-trial ; Mr Giddings – the caravan park owner – had had a stroke and was too ill to attend: Mrs Pearson, a motorist witness for the Crown, had emigrated to Australia, and Barbara Jones, who had helped Mrs Jackson into the Audi when she left Greyfriars, was still on holiday in Mexico. Summaries of their statements and evidence had been agreed by both sides and would be read aloud to the jury, with a proviso from the judge that these testimonies should be treated with extreme caution because the Defence would have no opportunity to cross-examine the witnesses.

The first witness for the Crown was Sarah Silberston, the assessment officer who testified to Sheila's reluctance to sign the form allowing Aunt Flo's flat to be sold. By calling her first, Glass was immediately trying to establish the motive of money, just as he had at the original trial.But in cross-examination she agreed with Jeremy Roberts that it was very common to find relatives of elderly people with rather unrealistic ideas about their care. There would, she admitted, have been no difficulty in Greyfriars fees eventually being paid. The local authority that ran the Home would have first call on Mrs Jackson's estate at the time of her death.

Next came the first of the Greyfriars staff. As Roberts cross-examined the care officers one by one, his game-plan slowly emerged. He treated all of them with enormous respect as trained professionals. He made it clear that no criticism was implied – not of them, nor indeed of Mrs Bowler herself – about the way Mrs Jackson was cared for. Of course, he conceded, Mrs Bowler – like so many other relatives of elderly people – could not be expected to understand her aunt's needs as well as professionally trained care staff. Mrs Bowler had had various ideas about the care of the old lady, 'and you and your colleagues offered every support and assistance.' There was none of the acrimony of the Hove trial, where the Greyfriars staff made it clear they had a very poor opinion of Mrs Bowler. Roberts defused their potentially damaging evidence with a successful charm offensive.

He listened patiently to their assessments of Mrs Jackson's mobility. The judge frequently intervened, anxious, it seemed to supporters in the public gallery, to show that he was familiar with the needs of elderly people, and well aware of the difficulties in caring for them and the special skills required to do so. He knew, he said, that old people had wandered off, 'sometimes in their pyjamas and dressing-gowns.' The first Greyfriars witness, Deborah Freeman, was asked about her description of Aunt Flo 'trotting along' and agreed that it was an accurate description. With each of the care staff, Roberts raised the subject of Mrs Jackson's accident on 16 April 1992 when she fell at Greyfriars and fractured her wrist. What a pity, he said gently, that the Greyfriars accident book had never been found. Not, of course, that he implied any criticism of anyone: accidents will happen. But it was strange, was it not, that only one of the care staff admitted to being on duty on the night of the fall, and even she had not witnessed the accident?

Five more Greyfriars witnesses and two Magdala House staff appeared for the Crown on the second day of the trial. The court heard that they had all come up from Sussex in the same coach. They all agreed that Mrs Jackson was frail both mentally and physically and could not, in their view, have left the Audi and walked down Station Road. Linda Hanson, Aunt Flo's key worker, said she herself lived in Station Road and she herself would find that journey difficult enough at night. Before her fall on 16 April Flo was able to walk with a zimmer frame but after that she was unable to use one. Could she use a walking stick? No, they all agreed. Joan Dobson, the matron in charge of the Home was most emphatic. As far as she knew, Flo had never used a stick, and in fact walking sticks were very difficult to use: 'It looks simple but in fact needs a lot of coordination. Lots of older people don't take to using one.'

The second day ended with the young motorist Christopher Beckett who had changed his mind about the times he left the two public houses he had visited. The jurors were so confused that they sent a note to the judge, asking for clarification. The judge asked Mr Glass whether he really needed to bring further Greyfriars witnesses as they had made their collective point. Yes, insisted Glass, 'the jury must decide on the *whole* of the evidence.'

The third morning opened with Mrs Val Wilding-Coe, formerly Mrs Nye but now remarried. She had been deputy head of the Home under Mrs Joan Dobson but unlike the other carers she had now retired from care-work and had come to the Old Bailey separately from her former colleagues. She looked nervous, constantly twisting a white handkerchief in her hands. Like the other Greyfriars staff she was asked about Mrs Jackson's mobility before and after her fall on 16 April 1992.

'Was she now in a wheelchair?' asked the judge.

'She used to walk with the aid of a stick,' said Mrs Wilding-Coe.

Glass paused. 'A walking stick?' he asked incredulously. All the other Greyfriars staff had told the court Mrs Jackson never used a stick. 'Did she manage with it?'

'Fairly well.'

Roberts in cross-examination was quick to pick up the point.

'It was one of Greyfriars' sticks: it was measured for her by a physiotherapist,' added Mrs Wilding Coe helpfully, 'she held it in her left hand.'

'She obviously knew how to use a stick?'

'Yes.'

Sheila's solicitor whispered, 'We've been trying for months to find someone to give evidence that Aunt Flo could use a walking stick, and now here's one of the main Prosecution witnesses saying so. Mr Glass must regret insisting on more Greyfriars witnesses giving evidence today!'

Tom Day, smart in blazer and tie, refused to budge on his assessment of Sheila's arrival time at his house, though it was contradicted by all the other witnesses. Nor would he change his opinion about the time she set off to drive home. He was sure the sun was setting because it shone through the copper beech trees in his garden – a beautiful sight, he told the court. He had even taken the trouble to test the time on May 13 every year since 1992. He did not recall the interview with the police some time before 22 May when he had been unable to be more specific about Sheila's arrival than 'between eight and nine.'

But perhaps, he conceded, plainly rather rattled by the Defence counsel's polite scepticism, a doubt had been put in his mind by Mrs Bowler's telephone call a few days after her visit. She told him the police had got it wrong: she said she had actually arrived at least half an hour later than they claimed.

During the lunch break Sheila told us that this was part of a general phone conversation she had had with Mrs Day, but to those listening it seemed as if she had made a special call to try to make Tom Day change his story in her favour. Mistaken or not, Mr Day's allegation was a point to the Crown.

Harry Kershaw was questioned by Tom Kark, once again acting as junior counsel for the Prosecution as he had done throughout all the hearings. Mr Kershaw asked Kark to speak up as he was rather hard of hearing. He said he had driven past the parked Audi at about 10.35 after an evening in the Robin Hood pub, the same one visited by Christopher Beckett. He drew alongside the car to see if anyone needed help. He said he was in a minibus-type vehicle high enough for him to look into the car. He saw nobody there, but nor did he see any pedestrians. It seemed plain that his eyewitness evidence was placed too late to be of any help to the Crown. By 10.35 the search was already under way and the searchers would have been in Station Road.

Did he drive on past the garage near the Bridge Inn, wondered Mr Kark? And if so, was it open?

'No, it always closes at tea-time,' said Mr Kershaw firmly. Another Crown witness bit the dust.

The high point of that third day was Jeremy Roberts's cross-examination of Mrs Cameron-Clarke, the magistrate called out to help in the search for Aunt Flo. A squat woman dressed all in black, she glared round the court with an expression of magisterial outrage as she described with apparent relish how strangely, in her view, Sheila Bowler had behaved when her aunt went missing. At one point, said Mrs Cameron-Clarke, 'She went like this...!' The magistrate gave a piercing shriek which echoed chillingly round the courtroom. Some of the jurors looked startled and Sheila's supporters in the public gallery stared at the witness in amazement.

Mrs Cameron-Clarke warmed to her theme: 'I got the impression that Mrs Bowler didn't want me to go further down Station Road. Throughout the night I got more and more anxious about Mrs Jackson. So in the morning I decided I would try to go down there. I thought it very odd,' here a note of sinister melodrama crept into her voice, 'I though it *very* odd that the gate near the pumping station was open. It was a five-bar gate.'

Roberts began his cross-examination gently enough and Mrs Cameron-Clarke answered confidently, adding still more details. Roberts asked, 'You were all very puzzled, very concerned?'

'Well,' said the magistrate, 'Mrs Bowler was not so concerned as the rest of us.'

Suddenly Roberts's tone changed: 'You were under the impression that Mrs Bowler didn't want anyone going down the road very far. Don't you think you were quite wrong and unfair to Mrs Bowler?'

Mrs Cameron-Clarke looked shocked and angry: 'No I don't! Why should I worry in the night and get up and go and look, wishing I'd gone down there that night?'

'Are you not prepared to concede that you've made a serious error and been very unfair to Mrs Bowler?'

'No, I'm not!'

'You said you noticed something strange. When you went along the road next day you found it strange that the gate was open. Is that true?'

'Yes, it was most unusual for the gate to be open.'

'Are you aware that for ten months at least before the 13th of May that gate remained wide open? It was permanently open so that grass had grown all round it. We will hear evidence about that gate later. I suggest you are *completely mistaken* about this. I am suggesting you are completely mistaken in quite a lot of the things you are saying, Mrs Cameron-Clarke!'

'Well I'm *not!* I'm absolutely sure! You can say what you like but I know what I know!'

A ripple of amusement ran through the public gallery as the magistrate stumped angrily down from the witness box. 'It's good to know he's got a Rottweiller streak beneath that smooth manner,' whispered one of Sheila's supporters.

As the afternoon drew to a close the tension was lightened still further when PC Millington gave his evidence and revealed that he had lost his policeman's notebook. Had he searched for it, Jeremy Roberts asked? It was after all almost five years since the first trial.

'Yes, I have,' said the constable earnestly. 'I've been trying to chase it up *all morning.'* Another titter went round the courtroom.

The following day, said the judge, the jury would be transported by coach to view the site. They would be joined there by himself and counsel. Mr Justice Wright warned the jury to wrap up warm and bring their own refreshments – he knew that part of the world and it could be bitterly cold and wet – and they should bring their wellington boots. Some of the younger jurors in their jeans and trainers looked confused. The judge issued dire warnings to members of the media to keep well away from the scene. There could be no filming – television or still photographs. At that stage, late in the afternoon, *Trial and Error's* Steve Haywood sat alone on the press benches. The judge fixed him with a grave stare: 'Perhaps those of you who are here will make sure to tell your colleagues.'

In the event the entire area was cordoned off by the police while the judge, jury and counsel visited the site, walked up to Number 4 Tanyard Cottages and then along Station Road to the pumping station. It was a cold January day, but the judge's warnings of Arctic conditions proved over-cautious. The sun came out from behind the scudding clouds and shone brightly over Romney Marsh, just as it had that summer's afternoon five years before when the first jury visited the site.

That Friday morning, an appointment had been made by Sheila's lawyers for her to visit a woman psychiatrist at one of the London hospitals, to see if she was fit to give evidence. The psychiatrist felt it would be helpful also to see Jane to get a fuller picture of her mother's character. Eventually she spoke to her on the telephone. When the Defence team received her report the following week it was clear that though Sheila was tired, she had given a good account of herself and would be fit to take the stand.

The court reconvened on Monday 19 January – Day Five of the hearing, counting the site viewing as Day Four. This was the chance for Patrick Thomas, junior Defence counsel, to begin his systematic demolition of the Crown's evidence about the Audi's front nearside tyre. Thomas is a distinguished Birmingham barrister who often sits as a judge. It cannot have been easy for him to play second fiddle to Jeremy Roberts. But when he was approached by Glaisyers to take on the case he was prepared to drop everything to do it. He had been working day and night on it for the last few months. At the start of the trial he set up his laptop and had been making rapid notes on it throughout. The clocking-in panel on the computer screen frequently revealed times of 3am or later when he had finally logged off for the night.

Director Steve Rankin, researcher Yasmin Mahamdallie, and the same *Trial and Error* film crew who had been with Sheila and Jane almost continuously for the past six months had filmed all the conferences with the Bowlers and their lawyers at 9 Gough Square, Jeremy Roberts's chambers.

It was a pity there were no TV cameras on hand now to record Thomas's skill as he deftly undermined the Prosecution case by raising grave doubts about police procedures in their handling of the tyre from the time it arrived at Rye police station to the time it was inspected by an expert in a Home Office laboratory. PC Derrick Watson had told Mr Glass that he had examined the tyre in the police station yard. Under cross-examination he said he had recorded the tyre pressure as 15 pounds per square inch on an entirely accurate gauge which was regularly checked. He had recorded the tyre as being 'in poor condition with cracks on the side walls.' Now he added that there were also 'cracks between the treads.' He had himself removed the tyre and had given it to Scene Investigator Victor Booth.

Three days later, on Day Eight, Victor Booth was to tell the court that on the contrary it was *he* who had removed the tyre and that the examination took place not in the police station yard but in the garage.

These may have seemed minor points, but Thomas was building up to his cross-examination of the next witness. This was David Price, a key witness for the Crown. Mr Price took the oath, preferring to affirm his allegiance rather than to swear by Almighty God.

During his examination-in-chief by Mr Glass, Mr Price explained that at the time he was asked to examine the tyre he was employed at the Home Office forensic laboratories at Aldermaston, where he specialized in assessing damage to vehicle components, usually in traffic accident cases.

He told Mr Glass that he had received the Audi tyre on 21 May, over a week after the alleged breakdown, but had not actually tested it until 27 May. He said he kept it in the vehicle lab storage shed where the temperature was known to fluctuate. When he finally measured the tyre's pressure his gauge showed it as 19psi, but, he added, as his gauge 'did not have a yearly calibrated certificate I applied a correction factor so the true pressure was 18.5psi.' He admitted that PC Watson's gauge was more accurate than his own. The pressure might have gone up because of the heat in the storage shed.

He had tested the tyre in a water bath and with a special aerosol spray to show up any defects. There were none, and he had concluded in his written report that the tyre was in good condition, without any of the defects mentioned by PC Watson. In evidence at the first trial he had told Mr Glass: 'The tyre was in good condition with an adequate depth of tread pattern. The external damage to both the tyre and the wheel was very slight and consisted mainly of scuffs to the tyre and to the chrome trim of the wheel. This is the sort of thing one gets from normal use.'

Price's measurement of the tyre's pressure and his assessment of its general condition were both radically different from Watson's. He was asked to produce the tyre and show it to the jury. As they peered at it, he told them there was nothing wrong with the rubber, the beading or the valve which would cause the tyre to lose air.

The following day, in cross-examining Price, Patrick Thomas was able to press his points home: how on earth was it that the tyre had *increased* in pressure from 15psi to 18.5psi or even 19psi *while it remained in police possession?* How was it that the police vehicle inspector recorded it as being in poor condition, while the Home Office tyre expert said it was in good condition? Why was there so much disagreement between Booth and Watson about their handling of the tyre? Could it, wondered Thomas, even be the same tyre? Although two days later Tom Kark was to lead Victor Booth meticulously through the standard police labelling, sealing and recording procedures for any exhibit, doubts had now been voiced and were to remain.

The tyre point seemed won, but meanwhile the Defence had suffered a setback. The Crown had decided not to call Dr Jeelani as one of their witnesses because they no longer felt him to be credible: he had, they claimed, changed his story about Mrs Jackson's mobility. Although the Defence were at liberty to call him as one of their own witnesses, Roberts feared that the affable local GP would not fare well under savage cross-examination by Glass. The judge agreed that instead, a summary of Jeelani's evidence and witness statements could be put before the jury. This was a low point for Sheila and her family and supporters. We all felt that Jeelani's testimony had been a vital element in persuading the Home Secretary to refer the case back to the Court of Appeal and if the jury were not now to see him in person, this important plank would be removed. As Sheila descended the austere marble stairway from Court Three that afternoon she broke down in tears. We comforted her as best we could, wishing the jury had been able to see the effect this terrible stress was having.

Next day the mood in court was lightened, as it had been at the first Hove trial, when Dr Heath, the Home Office pathologist, attempted once more to explain how a woman of 62 had managed to lead a woman of nearly 90 down the steep bank of the Brede without both of them tumbling in. Again an embarrassed titter rippled round the court as he elaborated on his already fanciful theory, this time speculating that perhaps the two ladies had gone down the bank side by side, or even backwards. He agreed that 'it is unlikely you could maintain your balance side by side. You could certainly walk down backwards, half in front.'

Dr Heath said he had not weighed Mrs Jackson at the post-mortem examination: 'I would have thought she was six to seven stones. But I am not good at this.' He agreed in cross-examination that there was no disease or injury to her lower limbs and that there was nothing in his pathological findings inconsistent with her having walked 500 yards. 'I can't say if she could walk a foot or two miles.' He agreed it was a possibility that the bruises he had said were 'consistent with a blow from a fist' could have happened while she was in the water. He could not exclude the possibility that the bruises to Mrs Jackson's arms were caused by 'her being held to assist her. If she is slumped down and you pull her up by the arms you could do that.'

Day Seven began in an altogether more sombre mood. Sheila's supporters in the public gallery noticed that a large embossed gold and red sword had suddenly appeared, hung like the sword of Damocles behind the judge's chair. The lawyers explained that this emblem was there to show that Mr Justice Wright was the most senior judge sitting in the Old Bailey that day. When he appeared, preceded by an official in blue velvet court dress with a lace *jabot* at the neck, Patrick Thomas, the forthright Birmingham barrister, joked, *sotto voce,* 'Remind me what century we're in!'

The whole of the day was taken up with the evidence of Dr Roger Lewis, Director of the Department of Geriatric Medicine at Guy's Hospital. As at the Court of Appeal hearings, Lewis made it absolutely clear that he rejected the possibility that Mrs Florence Jackson could have walked the 500 yards to her death in the River Brede. He rehearsed every step of the process required for the old lady to get from the car to the pumping station, with much grim technical discussion of the causes of dementia, the extent of Mrs Jackson's brain damage and its effect on her mobility.

There was a dispute about Mrs Jackson's weight. This was important in view of the Crown's proposition that Mrs Bowler had somehow got her aunt into the water single-handed. At one stage the old lady's weight was recorded as dropping to seven stones, a figure eagerly embraced by the Crown. But at Greyfriars she had eaten well, and the Defence team found a weight of 8st 3lb in the medical records. But they recalled reading somewhere that in fact at the time of her death she was almost a stone heavier still.

Fortunately Brian Mummery was in the public gallery. His wife Audrey had spent years analysing the papers of the case in great depth. Next morning Brian was able to contact Roberts's chambers with an exact reference in the hospital notes proving that just before she died Mrs Jackson was 9st 1lb: this weight was duly recorded in the Agreed Facts document given to the jury. It was of material importance because of the theory expanded by Dr Heath that Sheila had 'half-lifted' her aunt down the bank.

This was just one of many examples proving the worth of Sheila's support group which gave her lawyers access to such a wide range of expertise and experience. In view of her dreadful misfortunes over the past six years, Sheila was indeed fortunate that her final legal team was accessible and open enough to accept advice and information from every quarter. It meant that unlike many barristers, Jeremy Roberts had a wealth of detailed information about his client's character and background well before the case began. Most unusually he had visited her at home and got to know her and her family and friends very well.

Dr Lewis's evidence went on for hours and it was a welcome diversion when at one point he stepped down from the witness box and gave a demonstration of the way Aunt Flo walked with her zimmer. The jury craned forward to see him. To those watching from the public gallery he seemed to move surprisingly quickly.

'Can we exclude the possibility that she could have got out of the car and walked to her death?' asked Mr Glass.

'I believe we can' said Dr Lewis.

Next Glass turned to what he scathingly referred to as the Defence's 'anecdotal evidence.' Jeremy Roberts had prepared a twelve-page document headed *Incidents described by members of the public*. The document contained extracts from 38 of the letters sent to us via newspapers and the *Trial and Error* programmes, each relating a story of the extraordinary and unexpected exploits of elderly people previously believed to be immobile. We had typed them out and sent them with the originals to the lawyers, who had taken statements from some of the writers so that they could come to court and give evidence in person. Now Lewis set about rubbishing the case histories. They were, he said, 'valueless' in evaluating the capabilities of Mrs Jackson.

The judge intervened and asked for details of the material. Roberts explained how they had been collected. It was only fair, he said, to allow

Dr Lewis to comment on them, just as the Defence expert, Professor Archie Young, would be asked to comment. Glass objected: the case histories were not evidence, and they were valueless.

Meanwhile copies of the Defence document were handed to the jurors who seemed to peruse them with interest. The prosecuting counsel was plainly disconcerted. He had been led into accepting Roberts's proposal to show the jury the document. The best he could now hope for was damage limitation: 'It will be the Crown's submission that the jurors do not have this information when they come to consider their verdicts,' he snapped. Roberts pressed the point home by reading aloud two of the case histories. One was a letter from a home-help in Scotland, the other from the neighbour of an old lady in Hampshire. Both told tales of exploits even more remarkable than the 500 yard walk allegedly made by Aunt Flo.

Next day Dr Lewis returned in the afternoon to face the rest of his cross-examination. Now Roberts raised another issue: Dr Lewis's visit to Greyfriars. From Lewis's evidence and his demonstration the previous day it was plain that the staff had actually shown him physically the way Mrs Jackson walked. Was he aware, asked Roberts, that the staff had refused to give the same information to the Defence expert, Professor Young? Was he aware that they had refused to speak to the Defence side at all, despite persistent requests from Mrs Bowler's solicitors? Was he aware that East Sussex Social Services had sent the Home a memo ordering them to speak to nobody but their press officer?

Mr Glass objected: 'I must interrupt. I will address Your Lordship. Could the jury just pop out? It may be best they do not hear this.'

The jurors trooped out, some looking confused. In their absence the judge was persuaded to accept Roberts's request for two Greyfriars witnesses to be brought back to court the following day to give their demonstrations of Mrs Jackson's shuffling walk so that Professor Young would no longer be at a disadvantage.

When the jury had finally left at the end of the afternoon session, Roberts insisted that the two Greyfriars ladies should travel from Sussex with an independent driver so that they should not know the reason for their return to court. 'This is a very sensitive issue,' he said, 'in view of the fact that there was an official Greyfriars lie about Mrs Jackson not using a walking stick. I wouldn't like there to be any room for the suggestion that the ladies had spoken to each other or to anyone else. I don't want the ladies to confer.'

Next morning the entire court (apart from people in the public gallery) repaired to the marble-floored hall outside Court Three. The judge, jurors and lawyers stood in a large semi-circle. It was an incongruous, almost comical scene, the judge and counsel in their robes and wigs looking oddly theatrical out of context, next to the casually dressed jurors, and Sheila with her Securicor guard on one side and Jane on the other. In the middle of it all, first Erica Britton, and then Linda Hanson, hobbled a few steps on a zimmer frame brought into court for the purpose. Dr Lewis had had to do his demonstration without a frame. Professor Young stood by, timing them with a stopwatch. The care-workers did not see each other's demonstrations and indeed there were marked differences in their perceptions of Mrs Jackson's shuffling steps. But like Dr Lewis they both moved far more quickly than anyone had expected – a point very much in the Defence's favour.

The Crown's witnesses were nearly through. On Day Eight, Thursday 22 January, there was a chilling period during the testimony of Scene Investigator Victor Booth when Anthony Glass asked him to produce the clothes of Mrs Florence Jackson. One by one the artefacts were drawn out of their brown paper bags. The right slipper was handed to the jurors who passed it round, visibly recoiling as they balanced it gingerly on top of its brown envelope. In the dock Mrs Bowler sat with her head in her hands. Next Booth showed the jury the paper tissue retrieved from the deceased's hand, in a transparent plastic wallet. Then came the buff-coloured coat, crumpled and with a jagged tear; then the shrunken cardigan, sky-blue and incongruously childlike; and finally and most pathetically, an oyster pink girdle with tan-coloured stockings still attached to the front suspenders. A hush fell as Anthony Glass paused for the exhibits to take their full effect. However Florence Jackson had met her death, she was present there for a moment in that silent courtroom.

One witness who had appeared at the Hove trial was Monica Steward. She was now Deputy Head of Battle Abbey School and as at the first trial she was asked about the conversations she had had with Mrs Bowler the week after Aunt Flo's death. She volunteered to Tom Kark that 'Sheila was very worried about her daughter who I believe was doing her finals at the time, her music exams.' In cross-examination she told Jeremy Roberts that Sheila was not one to show her emotions.

Then Roberts came to his final set of questions: 'She said the police would find things which seemed incriminating but which had a rational and sensible explanation?'

'She said the police had suspicious minds and might think...,' Mrs Steward's voice trailed away and she looked embarrassed. But Roberts interrupted to press home the point: 'She talked, I believe, about the reputation of the Hastings police and their reputation for rigging evidence?'

'Yes,' said Mrs Steward, 'She was worried about that, yes.'

The only remaining witnesses for the Crown, apart from a few minor ones whose statements were read, were indeed those very same Sussex police officers. Linda Booth and David Renno were the detectives who had interrogated Sheila back in 1992. Renno, still distinctive in appearance – though his badger-like streaked black hair was now a little greyer and less striking – had attended all the hearings since that time, but Booth only appeared at the Old Bailey the day before she was due to give evidence. From local people we heard she had taken early retirement from the police force and now worked as a holistic therapist: Sheila's friend Anne Wood had read an account of her work in the Icklesham parish newsletter, which explained that she had left the police force and had retrained as a practitioner of kinaesthetics.

Mrs Booth took the witness stand, looking nothing like a police officer. It was hard to believe hers was the harsh voice behind the transcripts of the taped interrogations almost six years earlier. She wore a flowing pink silk shirt and matching trousers, high heeled shoes and a long flowered scarf in soft pastel shades.

Mr Glass spent many minutes establishing the integrity of Linda Booth's professional behaviour during the periods she was alone with Mrs Bowler following Mrs Jackson's death. He raised the points about Sheila having no food in the house and no bed prepared and touched upon Sheila's apparent lack of concern about her relative's death.

In cross-examination Jeremy Roberts addressed Mrs Booth with quiet courtesy, complimenting her on her 'handwritten rough notes' which were 'very helpful' and all part of 'proper police procedure.' He was puzzled, however, by her doubts about Mrs Bowler's timings on the night of 13 May. He quickly established that Booth's briefing notes from other police officers had adopted Carol Pierce's estimate. Pierce was the only Greyfriars worker to suggest that Sheila arrived between 7 and 7.30. All the others had said she arrived after 7.50 and Mrs Dobson had checked with her clock and saw her leave at 8.03. This, said Roberts, explained Booth's initial suspicion.

Still in the same quiet and civil tones, Roberts carefully explained to Booth why it was that Sheila had seemed to 'usher the officers out of the house' on the evening of May 14. By charting Sheila's movements since she had returned to the Audi to find Aunt Flo missing, he made it clear that she had had very little sleep or food. Of course – here he permitted himself a slight chuckle – Booth could not have thought Mrs Bowler had *literally* no food in the house. She must have realised she simply meant there was no supper prepared.

'It could be inferred either way,' replied Linda Booth.

Jeremy Roberts dealt in the same calm way with Detective Sergeant David 'Badger' Renno. In fact he used the cross-examination as a means of putting before the jury any information he thought they ought to know.

'You made enquiries into the background of Mrs Bowler?' he began.

'That is correct,' said Renno.

Roberts continued to give the jury a potted history of the case, covering the Home Secretary's referral back to the Court of Appeal, Sheila's prison sentence, and the quashing of the conviction the previous year. Although Renno had played no discernible part in the case's later history, he continued in true police mode to reply to every question like an automaton, 'That is correct, yes, that is correct.'

Roberts persisted, the model of smiling charm; 'I suppose that having regard to motive as to the murder of Florence Jackson you made enquiries into the financial affairs of Mrs Bowler?'

'That is correct.'

'She owned a detached house, the mortgage was paid off before her husband died. She got £8,000 a year from his pension and as you know she had three part-time music teaching jobs that brought in the region of £6,000 and she had a widow's pension of £3,000 a year.'

'I didn't know that.'

'But you see, don't you,' Roberts smiled, 'that that amounts to £17,000 a year?'

Next Roberts moved on to the motorcyclists.'One of the enquiries you made was about the motorcyclists at the bottom of Ferry Hill. You did make enquiries, and found there were two meetings of motorbike clubs that evening?'

'That is correct.'

'One was at the Royal Oak pub in Pett, between Hastings and Winchelsea. That was the Triumph Owners' Club. The other was a meeting at the Ash public house in Ashburnham, the other side of Hastings. These are vintage motorcycle clubs, aren't they? Do you know what they do at these meetings?'

'I have no idea, Sir.'

Roberts laughed, nodding conspiratorially at the detective, man to man: 'It may be an excuse for a night at the pub.' The policeman smiled back warmly.

Jeremy Roberts's handling of the Prosecution witnesses had been masterly. From the very outset he had managed to maintain such an air of urbane and civil good humour that it was sometimes hard to believe we were attending a murder trial. In this way he defused potentially hostile witnesses and created an atmosphere in the courtroom where any suggestion of sinister wrongdoing seemed extraordinary, indeed almost outrageous. Here we all were, civilized middle-class citizens behaving politely to each other. The very idea of *murder* seemed thousands of miles away.

Jeremy Roberts's strategy was to isolate Anthony Glass so that his melodramatic posturings seemed more and more absurd, and his suggestions of cold calculated murder more and more bizarre.

The last piece of Crown business that Friday morning, the tenth day of the trial, was to show the jury two police videos. The entire court repaired downstairs to Court Nineteen.

Sheila was taken there separately by her Securicor guard. For the first time she went down the stairs from the dock into a cold white-tiled area like a public lavatory. It was in stark contrast to the elegant oaken splendour of the courtroom. Like any common criminal Sheila was led down the narrow stairs into the bowels of the Old Bailey, along a corridor lined with cells, then back up another stairway into Court Nineteen.

Meanwhile in the corridor outside the new courtroom there had been a delay of five minutes or so and Jane stood back beside a pillar, embarrassed to be waiting so close to the jury members. But she took some heart from the jurors' manner. They seemed very relaxed and were smiling and whispering together. Several took the opportunity for a quick cigarette. Could these be the twelve people who would send Sheila Bowler back to Holloway Prison and an almost certain death in custody?

At last the court usher opened the door of Court Nineteen. Inside, a mini-courtroom had been set up, combined oddly with what looked like a small television studio. The judge's bench was there, complete with an imposing green leather chair like the one upstairs. On his desk stood a television monitor. In the body of the room were twelve chairs for the jurors, and in front of them a larger television screen. Behind them sat the lawyers with a third smaller TV monitor in front of them.

There was one remaining seat left. The usher directed Jane towards it. Jane found it acutely embarrassing to have to walk past the jury and she kept her head lowered as she took her place towards the back of the room. 'Sitting so close to the police I felt I was in the middle of the enemy and I didn't even dare look round to see if Mum was there.'

Sheila was led by her guard into the dock at the back of the courtroom. In front of her was a fourth small television monitor.

The videotape, operated by Jeremy Roberts, showed the scene at the river bank on the morning of 14 May 1992, as it was filmed by Jonathan Ashe, the police photographer. It had been set to begin a few minutes into the tape so that the jury would not have to view the distressing sight of Mrs Jackson's body lying on the bank.

The first film was silent but for the singing of the birds over Romney Marsh. It showed various views of the pumping station, the bank, the culvert with the slipper just above the concrete ledge, and the dry hard ground with various tyre impressions.

The second film was shot from a car making the journey that Aunt Flo would have to have made from the junction of Station Road and the A259 to the pumping station. Cow parsley edged the winding road and the sky was a beautiful blue. Once again the birds were singing. It was hard to believe that this was the scene of a sinister crime. One of the jurors asked for the films to be repeated and Roberts ran them through again.

The jurors were dismissed until the following Tuesday. (The judge had a long-standing engagement on the Monday). Everyone else returned to Court Three.

Now Jeremy Roberts announced that the Defence would make a submission of No Case to Answer. He had privately told Sheila and her family and supporters that there was almost no hope of the submission being accepted, but he wanted to put it forward for tactical reasons.

Now he repeated his opening submission that 'there is no direct evidence to convict Mrs Bowler. There are no eyewitnesses, no forensic evidence and no admission. The case is entirely circumstantial.' The evidence of the Crown's witnesses – Mrs Pearson, Mr Kershaw and Mr Beckett – had, he said, been demolished. Mr Day's timings had been dismissed. The tyre evidence merely corroborated Mrs Bowler's own view that there was something wrong with the Audi. All that remained was a period of 35 minutes when 'something happens which can never be known. It is unanswerable.'

Mr Glass naturally disagreed: 'The Crown's case is that this is a strong circumstantial case. There is no evidence of any other alternative. This is a case for the jury not for the trial judge.'

The judge agreed with the prosecuting counsel: 'This is the point. Nobody can gainsay the right of the jury to say, "This is a totally baffling conundrum. We don't think Mrs Jackson would have gone from the car. If she didn't it was either Mrs Bowler or it is a wholly unexplained phenomenon." Any jury is entitled to do that. A judge can't do that.' Although, he said, 'this is a *highly* unusual case... a judge must say it is open to a jury. This,' concluded Mr Justice Wright, 'is a case for the jury.'

So the case would have to go on. The Defence team had now received the full report from the psychiatrist who had examined Sheila a week earlier. It concluded that there was no medical reason why she should not give evidence.

Tom Kark spoke to Helen Barton. As there was a possibility that Mrs Bowler would not wish to give evidence, the Crown would also require a psychiatric report, and an appointment with another psychiatrist had to be made for the following Monday, when the court was not sitting.

As they left the Old Bailey, Sheila's lawyers tried to persuade her to relax during the long weekend ahead. Patrick Thomas discussed the state of play with the family. Only by a miracle would the case ever have been thrown out by the judge half way through, he said. But he sounded optimistic: 'We've won on the tyres and the timings,' he said, 'and I hope we've won on the walking theory. Now it's our turn to have some fun!'

Over that long and tense weekend, Sheila had to make a crucial decision: should she give evidence in her own defence? Jeremy Roberts and Patrick Thomas were plainly worried, as was Helen Barton, who thought Sheila was very tired and strained, although the psychiatrist's report had found no medical reason for her not to take the stand.

We all knew from the Hove trial that Sheila had been a poor witness. Indeed Nicholas Purnell had said she was one of the worst witnesses he had ever seen. Jane recalled how terror had transformed her mother's face into a white motionless mask which the jury might have interpreted as the face of a cold, calculating killer. Sheila herself said her mind had gone so blank that she tended to agree with every question put to her by both the Prosecution and the Defence counsels. The lawyers knew that although this was supposed to be a fresh trial, Glass had every right to pillory Sheila and confront her with the transcript of her disjointed testimony at Hove. He was likely to use the same tactics again to frighten and confuse her. Roberts and Thomas had taken pains to construct an elegantly argued case for the Defence. Would their client now go crashing through it like a bull in a china shop and wreck her own chances, just as she had before?

But, they had told Sheila at that Friday evening's conference, before she left London for the weekend, this had to be her own decision. In fact on the train home to Rye that night, she made up her mind. Over the weekend she rang Ewen Smith. He could cancel the appointment with the Crown psychiatrist, she told him. The jury needed to hear her tell them what really happened on the night of 13 May 1992. She would take the stand.

Although we all tried to keep up our own spirits and Sheila's, it was with some trepidation that we approached the Old Bailey on the morning of Tuesday 27 January, Day Ten of the trial.

The newspaper sellers outside St Paul's tube station shouted the latest news about the Queen Mother's health. She had had a bad fall over the weekend and was undergoing a hip replacement operation. The papers and television newsreaders praised the courage of the 97 year old in surviving a series of recent falls. Yet despite Her Majesty's history of falling, they said, she had been determined to walk with a walking stick the whole length of Westminster Abbey at Princess Diana's funeral. Was it naive of us to hope that the jurors would make a connection with Aunt Flo?

We had been informed that the case had been moved from Court Three to Court Two, an altogether larger, more ornate and more imposing courtroom than Court Three: it is commonly used for IRA cases and other high profile or top security trials. It seemed unfortunate that Sheila, of all the witnesses, would be the first to give her evidence in this lofty and intimidating space. The only advantage was that she could now see her supporters in the public gallery and we hoped she would draw strength from them. In Court Three they had been invisible above her head.

The day began badly with the judge refusing to allow two of the 'anecdotal' witnesses to come to the court and give evidence in person.

Although these ladies had had considerable difficulty in arranging to leave their elderly relatives, the judge was adamant. Sheila's spirits sank. Would the jury have understood how elderly people can behave simply from their rapid glance at the Defence list of case histories put before them? Jane was feeling angry: it seemed so unfair that the jury had heard nine days of Prosecution witnesses, yet they would not now have the opportunity of hearing Defence evidence from these experienced carers.

As if the Crown had not taken up enough court time, Tom Kark now announced that he had a few more Prosecution documents to put before the jury. The first was a statement from Detective Constable Poplett, the officer who had arrested Sheila, describing her reactions. Kark read it aloud, his cool, measured tone belying the horror of the arrest. In fact, Sheila's supporters agreed later, the reading had the effect of reinforcing her innocence, as Poplett's words described her shock at being arrested. Then Kark handed over to the jury a copy of the Missing Persons form completed by Sheila on the night of 13 May 1992.

At last Jeremy Roberts got to his feet to open the Defence case. He announced immediately that he would be calling Mrs Bowler to give evidence. She had, he said, 'consistently maintained her innocence through thick and thin.' There was not a shred of forensic evidence against her. The jurors seemed to sit up more alertly on their benches and several peered across at Sheila in the dock.

Roberts dismissed as utterly ludicrous Dr Heath's 'extraordinary theory that Mrs Bowler manoeuvred Mrs Jackson down the bank.' It was, he said, 'wholly, incredibly absurd and unbelievable. It would have resulted in both of them ending up in the river.' Then he ran through the motorist witnesses, convincingly dismissing them one by one.

'And now,' said Roberts, 'I'm afraid I'm going to say a harsh word about Mrs Cameron-Clarke. What an *appalling* piece of evidence from a magistrate of all people, especially in a murder trial. A magistrate, of all people, should know how in *these* courts we work on the facts, not on impressions and suppositions. It was Mrs Cameron-Clarke's *impression* that it was of significance that the gate to the pumping station was open. Yet it is an agreed fact that that gate had been open for the last ten months. But that did not stop Mrs Cameron-Clarke! It really is scraping the bottom of the barrel for a Prosecution witness – and a magistrate at that – to attach a sinister motive to her *impressions.'*

Next he turned with equal ferocity on Mr Price, the tyre expert. 'Mr Price assured the previous jury in Hove that his reading of 18.5psi was accurate and could be relied upon. Now he says his gauge had not been checked for three years and that the pressure in the tyre could have gone up because it was kept in a store where it was hot. So what is his evidence for the difference between 1993 and 1998? Well, you could call it barefaced! He says, "Oh, in 1993 I hadn't heard Watson's evidence"! What *business* has a Home Office forensic scientist to be changing his evidence by what he hears in other evidence? He is supposed to be a scientist, accurate and reliable, not tuning it according to what other witnesses say. What *business* has a Home Office forensic scientist to be indulging in guesswork and saying it doesn't matter? Scientists are supposed to deal in accurate figures, especially Home Office forensic scientists in criminal cases. So what is the one correct fact to emerge from the tyre evidence? That the tyre did lose pressure in police possession. That is a *devastating* fact against the Prosecution. It makes it clear that Mrs Bowler's account of trouble with her steering is not part of a cover story to cover up a murder.'

Finally Roberts turned to the defendant herself. 'This lady has gone through the most appalling trauma. At the end of January 1992 her husband died and her grief must have been devastating. In May 1992 Mrs Jackson went missing and Mrs Bowler was arrested and charged with her murder. At her trial in 1993 she said, "It just felt unreal sitting in the dock." If you are innocent it must feel unreal. Then the jury convicted her and she spent four years in prison.'

Last of all, he said, 'people who know Mrs Bowler are coming here to tell you about her, warts and all. They will tell you she may have a chilly exterior but she is a warm and caring person.'

Sitting listening at the back of the court with Jane was Sheila's step-daughter Elizabeth, who had travelled from her home in Paris to give support at this most critical point in the trial. During the weekend she and Jane had recalled how at the Hove trial Sheila's energy and concentration had flagged during the long hours of questioning. Now she was five years older and had suffered all the deprivations of prison life. Indeed a few days into this trial she had actually fallen asleep in the dock. Helen Barton had noticed and the hearing had had to be suspended for a short break. That morning Jane and Elizabeth had asked Jeremy Roberts how the trauma of giving evidence could best be mitigated.

Roberts felt that in view of the defendant's age and the stress of the last five years, she might be allowed to give her testimony sitting down, and to have frequent short breaks. In the event this worked very successfully by a kind of bush telegraph system. Jane, sitting at the back of the court, would watch her mother carefully and when she saw signs of exhaustion would give a signal to Helen Barton across the courtroom. Helen would tap Patrick Thomas on the shoulder and Jeremy Roberts would ask the judge's leave for a break. The judge was very understanding and everyone, not least the jurors, benefited from a ten minute break every hour.

Anthony Glass however was not best pleased. He was heard to remark to his junior, 'All these breaks! Just as you're getting up a head of steam there's another break!'

Now Sheila Bowler walked slowly down from the dock and up the steps into the witness box. She was wearing the same dress she had worn on her birthday three weeks earlier – a Laura Ashley floral print with a wide lace collar. Jane had had a real battle to get her to put it on that morning. 'I *can't* wear that!'she remonstrated. 'The jury will think I'm dressing up for them.'

Later Jane and Elizabeth were to say that the difference between Sheila's performance at the Hove trial and her testimony that day was phenomenal. At the end of her evidence Sheila told her friends that what had really made the difference was her knowledge that the *Trial and Error* team and hundreds of people all over the country had kept faith with her, and she must not let them down. She was also by now well practised in speaking publicly about herself and her feelings about the events of May 1992. For the last six months she had been interviewed almost daily by director Steve Rankin for his 'fly-on-the-wall' documentary. She liked and trusted Rankin and sharing her thoughts and fears with him had given her confidence.

Sheila did not let her supporters down. She gave her evidence calmly and pleasantly, not only during the 'bedding down' process when her own counsel led her gently along, but later when Mr Glass went on the attack. She spent the rest of that day in the witness box, returning the following morning – Wednesday 28 January – for Glass to continue his cross-examination.

That Wednesday morning, Day Eleven, there was a long delay and rumours flew around that one of the jurors might not be able to appear in court that day. The explanation when it came was shocking. The daughter of one of the male jurors, a tall West Indian man, had died suddenly in childbirth. The man, distraught with grief, had nevertheless turned up to do his duty. He was summoned before the court and honourably discharged by the judge, who expressed his deepest sympathy and the sympathy of the assembled court.

So the mood of the court was sombre as Sheila once more took the stand. Mr Glass remarked crossly to his junior, 'There's no need for her to have a prison guard with her!' Was the remark made out of sympathy for the elderly lady in the witness box – or was Mr Glass worried that the presence of a guard would invite the jurors' pity?

Glass began mildly enough, though in pained tones he said he was unable to understand why on earth Sheila hadn't driven the Audi on to the Bridge Inn to get help. Just as he was getting into his stride the jurors asked to adjourn for an early and extended lunch break. They were so shocked, they said in their note to the judge, by the tragic news about their colleague's bereavement that they could not concentrate on the evidence.

When the court finally reconvened, Sheila continued to deal calmly and sensibly with Glass's questions, turning to face the jury whenever she needed to explain anything in detail, and answering the questions interposed by the judge with clarity and dignity. After all, she, not the prosecuting counsel, was the 'expert' on the subject of Aunt Flo's capabilities and the events of 13 May 1992.

As the afternoon wore on, the prosecutor's questions became more and more aggressive. Just before the end of that day's session, he touched on the motive of money: 'If she had four or five years to live, that was the end of the proceeds of the flat – £30,000 you told the court you thought it was worth?'

'Yes, that was the estimate at the time.'

'Is that why you pushed her in the river?'

Sheila stared fixedly at Anthony Glass and in a firm, strong voice she said, 'I *didn't* push her in the river!'

At that, every juror turned round to face her. The day's hearing was over and they left the courtroom with those words ringing in their ears.

Although everyone congratulated Sheila on her *bravura* performance so far, she had been exhausted by the ordeal, and that night she confided to Jane that she was not at all sure whether she could face up to the continued onslaught the following morning. 'For once I had to get tough with her!' said Jane later. 'I told her there were hundreds of people relying on her and she daren't let them down now!'

Day Twelve – Thursday 29 January – began with alarming news. As we entered the court room, Patrick Thomas told us that Jeremy Roberts was ill with suspected food poisoning. Thomas would have to do the re-examination, picking up any points raised by Mr Glass.

Could the news be kept from Sheila until after Glass had finished questioning her? Although she greatly admired Thomas, she trusted Roberts implicitly, and in the fragile state she must now be in, the news might have a devastating effect on her final testimony. On the other hand, she was bound to notice Roberts's absence and might lose her concentration speculating about it. Thomas decided he must break the news.

Just at that moment the court doors swung open and in came Jeremy Roberts, looking decidedly green around the gills. Was it the sandwich he had eaten in the Inner Temple the previous evening? Or the Thai meal he had eaten later on? Whatever the cause, he felt well enough to soldier on, taking breaks like his client.

Now Sheila felt an even greater moral obligation to do her best. She continued to answer Glass's questions so disarmingly that his ever more desperate accusations of murder sounded more and more bizarre. Everyone who saw her felt sure the jury believed her. Towards the end of the case we heard via a journalist friend that one of the regular court reporters thought her testimony as a defendant in the dock was one of the best he had ever seen at the Bailey.

From that moment the case seemed to turn in Sheila's favour. Next Mrs Elizabeth (Biddy) Cole, the aunts' neighbour in Ferry Road, was called to the witness box. Her evidence was full of gifts for the Defence. The forthright Biddy said she found Sheila quite annoying, especially when she told her in graphic detail about the messes she had to clean up after the aunts. But the old ladies, she said, 'were *devoted* to Sheila. They used to wait for her to come. She'd take them out on drives, on mystery tours, jolly little rides round the countryside. They were always in the car.' One of the main reasons, said Biddy, that she was convinced of Sheila's innocence was her devotion to her daughter Jane and her pride in her musical career. 'I *can't* believe she'd have picked that moment, in the middle of her exams. I *can't* accept it.'

Professor Archie Young was the key witness for the Defence. He was first called that Thursday morning, and continued with his testimony until the Friday afternoon, apart from a brief interlude when Canon David Maundrell appeared as a character witness.

The former Rector of Rye, who had so faithfully visited Sheila over those long years in prison, now took the stand in her defence. Asked by Patrick Thomas what she was like, he said, 'She was a *very nice* person with many friends. To use an old-fashioned expression she is downright, and you could be slightly worried when you first meet her. But she is a very nice person.'

'And what is her reputation for truthfulness and honesty?'

'She is *entirely* honest and truthful.'

'Would you believe her on her oath?'

'I would.'

Professor Young's great achievement was to retain his good humour throughout the long hours of questioning and cross-examination. Though the evidence he was dealing with was technical in the extreme, he somehow managed to make it intelligible to those listening in court, without ever seeming to patronise.

The professor's thesis was that Aunt Flo was more likely to have suffered from Alzheimer's Disease than from another form of brain damage called multi-infarcts disease. His reasons for this diagnosis were that she failed to recognize her sister at one point, that she was cheerful, and that she did not suffer from very high blood pressure – all factors common in Alzheimer's patients. This diagnosis was helpful to the Defence because Alzheimer's is not known to affect mobility. Professor Young's other main point was that because Mrs Jackson's medical records showed no physical, mechanical disability or muscular atrophy in her legs, her immobility while she was at Greyfriars was more likely to be behavioural and the result of lack of confidence or over-supervision by care staff which, though well-intentioned can, he explained, make elderly people flustered and less effective in their actions.

Young maintained that under a sudden impulse, such as being left alone in the dark in the car, Mrs Jackson might well have been motivated to mobilize spontaneously. Although because of her senile dementia she would not have been able to *reason* how to undo the seatbelt and the door and get out of the car, she might well be able to do it impulsively. Her brain, reacting to environmental cues around her, might tap *automatically* into a pattern of behaviour she had learned from her many car trips in the past. The professor smiled at the jury as he gave them an analogy: 'It's easy to switch on a light switch in the dark without thinking. But if you try to measure its distance from the ceiling or from the door frame you won't be able to do it. Try it when you get home tonight.'

Now Roberts revealed that a few weeks before the re-trial began, the Defence had obtained from the Crown Prosecution Service the Greyfriars day and night books, which were full of valuable information about Mrs Jackson. Professor Young had discovered that on 1 May, twelve days before her death, she was noted as ringing the call bell at night to attract the nurses' attention. This, he said, was 'an indication of a spontaneous action' and, equally important, he had discovered that the button on the call bell was very similar indeed to the button on the Audi's seatbelt release mechanism. If Mrs Jackson could manage one, she could manage the other.

The Greyfriars night book also showed that on the night of 9 May, just four days before she died, Mrs Jackson had got out of bed on her own to use the commode. The only reason the Greyfriars night duty staff noted it in the record book was because she was found have got back into bed and to be lying the wrong way round. If she could perform this complex set of movements unaided, the professor concluded that she could have lifted her legs over the car sill and out on to the road, a far less onerous feat.

From experiments conducted in his own laboratory on walking speeds of elderly people, he estimated that Mrs Jackson, whose lower limbs, the post mortem examination showed, were undamaged by arthritis or muscular atrophy, could have made the journey to the pumping station in as little as 20 minutes. Taken as a whole, Professor Young gave striking evidence to support the Defence case.

Once again Jeremy Roberts asked the judge to allow him to admit as witnesses those who had written letters about their own experiences of the elderly. He would like Professor Young to question them in person.

No, said the judge: 'I would prefer him to do it from the basic evidence rather than from letters sent to a television programme.' Nevertheless he nodded amicably to the professor and said a few words to him privately.

'This is nothing untoward, Mr Glass,' chuckled Mr Justice Wright before the jury returned. 'The professor and I have a mutual acquaintance and I was just sending him my regards.'

Glass began his cross-examination by launching an assault on Professor Young's integrity, suggesting he had been hired by 'a television company.' Then he asked the professor about the name of a kind of walk common in elderly people, known as Petren's Gait. It was a term that had been used by Dr Lewis in his evidence. Young said he was not familiar with the term, though after hearing it from Lewis he had searched for it using the Mediline computer programme. He had also looked through most of the standard text books.

When the professor later returned to the witness box for Glass to complete his cross-examination, he was quizzed once more on the term. Glass sneered that the professor should have asked one of his own students, because the term appeared in a basic medical textbook. The judge looked amused but mildly irritated:

'Haven't you tweaked the professor's tail enough, Mr Glass?' he asked.

'I'm afraid I'm going to tweak it some more,' persisted Glass.

He handed Young a printed page with the definition of Petren's Gait highlighted. He demanded that the professor read it aloud to show that Petren was an early twentieth-century geriatrician who gave his name to a shuffling walk. The judge looked unimpressed, the jury looked blank. It may have been a tactical error on the Prosecutor's part. Whatever his strategy to discredit the professor, Glass failed to move him from his continuing assertion that he saw no reason to exclude the possibility that Mrs Florence Jackson could have walked to her death.

The last witnesses for the Defence were seven women 'proofed' by Helen Barton on the advice of Audrey Mummery to represent Sheila's character to the judge and jury. Helen had spent hours on the telephone arranging and re-arranging their appointments at the Old Bailey because of the many delays in the case. But they had all responded with good humour and that morning they all met round a table in the fourth floor cafeteria, smiling at Sheila across the room but studiously avoiding speaking to her, as they had been instructed.

They all looked well-dressed and eminently respectable. Indeed *Guardian* crime correspondent Duncan Campbell, reporting on another case in the building, raised his eyebrows and remarked to a colleague that the bevy of middle-class ladies being shepherded into Court Two had little in common with the kind of character witnesses he was accustomed to seeing at the Old Bailey.

Each was questioned by Patrick Thomas. Susan Catmur, who had supported Sheila so steadfastly in prison, came and spoke about their 50 year friendship. The judge asked whether Sheila under stress would 'rabbit on a bit.' 'Yes,' said Susan ruefully, 'my phone bill proves it!' Anne Wood in her slow, calm voice described Sheila's reliability and kindness. Carol Brigham spoke of her daily care for the aunts and her support when Carol's husband died of cancer: 'She hides her emotions, but she is a very, very vulnerable person.'

Audrey Mummery described her Methodist upbringing with Sheila, who used to look after her as a child in chapel. 'Sheila is,' she said, 'just like her father – she keeps her feelings to herself.' Sheila would never, said Audrey, do anything to jeopardize Jane's exams.

Audrey was cross-examined by Mr Glass. He asked about Sheila's driving.

'Is she a careful driver?'

'Very, very careful!'

'Is she a practical person?'

'Yes, she is.'

Sheila's friends held their breath: surely Audrey was aware that Sheila would not have any idea how to let down a tyre.

Mr Glass leaned forward eagerly: 'In what way is she practical?' Audrey smiled sweetly: 'About the house, with cleanliness, tidying up, doing the household chores.'

The judge beamed benignly at the good housekeeper sitting demurely in the dock.

The other character witnesses recalled Sheila in her student days, as an NSPCC committee member and as a work colleague. All said she could seem austere at first but was a kind and loyal friend.

The judge addressed an astute question to the last witness, a teaching colleague called Judith White: 'You said she was forthright. Did she upset other people?'

'Yes, I think she did.'

'There must have been people who didn't like her?'

'Yes, she could put people's backs up.'

Just before each witness left the box, Patrick Thomas put to them the same two questions:

'What is Sheila Bowler's reputation for truthfulness and honesty?'

All replied that it was unimpeachable.

'And would you believe her on her oath?'

All said that unquestioningly they would. The cumulative effect of the repeated questions and identical answers was powerful.

Anthony Glass's closing speech seemed to Sheila's supporters to be long, plodding and rather lacklustre. He began with the old stalwart legal metaphor that a case based on circumstantial evidence is like a strand of rope: each strand by itself may not be strong, but wound together they make a strong combination. ('That'll annoy the judge!' joked one of the journalists on the press benches. 'He'll want to use that old chestnut in his own summing-up!').

In fact for Glass the image seemed to us to fail: as he went through the Crown witnesses' evidence he seemed to be conceding their points one by one to the Defence, especially on the topic of the timings and the tyre. The rope analogy came in useful, but by the end of Glass's speech each of its strands was now so frayed that even taken together they had little strength.

Glass also attacked 'the Prof' as he persisted in calling Professor Young: 'I invite you to conclude that you should be very careful that because he is a professor and has written learned articles you may think "Gosh!" and accept his opinion.'

'Finally,' said Glass, 'It is hardly necessary to say that this case is very important. It is very important for Mrs Bowler and it is important for justice at large. Because there is no-one to speak for Florence Jackson. Her voice is silent. Mrs Bowler has obviously been through an ordeal. But it was an ordeal of her own making because that night in May 1992 she assumed responsibility for Mrs Jackson as a parent does for a child. She discharged that responsibility by pushing her in the River Brede. That was *murder.*'

Glass's doom-laden closing words seemed hollow as they echoed round the lofty courtroom. The testimonies of the character witnesses had lifted everyone's spirits and the supporters could not believe that the jurors would accept the Prosecutor's lurid case.

But it was the end of a tiring week and Jane, Sheila and Simon felt almost too exhausted to think at all as they set off for Jeremy Roberts's chambers at 9 Gough Square for the final conference before the concluding speeches. The *Trial and Error* film crew decided everyone needed a rest: this was one conference they would miss.

That evening we telephoned Jane and Sheila to see how the conference had gone. Both told us separately that they felt uneasy. Over the weekend Jeremy Roberts would be planning his closing speech for the Defence, to be delivered on Monday morning when everyone would be feeling refreshed after the two day break. The trial had gone far better than he had expected, with most of the Crown's evidence demolished and Sheila giving such a good account of herself in the witness box.

But, the family told us, the lawyers were still worried that the jury might not have been entirely convinced by 'the walking theory.' If they failed to believe that, they might – like the Hove jury – decide there was no realistic alternative to murder, and no credible culprit but Sheila. Like the Hove jury they might convict.

Roberts was therefore keen to propose the 'middle ground' – to suggest other theoretical alternatives that the jury might be prepared to consider. For instance, there was the theory of the Good Samaritan. Perhaps some kind passing motorist had picked up Aunt Flo as she began to shuffle down Station Road trying maybe to get home. (Sheila had nodded, remembering that years ago Flo used to walk along that river bank towards her Ferry Road flat). But perhaps that motorist had taken fright when the old lady panicked and dropped her near the pumping station. Perhaps the bikers had abducted her. There were many possibilities. Or, said Roberts, 'we could suggest – though of course this is not our case – that on the way back from Bexhill, Aunt Flo suddenly decides she wants to spend a penny. Sheila drives her down Station Road, helps her out and turns the car while she does what she has to do, then finds to her horror that Aunt Flo has slipped into the river.'

We were amazed.

'What on earth did you say to that?' we asked Jane and Sheila separately. Both said they felt so stunned they thought they must have been mistaken. But they were both terribly worried about any such suggestion being put to the jury.

'I've told the truth consistently for the past six years,' said Sheila. 'If I start lying now, where will I be?'

We agreed wholeheartedly. To include what we now called the 'spending a penny theory' might undermine every word of Sheila's evidence, and indeed betray the integrity and honesty of all her character witnesses. Late that Friday night we called Steve Phelps at *Trial and Error* in some alarm. He said he would look into the matter. The following morning we rang Jeremy Roberts who said he had been tired and had probably failed to explain himself very well. He invited us to attend the pre-hearing conference early on the Monday morning.

We felt quite reassured – perhaps everyone at the conference had been exhausted and there had been misunderstandings. Nevertheless we were grateful to hear that the programme director Steve Rankin had also spoken to Jeremy Roberts over the weekend and would be there on Monday too.

That weekend we discussed the matter at length with Sheila. The more she thought about the scenario Roberts had suggested putting before the jury, the more it filled her with horror. It seemed obvious to her, as it did to all of us, and to a number of trusted friends we had telephoned over the weekend, that to suggest such a story at the eleventh hour could only raise grave doubts in the jurors' minds. It would sound like a last-minute confession and suggest that even Sheila's lawyers no longer believed her.

The Monday morning conference was tense. The cameras were running and Jeremy was miked up. Patrick Thomas, Ewen Smith and Helen Barton were there. As soon as we arrived Jeremy began reading aloud to us the first part of his closing speech – an eloquent panegyric to Sheila's good character and the absolute honesty of her testimony in the witness box. In the light of this he would then outline the utter implausibility of the Crown's allegations. He would demolish the Prosecution case in terms of the motive, the cover story, the timings, the tyre evidence and Dr Heath's unlikely theories. He would uphold Professor Young's assessment that Mrs Jackson could well have walked to her death. So far, so good.

But then, went on Roberts, he would like to offer the jury a 'middle ground,' to suggest to them that should they refuse to accept the walking theory, there were other alternatives.

Sheila, sitting between Angela and Jane, listened intently. For instance, said Roberts, there was the Good Samaritan theory, or the theory that the motorcyclists or someone else could have abducted Aunt Flo.

'Or suppose,' – he paused, peering across the conference table over his half-moon spectacles – 'I know you're dead set against this – but just suppose a 62 year old niece takes an 89 year old aunt out, the aunt wants to spend a penny...' Roberts went on in front of the TV cameras to outline his new scenario for suggesting a 'middle ground' alternative to the jury, while making it clear that this was not the Defence case.

Sheila and Jane shook their heads, still concerned at the effect this might have on the jury. Angela was more forthright.

'If you do that,' she said, 'I think it'll be a total disaster!'

She said she had watched the jury as they listened to Sheila's evidence and she was sure they believed in her. This was a case about people speaking to people, and if the jury heard this new story at this late stage, every shred of Sheila's credibility and that of her character witnesses would be destroyed.

There was a long pause. Then Patrick Thomas agreed. 'We barristers don't really look at the jury,' he said. 'I think Angela's right. She's the nearest lay person we've got to a juror, and if she's been watching their reactions she's probably got it right.'

Jeremy agreed to find a form of words which would allow the jury to speculate about Aunt Flo's fate if they rejected the walking theory – without any reference to the 'spending a penny theory.' When he finally read his new draft aloud, everyone was satisfied that it offered vague alternatives without suggesting for a moment that Sheila had ever lied. If the jury could not accept that Aunt Flo had walked, yet they were sure that Sheila did not murder her, it was up to them to speculate what else might have happened. Aunt Flo's death was likely always to remain a mystery.

The sun was shining brightly as we walked with Sheila and Jane from Gough Square to the Old Bailey. The last battle seemed to have been fought and there was optimism in the air.

But at Court Number Two there was yet another delay. A second juror was likely to be discharged. She had become ill and the hearing would be adjourned until the afternoon when a doctor would make a pronouncement. Everyone sat around despondently. Now Jeremy's closing speech would have to fill the 'graveyard slot' after lunch when it would have less impact on the jury.

As they climbed the stairs once more to wait in the fourth floor cafeteria, Sheila and her family wondered how many more cups of coffee and dreary sandwiches they would have to consume in this joyless building. At the next table sat Patrick McKinley, one of the defendants in the Docklands bombing case, soon to be exonerated when the judge threw out his case.

Gareth Peirce, the solicitor in the case, was with him as usual. She was well known for her part in the release of the Birmingham Six and was famously portrayed by actress Emma Thompson in the film about that case, *In the Name of the Father*. (She also represented Roisin McAliskey whom Sheila had met in Holloway.) She has a reputation for thorough preparation of her cases, and indeed she was always quietly at work early each morning in the café, where she would often ask about the progress of Sheila's case during the long weeks of the trial.

After lunch Sheila's lawyers asked us all to join them for coffee in a corner of the cafeteria. They had with them a weighty legal tome and Jeremy Roberts said that together they had reached a decision. Though, as we had requested, he would not put the 'spending a penny' theory to the jury, he intended instead to put it before Mr Justice Wright before the judge made his summing up.

He planned to ask the judge for a Lucas ruling. This, explained Roberts, was a direction from the judge to the jury telling them that if the defendant has lied about another matter it should not affect the jury's decision to acquit on the central allegation of the case.

Sheila and Jane looked puzzled. Why was 'lying' being mentioned at all, when everyone knew Sheila had been patently honest throughout? They had thought Jeremy had finally abandoned this strange theory. But the lawyers insisted that the jury needed to be given the 'middle ground' option, and it would be better coming from the judge than from the Defence. Angela still protested, fearing that even putting this entirely erroneous idea in the judge's mind could damage Sheila's hard-won credibility.

But now the barristers and solicitors closed ranks. This, they said, was a matter between them and their client. It was a matter of law which might be difficult for a lay person to comprehend, but if they failed to do it, they would be jeopardizing their client's chances of an appeal should there be a guilty verdict. Steve Phelps turned up and said there were some things we would just have to leave to the lawyers. He only hoped they knew what they were doing. We were all too exhausted to argue.

At two o'clock the court reconvened. There would now only be ten jurors. The judge was all for pressing on, as it might take at least four days for the sick woman to recover, and as nobody wanted further delays, that decision was made.

Jeremy Roberts delivered his speech with panache, ending with a moving plea to the jury:

'Mr Glass ended his speech by saying rather dramatically that there was no-one here to speak up for Mrs Jackson. Mr Glass is sure that Mrs Bowler is guilty. But if you think *we're* right, then this lady who cared for Mrs Jackson for so many years has been wrongly convicted. If Mrs Jackson could send a message to you now, we suggest she would say to you, "Please don't make the same mistake again"'.

The day's hearing was over. The jurors were dismissed with Jeremy Roberts's earnest plea ringing in their ears.

Now Roberts put to the judge the suggestion that His Lordship's summing-up should put forward to the jury some other explanation to fill the 'middle ground.'

'Say,' said Roberts, 'that the jury had come to the conclusion that Mrs Bowler had lied in her evidence to the extent that she was *aware* of how Mrs Jackson met her death, but she had not murdered her?'

Sheila leaned forward in the dock. We had privately agreed with Sheila that if Roberts made his 'spending a penny' suggestion, she would shake her head vigorously to show the judge she disagreed – a crude and naive ruse maybe, but it was all anyone could think of.

Anthony Glass leapt to his feet. 'Is my friend suggesting that your Lordship gives a Lucas direction?'

The judge looked puzzled.

'I wasn't even thinking of it,' he said. 'It's only a lie that is really an issue in a Lucas direction, a fundamental lie'

'We find this very difficult,' Roberts began, but the judge interrupted.

'It's simply not on in this case, Mr Roberts, because a Lucas direction is only used where the defendant has admitted a lie, and here that is demonstrably untrue.'

Again Roberts tried to put forward his thesis.

Again Mr Justice Wright interrupted.

'Mr Roberts, I'm always anxious to hear from experienced leading counsel. But quite frankly Lucas never entered my mind. We must use great caution in a murder case. I will say no more. If I gave this direction the jury would be puzzled and confused. They would say, "What on earth is he talking about?"'

Sheila and her family and friends breathed a sigh of relief.

The judge's summing-up was very eloquent and seemed to us a model of fairness. He began with a summary of the cases for the Prosecution and the Defence. Then very deftly he covered the contentious 'middle ground'. Perhaps the Defence strategy had worked even more successfully than they could have hoped:

'Mrs Bowler now contends that in fact Mrs Jackson may have been able to walk along Station Road and that's what she did. Alternatively, if that was not possible, the only other explanation must be that Mrs Jackson was removed by an unknown third party who either pushed her in the river or abandoned her and left her wandering. Either that, or her death will forever remain a mystery.'

He told the jury they must be *sure* of Mrs Bowler's guilt before convicting. 'That is a short, simple, English word. You must be *sure*. You may have heard an old-fashioned word for it. Mr Glass used it because he's an old-fashioned sort of chap. That is, "beyond reasonable doubt." I suggest you should be *sure.*'

He moved on to Mrs Bowler's character: 'She has an *impeccable character.* When you make up your mind if you should believe her, you should put in the scale in her favour that she is so well thought of and that her character is spotless. You should take into account the unlikeliness, the *incredibility,* of the proposition that such a person *could* commit such a crime – indeed could commit *any* crime.'

He went on to give a masterly summary of the evidence on both sides. He ended: 'We all grieve for Florence Jackson who had a cold and lonely death in the river when she should have lived out her life in comfort among her family and friends. But we also equally cannot fail to feel for Mrs Bowler who has been through a terrible ordeal. She has had to face two full-scale murder trials, two appeals at the Court of Appeal, and now she is back here again. What a terrible experience after four years in prison.'

As Mr Justice Wright drew to a close he told the jury, 'Of course we grieve for Florence Jackson, of course we feel for Mrs Bowler. But now put all those emotions out of your heads. Because sympathy and emotion have no part in the awesome task you face, which must be a cool, calm, dispassionate analysis of the evidence you have heard and the conclusions you draw from it. Emotion is the enemy of clear thought. Put it out of your minds. Finally, any verdict must be unanimous. At this stage this must be the verdict of you all.'

At 2.35pm on Wednesday 4 February the ten remaining jurors retired to consider their verdict.

As Sheila was led from the dock, some of us standing beside it caught another glimpse of the white tiled walls below which Sheila had seen earlier in the trial on her way to Court Nineteen. Within a few hours, would Sheila Bowler be walking down those cold stairs towards the cells and the endless years in prison? Or would she walking out of the court room to freedom?

We all returned to the cafeteria to begin the long vigil.

Journalists had begun to gather in the cafeteria too. But they respected Sheila's privacy at this tense time. Nobody expected a verdict for several hours, but every time a voice came over the tannoy system everyone's heart missed a beat.

At 4.30 the tannoy announcement finally came.

'All parties in Bowler to Court Two.'

'It can't be a verdict yet,' we all told one another as we walked down the marble staircase to the courtroom.

The jurors looked tired and strained. They had not reached a verdict and would like to start afresh the following morning.

For anyone involved in the case of Sheila Bowler, the night of Wednesday 4 February was one of the longest of their lives. Jane told us later that Sheila was up at 3am, making lists and finishing packing a plastic carrier bag with clothes for prison.

When we arrived at the Old Bailey early next morning the television film crews were already gathering outside. One of the other big cases, the playground rape case, was also due to end that day.

Once again we all took up residence in the fourth floor cafeteria, strangely empty of lawyers, defendants and witnesses now that all the other courts were in session. The tension was palpable and those of us who had had too little sleep made the mistake of drinking too much coffee. Nobody felt like eating much. The oddest feeling of all was that in another room in that very building, ten complete strangers were sitting round a table just as we were. But they were making a decision that would change all of our lives in one way or another.

The journalists busied themselves making plans for the easiest form of press conference should Sheila be acquitted. They promised to be understanding if it went the other way. Sheila and her family and the *Trial and Error* team chatted and did crosswords.

Waiting in Jane's flat was Sheila's plastic holdall packed with prison clothes. Without anybody noticing, Sheila now scribbled a note to her friend Susan Catmur, telling her the place in Fair Meadow where she had hidden the money for Tinker's cattery bill. It might prove necessary, she told Susan, to find the kitten a new home.

The many friends and supporters who had packed the public gallery had had to repair to the Bar Roma on the opposite side of Newgate Street. A helpful court officer promised to go across and summon them back when the verdict was due.

The tension relaxed a little between one and two o'clock. The jurors were allowed an hour's lunch break and no announcement would be made then. We took it in turns to keep the supporters in the Bar Roma informed. Jane went and gave a brave interview to the *Trial and Error* film crew waiting on the pavement outside.

Just after two o'clock the tannoy announcement came once more: 'All parties in Bowler to Court Two.' We tried to stay calm. We knew the judge had decided to give the jury a majority direction if no unanimous verdict had been reached by this point. In a jury of ten, a majority has to be nine to one either way. A verdict of eight to two is a hung jury and could result in another re-trial should the Crown Prosecution Service decide to continue pressing their case.

But as we entered the courtroom, a whisper went round.

'We've got a verdict,' said solicitor Ewen Smith, his fingers firmly crossed.

It could only have been a three minute wait, but it seemed like hours. Then in walked the jurors one after another, their faces terrifyingly grim.

Our hearts almost stopped beating as the foreman rose to his feet.

'Are you the foreman of this jury?' asked the clerk to the court.

'I am,' said the young bearded man in spectacles.

'And how do you find the defendant, Guilty or Not Guilty?'

There was a tiny pause, then the foreman spoke the fateful words: 'Not Guilty.'

The public gallery erupted in shouts and cheers. From the back of the court Jane could be heard sobbing loudly in the arms of her brother and step-sister.

'Silence in court!' The Clerk's voice was harsh and her face was grim. The judge's geniality evaporated. Like a beleaguered schoolmaster faced with a mutinous class, he glared up at the gallery. To some of the supporters there it seemed ironic that now it was all over they were meant to show no emotion in a case that from the outset had turned on a woman's inability to weep. Furiously the judge threatened to impose contempt of court orders on people in the public gallery, and he glared at the journalists rushing to the courtroom door.

'*Sit still!*' he trumpeted.

The Clerk cleared her throat and continued, addressing her second question to the foreman: 'And is that the verdict of you all?'

'It is.'

In the dock Mrs Sheila Bowler, the woman who never cried, sat with her head in her hands and wept.

'Mrs Bowler, you may go,' said the judge. He thanked the jury and told them that after this long and taxing case they were now discharged from further jury service for life.

Suddenly the faces of the jurors were wreathed in smiles and some of them wiped away tears. Throughout this long trial they had remained entirely professional, and people in the public gallery could see them making neat and thorough notes in the blue-covered exercise books provided by the court ushers. They had banished all emotion from their faces as they listened intently to the witnesses.

Now they became human again.

When at last Sheila emerged at the front of the building to face the cameras, she was amazed to see most of the jurors standing on the opposite pavement in a tight-knit band, waving and clapping at the woman they had set free. As Sheila, Jane and Simon left in a taxi with David Jessel, they waved goodbye to the jurors, some still in tears, others hugging one another.

That evening's television news bulletins and the following morning's newspapers were full of Sheila's victory. It made the front pages of *The Times* and the *Express*. An *Express* journalist later told us it had been a choice between President Clinton, Saddam Hussein and Sheila Bowler for the front page splash. Sheila had won!

For the next few days in the run-up to the final *Trial and Error* programme about this case, Sheila and Jane felt obliged to give as many interviews as possible to publicize it and repay their enormous debt of gratitude to the television team. Undoubtedly without David Jessel, Steve Phelps, Steve Rankin and all the researchers over the years, Sheila would be facing eight more years in prison.

Mother and daughter appeared on ITV's *Good Morning* show, Sheila made up and backcombed into a vision of elegance, Jane natural as ever as they sat together on the sofa.

When they returned to Jane's South London flat, they stopped on the way to buy some broccoli and potatoes at her usual greengrocer's where they had shopped most evenings after court. The shopkeeper was ecstatic. They were TV stars, he said. He would take no payment for the vegetables.

Three days later they watched the *Trial and Error* programme at a party at the home of producer Steve Phelps amid laughter, rejoicing and some tears. Tinker the ginger kitten was voted star of the show. They were travelling back to Jane's flat after the party with some of the programme team when suddenly Sheila smelt burning. Ben, one of the cameramen, got out to see what was wrong. Sure enough one of the nearside tyres was completely flat. Everyone was struck by the irony of the situation. Luckily they were less than 500 yards from Steve's home – and someone had a mobile phone to call a recovery service!

Next day Mrs Sheila Bowler returned home to Rye and the hundreds of cards, letters and flowers from wellwishers. Ian Newton wrote movingly: 'I cannot escape the reality that it took the combined effort of many people working for five years to produce this result. I am also aware of the many who are still in prison, waiting and hoping. I will use this case to convince those who still believe that the death penalty is the solution to serious crime. And I would hope to convince them how easily it could have been them.'

Ironically, a few days later the Court of Appeal made an unprecedented condemnation of capital punishment when it quashed the conviction of a Somalian seaman wrongly hanged for murder 46 years earlier. Lord Justice Rose said the case showed that 'capital punishment was not perhaps a prudent culmination for a criminal justice system which is human and therefore fallible.'

We received a letter from former Home Secretary Michael Howard about the wrongful conviction of Sheila Bowler: 'Such cases of miscarriage of justice are always dreadfully distressing. I am grateful to you for the part which you played in persuading me to refer her case to the Court of Appeal.'

Tinker was retrieved from the cattery and raced about the garden at Number 25 Fair Meadow as Mrs Bowler waged war once more on five years of weeds. The exceptionally warm spring sunshine shone on the old green Audi and Mrs Bowler said it needed a good polish. She'd get down to it when she'd finished her thank-you letters.

Back at the television studios Steve Phelps smiled as he finally closed the file on Mrs Sheila Bowler.

'That's what we're all about,' he said. 'Giving people back their lives.'

EPILOGUE

IN HINDSIGHT

5 March 1998

It is now a month since the name of Sheila Bowler was cleared. The nightmare is over, and amazingly, because of the dignity and extraordinary lack of bitterness with which Sheila has returned to her old life in Rye, it appears to her friends and neighbours as if nothing much really happened.

But something of national importance did happen.

An entirely innocent woman of 62, widely acknowledged to be a pillar of respectability, was just twelve weeks widowed and privately grieving for her late husband when she was engulfed in a terrifying nightmare. She was deprived of her freedom, locked up for four years and subjected to the indignity of being handcuffed, herded about, bawled at and strip-searched for drugs. As these pages have shown, her health has been jeopardized and her family life stalemated while her daughter's professional music career was put on hold, and her visually impaired son was put under almost unendurable stress. Her previously impeccable reputation has been vilified, her previously untarnished name bandied about in lurid headlines and in a particularly vicious article in the *News of the World* and a devastating *Crime Monthly* television programme, both of which reproduced the police version of events, blackening the name of Sheila Bowler to audiences of millions.

The law has been proved, as Dickens's Mr Bumble put it, to be an ass. In hindsight you only have to read the judgement of the first Court of Appeal to know how terribly wrong eminent intellects can be. Consider this passage justifying the decision of their lordships not to hear in person the evidence of Professor Archie Young.

'*Professor Young's report is of necessity theoretical. Unlike the many witnesses who gave evidence, including Dr Jeelani, he never observed the deceased. The evidence given at the trial that Mrs Jackson would be unable to do that which is now suggested was in reality quite overwhelming. It is our view that, if such a theory had been placed before the jury, it would have been possibly damaging to the Appellant's case as being manifestly incredible.*

'*If we had come to the conclusion that there was any real possibility that a jury would or could come to a conclusion that Mrs Jackson might of her own volition have walked to her death, we would have had no hesitation in admitting the fresh evidence and, if appropriate, quashing the conviction. However, for the reasons we have given, we came to the conclusion that such a theory was, on the evidence, wholly untenable.*'

Yet after a full-scale murder re-trial at the Old Bailey, when all the evidence was put in front of the jury, that jury took just a few hours to reach a unanimous verdict of Not Guilty.

This case was a chapter of legal accidents that must make every lawyer uneasy. There must be some legal heartsearching about what went so very wrong. In particular, this case has demonstrated the grave danger of attaching too much weight to circumstantial evidence alone. There was not a shred of forensic evidence to link Sheila Bowler with the drowning of Florence Jackson. Mrs Bowler's character, which was never fully explored until the re-trial, was then shown to be of such a high quality that it was inconceivable that she could ever be capable of the terrible crime of murder. The alleged motive was ludicrous for a woman of some substance. The alleged plot was laughable for a woman of some intelligence.

Should the first trial judge ever have allowed the case to go before a jury after every main plank of the Crown's evidence had been demolished by the Defence? Why were the jurors allowed to ask themselves, 'If not the Defendant, then who?' when really they should have been directed to ask themselves, 'Has the case against Sheila Bowler been proved beyond all reasonable doubt?'

Why did the judges at the first Court of Appeal not accept that there was plenty of medical evidence to suggest that Aunt Flo was capable of performing this unsuspected feat of mobility? The re-trial jury acquitted, but should the jury not have been allowed a proper reading of the case-histories scornfully dismissed as 'anecdotal' evidence and generally accepted by the Crown and the re-trial judge to be 'valueless' – even though there is an acknowledged dearth of documented medical precedents?

In view of Sheila Bowler's nightmarish ordeal, it may seem strange to describe her as lucky. But in some ways she was fortunate, compared with many others who remain in prison protesting their innocence. The adversarial system is a lottery, particularly in legal aid cases like Sheila's. She was fortunate in having a legal team prepared to work in partnership with lay people like us and many of Sheila's other supporters, and to allow the direct access which is so often denied to defendants. She was fortunate too in having advocates prepared to try to understand their client's character. David Martin-Sperry worked closely with us and was the first to examine exactly why Sheila seemed to react so strangely on the night of 13 May 1992. Ewen Smith showed endless patience when we had to telephone him at home at weekends. Jeremy Roberts QC, like Ewen, gained a true insight into Sheila's character by visiting her home and meeting many of her supporters. He has the humility to believe that lawyers do not always have the monopoly of the best arguments, and he was prepared to listen to lay advice until the very end of the case.

In the absence of properly resourced investigative machinery to examine possible miscarriages of justice, what alternative is left to campaigners except to harness the support of the media? We were lucky because one of Sheila's friends was a constituent of Chris Mullin MP. Had it not been for Mullin's connection with Channel Four's *Trial and Error*, and had it not been for the perseverance and generosity of the programme's investigative journalists, we would have had no hope of success. We were fortunate too in the support of a number of national newspapers whose journalists had direct access to Sheila in prison. They visited her and were convinced of her innocence. Now journalists have been banned from visiting prisoners for this same purpose by a recent judgement in the Court of Appeal in favour of the current Home Secretary.

There has been another curb on investigative journalism with the passing of the Criminal Procedures and Investigations Act, which became law on 1 April 1996. It deals with the disclosure of evidence by the police to the Defence in criminal cases. Clause 17 of the Act makes that material confidential and it is a contempt of court to use it outside the court case it was gathered for. Had Sheila's first trial taken place after that date, her solicitors would have been forbidden to disclose any unused material to the *Trial and Error* team, and much of the material in this book would have been suppressed.

So compelling were the articles and TV programmes about Sheila's case that newspaper readers and television viewers rallied round her, often drawing on their own experience of elderly relatives. They joined her already large band of personal friends to form The Friends of Sheila Bowler. A strong supporters group is vital – not just because it can lobby for the political support which can be so important. Supporters give hope, boost fragile morale and enable a prisoner to 'live' outside the walls of the jail. Sheila says that although her body was in Holloway, her mind and her spirit remained outside with her friends and supporters. On the night before her terrifying final ordeal in the Old Bailey witness box, she says she only had the courage to carry on because she knew that hundreds and hundreds of supporters were behind her and she must not let them down. That is why journalists called this 'the people's case.'

And that is why this book is dedicated to The Friends of Sheila Bowler.

OTHER BOOKS BY ANGELA DEVLIN

Criminal Classes: Offenders at School

This book examines for the first time in detail the links between educational failure and future criminal offending. In their own words prisoners tell the stories of their schooldays – sometimes shocking and often moving – as they try answer the central question, 'Could anything have been done at school to prevent you being in custody now?'

'This is a book of considerable public importance on a subject which calls for attention.' Sir Stephen Tumim

'I found it fascinating and very disturbing.' Lord Scarman

'A wise and absorbing volume.' Marcel Berlins, *The Guardian*

Paperback ISBN 1 872 870 30 9 Price £16 plus £1.50 postage and packing
Published by Waterside Press, Domum Road, Winchester SO23 9NN
Telephone or fax: 01962 855 567

Prison Patter: A dictionary of prison words and slang

An informative and fascinating handbook with some 2,500 entries collected from serving prisoners.

'A scholarly work of major sociological value.' John Izbicki, *The Independent*

Paperback ISBN 1 872 870 41 4 Price £12 plus £1.50 postage and packing
Published by Waterside Press, Domum Road, Winchester SO23 9NN
Telephone or fax: 01962 855 567

Invisible Women: What's wrong with women's prisons?

This new book (first edition scheduled 30 June 1998) is the result of five years of research in women's prisons. In a book that is deliberately accessible to the general reader as well as to the prison professional, the author vividly recreates the realities of prison life as conditions worsen with overcrowding, staff shortages and expenditure cuts. Some of her findings will shock as well as inform. *Invisible Women* is a comprehensive and graphic update on the state of women's prisons which enables readers – especially people who have never set foot inside a prison – to 'see' the invisible women behind the bars.

Paperback ISBN 1 872 870 59 7 Price £18 + £1.50 postage and packing
Published by Waterside Press, Domum Road, Winchester SO23 9NN
Telephone or fax: 01962 855 567

ORDER FORM

Please supply (insert title/s and number of copies)

....

....

....

....

....

I enclose cheque for £........................./or please invoice my organization

Address for delivery (state invoice address separately if different)

....

....

....

....

....

Postcode .... Telephone ....

The direct mail price of each book appears against each title. Please add £1.50 per book p&p to a maximum £6 (UK only. Postage abroad is charged at cost). Please send your order to WATERSIDE PRESS, Domum Road, Winchester SO23 9NN. Tel or fax 01962 885 567. Cheques should be made out to Waterside Press. Organizations invoiced for two or more books on request.